INTRODUCTION TO
EXERCISE
SCIENCE

FOURTH EDITION

editors

Terry J. Housh
UNIVERSITY OF NEBRASKA–LINCOLN

Dona J. Housh
UNIVERSITY OF NEBRASKA MEDICAL CENTER

Glen O. Johnson
UNIVERSITY OF NEBRASKA–LINCOLN

H·H·P

Holcomb Hathaway, Publishers
Scottsdale, Arizona

Library of Congress Cataloging-in-Publication Data

Housh, Terry J.
  Introduction to excercise science / edited by Terry J. Housh, Dona J.
Housh, Glen O. Johnson. — 4th ed.
    p. cm.
  ISBN 978-1-934432-46-4 (print book) — ISBN 978-1-934432-47-1 (ebook)   1.
Exercise—Textbooks.   2. Sports sciences—Vocational guidance.   I. Housh,
Terry J.   II. Housh, Dona J.   III. Johnson, Glen O. (Glen Oliver). Title.
  QP301.I65 2012
  612'.044—dc23

                                                    2010038040

Holcomb Hathaway, Publishers, Inc.
8700 E. Via de Ventura Blvd., Suite 265
Scottsdale, Arizona 85258
480-991-7881
www.hh-pub.com

10 9 8 7 6 5 4 3 2 1

PRINT ISBN: 978-1-934432-46-4
EBOOK ISBN: 978-1-934432-47-1

Photo Credits

Front cover, Ostill; back cover *(left to right)*, Stockbyte, Paviem/123RF, Wavebreak Media Ltd/123RF; Chapter 1, Benis Arapovic/123RF *(top)*, Joe Belanger/123RF *(bottom)*; Chapter 2, Lori Sparkia/123RF *(top)*, Imagesource/123RF *(bottom)*; Chapter 3, Gabriel Moisa/123RF *(top)*, Stylephotographs/123RF *(bottom)*; Chapter 4, Sphotography/123RF *(top)*, Shariff Che'Lah/123RF *(bottom)*, Andrea Crisante/123RF *(page 80)*; Chapter 5, Stevanovicigor/123RF *(top)*, Daniel Sroga/123RF *(bottom)*; Chapter 6, Igor Golovnov/123RF *(top)*, Cathy Yeulet/123RF *(bottom)*; Chapter 7, Marcin Balcerzak/123RF *(top)*, Mezzotint/123RF *(bottom)*; Chapter 8, Warren Goldswain/123RF *(top)*, Auremar/123RF *(bottom)*, Denys Kurbatov/123RF *(page 165)*, Rafal Olkis/123RF *(page 167)*; Chapter 9, Dimaberkut/123RF *(top)*, Peter Bernik/123RF *(bottom)*; Chapter 10, Benis Arapovic/123RF *(top)*, Galina Barskaya/123RF *(bottom)*; Chapter 11, Benis Arapovic/123RF *(top)*, Kzenon/123RF *(bottom)*

Contents

3 Measurement in Exercise Science   37

FIELDS OF STUDY CHAPTERS

Anatomy in Exercise Science   61

Exercise Physiology   85

Exercise Epidemiology   123

Athletic Training   139

8   Exercise and Sport Nutrition   157

Biomechanics   191

Motor Control and Motor Learning   219

11 Exercise and Sport Psychology   241

Introduction to Exercise Science, Fourth Edition, is designed to expose undergraduate students to important aspects of the discipline, including areas of study, technology, certifications, professional associations, and career opportunities. It also helps students develop an appreciation for the history of, as well as current and future trends in, exercise science. This textbook is not designed as an in-depth discussion of the individual areas of study (e.g., exercise physiology, biomechanics) in exercise science; rather, each chapter identifies prominent and timely lines of inquiry without exhaustive reviews of the primary literature.

Chapter features include highlighted Focus Points, journal abstract examples, study questions, learning activities, and suggested readings. Following chapters that provide introductory and background information about the exercise science field, the remaining chapters focus on specific areas of study in exercise science. Chapters 3 through 11 present brief histories, health- and sports performance–related issues, technology and related tools, educational preparation, professional associations, employment opportunities, and future directions concerning those areas of study. Following is a brief summary of chapter content.

CHAPTER 1, An Introduction to Exercise Science. In Chapter 1, Terry Housh, Dona Housh, and Herbert A. deVries provide basic information about exercise science. The chapter defines exercise and science and provides a working definition of exercise science as "how and why the human body responds to physical activity." It also describes the course work typically included in an undergraduate major in exercise science. Furthermore, this chapter synopsizes the recommendations of the Committee on Accreditation of the Exercise Sciences as well as the *Basic Standards for the Professional Preparation in Exercise Science* prepared by the Applied Exercise Science Council of the National Association for Sport and Physical Education (NASPE) of the American Alliance for Health, Physical Education, Recreation and Dance (AAHPERD).

CHAPTER 2, Reading and Interpreting the Literature in Exercise Science. Joel Cramer and Travis Beck provide information designed to help students become wise consumers of the literature in exercise science. Chapter 2 describes the characteristics of primary and secondary literature sources, as well as scientific and nonscientific sources. In addition, this chapter describes the typical contents of the abstract, and the introduction, methods, results, discussion, conclusions, and reference sections of a research article. The authors also answer the question "Where do I look to find basic and applied scientific articles?" in the section Tips for Conducting Online Searches.

CHAPTER 3, Measurement in Exercise Science. Measurement theory and procedures have many applications in exercise science. In Chapter 3, Dale Mood explores the roles of measurement in exercise science. In addition to the assessment of cognitive, affective, and psychomotor aspects of human performance, the discussion of measurement includes issues related to statistical procedures and computer applications.

CHAPTER 4, Anatomy in Exercise Science. An understanding of human anatomy is essential to the development of knowledge in exercise science. In Chapter 4, Glen Johnson provides a history of anatomy and defines the subspecialties of gross anatomy, cytology, histology, comparative anatomy, developmental anatomy, and pathological anatomy. Furthermore, Dr. Johnson ties the study of anatomy to exercise science by relating it to research in growth and development, body composition, and the cellular adaptations to training.

CHAPTER 5, Exercise Physiology. Exercise physiology is central to an understanding of exercise science. In Chapter 5, Joe Weir describes many areas of basic and applied research. Exercise physiologists enjoy a number of employment opportunities in academia as well as in the private sector. Professional organizations such as the American College of Sports Medicine (ACSM) and National Strength and Conditioning Association (NSCA) provide certifications that require mastery of topics in exercise physiology and that supplement the formal college and university training for exercise science students.

CHAPTER 6, Exercise Epidemiology. Typically, exercise epidemiologists study the associations among the various modes of physical activity and the risks of developing specific diseases or becoming injured. In Chapter 6, Travis Beck describes the primary areas of study in exercise epidemiology, including cardiovascular disease, cerebrovascular disease and stroke, hypertension, diabetes, osteoporosis, cancer, and mental health. In addition, this chapter includes information regarding the common research methods and tools used in the developing area of exercise epidemiology.

CHAPTER 7, Athletic Training. In this chapter, Kyle T. Ebersole and Ronald Pfeiffer describe the profession of athletic training, the Board of Certification for the Athletic Trainer (BOC) examination, and employment opportunities. Athletic training provides a unique opportunity for exercise science professionals to combine work in the area of sports performance with health-related, clinical careers. The national certification process is highly structured, and Drs. Ebersole and Pfeiffer outline the expectations for professionals in athletic training.

CHAPTER 8, Exercise and Sport Nutrition. Proper nutrition is important for optimal health as well as successful sports performance. In Chapter 8, Joan Eckerson provides information about nutrition as it relates to chronic disease and athletic performance and also discusses nutritional supplements as ergogenic aids. In terms of employment opportunities, Dr. Eckerson outlines the growing trend toward combining formal training in nutrition with exercise science to meet the needs of health clubs and wellness centers.

CHAPTER 9, Biomechanics. This chapter is coauthored by Nicholas Stergiou, Daniel Blanke, Sara A. Myers, and Ka-Chun Siu. Biomechanics has many applications in exercise science, and this chapter outlines various sports performance and health-related aspects. In addition, the chapter discusses a number of new technologies that are used for in-depth analyses of human movement.

CHAPTER 10, Motor Control and Motor Learning. In this chapter, David Sherwood provides basic information concerning the psychological and neurological theories underlying motor control and motor learning. The application of these theories has implications for health-related fields such as physical therapy and rehabilitation, as well as sports performance. A basic knowledge of motor learning and motor control is valuable for allied health professionals and athletes.

CHAPTER 11, Exercise and Sport Psychology. In Chapter 11, Richard Schmidt provides information regarding various aspects of exercise and sport psychology. Exercise psychology deals with factors related to motivation, exercise initiation, adherence, and compliance as well as the psychological changes associated with exercise training. Sport psychology includes factors that limit as well as enhance the ability to perform athletic events. Dr. Schmidt also discusses ways in which participation in sport and physical activity can enhance psychological growth and development.

ABOUT THE WEBSITE AND EBOOK

The fourth edition of *Introduction to Exercise Science* includes a companion website. The site works as a review tool, through key term lists and study questions, and also gives students an opportunity to apply their learning through a series of hands-on labs. A lab is provided for each chapter, allowing students to perform basic exercise science tasks such as administering a PAR-Q, measuring heart rate, assessing body composition, and conducting a research review.

Introduction to Exercise Science is also available as an ebook. It features color formatting, active web links, and digital note taking and book marking. It also ties directly to the companion website, making it easy for readers to review key concepts.

www

Introduction to Exercise Science Companion Website
http://hhpcommunities.com/exercisescience

ACKNOWLEDGMENTS

We wish to thank the following reviewers for their helpful suggestions: *For this edition:* Tal Amasay, Barry University; Brett Bruininks, Concordia College; Melissa Cook, Indiana Wesleyan University; Robert W. Hensarling, Samford University; Trent J. Herda, The University of Kansas; Timothy Hilliard, Fitchburg State University; Louise A. Kelly, California Lutheran University; David H. Leigh, Marquette University; Russell H. Lord, Montana State University Billings; Astrid Mel, Mercy College; Jennifer Petit, The University of Akron; and Christine Rockey, Coastal Carolina University.

For prior editions: Paul Arciero, Skidmore College; Ted Baumgartner, University of Georgia; Jay Bradley, Indiana University–Purdue University Indianapolis; Cynthia Butler, Florida Atlantic University; Sue Graves, Florida Atlantic University; Kirkland J. Hall, Sr., University of Maryland Eastern Shore; Michael Nordvall, Marymount University; Marnie Vanden Noven, Marquette University; Seth Paradis, Bethel University; Carrie Quinn, Avila University; and Bret Wood, University of North Carolina at Charlotte.

About the Editors and Contributors

This textbook includes contributions from four generations of exercise scientists. Dr. Herbert A. deVries (1918–2009) was truly a pioneer in the study of exercise and its relationship to sports performance and health across the life span. In 1986, we, Terry and Dona Housh, were at Portland State University in Oregon. A faculty member, Dr. Mike Tichy, asked whether we would be interested in helping with a research project organized by Dr. deVries at PSU. It turned out that Mike and Herb attended undergraduate school together at East Stroudsburg University in Pennsylvania and were lifelong friends. It was to our great benefit to have the opportunity to assist Herb with that initial project. Following that project, Dr. deVries came to the University of Nebraska–Lincoln periodically to continue our research on electromyography and muscle fatigue. We were fortunate to be in the right place at the right time in 1986, and it was our personal and professional pleasure to work with Dr. deVries for over 20 years.

Glen O. Johnson and Dale P. Mood attended graduate school together at the University of Iowa. They have continued their friendship over the years, and we were fortunate to persuade them to contribute to this textbook. Glen was a doctoral advisor at the University of Nebraska–Lincoln for both of us (Terry and Dona Housh). It was through Glen that we were introduced to Dale, and we have greatly enjoyed attending professional conferences together.

Joan M. Eckerson, Joseph P. Weir, Kyle T. Ebersole, Joel Cramer, and Travis Beck earned their doctoral degrees at the University of Nebraska–Lincoln. Glen Johnson, Terry Housh, and Richard J. Schmidt were doctoral advisors for Joan, Joe, Kyle, Joel, and Travis, and the succession of exercise scientists has continued with their students.

Editing this textbook gave us the opportunity to further develop existing friendships and make new ones. In this regard, it has been our pleasure to work with Daniel L. Blanke, Nick Stergiou, Sara A. Myers, and Ka-Chun Siu from the University of Nebraska at Omaha, Ronald P. Pfeiffer from Boise State University, and David E. Sherwood from the University of Colorado–Boulder.

One of the true joys of academic life is the long-term associations with students and colleagues who have similar professional interests. It is our hope the collective insights of the four generations of exercise scientists represented in this textbook will contribute to the professional development of future generations of exercise scientists.

THE EDITORS

Terry J. Housh, Ph.D., FACSM, FNSCA, is a professor in the Department of Nutrition and Health Sciences, Director of the Exercise Physiology Laboratory, and Co-Director of the Center for Youth Fitness and Sports Research at the University of Nebraska–Lincoln (UNL). He has coauthored more than 230 peer-reviewed research articles and nine college textbooks, and has given more than 250 presentations at annual meetings of professional organizations including the American College of Sports Medicine (ACSM), National Strength and Conditioning Association (NSCA), American Alliance for Health, Physical Education, Recreation, and Dance (AAHPERD), and National Athletic Trainers' Association (NATA). He was the 1998 recipient of the NSCA Outstanding Sport Scientist Award, 2002 Doane College Honor D Award, 2006 NSCA Educator of the Year Award, 2008 NSCA President's Award, and 2008 *Journal of Strength and Conditioning Research* Editorial Excellence Award. In 2009, the NSCA named its annual award the "Terry J. Housh Young Investigator Award."

Dona J. Housh, Ph.D., FACSM, is a professor in the Department of Oral Biology, College of Dentistry at the University of Nebraska Medical Center. She teaches Human Physiology to first year dental students as well as postdoctoral graduate students in various dental specialities. Dr. Housh's research interests include muscle function, neuromuscular fatigue, and hypertrophic responses to resistance training. She has authored numerous peer-reviewed articles in prestigious scholarly journals and has presented research findings at annual meetings of the ACSM and NSCA.

Dr. Glen O. Johnson (together with Dr. Bill Thorland) began the Ph.D. program in Exercise Physiology at the University of Nebraska in the late 1970s. He taught human anatomy at UNL for 36 years. Today, Dr. Johnson is a professor emeritus in the Department of Nutrition and Health Sciences at UNL and continues to help advise Exercise Physiology doctoral students. He received his B.S. and M.S. degrees from Winona State University and his Ph.D. from the University of Iowa under Dr. Charles M. Tipton. He is a Distinguished Alumni of Winona State as well as a member of its Athletic Hall of Fame. He helped develop and served as co-director of the Center for Youth Fitness and Sports Research at UNL. He is a Fellow of ACSM and a Research Consortium Fellow of AAHPERD. He has coauthored over 150 peer-reviewed articles and given numerous presentations at national conferences of ACSM and AAHPERD. He is co-editor of two college textbooks.

THE CONTRIBUTORS

Travis W. Beck, Ph.D., earned his B.S. in Biology from Doane College and M.P.E. in Health and Human Performance and Ph.D. in Human Sciences from the University of Nebraska–Lincoln. He is currently an Assistant Professor in the Department of Health and Exercise Science at the University of Oklahoma. Dr. Beck's main research interests include evaluation of muscle function using electromyography and mechanomyography and digital signal processing.

Daniel Blanke, Ph.D., is a Professor and Director in the School of Health, Physical Education and Recreation at the University of Nebraska at Omaha. He directs both Campus Recreation and the academic Department of the School of HPER. Dr. Blanke continues his contribution to scholarly work by participating in ongoing research within the Nebraska Biomechanics Core Facility, as well as procuring grant funding. He led a significant $38.6 million renovation of the HPER building and recently he was able to secure $6 million to build the first exclusive research building on the UNO campus for Biomechanics Research.

Joel T. Cramer, Ph.D., is an Associate Professor in the Department of Nutrition and Health Sciences at the University of Nebraska–Lincoln. He received a bachelor's degree in Exercise Science from Creighton University in 1997 and completed master's and doctoral degrees with Dr. Terry J. Housh at UNL in 2001 and 2003, respectively. Dr. Cramer studies the safety and efficacy of nutritional supplements across the lifespan as well as neuromuscular responses to resistance training and stretching. He has published over 135 scientific articles, coauthored a book entitled *Physical Fitness Laboratories on a Budget,* and is actively involved in NSCA.

Herbert A. deVries (1918–2009), Ph.D., FACSM, was Professor Emeritus of the Department of Physical Education at The University of Southern California. He was world-renowned for his research on the physiological adaptations to exercise training in the elderly and in research involving the application of electromyography to various aspects of neuromuscular fatigue. He published extensively in prestigious peer-reviewed journals and was the author of eleven books, including five editions of his classic text *Physiology of Exercise for Physical Education, Athletics, and Exercise Science.* For his lifetime of scholarly work, Dr. deVries was honored with the Alumni Honor Award from East Stroudsburg University, the Silver Anniversary Award by the President's Council on Physical Fitness and Sports, and the Citation Award from The American College of Sports Medicine. In addition, the Council on Aging and Adult Development of AAHPERD named the CAAD Research Award the Herbert A. deVries Research Award.

Kyle T. Ebersole, Ph.D., ATC, is an Associate Professor in the Department of Kinesiology and Director of The Human Performance & Sport Physiology Laboratory at the University of Wisconsin–Milwaukee. Dr. Ebersole earned his B.S. in Kinesiology from the University of Illinois at Chicago and M.P.E in Exercise Science and Ph.D. in Exercise Physiology from the University of Nebraska–Lincoln. Dr. Ebersole is a Licensed Athletic Trainer and currently teaches within the undergraduate Athletic Training program and Doctor of Physical Therapy program. Dr. Ebersole's research interests are related to the physiological basis for injury prevention, re-conditioning, strength training, and sport performance.

Joan M. Eckerson, Ph.D., is a Professor in the Department of Exercise Science at Creighton University in Omaha, Nebraska. She has over 40 publications in the area of body composition and dietary supplementation and in 2008 received the NSCA William J. Kraemer Outstanding Sport Scientist Award in recognition for her contributions to the field of applied exercise and sport science. Dr. Eckerson also serves as an editorial board member for the *Journal of Strength and Conditioning Research* and the *Journal of the International Society of Sports Nutrition.*

Dale P. Mood, Ph.D., is Professor Emeritus and former Associate Dean of Arts and Sciences at the University of Colorado–Boulder. Dr. Mood has taught measurement and evaluation, statistics, and research methods courses since 1970 and has published extensively in the field, including 51 articles and five books. He is one of four authors of *Measurement and Evaluation of Human Performance,* now in its fourth edition. He has served as a consultant for five NFL teams, chair of the Measurement and Evaluation Council of AAHPERD, and reviewer for many exercise science journals.

Sara A. Myers, Ph.D., is an Assistant Professor in the School of Health, Physical Education, and Recreation, Director of the Gait Analysis Laboratory, and Assistant Director of the Nebraska Biomechanics Core Facility at the University of Nebraska at Omaha. She has presented her research at the American Society of Biomechanics, AAHPERD, Society for Neuroscience, and North American Society for the Psychology of Sport and Physical Activity annual meetings. She has received research funding from several of these organizations, as well as from the National Institutes of Health.

Ka-Chun (Joseph) Siu, P.T., Ph.D., is an Assistant Professor at the University of Nebraska Medical Center and a faculty member of the Nebraska Biomechanics Core Faculty, University of Nebraska at Omaha (UNO). Dr. Siu obtained his B.S. in Physical Therapy from the Kaohsiung Medical University, School of Rehabilitation Medicine in Taiwan, and his Ph.D. in Human Physiology (motor control and learning) at the University of Oregon. Dr. Siu also received his post-doctoral training in Biomechanics at the Nebraska Biomechanics Core Facility, UNO. His research interests include motor control, biomechanics in aging, simulation technology, and rehabilitation.

Richard J. Schmidt, Ph.D., is an Associate Professor in the Department of Nutrition and Health Sciences at the University of Nebraska–Lincoln, where he teaches courses in exercise science. Dr. Schmidt is the adviser for the graduate M.S. degree specialization in nutrition and exercise.

David E. Sherwood received his Ph.D. from The University of Southern California and is an Associate Professor in the Department of Integrative Physiology at the University of Colorado–Boulder. His research interests include the learning and control of motor skills, including discovering the principles of bimanual coordination and how the focus of attention affects motor performance. Dr. Sherwood has published in journals such as the *Journal of Motor Behavior, Research Quarterly for Exercise and Sport,* and the *Journal of Experimental Psychology.* He is an active member of the North American Society for the Psychology of Sport and Physical Activity.

Nicholas Stergiou, Ph.D., is the Isaacson Professor of the School of Health, Physical Education, and Recreation at the University of Nebraska at Omaha. He is also the Graduate Program Chair of the Department of Environmental, Agricultural, and Occupational Health of the University of Nebraska Medical Center. Dr. Stergiou is the director of the Nebraska Biomechanics Core Facility, where his research focuses on understanding variability inherent in human movement. This research spans from infant development to older adult fallers, and has impacted training techniques of surgeons and treatment and rehabilitation techniques of pathologies, such as peripheral arterial disease and multiple sclerosis.

Joseph Weir received his Ph.D. in Exercise Physiology from the University of Nebraska–Lincoln. He is a Professor in and Chair of the Department of Health, Sport and Exercise Sciences at the University of Kansas. Previously, he was on the faculty at Des Moines University and at Teachers College, Columbia University. Dr. Weir is a Fellow of the American College of Sports Medicine and the National Strength and Conditioning Association. His primary research interests focus on muscle strength and muscle fatigue.

INTRODUCTION TO
EXERCISE SCIENCE

FOURTH EDITION

An Introduction to Exercise Science

TERRY J. HOUSH ■ DONA J. HOUSH ■ HERBERT A. deVRIES

WHAT IS EXERCISE SCIENCE?

Exercise can be simply defined as "the performance of any physical activity for the purpose of conditioning the body, improving health, or maintaining fitness, or as a means of therapy for correcting a deformity or restoring the organs and bodily functions to a state of health" (*Mosby*, 2006). **Science** is "a systematic attempt to establish theories to explain observed phenomena and the knowledge obtained through these efforts" (*Mosby*, 2006). Simply stated, **exercise science** is concerned with how and why the human body responds to physical activity. The principles of exercise science are sometimes applied to nonhuman animals, such as racehorses, show horses, and racing dogs, and animal models are valuable in research; nonetheless, the primary application of exercise science knowledge is to benefit human health, exercise, or sports performance. From this generic description, it is clear that exercise science is a very diverse field of study that encompasses many areas of inquiry. For example, the simple act of walking can be viewed from many different perspectives. An anatomist can describe the muscles involved in walking. An exercise physiologist may study how the systems of the body respond to the stress of walking, and a biomechanist can apply the laws of physics to examine the efficiency of each stride. An exercise psychologist may be interested in what motivates the subject to walk, and a sports nutritionist can describe how the food that we eat is used to supply the energy for the walk. An exercise epidemiologist can determine the relationship between walking regularly and the risk of developing such diseases as coronary heart disease (CHD) or cancer. This exemplifies the integration of the various areas within exercise science. Although they often stand alone as individual courses within the exercise science curriculum, these various areas of study make up an integrated picture of the complexity of physical activity.

Furthermore, each of these exercise scientists can study how we respond during an exercise bout (acute responses to exercise) or how we adapt to exercise training (chronic responses to exercise). For example, an exercise physiologist may find that as we begin to walk, our cardiovascular and pulmonary systems respond to the demands of the activity by increasing our heart rates and ventilatory rates. These are examples of acute responses to exercise. In contrast, if we change from a sedentary lifestyle and begin to walk regularly, our cardiovascular and pulmonary systems become more efficient, resulting in reduced heart rates and ventilatory responses to exercise. These improvements in physical fitness are examples of chronic responses to exercise.

science ■

exercise science ■

It is likely that as a student of exercise science, you will discover that even simple acts of physical activity, such as walking, can be more complex and thought provoking than they initially appear. This, however, is the exciting challenge of studying exercise science and learning how and why the human body responds to physical activity.

WHAT DO EXERCISE SCIENTISTS STUDY?

Two primary areas of inquiry for exercise scientists are (1) the health-related aspects of physical activity (see Box 1.1) and (2) sports performance (see Box 1.2). Research provides valuable information concerning various aspects of the relationship between physical activity and health (Blair, 1994; Blair, Kohl, Barlow, et al., 1995; Blair, Kohl, Paffenbarger, et al., 1989; Kaplan et al., 1987; Lee, 1994; Linsted, Tonstad, & Kuzma, 1991; Mackinnon, 1992; Morris et al., 1990; Nieman, 1994; Paffenbarger et al., 1993;

Issues in Health-Related Aspects of Physical Activity

Obesity: Halting the epidemic by making health easier

box
1.1

Centers for Disease Control and Prevention, 2011, http://www.cdc.gov/chronicdisease/resources/publications/AAG/obesity.htm

THE OBESITY EPIDEMIC

More than one third of U.S. adults (over 72 million people) and 17 percent of U.S. children are obese. From 1980 to 2008, obesity rates doubled for adults and tripled for children. During the past several decades, obesity rates for all population groups—regardless of age, sex, race, ethnicity, socioeconomic status, education level, or geographic region—have increased markedly.

OBESITY AND HEALTH DISPARITIES

Reports show substantial differences in obesity prevalence by race/ethnicity, and these differences vary by sex and age. For example, according to 2005–2008 data from the National Health and Nutrition Examination Survey, 51 percent of non-Hispanic black women age 20 years or older were obese, compared with 43 percent of Mexican Americans and 33 percent of whites. Among females age 2–19 years, 24 percent of non-Hispanic blacks, 19 percent of Mexican Americans, and 14 percent of whites were obese. Efforts are being made to reduce these disparities by focusing interventions on subgroups having a high prevalence of obesity.

HEALTH CONSEQUENCES OF OBESITY

Obesity increases the risk of many health conditions, including the following:

- Coronary heart disease, stroke, and high blood pressure
- Type 2 diabetes
- Cancers such as endometrial, breast, and colon cancer
- High total cholesterol or high levels of triglycerides
- Liver and gallbladder disease
- Sleep apnea and respiratory problems
- Degeneration of cartilage and underlying bone within a joint (osteoarthritis)

- Reproductive health complications such as infertility
- Mental health conditions

OBESITY IS COSTLY

In 2008, overall medical care costs related to obesity for U.S. adults were estimated to be as high as $147 billion. People who were obese had medical costs that were $1,429 higher than the cost for people of normal body weight. Obesity also has been linked with reduced worker productivity and chronic absence from work.

POLICY AND ENVIRONMENTAL APPROACHES NEEDED

The causes of obesity in the United States are complex and numerous, and they occur at social, economic, environmental, and individual levels. American society has become characterized by environments that promote physical inactivity and increased consumption of less healthy food. Public health approaches that can reach large numbers of people in multiple settings—such as in child care facilities, workplaces, schools, communities, and health care facilities—are needed to help people make healthier choices.

Policy and environmental approaches that make healthy choices available, affordable, and easy can be used to extend the reach of strategies designed to raise awareness and support people who would like to make healthy lifestyle changes.

CDC'S RESPONSE

The CDC's Division of Nutrition, Physical Activity, and Obesity (DNPAO) is working to improve nutrition and physical activity and reduce obesity through state programs, technical assistance and training, surveillance and applied research, program implementation and evaluation, translation and dissemination, and partnership development.

Rowland, 1990; U.S. Department of Health and Human Services, 1996). For example, exercise epidemiologists found compelling evidence to suggest that an active lifestyle reduces the risk of developing diseases such as CHD and some forms of cancer (Blair, Kohl, Paffenbarger, et al., 1989; Lee, 1994). Furthermore, studies indicate that disease risk factors can be favorably modified with appropriate exercise and dietary interventions (Blair, 1991; Blair, Kohl, Barlow, et al.,

Issues in Sports Performance Research
Should children be allowed to run marathon races? A virtual roundtable.

THE CASE FOR

In the November 2003 issue of the *Clinical Journal of Sport Medicine,* Stephen Rice and Susan Waniewski presented a position statement entitled "Children and Marathoning: How Young Is Too Young?" that was reportedly unanimously approved by the General Assembly of the International Medical Marathon Directors Association (IMMDA). This statement was, to say the least, cautionary. The authors note that the concept that children are developmentally immature compared with adults is "intuitively understood," but in athletic competitions "these distinctions are forgotten or ignored." They go on to express concerns that marathon running by children might place growing athletes at risk for musculoskeletal injury and psychological "burnout" as well as the female athlete triad of disordered eating, amenorrhea, and osteoporosis. They conclude that training to participate in a marathon by young athletes is "ill advised." And race directors who permit children to run marathons, they contend, only serve to sanction this behavior. They argue that the age of 18 is the appropriate time for a runner to increase training volume to engage in marathon events.

THE CASE AGAINST

"Phooey" [I, Rowland, am paraphrasing here], replied Bill Roberts in a letter to the editor after publication of the IMMDA statement. Dr. Roberts is a past president of IMMDA and is medical director of the Twin Cities Marathon. He finds little substance to the argument proscribing marathon running by children, suggesting that, although well-intentioned, the IMMDA statement provides little advice beyond "just say no." Dr. Roberts does not believe that children and adolescents should be *encouraged* to run marathons. But with no clear data indicating that such participation is any more risky for youth than adults, he feels that this age group can enter marathon races under certain circumstances: The child should be involved in a supervised, appropriate training program (with attention to proper nutrition and injury prevention), should be monitored in his or her training by a physician, and should be self-motivated to participate.

1995; Paffenbarger et al., 1993; U.S. Department of Health and Human Services, 1996). Other studies found that exercise can affect the immune system and potentially influence the risk of developing infectious diseases (Mackinnon, 1992; Nieman, 1994). The total picture regarding the health-related benefits of physical activity, however, is far from complete. For example, perhaps the greatest public impact from exercise science research is the study of how low-to-moderate levels of exercise improve health and well-being throughout the lifespan (American College of Sports Medicine, 2010; Blair, 1991; Kaplan et al., 1987; Siedentop, 1994). We still know very little about how much exercise is needed to reduce the risk of developing specific diseases. Thus, with our present level of knowledge we are limited in the ability to provide "safe and effective" exercise prescriptions for various age groups (Blair, 1994). Future generations of exercise scientists will carry on these important lines of research.

Exercise scientists, sometimes called sport scientists (Stone, Stone, & Sands, 2005), also study factors related to the improvement of sports performance. The study of sports performance includes a wide range of diverse areas: the growth and development of young athletes, the nutritional needs of adult athletes, biomechanical analysis of Olympic athletes, and the psychological characteristics of Masters age-group athletes. Applied research involving the development and application of training techniques for athletes is a primary interest of strength and conditioning coaches associated with universities and professional teams. In addition, athletic trainers often study methods of preventing athletic injuries and rehabilitating athletes injured in competition or practice. Clearly, there are many opportunities for exercise scientists with regard to the development and application of knowledge related to sports performance.

EXERCISE SCIENCE: A HISTORICAL PERSPECTIVE

Exercise science as an academic discipline in colleges and universities has existed only since the mid-to-late 1960s. Although the value of exercise was recognized for centuries and interest was taken in it by earlier civilizations (notably by the Greeks, who were the progenitors of Olympic competition), prior to the early 1900s the basic sciences were not yet sufficiently developed to be used in such diverse fields as athletic competition, military conditioning, medical applications, and physical fitness. Methods for measuring human functions at rest were difficult in themselves; measurements in the course of vigorous exercise or involvement in athletic activities such as walking, running, jumping, swimming, and cycling had to wait for the future development of electronics, which did not occur in any practical sense until the 20th century.

It was not until the 1960s that various areas of study within exercise science, such as anatomy, biomechanics, athletic training, exercise physiology, exercise and sport nutrition, exercise and sport psychology, measurement, **epidemiology**, and motor control and learning, coalesced into a cohesive academic major in colleges and universities. Now, as a result of the divergent interests, curricula in many of our universities are divided into separate majors in physical education and exercise science.

■ *epidemiology*

Evolution of Exercise Science

Over the last few decades, exercise science evolved as a result of advances in physiology, anatomy, kinesiology, and health and fitness as well as from the formation of the American College of Sports Medicine (ACSM), which promotes the interests of exercise scientists.

Physiology

It has been said that **physiology**, or the study of the processes and functions of the human body, is the meeting place of the sciences. This is so because understanding the function of biological systems requires an understanding of anatomy, biology, physics, and chemistry as well as the mathematical principles undergirding the analysis of findings in the laboratory.

■ *physiology*

As our knowledge base increases in sophistication, we must add molecular biology to general biology. Some aspects of biology merge with physical principles to become biophysics. Biology merges with chemistry to become biochemistry, and chemistry, which started out as simple general inorganic and organic chemistry, now requires special applications of physics and mathematics to become physical chemistry. So it is easy to see how all the sciences contribute to our understanding of the functions of the human body. Furthermore, as sophistication progresses, our methods of measurement of human movement and exercise require a knowledge of technology to utilize the complex instrumentation in use today, and a thorough understanding of statistics and computer applications is needed to digest and report the findings of the laboratory.

Anatomy

anatomy ■ Modern study of **anatomy** had its beginning in the 1500s as the gross study of organ structure and function. However, the study of cellular structure within the tissues of muscles and organs remained to be discovered after the invention of the microscope by Anton van Leeuwenhoek around 1660. Only then were muscle fibers identified as the cellular element of muscle tissue. However, a true understanding of how force was developed by muscle fibers through changes in molecular structure remained to be studied by the electron microscope, which was not developed until the 1950s.

Histology, the study of the anatomy of tissues and their cellular basis, opened the door to a much better understanding of organ structure and function by the medical profession.

A subdivision of anatomy, **embryology,** or developmental anatomy, developed largely in the 1800s as scientists studied the changes in form and structure of the embryo and fetus in chicks and pigs. This work was of great importance to

histology ■
embryology ■

physicians and especially to obstetricians in their applications to humans. Exercise scientists who deal with questions regarding exercise and pregnancy also benefit from this work.

Kinesiology

kinesiology ■ **Kinesiology** can be defined most simply as the study of human motion; indeed, some universities use this term for the name of a department that includes exercise science and physical education (among others) programs. In the early days of physical education, when few activities were taught besides gymnastics and dance, the contents of a course in kinesiology were confined largely to functional anatomy. In any event, the unique contribution of kinesiology is that it selects from sciences such as anatomy, physiology, and physics the principles that are pertinent to human motion and systematizes their application. Gradually, as sports assumed a more important place in the physical education curriculum, the concept of kinesiology was broadened to include the study of mechanical principles that applied to sports techniques. The advent of the computer facilitated highly technical analyses of human movement, and this area of study is

biomechanics ■ frequently referred to as **biomechanics.**

Health and fitness

The nature of the illnesses that beset the U.S. population in recent times has undergone a transition from a predominance of infectious diseases to the present predominance of degenerative diseases. This change represents the contribution of the medical profession, both in research and in clinical practice, toward the virtual control and the imminent eradication of a large portion of the formerly dreaded infectious scourges.

The increase of such degenerative diseases as cardiovascular accidents (heart attacks and strokes), hypertension, neuroses, and malignancies offers a challenge not only to medicine but to exercise science as well. It seems that as improvements in medical science allow us to escape decimation by such infectious diseases as tuberculosis, diphtheria, and poliomyelitis, we live longer only to fall prey to the degenerative diseases at a slightly later date. Whether this involvement with the degenerative problems follows from our living longer or is the result of our simultaneous change in lifestyle cannot yet be answered.

The influence of lifestyle on the health and illnesses of a lifetime has been suggested in the past, but hard, epidemiological evidence has only been available since the 1970s. For example, in a survey of 6,928 adults of Alameda County, California (Belloc & Breslow, 1972), individual health practices were related to health and also to mortality statistics. The health practices surveyed included (1) smoking, (2) weight in relation to desirable standards, (3) use of alcohol, (4) hours of sleep, (5) breakfast eating, (6) regularity of meals, and (7) physical activity. It was found that the average life expectancy of men age 45 who reported six or seven "good" practices was more than 11 years greater than that of men reporting fewer than four. For women, the difference in life expectancy was 7 years. It was also found that good health practices were reliably associated with positive health and that the combined effect of the different health practices was cumulative; those who followed all the good practices, even though older, were in better health than those who failed to follow them. This association was found to be independent of age, gender, and economic status. Furthermore, epidemiological studies over the last 40 years continue to support the relationships among lifestyle behaviors, exercise, and health (see Chapter 6, Exercise Epidemiology).

American College of Sports Medicine
www.acsm.org

American College of Sports Medicine (ACSM)

It is not surprising that many of the pioneers in the development of exercise science were trained as medical doctors. The ACSM was formed in 1954 in recognition of the need to promote and integrate scientific research, education, and practical applications of sports medicine and exercise science to maintain and enhance physical performance, fitness, health, and quality of life.

In 1954 there were only 11 charter members in ACSM. Today that membership has grown to over 20,000, whose interests are divided into (1) basic and applied sciences, (2) medicine, and (3) education and allied health.

Impetus for the Emergence of Modern Exercise Science

A number of factors have served as an impetus for the emergence of modern exercise science: the need for science-based principles of exercise, the need to correct myths regarding exercise, the need for methodology for training athletes, and the need for methodology for developing optimal health and fitness.

Need for science-based principles for exercise

Today more and more people, laymen as well as physicians and other health scientists, realize the potential health benefits derived from the pursuit of physical fitness. This interest in physical fitness initially was accelerated by the need for physically fit young men for the armed forces during World Wars I and II. Our leaders recognized the need to develop scientific bases for the conduct of exercise programs, whether directed toward health enhancement, physical fitness for work and play, sports performance, or rehabilitation after injury. That is, we needed to be guided by evidence developed from scientific experiments that were conducted under laboratory-controlled conditions wherever possible.

Need to correct myths regarding exercise

In the early years, there was very little scientific data by which exercise programs could be governed. To exemplify the problem, consider the following *myths,* which were widely accepted as fact until recently.

1. Heavy exercise, such as weight training, was said to make a person "muscle bound." This was believed to slow the athlete and restrict range of motion. Consequently, athletic coaches of the 1930s and 1940s strictly forbade their athletes from lifting weights. Scientific research in the 1950s completely reversed this thinking, and now weight rooms are necessities in any athletic program.

2. "Athlete's heart" was thought to result from heavy endurance training, such as long-distance running and swimming. This myth resulted from the well-known fact that the hearts of well-trained athletes grew larger. In some types of heart disease, the heart also grows larger, but for very different reasons. In any event, cardiologists now recognize that endurance exercise programs are beneficial, not detrimental, for the normal individual.

3. As recently as the 1950s, it was believed, even by many members of the medical profession, that older individuals (after 40 years of age) would not benefit from physical conditioning. They were no longer capable of the usual training response found in younger people. One of this chapter's authors was among the pioneers who disproved this myth by bringing about significant training effects in men who averaged 70 years of age (deVries, 1970). Subsequently, this work was extended to show that even in the 90s age group, significant benefits occur through appropriate conditioning (Dill, Arlie, & Bock, 1985).

4. Another myth of long standing was corrected in the late 1990s: "No pain, no gain" was the philosophy of many coaches and physical educators who worked their charges unmercifully to supramaximal efforts in the belief that anything less would be ineffective. Although this belief may have some merit when training champion athletes, it is definitely not a valid concept for training those members of the general public interested in improvement of their health and/or fitness levels. For example, we now know that even walking constitutes a training challenge and elicits a beneficial response for the untrained individual and, especially, for the elderly.

Need for methodology for training athletes

A major problem in developing scientific bases for exercise science lies in the great diversity of what falls within the realm of sport and exercise. It is abundantly obvious that the exercise that will improve a distance runner will not be the method of choice for the shot putter or weight-lifter. Then consider the many different sports and it is easy to see that instead of a "cookbook" for each conceivable activity it is far preferable to have scientifically based principles that can be applied to any given type of activity. For these reasons, textbooks in exercise physiology often break down into chapters organized by the element of performance involved, such as strength, endurance, or speed. The research-based knowledge concerned with these elements of performance is already voluminous and is growing exponentially. Exercise science is now an established area of study.

Need for methodology for developing optimal health and fitness

Over the past five decades, much evidence has been furnished that supports the value of exercise as a prophylactic and therapeutic measure. Although we can confidently say that the available evidence indicates that a vigorous lifestyle maintains optimum levels of health and well-being, we do not yet have all the answers as to how and why. At the rate at which scientific investigation has proceeded in the past few decades, it may not be unrealistic to expect the ultimate development of a "pharmacopoeia of exercise" in the coming decades.

ACADEMIC PROGRAMS IN EXERCISE SCIENCE

Most current college and university academic programs in exercise science grew out of the applied, professional discipline of physical education, which in the 1960s encompassed various aspects of sports, fitness, and physical activity (Siedentop, 1994). Today, however, physical education usually refers to the major that prepares students to teach in elementary and secondary schools while exercise science normally refers to a nonteaching option. At many universities, exercise science is one of the largest undergraduate majors in departments such as Kinesiology; Health and Human Performance; and Health, Physical Education, and Recreation (Siedentop, 1994).

Emergence of Academic Programs

Many academic programs in exercise science emerged in response to public concerns about our society's lack of physical fitness and the aerobic fitness movement of the 1960s and 1970s. Even with this increased interest in exercise, studies show that people today are generally not very fit or active, which increases the risk of developing a number of diseases (U.S. Department of Health and Human Services, 1996). This, combined with the results of other studies that showed that we can improve our health and quality of life through regular physical activity (Blair, Kohl, Barlow, et al., 1995; Blair, Kohl, Paffenbarger, et al., 1989; Paffenbarger et al., 1993), has sparked an interest in understanding the responses of the body to exercise. As the role of exercise in maintaining fitness and healthy lifestyles becomes better understood, researchers are able to obtain government as well as private funding to study the health-related aspects of exercise. The increased funding is, in part, responsible for the development and continuation of programs in exercise science in postsecondary institutions. There is, however, far less funding available for sport-related research than health-related research (Stone et al., 2005). This lack of funding opportunities threatens the ability of university researchers to address the critical questions related to sports performance that can help athletes remain competitive in international competitions (Stone et al., 2005).

Growth of Academic Programs

Initially, many students are drawn to the undergraduate major in exercise science because they enjoyed athletic participation during childhood and adolescence. The opportunity to study the scientific bases of sport performance is often appealing. Some students also find it interesting to apply this scientific knowledge to their own training as competitive athletes or to their own exercise programs, or to work with athletes in various settings. Other students major in exercise science because the rigorous scientific course work prepares them for future careers. The dramatic growth in exercise science programs in colleges and universities outlined above is also due to the diversity of career opportunities available to graduates. See Exhibit 1.1.

exhibit   1.1   Potential career and employment options for students in exercise science.

Option	Related Associations and Organizations	Selected Websites	Estimated Annual Salary Range*
AGENCY FITNESS			
Youth sport, fitness/wellness, personal training	The Y, the YWCA	www.ymca.net, www.ywca.org	$15,000–30,000
Military fitness	Armed Forces	www.benning.army.mil www.brooks.af.mil www.nomi.med.navy.mil	$25,000–40,000
CLINICAL AND REHABILITATION			
Cardiac rehabilitation	American Association of Cardiovascular and Pulmonary Rehabilitation (AACVPR)	www.aacvpr.org	$30,000–45,000
Pulmonary rehabilitation	AACVPR	www.aacvpr.org	$30,000–45,000
Athletic training	National Athletic Trainers' Association (NATA)	www.nata.org	$35,000–80,000
Massage therapy	American Massage Therapy Association (AMTA)	www.amtamassage.org	$15,000–25,000
Medical Technologist	American Medical Technologists (AMT)	www.amt1.com	$25,000–35,000
PROFESSIONAL SCHOOLS			
Allopathic Medicine (M.D.)	American Medical Association (AMA)	www.ama-assn.org	$100,000+
Osteopathic Medicine (D.O.)	American Osteopathic Association (AOA)	www.osteopathic.org	$100,000+
Physician's Assistant (P.A.)	American Academy of Physician's Assistants	www.aapa.org	$40,000–80,000
Dentistry (D.D.S.)	American Dental Association (ADA)	www.ada.org	$100,000+
Podiatry (D.P.M.)	American Podiatric Medical Association	www.apma.org	$80,000+
Physical Therapy (P.T.)	American Physical Therapy Association	www.apta.org	$40,000–60,000
Physical Therapy Assistant (P.T.A.)	Occupational Outlook Handbook	www.bls.gov/oco	$25,000–30,000
Occupational Therapy (O.T.)	American Occupational Therapy Association (AOTA)	www.aota.org	$40,000–60,000
Occupational Therapy Assistant (O.T.A.)	Occupational Outlook Handbook	www.bls.gov/oco	$25,000–30,000
Chiropractic (D.C.)	International Chiropractors Association (ICA)	www.chiropractic.org	$50,000+
Optometry (O.D.)	American Optometric Association (AOA)	www.aoa.org	$40,000–60,000
Nursing (R.N.)	American Nursing Association (ANA)	www.nursingworld.org	$30,000–70,000
PRIVATE SECTOR			
Corporate fitness and wellness	National Wellness Institute	www.nationalwellness.org www.HPCareer.net	$20,000–30,000
Health club employee	International Health, Racquet, and Sportsclub Association (IHRSA) Medical Fitness Association	www.ihrsa.org www.medicalfitness.org	$15,000–30,000
Personal training	International Dance Education Association (IDEA) National Strength and Conditioning Association (NSCA) Aerobic and Fitness Association of America	www.ideafit.com www.nsca-lift.org www.afaa.com	$15,000–30,000

(continued)

Continued.

exhibit **1.1**

Option	Related Associations and Organizations	Selected Websites	Estimated Annual Salary Range*
Ergonomics consulting	Human Factors and Ergonomics Society (HFES) Board of Certification in Professional Ergonomics (BCPE)	www.hfes.org www.bcpe.org	$25,000–40,000
Strength and conditioning coach for professional team	NSCA	www.nsca-lift.org	$30,000–80,000
Dietician	American Dietetics Association	www.eatright.org	$25,000–45,000
Occupational safety specialist	Occupational Health and Safety Administration (OSHA)	www.osha.gov	$25,000–40,000
Health and fitness writer	American Medical Writers Association (AMWA)	www.amwancal.org	$20,00–40,000
TEACHER, RESEARCHER, AND/OR COACH			
University, college, or community college professor	American Association of University Professors (AAUP)	www.aaup.org	$40,000–80,000
University or college strength and conditioning coach	NSCA	www.nsca-lift.org	$30,000–80,000
Athletic team coach	National Collegiate Athletic Association (NCAA)	www.ncaa.org	$20,000+
Institutional research (e.g., Cooper Institute or Olympic Training Center)	American College of Sports Medicine (ACSM) NSCA Olympic Training Center Cooper Institute	www.acsm.org www.nsca-lift.org www.olympic-usa.org www.cooperinst.org	$20,000+

This chart shows variability in what might be considered a "typical" salary range for the listings. Many factors, such as experience, specialty, geographic location, educational training, and professional certifications, influence salary.

Undergraduate exercise science programs are frequently used as the foundation for attending professional schools in medicine, physical therapy, chiropractic, occupational therapy, and dentistry as well as other **allied health** fields. In addition, an exercise science degree is valuable for careers in **corporate or agency fitness** (YMCA, YWCA, and the like), **personal training,** and **private consulting,** such as for health clubs. The expansion of fitness facilities by corporations is driven not only by a desire to provide a valued fringe benefit for employees but also by research that indicates that the company can benefit economically through reduced health insurance costs and absenteeism when their workforce is physically fit and active (Kaman & Patton, 1994). The need for qualified managers of such facilities contributed to the development of exercise science majors at colleges and universities as well as certification programs through professional organizations such as the American College of Sports Medicine, the National Strength and Conditioning Association (**NSCA**), the American Council on Exercise (**ACE**), and the International Society of Sports Nutrition (**ISSN**), among others (see Exhibit 1.2).

- *allied health*
- *corporate or agency fitness*
- *personal training*
- *private consulting*

- *NSCA*
- *ACE*
- *ISSN*

The combination of a degree in exercise science and certification from a reputable professional organization increases the likelihood of success in the job market. Another career option for undergraduate exercise science students

exhibit / 1.2   Selected professional certifications in exercise science.

Organization	Certification(s)
American College of Sports Medicine (ACSM) 401 West Michigan Street Indianapolis, IN 46202-3233 (317) 637-9200 • www.acsm.org	ACSM Certified Personal Trainer® This certification is for those who want to train individuals with no medical condition. Degree requirements: High school diploma. ACSM Certified Health Fitness Specialist® This certification is for those who want to train individuals having a low-to-moderate-risk and/or controlled diseases. Degree requirements: Exercise-based Bachelor's degree ACSM Clinical Exercise Specialist® This certification is for professionals who typically work in cardiovascular/pulmonary rehabilitation programs, physician's offices, or medical fitness centers. Degree requirements: Bachelor's degree in exercise-related field. ACSM Registered Clinical Exercise Physiologist® This certification is for allied health professionals who work in preventive or rehabilitative settings. Degree requirements: Master's degree in movement science, kinesiology, or exercise physiology.
American Council on Exercise (ACE) 4851 Paramount Drive San Diego, CA 92123 (858) 279-8227 • www.acefitness.org	ACE Personal Trainer Certification This certification is for those who want to train individuals having no medical condition. Degree requirements: None. Group Fitness Instructor This certification is for those who want to lead groups of individuals having no medical conditions in fitness settings. Degree requirements: None. Lifestyle & Weight Management Coach This certification is for those who want to develop weight management programs for individuals. Degree requirements: Bachelor's degree in exercise science or related field; various certifications. Advanced Health and Fitness Specialist This certification is for those who want to work with special populations. Degree requirements: Bachelor's degree in exercise science or related field; various certifications.
American Sport Education Program (ASEP) 1607 N. Market Street P.O. Box 5076 Champaign, IL 61825-5076 (800) 747-5698 • http://asep.com/index.cfm	National Coaches Registry This course is for those who want to become coaches. Degree requirements: None. National Officials Registry This course is for those who want to become officials. Degree requirements: None.
International Society of Sports Nutrition (ISSN) 600 Pembrook Drive Woodland Park, CO 80863 (866) 472-4650 • www.sportsnutritionsociety.org	Sports Nutrition Specialist (SNS) This is an entry-level certification for health, fitness, and medical professionals who work with athletes or active individuals. Degree requirements: None. Certified Sports Nutritionist (C-ISSN) This certification is more advanced than the SNS and is for health, fitness, and medical professionals who work with athletes or active individuals. Degree requirements: Bachelor's degree in exercise science, kinesiology, PE, nutrition, biology, or related biological science.

(continued)

Continued.

Organization	Certification(s)
	Body Composition Certification (BCC-ISSN) This certifies one to perform body composition assessments. Degree requirements: Bachelor's degree in exercise science, nutrition, biology, or related field.
National Athletic Trainers' Association (NATA) 2952 Stemmons Freeway #200 Dallas, TX 75247 (214) 637-6282 • www.nata.org	**The Certified Athletic Trainer (ATC)** This certification requires formal education and the successful completion of the ATC examination administered by the NATA Board of Certification. Degree requirements: Bachelor's degree in athletic training.
National Strength and Conditioning Association (NSCA) 1865 Bob Johnson Dr. Colorado Springs, CO 80906 (719) 632-6722 • www.nsca-lift.org	**NSCA-Certified Personal Trainer (NSCA-CPT)** This certification is for professionals who work with both active and sedentary clients in one-on-one situations. Degree requirements: None.
	Certified Strength and Conditioning Specialist (CSCS) This certification is for professionals who design and implement strength training and conditioning programs for athletes in a team setting. Degree requirements: Bachelor's degree in exercise science or related field.

is to attend graduate school. Generally, the graduate school options involve advanced preparation for students interested in corporate or agency fitness, specialized training in clinical aspects of exercise science such as cardiac rehabilitation, or the development of research skills for those interested in teaching and conducting research in university settings.

The Curriculum

The typical undergraduate exercise science curriculum includes a foundation in the basic sciences, followed by a series of courses related to exercise. Although differences exist among curricula from various institutions, they generally follow a similar format. For example, the science core usually includes courses in anatomy, biology, chemistry, and physiology. The exercise-related courses often include biomechanics, exercise physiology, laboratory techniques, and sports nutrition. Typically, one strength of undergraduate exercise science programs is the integrated approach to knowledge. The exercise-related courses draw on the information from the courses within the science core and apply the knowledge to physical activity.

The philosophy underlying the undergraduate exercise science curriculum is that there is a knowledge base that all students should have. In general, this knowledge base is important for all specialized areas of interest, whether it be cardiac rehabilitation, corporate and agency fitness, physical therapy, or medicine. There is also an underlying concept that, in addition to core courses, students should develop the skills and knowledge associated with their specialized area of interest in many ways, including elective courses, practicum experiences, volunteer noncredit activities, work experiences, and/or special training from professional certification programs during their undergraduate preparation. Many students also specialize through postbaccalaureate experiences, such as professional school (physical therapy, medicine, chiropractic,

www

Undergraduate training for exercise physiologists

http://faculty.css.edu/tboone2/asep/accredit.htm

www

Undergraduate training for strength and conditioning professionals

www.nsca-lift.org/erp/erpsc.shtml

and the like) or graduate school. In addition to traditional exercise science programs, more specialized curricula were proposed by the American Society of Exercise Physiologists (ASEP) for training undergraduate exercise physiologists and by the NSCA for preparing strength and conditioning professionals.

PROFESSIONAL STANDARDS FOR EXERCISE SCIENCE PROGRAMS

AAHPERD ■

www
Standards
www.acsm.org
www.aahperd.org
www.akta.org
www.cooperinst.org
www.aacvpr.org
www.nsca-lift.org

A number of fitness-related organizations, including the American College of Sports Medicine (ACSM), American Alliance for Health, Physical Education, Recreation and Dance (**AAHPERD**), American Kinesiotherapy Association (AKTA), Cooper Institute, American Association of Cardiovascular and Pulmonary Rehabilitation (AACVPR), National Strength and Conditioning Association (NSCA), American Council on Exercise, and National Academy of Sports Medicine, cooperated to establish undergraduate academic standards and guidelines for Exercise Science Programs. The standards are based on the recommendations of the Committee on Accreditation of the Exercise Sciences (CoAES), and programs that meet the standards can be accredited by the Commission on Accreditation of Allied Health Education Programs (CAAHEP). Currently, there are 28 CAAHEP-accredited Exercise Science programs in 16 states. The undergraduate program curriculum to meet the standards and guidelines for the Accreditation of Educational Programs in Exercise Science includes a sequence of classroom, laboratory, and clinical/practical activities that encompass the knowledge, skills, and abilities (KSAs) published in *ACSM's Guidelines for Exercise Testing and Prescription* (2010). In addition, the CoAES recommends that the program include culminating experiences such as an internship and a national credentialing examination such as ACSM Certified Health Fitness Specialist (CHFS), NSCA Certified Strength and Conditioning Specialist (CSCS), NSCA Certified Personal Trainer (CPT), or National Athletic Trainers' Association (**NATA**) Certified Athletic Trainer, among others.

www
Accreditation
www.coaes.org
www.caahep.org

NATA ■

www
Educational standards
www.fau.edu/divdept/exsci/
seacsm/qnews.htm

The Southeast Regional Chapter of the American College of Sports Medicine (SEACSM) developed a position statement titled *SEACSM Position on Educational Programs*. These educational standards provide a "minimum foundation upon which other educational/curricular objectives for training exercise science professionals can be based regardless of their future educational directions." At the undergraduate level (e.g., bachelor's degree), the suggested content areas include anatomy/physiology, biomechanics, kinesiology, physiology of exercise, nutrition/weight control, exercise testing for normal and special populations, exercise prescription for normal and special populations, first-aid/athletic training (including emergency and safety procedures for facilities), exercise leadership, practicum (applied) experience, and computer proficiency. In addition to demonstrating competence in the undergraduate content areas, the recommended graduate level (e.g., master's degree) content areas include research design and statistics, advanced or clinical exercise physiology, epidemiology of exercise and disease prevention, advanced exercise prescription and testing for normal and special populations, pharmacology, computer applications for exercise science, and research or clinical internship.

NASPE ■

The National Association for Sport and Physical Education (**NASPE**) is an association of AAHPERD. The Applied Exercise Science Council of NASPE developed a document called ***Basic Standards for the Professional Preparation in Exercise Science*** (AAHPERD, 1995), which was designed to provide guidance for curricular development for college and university programs that prepare undergraduate students for careers in exercise science. Basic standards are included in the major areas of

■ *Basic Standards for the Professional Preparation in Exercise Science*

- Foundational core
- Exercise prescription for normal and special populations
- Health promotion
- Administrative tasks
- Human relations
- Professional development
- Practical experience

Each area also includes specific behavioral objectives related to the knowledge and skills expected of entry-level exercise science professionals.

Foundational Core

The behavioral objectives associated with the foundational core indicate that exercise science students should have basic knowledge in the scientific areas of human anatomy, human physiology, exercise physiology, biomechanics, first aid, and the care and prevention of fitness-related injuries. Furthermore, students should maintain cardiopulmonary resuscitation (CPR) certification and be able to discuss and implement emergency and safety procedures for exercise settings.

Exercise Prescription for Normal and Special Populations

Entry-level exercise science professionals should be able to administer field and laboratory tests for evaluating cardiovascular endurance, body composition, muscular strength, muscular endurance, and flexibility and to develop safe and effective exercise prescriptions based on the results of these tests. Furthermore, exercise scientists should be able to modify exercise prescriptions for participation under various environmental conditions and by different populations, including the elderly. In addition to exercise prescription, it is important to be able to provide leadership for the implementation of aerobic, strength, and flexibility programs.

Health Promotion

Exercise scientists must be knowledgeable about factors related to nutrition and weight control, stress management, and substance abuse. Furthermore, it is important to have basic knowledge of available community referral services for individuals who need additional professional help with these issues.

Administrative Tasks

Exercise science professionals should have practical knowledge of (1) the equipment and facilities needed to develop and evaluate health and fitness programs, (2) trends related to health and fitness programming, (3) marketing strategies, and (4) legal and ethical issues involved in implementing health and fitness programs.

Human Relations

Entry-level exercise science professionals must possess sufficient verbal and written communication skills to speak clearly and concisely to individuals and groups and to prepare business letters, proposals, and technical reports. They must also demonstrate a basic knowledge of the motivational techniques related to exercise program adherence and retention.

Professional Development

It is important for exercise science professionals to understand the cultural environments and organizational structures within which fitness, wellness, and cardiac rehabilitation programs operate. Furthermore, exercise scientists should have knowledge of the professional organizations and publications related to their discipline and be able to articulate career planning strategies.

Practical Experience

Practical, hands-on experience is integral to the preparation of exercise science professionals. In this regard, students should have at least one observation experience at a work site and develop, with the site supervisor and university supervisor, a contractual agreement that includes specific learning experiences for an internship.

SUMMARY

E xercise science as an academic area of study is growing, as evidenced by the increasing number of undergraduate and graduate programs available to students. At many institutions, more students are now enrolled in the nonteaching option in exercise science than the traditional physical education teacher preparation major. The diversity of career options in areas such as agency and corporate fitness, personal training, **clinical rehabilitation**, allied health, consulting for the private sector, and **higher education** attracts many students to the exercise science major. Furthermore, the strong background in the basic sciences (e.g., anatomy, biology, and chemistry) associated with most undergraduate exercise science programs provides a solid foundation for students to meet the entrance requirements of many professional schools. In addition to the basic sciences, exercise science graduates are well grounded in the application of theory to practice by exercise-related courses and practical hands-on experiences such as practicums and internships.

clinical rehabilitation ■

higher education ■

Visit This Book's Companion Website

www

Introduction to Exercise Science Companion Website
http://hhpcommunities.com/exercisescience

Visit the *Introduction to Exercise Science* (IES) website for study aids and demonstration labs. You can review and take notes on the Study Questions and Learning Activities, review key terms, and try out a lab for each chapter, including this chapter's lab on pre-participation screening.

study / QUESTIONS

1. Define exercise science.
2. Name and describe the two primary areas of inquiry for exercise scientists.
3. Discuss the career opportunities available to an exercise scientist.
4. Discuss the skills that an entry-level exercise scientist should possess in order to prescribe exercise programs for normal and special populations.
5. Exercise science degrees are often used as a foundation for what future paths?
6. What are some health-related aspects of physical activity?
7. In order to promote a healthy lifestyle, exercise scientists must be knowledgeable about what factors?

learning \ ACTIVITIES

1. Visit the ACSM website (www.acsm.org).
   a. List five knowledge, skills, and abilities (KSAs) for the ACSM Certified Health Fitness Specialist (CHFS).
   b. Which ACSM membership should you apply for? What are the benefits of membership? How much does it cost?
2. Visit the NSCA website (www.nsca-lift.org). Select "Why Join?" Choose three of the reasons for joining and explain how they fit your situation.
3. Search online for any exercise science topic of your choice. Find two sites that you find interesting—one informative, one practical. Provide the site URL and a brief description, and explain why you like these particular sites.
4. Research exercise science curricula via the Internet. (*Hint:* Using Google, type "exercise science curriculum site:.edu"—using "site:.edu" limits the search to educational institutions.) Choose two other universities or colleges to compare their curricula to your university's curriculum.

suggested / READINGS

American College of Sports Medicine. (2010). *ACSM's guidelines for exercise testing and prescription* (8th ed.). Philadelphia: Lippincott Williams & Wilkins.

Chandler, T. J., & Brown, L. E. (2008). *Conditioning for strength and human performance.* Philadelphia: Lippincott Williams & Wilkins.

Howley, E. T., & Franks, B. D. (2007). *Fitness professional's handbook* (5th ed.). Champaign, IL: Human Kinetics.

references

American Alliance for Health, Physical Education, Recreation and Dance. (1995). *Basic standards for the professional preparation in exercise science 1995*. Reston, VA: Author.

American College of Sports Medicine. (2010). *ACSM's guidelines for exercise testing and prescription* (8th ed.). Philadelphia: Lippincott Williams & Wilkins.

Belloc, N. B., & Breslow, L. (1972). Relationship of physical health status and health practices. *Preventive Medicine, 1,* 409–421.

Blair, S. N. (1991). *Living with exercise: Improving your health through moderate physical activity*. Dallas, TX: American Health Publishing Company.

Blair, S. N. (1994). Physical activity, fitness, and coronary heart disease. In C. Bouchard, R. J. Shephard, & T. Stephens (Eds.), *Physical activity, fitness, and health: International proceedings and consensus statement*, pp. 579–590. Champaign, IL: Human Kinetics.

Blair, S. N., Kohl, H. W., Barlow, C. E., Paffenbarger, R. S., Gibbons, L. W., & Macera, C. A. (1995). Changes in physical fitness and all-cause mortality: A prospective study of healthy and unhealthy men. *Journal of the American Medical Association, 273,* 1093–1098.

Blair, S. N., Kohl, H. W., Paffenbarger, R. S., Clark, D. G., Cooper, K. H., & Gibbons, L. W. (1989). Physical fitness and all-cause mortality: A prospective study of healthy men and women. *Journal of the American Medical Association, 262,* 2395–2401.

deVries, H. A. (1970). Physiological effects of an exercise training regimen upon men aged 52–88. *Journal of Gerontology, 25,* 325–336.

Dill, D., Arlie, B., & Bock, V. (1985). Pioneers in sports medicine, Dec. 30, 1888–Aug. 11, 1984. *Medicine and Science in Sports and Exercise, 17,* 401–404.

Kaman, R. L., & Patton, R. W. (1994). Cost and benefits of an active versus an inactive society. In C. Bouchard, R. J. Shephard, & T. Stephens (Eds.), *Physical activity, fitness, and health: International proceedings and consensus statement*, pp. 134–144. Champaign, IL: Human Kinetics.

Kaplan, G. A., Seeman, T. E., Cohen, R. D., Knudsen, L. P., & Guralnik, J. (1987). Mortality among the elderly in the Alameda County Study: Behavioral and demographic risk factors. *American Journal of Public Health, 77,* 307–312.

Lee, I.-M. (1994). Physical activity, fitness, and cancer. In C. Bouchard, R. J. Shephard, & T. Stephens (Eds.), *Physical activity, fitness, and health: International proceedings and consensus statement*, pp. 814–831. Champaign, IL: Human Kinetics.

Linsted, K. D., Tonstad, S., & Kuzma, J. W. (1991). Self-report of physical activity and patterns of mortality in Seventh-Day Adventist men. *Journal of Clinical Epidemiology, 44,* 355–364.

Mackinnon, L. T. (1992). *Exercise and immunology*. Champaign, IL: Human Kinetics.

Morris, J. N., Clayton, D. G., Everitt, M. G., Semmence, A. M., & Burgess, E. H. (1990). Exercise in leisure time, coronary attack and death rates. *British Heart Journal, 63,* 325–334.

Mosby's Pocket Dictionary of Medicine, Nursing, and Allied Health. (2006). St. Louis: Mosby.

Nieman, D. C. (1994). Physical activity, fitness, and infection. In C. Bouchard, R. J. Shephard, & T. Stephens (Eds.), *Physical activity, fitness, and health: International proceedings and consensus statement*, pp. 796–813. Champaign, IL: Human Kinetics.

Paffenbarger, R. S., Hyde, R. T., Wing, A. L., Lee, I.-M., Jung, D. L., & Kampert, J. B. (1993). The association of changes in physical activity level and other lifestyle characteristics with mortality among men. *New England Journal of Medicine, 328,* 538–545.

Rowland, T. W. (1990). *Exercise and children's health*. Champaign, IL: Human Kinetics.

Siedentop, D. (1994). *Introduction to physical education, fitness, and sport* (2nd ed.). Mountain View, CA: Mayfield Publishing Company.

Stone, M. H., Stone, M. E., & Sands, W. (2005). The downfall of sports science in the United States. *Olympic Coach, 17,* 21–24.

U.S. Department of Health and Human Services. (1996). *Physical activity and health: A report of the Surgeon General*. Atlanta, GA: U.S. Department of Health and Human Services, Centers for Disease Control and Prevention, National Center for Chronic Disease Prevention and Health Promotion.

Reading and Interpreting the Literature in Exercise Science

JOEL T. CRAMER ■ TRAVIS W. BECK

INTRODUCTION

Formalized areas of study such as chemistry, biology, physics, and philosophy have existed for well over 2,000 years. The scientific and philosophical writings of Aristotle and Plato have shaped modern thought since 300 to 400 years BCE. Our scientific perspective on exercise science, however, has been cultivated by papers presented and published during the past 100 years, most of which were written within the last 50 years. As described in Chapter 1, academic programs in exercise science have existed only since the mid-to-late 1960s and are largely based on research dating back to the 1920s. Thus, exercise science is a relatively new area of inquiry, and many important discoveries have yet to be made. It is this dynamic, scientific nature of exercise science that has generated much excitement and popularity in recent times.

Due to its "scientific infancy," current knowledge in exercise science changes rapidly and often. New research findings that guide the direction of this field are regularly being published. Technological advances reinforce the need to continually reassess established theories and hypotheses as well as answer new questions or those that were once regarded as unanswerable. Therefore, staying abreast of the most recent scientific literature in exercise science is of paramount importance. Being regular consumers of scientific literature is important not only for researchers—such continuing education also ultimately advances all aspects of exercise science. Research informs teaching; thus, teaching the conceptual theory and applied tasks in exercise science is the primary vehicle by which current research findings are disseminated and integrated into practice. Overall, understanding the scientific literature enables us to distinguish fact from fiction, and in today's media, this can be a very difficult task.

As our field matures, the scope of exercise science broadens and diversifies, which is evidenced by the breadth of this book. Disciplines such as anatomy, athletic training, biomechanics, exercise epidemiology, exercise physiology, exercise and sport nutrition, exercise and sport psychology, measurement, and motor control and motor learning have emerged as specialized areas of scientific research. Exhibit 2.1 lists these disciplines and some representative peer-reviewed scientific journals that have helped define and shape them. However, with a plethora of scientific literature in a number of subdisciplines under the auspice of exercise science, the prospect of keeping up with the current findings may seem overwhelming. Therefore, the primary objective of this chapter is to teach you how to be an informed consumer of the scientific literature in exercise science.

LITERATURE SOURCES

The First Amendment of the U.S. Constitution allows people to write, disseminate, and sometimes publish just about anything. Supporting the growing excitement and interest in exercise science, the Internet provides access to a vast amount of literature in the field. Some Internet sources provide access to high-quality objective material, whereas others present subjective opinions that lack research support. Thus, it is important to teach consumers of the literature how to identify the quality and soundness of information. *Literature* in our field includes any written words related to exercise science that originate from both *scientific* and *nonscientific* sources.

List of exercise science subdisciplines and examples of representative scientific journals.

exhibit   2.1

Discipline	Journal Name	International Standard Serial Number (ISSN)	National Library of Medicine Identification Number (NLM ID)
Anatomy	Journal of Anatomy	0021-8782 (Print) 1469-7580 (Electronic)	0137162
Athletic Training	Journal of Athletic Training	1062-6050 (Print) 1938-162X (Electronic)	9301647
Biomechanics	Journal of Biomechanics	0021-9290 (Print) 1873-2380 (Electronic)	0157375
Exercise Epidemiology	Medicine and Science in Sports and Exercise	0195-9131 (Print) 1530-0315 (Electronic)	8005433
Exercise Physiology	European Journal of Applied Physiology	1439-6319 (Print) 1439-6327 (Electronic)	100954790
Exercise and Sport Nutrition	International Journal of Sport Nutrition and Exercise Metabolism	1526-484X (Print) 1543-2742 (Electronic)	100939812
Exercise and Sport Psychology	Journal of Sport and Exercise Psychology	0895-2779 (Print) 1543-2904 (Electronic)	8809258
Measurement	Research Quarterly for Exercise and Sport	0270-1367 (Print) 0364-9857 (Electronic)	8006373
Motor Control and Motor Learning	Perceptual and Motor Skills	0031-5125 (Print) 1558-688X (Electronic)	0401131
Strength and Conditioning	Journal of Strength and Conditioning Research	1064-8011 (Print) 1533-4287 (Electronic)	9415084

Scientific Literature Sources

Typically, **scientific literature** undergoes a **peer-review process,** whereas nonscientific literature is usually not reviewed (see Exhibit 2.2). When a scientific article or book chapter is submitted for publication, the manuscript is reviewed by two or three **external reviewers** who are chosen because of their expertise in the content area. The external reviewers rate the manuscript, recommend it for acceptance or rejection, and provide comments and suggestions for improvement. It often takes 1 to 6 months to organize the review of a single manuscript. Based on the recommendations and comments from the external reviewers, the editor must decide whether to reject or accept the manuscript, or request revisions from the author(s) before a decision regarding publication can be made. Typically, the author is given an opportunity to

- scientific literature
- peer-review process

- external reviewers

exhibit / 2.2	Examples of peer-reviewed research journals and non–peer-reviewed journals/magazines in exercise science.

Peer-Reviewed Research Journals	Non–Peer-Reviewed Journals/Magazines
Journal of Neuroscience Methods	Flex
European Journal of Applied Physiology	Iron Man Magazine
International Journal of Sport Nutrition & Exercise Metabolism	Men's Fitness
International Journal of Sports Physiology and Performance	Men's Health
Isokinetics and Exercise Science	Ms. Fitness Magazine
Journal of Applied Physiology	Muscular Development
Journal of Electromyography and Kinesiology	Muscle & Fitness
Journal of Strength and Conditioning Research	Planet Muscle Magazine
Medicine & Science in Sports & Exercise	Procycling Magazine
Pediatric Exercise Science	Runner's World
Research Quarterly for Exercise and Sport	Shape Magazine

revise the manuscript and respond to the reviewers' comments. Upon receiving the revised manuscript and responses to reviewers' comments from the author, the editor either conducts a second review or makes the final decision regarding its publication status. Overall, the review process for most scientific literature is extensive and rigorous and demands higher standards than nonscientific, non-reviewed literature. There are two types of peer-reviewed scientific literature: *primary* and *secondary references*.

Primary references

primary references ■

Consumers can be assured that each primary scientific literature source underwent a peer-review process, which brings a level of credibility to the content.

Primary references are the basic and applied research articles that present the purpose, methods, results, and conclusions of a scientific research study (see Exhibit 2.2). Reading and understanding primary references allow the reader to see firsthand the results of a single study and draw conclusions based on those results and/or the authors' interpretations. These references provide the most current information on topics in exercise science and expose the reader to the original report. The only potential drawback to primary sources is that there is usually a large amount of literature on a specific topic, making it difficult to draw sound conclusions that are based on the results of only one study. Thus, readers must be aware of the findings of many separate studies in order to fully understand the topic; for example, following are several primary sources that address the issue of central versus peripheral manifestations of muscular fatigue during exercise:

■ Bigland-Ritchie, B., Furbush, F., & Woods, J. J. (1986). Fatigue of intermittent submaximal voluntary contractions: Central and peripheral factors. *Journal of Applied Physiology, 61*(2), 421–429.

- Nordlund, M. M., Thorstensson, A., & Cresswell, A. G. (2004). Central and peripheral contributions to fatigue in relation to level of activation during repeated maximal voluntary isometric plantar flexions. *Journal of Applied Physiology, 96,* 218–225.

- Weir, J. P., Keefe, D. A., Eaton, J. F., Augustine, R. T., & Tobin, D. M. (1998). Effect of fatigue on hamstring coactivation during isokinetic knee extensions. *European Journal of Applied Physiology and Occupation Physiology, 78*(6), 555–559.

Secondary references

In contrast, **secondary references** include review articles and academic book or textbook chapters. These sources are still rigorously peer-reviewed, but they often summarize and/or synthesize the results of many research studies, which allows for a more inclusive understanding of the topic than any one research article. Consumers are not required to find and understand all of the primary references; rather, they can "get the big picture" all in one article review or book chapter. Secondary literature sources are also valuable for locating primary references that cannot be found using traditional literature searches. On the other hand, secondary references are often narrative reviews, which are subjective interpretations by their nature (some literature reviews are objective—see the discussion on meta-analyses later in this chapter). Thus, the reader receives a secondhand interpretation of several primary sources. In addition, secondary references can be somewhat out-of-date at the time of publication, a particularly important problem for book chapters that are often written 1 to 3 years in advance of their publication date and may not include the most recent information. Below are examples of opposing narrative literature reviews regarding the issue of central versus peripheral manifestations of muscle fatigue, along with two complementary secondary-source book chapters:

■ *secondary references*

LITERATURE REVIEWS

- Weir, J. P., Beck, T. W., Cramer, J. T., & Housh, T. J. (2006). Is fatigue all in your head? A critical review of the central governor model. *British Journal of Sports Medicine, 40*(7), 573–586.

- Noakes, T. D., & St. Clair Gibson, A. (2004). Logical limitations to the "catastrophe" models of fatigue during exercise in humans. *British Journal of Sports Medicine, 38,* 648–649.

BOOK CHAPTERS

- Smith, A. E., & Cramer, J. T. (2012). Endurance training program design. In J. R. Hoffman (Ed.), *Program design.* Champaign, IL: Human Kinetics.

- Ryan, E. D., & Cramer, J. T. (2012). Fitness testing protocols and norms. In J. W. Coburn & M. H. Malek (Eds.), *NSCA's essentials of personal training* (2nd ed.), Champaign, IL: Human Kinetics.

Nonscientific Literature Sources

Popular magazines, newspapers, and most Internet websites publish **nonscientific literature** in exercise science. These are usually subjective, opinion-based articles that have not been reviewed for credibility or content. For example, *Shape, Men's Health,* and *Muscle & Fitness* (see Exhibit 2.2 for further

■ *nonscientific literature*

examples) are magazines that publish nonscientific content that has not been peer-reviewed. However, nonscientific literature is not without value. Presented correctly, exercise science-related information disseminated to the lay public can increase awareness of critical issues in the field. For example, a newspaper article that reports the results of a recent study demonstrating that exercise can reduce the risk of heart disease (Fogoros, 2002) would likely result in a positive outcome for the general population. In addition, nonscientific articles can be used as an impetus for conducting a scientific study. To illustrate, if an article in an online magazine claims that drinking coffee prior to exercise

Popular magazines and websites do interview scientists in the field of exercise science, but often the scientist is not given an opportunity to review the resulting article prior to publication.

or athletic events will not improve performance (Raiciu, 2006), then this hypothesis can be tested by researchers in an experimental setting (e.g., Costill, Dalsky, & Fink, 1978). Therefore, although nonscientific literature is generally not cited as a legitimate source of information in exercise science, this type of information does have some value to society. Following are some examples of nonscientific literature sources on muscle fatigue.

- Cavazos, M. (2011, May 26). What are the causes of fatigue during endurance exercise? Retrieved from http://www.livestrong.com/article/380893.

- Parker-Pope, T. (2011, February 11). Picking up good vibrations at the gym. Retrieved from http://well.blogs.nytimes.com/2011/02/11/picking-up-good-vibrations-at-the-gym/.

READING PRIMARY REFERENCES

As stated previously, a primary reference is a research study that is designed to answer a very specific research question. In many cases, these studies are referred to as original investigations. Although there are exceptions to this general format, most primary references have seven sections: (1) Abstract, (2) Introduction, (3) Methods, (4) Results, (5) Discussion, (6) Conclusions, and (7) References.

Abstract

abstract ■ The purpose of the **Abstract** is to provide a very brief overview of the purpose of the study, the methods used to collect and analyze the data, the study's results, and the conclusions that can be drawn from the results. For many journals, the Abstract is required to be 150 to 250 words in length. As shown in Exhibit 2.3, the Abstract is very concise and does not contain detailed information regarding the study's experimental design and results. The Abstract can usually be accessed free of charge on specialized websites, allowing readers to determine within minutes whether or not they want to read the full-text article.

Introduction

introduction ■ The **Introduction** section of a research article has three primary functions: (1) to introduce the reader to important topics that are relevant to the manuscript, (2) to provide a purpose statement for the study, and (3) to propose one or more hypotheses regarding the study's outcome(s). Like the Abstract, the Introduction section is an important part of the research report because it

Example of an Abstract from a research article.

exhibit 2.3

Herda, T. J., Costa, P. B., Walter, A. A., Ryan, E. D., Hoge, K. M., Kerksick, C. M., Stout, J. R., & Cramer, J. T. (2011). Effects of two modes of static stretching on muscle strength and stiffness. *Medicine and Science in Sports and Exercise, 43*(9),1777–1784.

PURPOSE: The purpose of the present study was to examine the effects of constant-angle (CA) and constant-torque (CT) stretching of the leg flexors on peak torque (PT), electromyography (EMG_{RMS}) at PT, passive range of motion (PROM), passive torque during the range of motion (PAS_{TQ}), and musculotendinous stiffness (MTS).

METHODS: Seventeen healthy men (mean ± SD age = 21.4 ± 2.4) performed a PROM assessment and isometric maximal voluntary contraction (MVC) of the leg flexors at a knee joint angle of 80° below full leg extension before and after 8 min of CA and CT stretching. PAS_{TQ} and MTS were measured at three common joint angles for pre- and post-assessments.

RESULTS: PT decreased (mean ± SE 5.63 ± 1.65 Nm) ($P = 0.004$), and EMG_{RMS} was unchanged ($P > 0.05$) from pre- to post-stretching for both treatments. PROM increased (5.00 ± 1.03°) and PAS_{TQ} decreased at all three angles pre- to post-stretching (angle 1 5.03 ± 4.52 Nm; angle 2 6.30 ± 5.88 Nm; angle 3 6.68 ± 6.33 Nm) for both treatments ($P \le 0.001$). In addition, MTS decreased at all three angles (angle 1 0.23 ± 0.29 Nm°; angle 2 0.26 ± 0.35 Nm°; angle 3 0.28 ± 0.44 Nm°) following the CT stretching treatment ($P < 0.005$); however, MTS was unchanged following CA stretching ($P > 0.05$).

CONCLUSION: PT, EMG_{RMS}, PROM and PAS_{TQ} changed in a similar manner following stretching treatments; however, only CT stretching resulted in a decrease in MTS. Therefore, if the primary goal of the stretching routine is to decrease MTS, these results suggest CT stretching (constant pressure) may be more appropriate than a stretch held at a constant muscle length (CA stretching).

introduces the reader to the question the investigators are trying to answer. Thus, most of the Introduction section contains background information that informs the reader and provides justification for doing the study. For example, if the purpose of a study is to examine the effect of a particular sports supplement on muscular strength, the Introduction section should contain information regarding the physiological mechanisms by which the supplement could affect strength. This background material provides justification for doing the study (e.g., the authors may state that the study has never been done before or that the results from previous investigations are inconclusive).

After the background information, the Introduction section usually contains a purpose statement that describes the specific research question the study is designed to answer. Because most research questions usually cannot be answered conclusively with one study, a common approach taken in exercise science laboratories is to conduct a series of investigations that answer slightly different research questions. The results from the series of studies are then interpreted as a whole, which allows the researchers to make definitive statements regarding the research problem. After the purpose statement, the author often proposes one or more hypotheses regarding the study's outcome(s). The **hypotheses** are usually based on the background information presented earlier in the Introduction section and reflect what the author believes the study results will show. Exhibit 2.4 shows an example of a purpose statement and hypothesis at the end of an Introduction section.

■ *hypotheses*

exhibit / 2.4   Example of a purpose statement and hypothesis at the end of an Introduction section.

Herda, T. J., Costa, P. B., Walter, A. A., Ryan, E. D., Hoge, K. M., Kerksick, C. M., Stout, J. R., & Cramer, J. T. (2011). Effects of two modes of static stretching on muscle strength and stiffness. *Medicine and Science in Sports and Exercise, 43*(9), 1777–1784.

Therefore, the purpose of the present study was to examine the acute effects of CA versus CT static stretching of the hamstring muscles on peak torque (PT), electromyographic amplitude (EMG_{RMS}) at PT, passive range of motion (PROM), passive torque during the range of motion (PAS_{TQ}), and musculotendinous stiffness (MTS). Based on the results of previous studies it was hypothesized that CA and CT static stretching would have equivalent effects on all of the dependent variables.

Methods

methods ■   The **Methods** section provides detailed information regarding the characteristics of the study's participants, the type of equipment used and the tests performed, and a description of the *experimental design,* including all *independent* and *dependent variables* that were a part of the study. The Methods section is useful to others who are interested in replicating the study or conducting a study with a similar experimental design. For example, a researcher who wants to replicate or slightly modify a certain study must have information regarding the equipment and procedures that were used to collect the data and how the data were analyzed. Thus, the Methods section is important for establishing the study's *external validity.* The Methods section is important when comparing the results from different studies. For example, when two studies with similar experimental designs report different results, the discrepancy could be due to differences in such factors as the type of study participants or the procedures used to collect the data. Exhibit 2.5 shows an excerpt from the Methods section of a research article.

exhibit / 2.5   Excerpt from the Methods section of a research article.

Herda, T. J., Costa, P. B., Walter, A. A., Ryan, E. D., Hoge, K. M., Kerksick, C. M., Stout, J. R., & Cramer, J. T. (2011). Effects of two modes of static stretching on muscle strength and stiffness. *Medicine and Science in Sports and Exercise, 43*(9), 1777–1784.

This study used a randomized, repeated measures, crossover design to examine the acute effects of constant-angle (CA) and constant-torque (CT) stretching of the leg flexors on PT, EMG_{RMS}, PROM, PAS_{TQ}, and MTS. Each participant visited the laboratory three times, separated by 3–5 days. The first visit was a familiarization trial and the next two visits were experimental trials, in which the subjects were randomly assigned to either the CA or CT stretching treatment prior to the first experimental trial and then performed the other treatment on the second experimental trial. During each experimental trial, the participants underwent the pre-stretching tests (PROM assessments followed by MVC assessments), the stretching intervention, and the post-stretching assessments occurred immediately after the stretching. All experimental trials were performed at the same time of day (± 2 h).

Results

Like the Methods section, the **Results** section is usually very detailed and presents the results from all of the statistical analyses performed in the study. Thus, the Results section typically contains one or more figures and/or tables, along with text that describes the experiment's results. Although the Results section is usually written using somewhat technical and monotonous language, it provides comprehensive information regarding the results from the statistical analyses. This information is particularly important when examining the study's results. For example, suppose several statistical analyses were performed, but the author chose to discuss only the most interesting results or those results most directly related to the research question. Some readers, however, may be interested in results that are not directly related to the research question. Another reason why the Results section must be comprehensive is because the results from statistical tests may be used in review articles referred to as meta-analyses (see the Reviews section later in this chapter). Briefly, the meta-analysis is a review article in which the results from many studies are statistically combined. If the Results section of a particular study is not comprehensive, it may not be possible to use the data in the meta-analysis. Exhibit 2.6 shows an excerpt from the Results section of a research article.

■ *results*

Discussion

The **Discussion** section, one of the most important sections, is written such that it relates the study's results to the information presented in the Introduction section and to the results from previous investigations. This section also typically contains detailed information regarding how the results from the study fit within the **theory,** a comprehensive explanation of a given set of data that has been repeatedly confirmed by observation and experimentation and has gained general acceptance within the scientific community but has not yet been decisively proven. In most cases, this theory was developed in the Introduction section and provided a basis for conducting the study. The Discussion section usually contains information regarding the results from previous studies that have examined similar research questions, and the findings from these investigations are then compared and contrasted with those from the current study. Hypotheses can then be proposed regarding why the experiment turned out the way it did.

■ *discussion*

■ *theory*

Another important part of the Discussion section involves developing a basis for future studies. Because a particular research study is often a con-

Excerpt from the Results section of a research article.	**exhibit** 2.6

Herda, T. J., Costa, P. B., Walter, A. A., Ryan, E. D., Hoge, K. M., Kerksick, C. M., Stout, J. R., & Cramer, J. T. (2011). Effects of two modes of static stretching on muscle strength and stiffness. *Medicine and Science in Sports and Exercise, 43*(9), 1777–1784.

For PT, there was no significant two-way interaction (treatment x time, $F_{1,16} = 1.962$, $P = 0.180$, $\eta_p^2 = 0.109$) and no main effect for treatment ($F_{1,16} = 0.201$, $P = 0.654$, $\eta_p^2 = 0.013$), but there was a main effect for time ($F_{1,16} = 11.515$, $P = 0.004$, $\eta_p^2 = 0.418$). PT decreased from pre- to post-stretching (collapsed across CA and CT treatments) by an average of (mean ± SE) 6.41 ± 3.15%.

tinuation of work done previously in the author's laboratory, the Discussion section may provide the basis for the next experiment the researcher has planned. In fact, it is fairly common for scientists to spend their entire careers in one research area. Although extremely time-consuming, the process of conducting a sequence of slightly modified experiments helps researchers become very knowledgeable in a particular area, and the Discussion section is where they describe the results of their work. Exhibit 2.7 shows an excerpt from the Discussion section of a research article.

Conclusions

conclusions ■ The **Conclusions** section is typically presented either toward the end of the Discussion section or immediately thereafter. In the Conclusions section, the author briefly summarizes the most important findings from the study and whether or not the results support the hypotheses. In addition, the author may provide recommendations for future studies that should be done in the area. Exhibit 2.8 shows an example of a Conclusions section from a research article.

References

references ■ One of the most useful components of a journal article is the list of **References** presented after the Conclusions section. Specifically, the Reference list provides all of the information necessary to locate the publications cited by the author(s) in the article. For example, for each journal article cited in the text, the author must provide the authors' names, the article's title, the name of the journal that published the article, the year of publication, the

| exhibit / 2.7 | Excerpt from the Discussion section of a research article. |

Herda, T. J., Costa, P. B., Walter, A. A., Ryan, E. D., Hoge, K. M., Kerksick, C. M., Stout, J. R., & Cramer, J. T. (2011). Effects of two modes of static stretching on muscle strength and stiffness. *Medicine and Science in Sports and Exercise, 43*(9), 1777–1784.

The primary finding of the present study was that only the CT stretching decreased muscle stiffness, whereas both types of stretching (CT and CA) improved the range of motion. Specifically, 8 min of CA and CT stretching increased PROM and decreased PAS_{TQ} at all joint angles; however, MTS only decreased following the CT stretching and was unchanged following CA stretching. Previous studies have examined the effects of a 30-min bout of CA and CT stretching in stroke patients with ankle hypertonia.* The authors reported greater increases in range of motion and decreases in the viscoelastic properties of the muscle for the CT stretching treatment compared to the CA stretching treatment. Yeh et al.* hypothesized that the greater decreases in stiffness reported with the CT stretching protocol may have been due to "muscle creep" during the stretch. Ryan et al.* suggested that CT stretching protocols may place more tension and/or apply more work on the MTU, which would result in greater changes in the viscoelastic properties of the muscle when compared to holding a stretch at a constant joint angle. The results of the current study support these hypotheses and suggest that CT stretching is superior to CA stretching for decreasing muscle stiffness.

Reference citations omitted.

Example of the Conclusions section from a research article.   **exhibit**   **2.8**

Herda, T. J., Costa, P. B., Walter, A. A., Ryan, E. D., Hoge, K. M., Kerksick, C. M., Stout, J. R., & Cramer, J. T. (2011). Effects of two modes of static stretching on muscle strength and stiffness. *Medicine and Science in Sports and Exercise, 43*(9), 1777–1784.

> In summary, PAS_{TQ} and PROM changed in a similar manner for both treatments; however, MTS decreased following CT stretching but not CA stretching. If the primary goal of the stretching routine is to decrease MTS and reduce musculoskeletal injuries, these results suggest that a static stretch held with a constant pressure (CT stretching) would be more appropriate than stretching held at a constant muscle length (CA stretching). Practitioners should be aware that despite the greater changes in MTS following CT stretching, there will not be a greater decrement in strength compared to CA stretching. In addition, future research is needed to examine the acute effects of a smaller duration of time under stretch (<8 min) of CT and CA stretching on PROM, MTS, and muscle strength in both males and females.

volume and/or issue numbers, and the page numbers where the article can be found. Similar information must be provided for all books and book chapters cited. The Reference list helps readers quickly locate groups of articles that address a particular topic. The Reference list of a review article or book chapter often contains 100 or more entries. Because review articles and book chapters are comprehensive and written by experts in the field, they are an excellent starting point for beginning researchers or those interested in a particular topic. For example, delayed-onset muscle soreness (DOMS) is one of the most researched topics in exercise science. Anyone interested in DOMS should acquire one of the many DOMS-related review articles and begin collecting the articles, books, book chapters, and so on, provided in the Reference list. Although laborious, this is one of the quickest and most comprehensive methods for beginning research in a particular area.

READING SECONDARY REFERENCES

For many students, their first exposure to the literature in exercise science comes from textbooks, even though such books are only one of several types of secondary sources.

Textbooks

The purpose of textbooks in exercise science is to educate students and summarize the literature on various topics. A major advantage of textbooks is that they are usually written for teaching purposes; thus, the information may be presented at either an introductory or more advanced level. Most exercise science textbooks are very well organized, with chapters devoted to those basic areas that should be mastered by beginning students. For example, a particular textbook chapter may discuss muscle anatomy and physiology, while another might address cardiovascular responses to exercise. Furthermore, the text's reference list is usually comprehensive, which allows interested readers to quickly access many literature sources on a particular topic.

Professional Books

Although exercise science is still a relatively new area of study, many comprehensive books have been written by experts in the field on various specialized topics. The information usually summarizes the results from previous studies and facilitates the development of future studies. These books often have a comprehensive reference list that is useful for anyone interested in examining other sources of literature.

Reviews

Review articles are similar to specialized professional books in that they are often comprehensive, are usually written by experts in the field, and typically have an extensive reference list. Review articles are, however, even more focused than specialized books. For example, a specialized book may discuss DOMS, while a review article might address the factors that cause the cytoskeletal damage underlying DOMS.

narrative review ■   Although review articles can be written in various forms, there are two primary types in exercise science: narrative reviews and meta-analytic reviews. A **narrative review** summarizes the results from most, if not all, of the studies in a particular area. Usually, a narrative review is written after a substantial number of studies have been conducted on a particular research topic. The review's purpose is to discuss the studies' results collectively so that conclusions can be drawn and future research ideas developed. Although narrative reviews are excellent starting points for beginning researchers, they are usually written at an advanced level and may be difficult to understand.

meta-analysis ■   Unlike narrative reviews, meta-analytic reviews use statistical procedures to combine the results from several studies that address a similar research question. Briefly, the **meta-analysis** uses a standardized measure of effect size based on the quantitative results from various studies in the area. The primary purpose of the meta-analysis is to use the results to draw general conclusions regarding a particular research question. Although the meta-analysis is a very useful statistical technique for quantitatively summarizing the results of several studies, a background in statistics is usually necessary to fully understand the results. Thus, meta-analyses are very helpful for researchers but may be difficult to understand for beginning exercise science students.

LOCATING REFERENCES IN EXERCISE SCIENCE

Perhaps the first and most common question from students and others who wish to find basic and applied scientific articles in exercise science is *Where do I look?* The Internet has revolutionized the process of locating research literature. Government websites that host the PubMed and ERIC® (Exhibit 2.9) databases enable anyone with Internet access to locate scientific articles published in the allied health- and education-related fields, respectively. Other databases like PsycINFO® and SPORTDiscus (Exhibit 2.9) are usually available on university or college campuses (check with your campus librarian). When searches are conducted off campus, however, these databases usually require access fees.

Common databases for locating research literature in exercise science.   **exhibit   2.9**

Database	Website	Description
PubMed	www.pubmed.gov/	PubMed is made available via the National Center for Biotechnology Information (NCBI) at the National Library of Medicine (NLM), located at the U.S. National Institutes of Health (NIH). PubMed provides access to bibliographic information that includes MEDLINE, OLDMEDLINE, and other sources. MEDLINE is the NLM's premier bibliographic database covering the fields of medicine, nursing, dentistry, veterinary medicine, the health care system, and the preclinical sciences. PubMed is free for use by anyone with Internet access.
Web of Knowledge™	http://www.isiwebof knowledge.com/	Web of Knowledge is a research platform used to search, track, measure, and collaborate in the sciences, social sciences, arts, and humanities. So, for multidisciplinary research topics, Web of Knowledge (more specifically Web of Science®) allows the user to search across many disciplines' top databases at one time. Web of Knowledge also provides citation resources to determine how often particular articles or authors are cited by other journal articles. Users must pay to search with Web of Science unless access is granted through a university or public library. This is a comprehensive platform with many functions.
PsycINFO®	www.apa.org/psycinfo/	PsycINFO is an abstract (not full-text) database of psychological literature from the 1800s to the present. PsycINFO is updated weekly. Users must pay to search the PsycINFO database unless access is granted through a university or public library.
Educational Resources Information Center (ERIC®)	www.eric.ed.gov/	ERIC is an Internet-based digital library of education research and information sponsored by the Institute of Education Sciences (IES) of the U.S. Department of Education. ERIC provides access to bibliographic records of journal and non-journal literature indexed from 1966 to the present. ERI® users include education researchers, teachers, librarians, administrators, education policymakers, instructors and students in teacher-preparation programs, parents, the media and business communities, and the general public. ERIC is free for use by anyone with Internet access.
SPORTDiscus	EBSCOhost® www.epnet.com/ SIRC® www.sirc.ca/ OVID® www.ovid.com/	SPORTDiscus is a comprehensive, bibliographic database covering sport, physical fitness, exercise, sports medicine, sports science, physical education, kinesiology, coaching, training, sport administration, officiating, sport law & legislation, college & university sport, disabled persons, facility design & management, intramural & school sport, doping, health, health education, biomechanics, movement science, injury prevention rehabilitation, physical therapy, nutrition, exercise physiology, sport & exercise psychology, recreation, leisure studies, tourism, allied health, occupational health & therapy, public health, and more. This database includes hundreds of thousands of records with journal and monograph coverage going back to 1800 and thousands of dissertations, theses, and references to articles in over 50 languages. The content also consists of international references from journal and magazine articles, books, book chapters, conference proceedings, and more. SPORTDiscus is provided by the Sport Information Resource Centre. Users must pay to search the SPORTDiscus database unless access is granted through a university or public library.

The databases in Exhibit 2.9 can be searched for references on specific topics; however, due to copyright laws, they cannot provide the full-text article without an additional cost or paid subscription. Instead, online database searches yield the author(s), title, indexing information, and abstract. For example, Exhibit 2.10 shows the initial results of a PubMed search when the words *static stretching, muscle strength, stiffness* were used. There were 17 *hits,* or articles, for this search. The initial search results provide the authors, title, and indexing information for each hit, which allows the

exhibit / 2.10   Results of a PubMed search.

NCBI   Resources ⊙   How To ⊙

PubMed.gov
US National Library of Medicine
National Institutes of Health

[PubMed ⬦] static stretching, muscle strength, stiffness ◄───(A)

RSS   Save search   Limits   Advanced

Display Settings: ⊙ Summary, 20 per page, Sorted by Recently Added   Send to: ⊙

Results: 17

(B)

1. Effects of two modes of **static stretching** on **muscle strength** and **stiffness**. ◄───(C)
   Herda TJ, Costa PB, Walter AA, Ryan ED, Hoge KM, Kerksick CM, Stout JR, Cramer JT. ◄───(D)
   Med Sci Sports Exerc. 2011 Sep;43(9):1777-84.
   PMID: 21364485 [PubMed - indexed for MEDLINE]]───(E)
   Related citations

2. Acute effects of passive **stretching** and vibration on the electromechanical delay and musculotendinous **stiffness** of the plantar flexors.
   Herda TJ, Ryan ED, Costa PB, Walter AA, Hoge KM, Uribe BP, McLagan JR, Stout JR, Cramer JT.
   Electromyogr Clin Neurophysiol. 2010 Sep-Oct;50(6):277-88.
   PMID: 21061774 [PubMed - indexed for MEDLINE]
   Related citations

3. Achilles pain, **stiffness**, and **muscle** power deficits: achilles tendinitis.
   Carcia CR, Martin RL, Houck J, Wukich DK; Orthopaedic Section of the American Physical Therapy Association.
   J Orthop Sports Phys Ther. 2010 Sep;40(9):A1-26. Review. No abstract available.
   PMID: 20805627 [PubMed - indexed for MEDLINE]
   Related citations

4. Changes in the eccentric phase contribute to improved stretch-shorten cycle performance after training.
   Cormie P, McGuigan MR, Newton RU.
   Med Sci Sports Exerc. 2010 Sep;42(9):1731-44.
   PMID: 20142784 [PubMed - indexed for MEDLINE]
   Related citations

5. Concentric **muscle** contractions before **static stretching** minimize, but do not remove, stretch-induced force deficits.
   Kay AD, Blazevich AJ.
   J Appl Physiol. 2010 Mar;108(3):637-45. Epub 2010 Jan 14.
   PMID: 20075259 [PubMed - indexed for MEDLINE]   Free Article
   Related citations

6. Gender bias in the effect of dropping height on jumping performance in volleyball players.
   Laffaye G, Choukou MA.
   J **Strength** Cond Res. 2010 Aug;24(8):2143-8.
   PMID: 19834346 [PubMed - indexed for MEDLINE]
   Related citations

7. Isometric contractions reduce plantar flexor moment, Achilles tendon **stiffness**, and neuromuscular activity but remove the subsequent effects of stretch.
   Kay AD, Blazevich AJ.
   J Appl Physiol. 2009 Oct;107(4):1181-9. Epub 2009 Jul 30.
   PMID: 19644033 [PubMed - indexed for MEDLINE]   Free Article
   Related citations

A. The search terms.

B. The first seven hits for this search.

C. Title.

D. Authors.

E. Indexing information, including the journal name, year, issue, volume, page numbers, and PubMed identification number.

Today, the most commonly searched database for scientific articles in exercise science is PubMed because it is free, comprehensive, and updated frequently.

user to discern whether the article is of interest. In addition, much like other databases, each reference indexed by PubMed has a unique identification number called the PubMed Identification (PMID) number. This number is useful for quickly finding specific references in PubMed. Exhibit 2.11 shows the detailed information of the first article listed. The two primary benefits of this screen (Exhibit 2.11) are that the user can read the article abstract and a link to the full-text version of the article is provided.

Tips for Conducting Online Searches

Multiple strategies can be used to conduct online literature searches, with the most common using words in the title, the author's name, the year of publication, and keywords. In addition to indexing the words in the title, databases also index **keywords**—those words that describe the article's content but do not

The detailed information that is displayed after clicking on the first article listed in Exhibit 2.10.

exhibit **2.11**

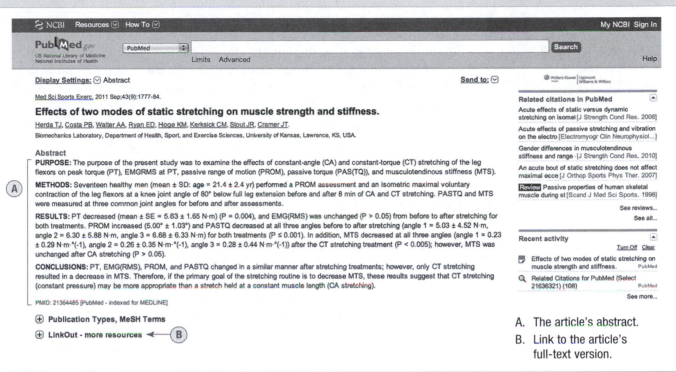

A. The article's abstract.

B. Link to the article's full-text version.

appear in the title. For example, the words used in the search in Exhibit 2.10— *static stretching, muscle strength, stiffness*—constitute an example of a keyword search. Although these words describe the articles' content, they may not appear in that particular order anywhere in the articles. The more specific the search terms, the smaller and more specific the search results. For example, using the search terms *exercise and cancer* yields over 6,300 hits—an impractical number to read. However, using the more specific search terms *exercise and non-Hodgkin's lymphoma* yields only 48 hits—a more manageable number.

■ *keywords*

Author searches are a very helpful tool for finding literature because there is usually a relatively small network of investigators who conduct research in a specific area. Therefore, if one is interested in finding articles authored by a particular individual, an author search can be conducted within a database. For example, searching for articles authored by Glen O. Johnson (a coeditor of this textbook) in PubMed is done by using his last name and first two initials (i.e., Johnson GO). The search may be narrowed by using the terms *Johnson GO 2010* to retrieve all of the articles authored by Dr. Johnson in the year 2010. Using keywords, title phrases, authors' names, and other information to narrow an online search is necessary to obtain specific articles from a database.

Accessing the Full-Text Article

Although more and more journals are beginning to allow online access to full-text article versions, there may be a cost involved. Many people pay for journal subscriptions that provide a mailed hard copy as well as online access. Students conducting online searches while on a university or college campus (or through proxy servers connected through the university) may access the full-text version of an article using the university's library subscription information. If the university or college does not own a subscription to a specific journal, students are encouraged to use a library service called an interlibrary loan. The interlibrary loan service allows students to request a copy of an article through the library. It often takes 1 to 3 weeks for delivery of the article; however, the copy can usually be accessed online. For more information about specific library services, contact your local librarian.

Due to the increased availability of online literature services (i.e., university library services or paid article retrieval systems), in most cases, an article can be delivered to your computer.

USING SCIENTIFIC LITERATURE TO LOCATE GRADUATE PROGRAMS IN EXERCISE SCIENCE

An often overlooked, yet extremely valuable tool for undergraduate and master's-level students is the ability to use sources of research literature to locate graduate programs and faculty mentors. One particularly effective strategy is to study the literature and determine where most of the research is being conducted. For example, if a student is interested in exercise endocrinology and hormonal responses to resistance training, there are many primary references in this area authored by Dr. William J. Kraemer at the University of Connecticut. Thus, studying these articles is an excellent way to begin focusing on a particular graduate program. Because the author's contact information is usually listed in the article or book, students can contact these individuals to inquire about potential graduate school openings. This is perhaps the most direct way of aligning the student's interests with the expertise of those capable of training graduate students.

SUMMARY

The rapid growth of exercise science in the last 50 years has resulted in the development of a broad literature base that covers such disciplines as anatomy, athletic training, biomechanics, exercise epidemiology, exercise physiology, exercise and sport nutrition, exercise and sport psychology, measurement, and motor control and motor learning. As in many fields, exercise science literature comes in two forms: scientific and nonscientific. Sources for scientific literature include research articles, reviews, books, textbooks, and book chapters, whereas nonscientific sources are usually in the form of popular magazines, newspaper articles, and Internet websites. It is important for exercise science students to understand the differences between these sources as well as how to obtain useful information from them.

The advent of the Internet revolutionized the way scientific and nonscientific sources are accessed. Government websites that host the PubMed and ERIC databases allow anyone with Internet access to locate research articles in various allied health- and education-related fields. Thus, the ability to efficiently access and understand the various sources is an important skill in many exercise science-related professions.

study / QUESTIONS

1. What are the differences between scientific and nonscientific literature sources?
2. What are the differences between peer-reviewed journals and non–peer-reviewed magazines?
3. Describe the general process that a research article must go through before it is published.
4. List the seven basic sections found in a research article and briefly describe the purpose of each section.
5. What are the differences between a narrative review and a meta-analysis?
6. Describe why primary references are useful for locating graduate programs.
7. Why has the Internet revolutionized the process of conducting a literature search?
8. What is the difference between a "keyword search" and an "author search"?
9. If a primary reference is not available in the university library, what is one of the best ways to access the article?

Visit the IES website to study, take notes, and try out the lab for this chapter.

learning \ ACTIVITIES

1. Go to the National Center for Biotechnology Information's PubMed website, www.ncbi.nlm.nih.gov. Search for articles concerning *central and peripheral manifestations of muscular fatigue during exercise*. Write an abstract for one article.
2. Search your library for secondary references on *oxygen uptake kinetics*. Create a list of five resources for this topic. Be sure to include the author's name, copyright date, and call number.
3. Search your library for secondary references on *electromyography*. Create a list of five resources for this topic. Be sure to include the author's name, copyright date, and call number.
4. Go to the PubMed website (see Learning Activity 1). Search for articles concerning *delayed onset muscle soreness (DOMS)*. Write an abstract for one article.

suggested / READINGS

Baumgartner, T. A., Strong, C. H., & Hensley, L. D. (2002). *Conducting and reading research in health and human performance* (3rd ed.). Boston: McGraw-Hill.

Hyllegard, R., Mood, D. P., & Morrow, Jr., J. R. (1996). *Interpreting research in sport and exercise science*. St. Louis, MO: Mosby.

Thomas, J. R., Nelson, J. K., & Silverman, S. J. (2011). *Research methods in physical activity* (6th ed.). Champaign, IL: Human Kinetics.

references

Bigland-Ritchie, B., Furbush, F., & Woods, J. J. (1986). Fatigue of intermittent submaximal voluntary contractions: Central and peripheral factors. *Journal of Applied Physiology, 61*(2), 421–429.

Costill, D. L., Dalsky, G. P., & Fink, W. J. (1978). Effects of caffeine ingestion on metabolism and exercise performance. *Medicine and Science in Sports, 10*(3), 155–158.

Fogoros, R. N. (2002, November 11). Even moderate exercise reduces risk. Retrieved from http://heartdisease. about.com/cs/exercise/a/modexer.htm.

Herda, T. J., Costa, P. B., Walter, A. A., Ryan, E. D., Hoge, K. M., Kerksick, C. M., Stout, J. R., & Cramer, J. T. (2011). Effects of two modes of static stretching on muscle strength and stiffness. *Medicine and Science in Sports and Exercise, 43*(9), 1777–1784.

Noakes, T. D., & St. Clair Gibson, A. (2004). Logical limitations to the "catastrophe" models of fatigue during exercise in humans. *British Journal of Sports Medicine, 38,* 648–649.

Nordlund, M. M., Thorstensson, A., & Cresswell, A. G. (2004). Central and peripheral contributions to fatigue in relation to level of activation during repeated maximal voluntary isometric plantar flexions. *Journal of Applied Physiology, 96,* 218–225.

Raiciu, T. (2006, January 16). Coffee and physical effort don't go together. Retrieved from http://news.softpedia. com/news/Coffee-and-Physical-Effort-Don-t-Go-Together-16357.shtml.

Weir, J. P., Beck, T. W., Cramer, J. T., & Housh, T. J. (2006). Is fatigue all in your head? A critical review of the central governor model. *British Journal of Sports Medicine, 40*(7), 573–586.

Weir, J. P., Keefe, D. A., Eaton, J. F., Augustine, R. T., & Tobin, D. M. (1998). Effect of fatigue on hamstring coactivation during isokinetic knee extensions. *European Journal of Applied Physiology and Occupation Physiology, 78*(6), 555–559.

Measurement in Exercise Science

DALE P. MOOD

DEFINITIONS IN MEASUREMENT

A ll disciplines rely on the accurate assessment of variables of interest. As intuitive as this statement is, it is sometimes forgotten in the excitement of proposing new ways to accomplish goals or designing research projects. For example, if we believe that exposure to a particular exercise regimen will improve a specific attribute of a group of individuals (e.g., physical fitness, attitude toward activity, or knowledge about heart rates), how do we determine whether our belief is true or not? Implicit in making such a determination is the fact that we can accurately assess the amount of the specific attribute the individuals possess. There exists an entire field of study—measurement—that involves examination of the procedures for developing, evaluating the accuracy of, and refining measurement practices associated with variables of interest to the exercise scientist. Because the measurement process is complex, there are several key concepts with which the measurement specialist must be familiar to develop, evaluate, and refine measurement practices.

Measurement Versus Evaluation

measurement ■

evaluation ■

In exercise science, the typical meaning of the word **measurement** refers to the act of assigning a number to each member of a group of individuals or objects based on the amount of a specific attribute each possesses. **Evaluation,** on the other hand, is a statement of quality, goodness, value, or merit about what was measured. The act of evaluation involves judgment and decision making, and the decision is usually based partially on measurements and partially on a knowledge of normative data. For example, if you use a stopwatch to determine the amount of time it takes an individual to run the 50-yard dash, you are making a measurement. When you comment to the individual, "Wow, that was fast," you are making an evaluation. Further, in the case of a 10-year-old girl, you would evaluate a time of 7.5 seconds as "fast," but you would evaluate the same measurement for a 15-year-old boy as "slow."

Measurement Accuracy

Some attributes can be measured very accurately and others cannot. Typically, the characteristics that can be measured directly (e.g., the time to run the 50-yard dash) can be assessed with higher precision than characteristics that are measured indirectly (e.g., the percent of body weight comprising fat).

Another element that affects measurement accuracy involves the clarity of the definition of the attribute to be assessed. For example, the measurement of response time, defined as the time elapsed between the presentation of a stimulus and the end of the required movement, is relatively unambiguous. However, even with the amount of attention physical fitness has received in recent years, exercise scientists do not universally agree as to the specific attributes that comprise it.

The two most fundamental questions to be answered regarding the accuracy of the measurement process are whether it actually measures what it is

validity ■

reliability ■

intended to measure (**validity**) and whether it does so consistently (**reliability**). Validity, then, is the degree of truthfulness in a measurement, and reliability is the consistency or repeatability of a measurement. This section also includes a discussion of the concept of objectivity, which is a subset of reliability.

Validity

As mentioned earlier, validity deals with the truthfulness of a measurement (i.e., does the measurement reflect the amount of the characteristic you actually are trying to measure). It is rather easy to see, for example, that weight in pounds is probably not a very good (valid) measure of flexibility. Sometimes, a measurement's invalidity is not so obvious. Consider a device to measure biceps strength consisting of a bar held in front of the body with both hands at a 90° angle to the elbows. Assume the bar is attached to a dynamometer anchored in the floor that records the force when the individual attempts to pull up on the bar.

At first inspection, this apparatus would seem to measure biceps strength, but what about those individuals who are unable to keep their hands extended? Perhaps their biceps strength scores would be lower than they could actually achieve if the test did not also rely on hand strength.

There are various situation-specific methods of examining a measurement's validity. Three types of validity—content, criterion, and construct—and the kind of evidence necessary for each are discussed next.

Content validity. **Content validity** considers the degree to which the sample of tasks or items on a test represent the actual content to be assessed. For example, you might examine the questions on a written examination to determine how well they cover the material to be tested. As another example, some might question the content validity of selecting offensive linemen for a football team on the basis of their time to run a 40-yard dash, a task they seldom perform in the game. Thus, content validity relies principally on a judgment as to the degree to which the content of the measurement process actually resembles the characteristic for which a measurement is desired.

■ *content validity*

Criterion validity. **Criterion validity** is determined by examining how well the measurement correlates with a criterion measure believed to be a true assessment of the characteristic of interest. For example, the $\dot{V}O_2$ max test performed on a treadmill is considered to produce an accurate measurement (the criterion measure) of cardiovascular endurance. However, this test requires a great deal of equipment, time, and personnel to administer. Because the correlations between $\dot{V}O_2$ max tests and various distance run tests (depending on the participants' age and gender) have been found to be quite high, the distance run tests are thought to be reasonably valid indicators of cardiovascular fitness.

■ *criterion validity*

The previous examples produce validity evidence that is also known as *concurrent validity*. This is because the "new" test and the criterion test are administered in the same time frame. If the criterion measure is not available until sometime in the future (e.g., a test given to predict swimming performance before the beginning of the season, correlated with swimming performance at the end of the season), the criterion validity evidence is called *predictive validity*.

Construct validity. **Construct validity** refers to the degree to which a test measures an intangible quality or attribute (a construct). For example, the concept of IQ is a construct. It is not tangible. The typical procedure for collecting construct validity evidence is to conduct experiments using the hypothesis that a particular construct does exist. For example, is it possible that some individuals possess a higher degree of kinesthetic awareness than others? If so, and if a test of jumping forward while blindfolded to land at a certain spot on the floor actually measures the construct of kinesthetic awareness, it might be hypothesized that divers and

■ *construct validity*

gymnasts should perform better on the test than non-athletes. If this is confirmed, it is evidence (not conclusive) that the test measured the construct.

Reliability

Typically, a measurement is made by using some test, device, or procedure to assign a numerical score that reflects the amount of some characteristic possessed by an individual. Unfortunately, no matter how carefully this is done, it is possible to introduce error into the process. For example, we could misread the scale, record an incorrect number, or fail to record the individual's best effort. Only when no error is present (a condition seldom, if ever, achieved) is a measurement perfectly reliable. As the amount of error increases, the reliability of the measurement decreases.

One way to think about this is to consider an observed score (the one that you assign) to be the sum of the true score and any error that might have occurred. For any set of individuals measured, there are three columns of scores—observed, true, and error. Each column has a mean and some variability in the values listed, as shown in Exhibit 3.1.

In theory, if the error that occurs is random (i.e., due to imprecision in the process rather than a systematic error, like a scale that is off by 2 pounds for everyone), the sum of the error scores and thus the average (x) error score should be zero. As shown in Exhibit 3.1, an error of measurement did occur for all individuals except F and J. The variability of the scores in the three columns is reflected by a statistic called *variance (s^2)*. Notice that the sum of the true score variance and the error score variance is equal to the observed score variance. One method of expressing a measurement's reliability is to calculate the ratio of the true score variance to the observed score variance. In this example,

exhibit 3.1   Example of observed, true, and error scores.

Individual	Observed	=	True	+	Error
A	3		5		−2
B	17		15		+2
C	16		20		−4
D	23		25		−2
E	27		25		−2
F	25		25		0
G	35		25		+10
H	26		30		−4
I	33		35		−2
J	45		45		0
x	25		25		0
variance (s^2)	120.2		105.0		15.2

the ratio is 105.0/120.2 or .87. It can be seen that if no error was present, the ratio would be 105.0/105.0 or 1.00, indicating perfect reliability.

Of course, this is a fictional example because the only scores you actually ever know are those that are "observed" and not the "true" scores. It is helpful to use this example, however, because reliability can be calculated through various procedures, and it is most often expressed as a correlation coefficient (a statistic having a range of −1.0 to +1.0). Thus, if a test is reported to have a reliability of .87 (calculated by using a test–retest or some other procedure), we would be able to interpret what this represents in terms of true and observed variance and thus have some notion of the meaning of a measure's reliability.

Methods for assessing reliability include test–retest (the same test is administered to the same participants twice; actually a stability indicator), equivalence (two "equivalent" but not identical measurements of the same characteristic are compared), split-halves (one-half of a measuring instrument is compared with the other half; for example, the odd numbered items on a written test are compared with the even numbered items), and intraclass (used when more than two trials of a test are available; for example, four trials of the standing long jump are measured for a group of individuals). Each method has its proper situation for use, but the net result is a reflection of the measurement's consistency expressed as a correlation coefficient.

Another helpful way to interpret a reliability coefficient is to determine its square root. This produces a statistic called the index of reliability and is the theoretical correlation between the observed scores and the true scores. In our example (rel = .87), this value would be .93.

To be of any value, a measurement process must result in a consistent score being assigned to an individual. How much confidence would you have, for example, in a scale that gave you a different weight each time you stepped on it? However, reliability alone is not the only concern regarding the accuracy and usefulness of a measurement. As discussed earlier, if you had a very reliable scale to measure your weight, but someone told you it was a measure of your flexibility, you might raise questions about the measurement reflecting much, if anything, about flexibility. This is the issue of validity, which was discussed earlier.

The concepts of validity and reliability are critical to all scientists. Without accurate measurement, research and experimentation are impossible. This, of course, is as applicable to the exercise scientist as to the physicist or chemist.

Importance of validity and reliability

It is important to note that a measurement does not have *a* validity or *a* reliability. The validity and reliability of a measurement are situation specific and relative. For example, one individual might produce very reliable skinfold measurements and another might not. A shuttle run test designed to validly measure the agility of 14-year-old boys may not measure this characteristic at all for 6-year-old girls. Thus, it is imperative to clearly understand the concepts of validity and reliability to evaluate the worth of any measurement process.

Objectivity

Objectivity is actually a subset of reliability. It assesses differences in test administrators, a very important potential source of error. Suppose an examiner administered a pull-up test to a group of athletes one day, and a   ■ *objectivity* different examiner administered a pull-up test to the same group of athletes a few days later. If all conditions under which the tests were administered were the same, we would expect the resulting two sets of scores to be reasonably similar (thus, reliable). However, if one examiner was very strict in administering the test (e.g., allowed no kipping action, made certain the chin was fully over the bar and that the arms were fully extended at the bottom of the exercise, did not permit any resting) and the other examiner was not diligent in applying these rules, the resulting two scores for each individual might differ considerably. If the athletes' scores varied under the two test administrators, not because they possessed differing amounts of upper arm strength and endurance, but because the administrators applied the measurement differently, the test would be considered to be low in objectivity and thus demonstrate low reliability. Tests that have standardized procedures for their administration, which are followed carefully, tend to be more objective than tests that involve subjectivity in their administration or scoring procedures. In the cognitive domain, multiple-choice tests are considered objective, whereas essay tests are less so because of the subjectivity that often accompanies the assessment of the answers' quality. It is important to administer tests carefully and according to their instructions to increase their objectivity.

Measurement Levels

Measurements may be classified on the basis of the type and amount of information they yield. For example, it is possible to rank a group of individuals in height either by inspection or by using a measuring tape and recording the height of each individual in inches or centimeters. The type of information obtained from each procedure is different. In the inspection procedure, the results permit only statements such as "Sally is shorter than Betty," but in the measuring procedure, it is possible to determine how much shorter Sally is than Betty. Measurements can be placed into four categories—nominal, ordinal, interval, and ratio—based on the information they provide.

Nominal measurement

nominal measurement ■ **Nominal measurement** conveys a minimal amount of information. It permits only the assessment of equality or difference. Nominal measurement often uses word descriptors to classify people or objects into categories. For example, a person may be classified as a letter winner, a girl, having brown hair, and so on. Occasionally, numerals are used in a nominal way. Baseball players, for example, are identified by numerals on their uniforms, but statements about their order, or about their quality, based on their identification numbers are not possible.

Ordinal measurement

ordinal measurement ■ **Ordinal measurement** permits the ranking of the people or objects measured. Information regarding greater than or less than becomes relevant with ordinal measurement. For example, individuals' ability in handball may be ranked at the completion of a round-robin tournament.

Interval measurement

Interval measurement permits the making of statements about the equality of intervals. Temperature is an example of an interval measurement. The same distance exists on the Fahrenheit scale between 0° and 40° as exists between 40° and 80°. However, it is not appropriate to say that 80° is twice as hot as 40°, because the zero point on the Fahrenheit scale is an arbitrary point and does not really indicate an absence of heat. Likewise a fifth-grade boy who can do four chin-ups is not twice as strong as another fifth-grade boy who can do only two chin-ups, because doing zero chin-ups does not indicate the absolute lack of any upper-arm strength.

■ *interval measurement*

Ratio measurement

Ratio measurement permits statements of comparison such as twice as much or one-third as much. To achieve this level of measurement, an absolute zero point is necessary. It is possible to say, for example, that a high jump of 6 feet is twice as high as a high jump of 3 feet.

■ *ratio measurement*

Selecting the appropriate measurement level

The higher the level of measurement, the more information is gained and thus the more useful it is. Although it is true that one should always use the highest level of measurement possible, there are times when only a lower level of measurement is available. For example, if an athletic trainer is interested in evaluating various modalities for treating muscle soreness, the measurement of this condition relies on ordinal measurement—"On a scale from 1 to 5, how sore is your muscle?" Currently, no calipers are available to assign any sort of interval score that reflects the degree of soreness.

Note that it is possible to move from a higher level of measurement to a lower level, but it is not possible to go in the other direction. For example, if you measure the heights of several individuals (ratio measurement), you could line them up according to their height. However, if you simply line them up by height, you can rank them, but you cannot determine the difference in inches between their heights.

Statisticians have devised many statistical tools that assume the use of at least the interval level of measurement. These statistical tests are categorized as parametric statistics. Another branch of statistics, called non-parametric statistics, consists of procedures that allow measurement at the nominal and ordinal levels. As expected, non-parametric statistics are not as powerful as parametric statistics, due to the reduced amount of information derived from the level of measurement employed.

Domains of Human Experience

Another way to classify measurement associated with exercise science (or almost any academic discipline) is by using three domains: cognitive, affective, and psychomotor. The **cognitive domain** involves objectives in knowledge and mental achievement. The **affective domain** (sometimes called psychological) is concerned with attitudes and perceptions. And of major interest to the exercise scientist, the **psychomotor domain** involves physiological and physical performance.

■ *cognitive domain*
■ *affective domain*

■ *psychomotor domain*

From information gleaned from studies conducted over the years, structures called taxonomies (classification systems) were devised to reflect a hierarchical nature in elements in each domain. An example of a taxonomy for each domain is presented in Exhibit 3.2, but realize that others exist; for example, a revision of Bloom's taxonomy (Anderson & Krathwohl, 2001).

These hierarchical taxonomies are of value to the measurement specialist when devising assessment procedures. The assumption is that each level of the taxonomy is based on the notion that earlier levels were achieved.

exhibit / 3.2   Taxonomies for the cognitive, affective, and psychomotor domains.

I. Taxonomy of the Cognitive Domain (Bloom, 1956)
 1. Knowledge
   a. Knowledge of specifics
   b. Knowledge of ways and means of dealing with specifics
   c. Knowledge of the universals and abstractions in a field
 2. Comprehension
   a. Translation
   b. Interpretation
   c. Extrapolation
   d. Application
 3. Analysis
   a. Analysis of elements
   b. Analysis of relationships
   c. Analysis of organizational principles
 4. Synthesis
   a. Production of unique communications
   b. Production of a plan for operations
   c. Derivation of a set of abstract relations
 5. Evaluation
   a. Judgments in terms of internal evidence
   b. Judgments in terms of external evidence
II. Taxonomy of the Affective Domain (Krathwohl, Bloom, & Masia, 1964)
 1. Receiving
   a. Awareness
   b. Willingness to receive
   c. Controlled or selected attention
 2. Controlled or selected attention
   a. Responding
   b. Acquiescence in responding
   c. Willingness to respond
   d. Satisfaction in response
 3. Valuing
   a. Acceptance of a value
   b. Preference for a value
   c. Commitment

 4. Organization
   a. Conceptualization of a value
   b. Organization of a value system
 5. Characterization by a value complex
   a. Generalized set
   b. Characterization
III. Taxonomy of the Psychomotor Domain (Harrow, 1972)
 1. Reflex movements
   a. Segmental reflexes
   b. Intersegmental reflexes
   c. Suprasegmental reflexes
 2. Basic-fundamental movements
   a. Locomotor movements
   b. Nonlocomotor movements
   c. Manipulative movements
 3. Perceptual abilities
   a. Kinesthetic discrimination
   b. Visual discrimination
   c. Auditory discrimination
   d. Tactile discrimination
   e. Coordinated discrimination
 4. Physical abilities
   a. Endurance
   b. Strength
   c. Flexibility
   d. Agility
 5. Skilled movements
   a. Simple adaptive skill
   b. Compound adaptive skill
   c. Complex adaptive skill
 6. Nondiscursive movements
   a. Expressive movement
   b. Interpretive movement

Using Bloom's taxonomy in Exhibit 3.2 as an example, it is possible to *know* that the valence of oxygen is –2. In fact, if you read the previous sentence and accept it as true, you now have this knowledge. Without this type of knowledge you cannot move to the next level—comprehension. To *comprehend* that valence has to do with the degree of combining power of an element based on its atomic weight requires knowledge of particular valences and much more, but it would not be possible to explain what would happen— *analyze*—in a new situation without this comprehension. Notice how each level builds on the previous ones.

As another example, it is not appropriate to measure complex motor skills in a young child who has not yet developed to that level of a psychomotor domain. The measurement specialist must be cognizant of these domains and taxonomies to develop measuring instruments and procedures that are appropriate for each situation.

MEASUREMENT ACTIVITIES

Because the exercise scientist works in such a variety of settings, the array of possible measurement applications is vast. The information presented in this section is limited to discussing those factors that should be considered when constructing valid measurement instruments; in addition, examples of some measurement instruments are described. Several excellent textbooks (see Suggested Readings at the end of this chapter) are available that describe the actual construction, validation, and use of exercise science measurement techniques. The discussion that follows is organized around the three domains described earlier: cognitive, psychomotor, and affective.

Cognitive Domain

In many instances, the primary objective of an exercise scientist is to determine the level of, or increase in, individuals' knowledge and understanding about physical activity. This typically requires measurement of cognitive processes and is usually done through the use of a written examination.

The multiple sources of written tests include textbook publishers, state agencies, and national corporations that specialize in test construction. In the field of exercise science, however, outside sources of written tests are rather limited—in fact, the most common test source is the exercise scientist. The upside is that the person making the assessment should be able to construct the most valid test (one that measures what it is intended to measure). The downside is that knowing what to measure is not the same as knowing how to measure it—the exercise scientist must learn the principles of written test construction.

To develop an effective written test, the constructor must meet five requirements. The first requirement is to be aware of the proper techniques for written test construction (more about this later). The second is to have a very thorough knowledge about the subject area to be tested. The third qualification is to be skilled at written expression. Test questions constructed by those whose skill is lacking are often ambiguous and lead to incorrect conclusions, which reduces the instrument's usefulness. The fourth requirement is to be aware of the range and level of understanding possessed by those individuals to be assessed. Questions that are too difficult or too easy do not effectively discriminate among individuals. Finally, test constructors must realize that

WWW

The Cognitive Domain
www.uwsp.edu/education/ lwilson/CURRIC/cognitiv.htm

building adequate written tests takes a considerable amount of time and trial and error. Potential questions must be tested and revised, often many times, before they function appropriately.

Of these five requirements, the last four are characteristics of a careful researcher or exercise scientist. It is really only the first requirement, knowledge of proper test construction techniques, that requires study. Again, this section presents only an outline of the types of issues to be considered.

Planning the written test

The first issue when planning the written test is to determine whether the test is to be a mastery test (designed to measure whether the examinee has enough understanding to achieve a prescribed standard) or an achievement test (designed to discriminate among various levels of understanding).

The next (and very important) decision in the planning process is to determine *what* is to be measured. This involves building a table of specification, which is a matrix involving educational objectives on one axis and content objectives on the other. It is a blueprint for the written test.

How to measure

Issues to consider include (1) when to test, (2) how many questions to include, (3) the format to use, and (4) the type of questions to use.

Administering the written test

Such concerns as examinee anxiety, test distribution, security, and the prevention of cheating are involved in the test administration.

Analyzing the written test

The major concerns when analyzing the written test are determining its reliability and validity as a measuring instrument and assessing the effectiveness of each test item. These procedures are somewhat complex but are necessary and important to ensure that the written test accurately assesses what it is intended to measure.

Psychomotor Domain

Physical educators and exercise scientists are interested in the measurement of physical fitness, physical activity, and sports skills and motor abilities. This section is divided into three brief discussions of each topic.

Early measurement of physical fitness included assessing such elements as muscular strength, posture, speed, power, agility, and muscular endurance.

Physical fitness

In the 1970s, a concept involving *health-related fitness* emerged that focused on cardiovascular endurance, body composition, and musculoskeletal function. Precisely how these elements are to be measured is still being debated among exercise scientists, but most physical fitness tests now include some of the following measurement types:

1. Endurance runs (see Exhibit 3.3a; distances vary according to the participants' ages).

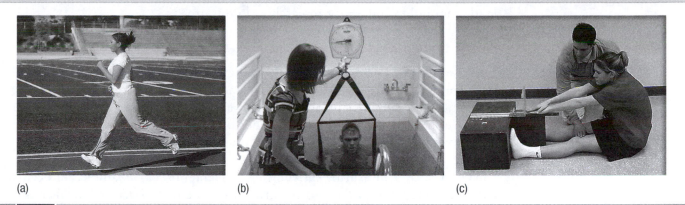

exhibit **3.3**

Three types of physical fitness tests: (a) endurance runs, (b) body fat calculations, and (c) muscular performance.

(a)   (b)   (c)

2. Calculation of the percentage of body fat (see Exhibit 3.3b; assessment techniques vary from weighing individuals underwater to measuring skinfold thickness and various body girths).

3. Musculoskeletal function (see Exhibit 3.3c; assessment of muscular performance using repetitive exercises such as sit-ups, pull-ups, and sit-and-reach).

Exercise scientists, including measurement specialists, are currently working on many aspects of the assessment of physical fitness. Among the issues are defining the concept (i.e., precisely what is physical fitness?), determining how to most accurately assess those elements deemed essential, identifying the minimal amount of each characteristic that is deemed sufficient to be considered healthy, and determining how to define and measure physical fitness for various subsets of the population—children through older adults, males versus females, individuals with physical disabilities, and so on.

Physical activity

Although important research continues to be done in the area of physical fitness, in the early 1990s an increased interest in and emphasis on measuring physical activity developed. Several recent epidemiological studies convinced many exercise scientists that even minimal levels of physical activity can elicit many of the health benefits once thought to require relatively large amounts of exercise. To study the validity of this notion, it has become increasingly important to quantify and assess physical activity.

Measuring the amount of physical activity a person engages in is not an easy task, because it is necessary to assess not only the activity's frequency and duration but also its intensity. The many measurement methods currently being investigated can be classified into self-report surveys and direct observation. Many self-report surveys have been devised for various segments of the population and situations, including task-specific diaries, recall questionnaires, and global self-reports. Direct observation techniques include behavioral observation, job classification, gait assessment, direct and indirect calorimetry, and the use of heart rate monitors, motion sensors, pedometers, and accelerometers.

Each procedure has advantages and disadvantages, and in general, the measurements' validity and reliability seldom reach the levels deemed acceptable by most exercise scientists; however, improvements are continually being made that hold promise for researchers in this area.

Sports skills and motor abilities

Exercise scientists involved primarily in the area of teaching sports skills and motor abilities (i.e., physical educators and coaches) are very interested in assessing these qualities prior to, during, and after engaging in activities to improve them. Although a large number of tests and procedures have been developed over the years to make such assessments, the exercise scientist is often faced with a unique situation in which the knowledge of how to construct such a measuring instrument is invaluable. For example, an occupational therapist may have to construct a unique test to determine when an injured worker is ready to return to work.

In this chapter, it is not possible to list all of the tests and measuring devices that already exist (several measurement books are available for this), nor is it possible to discuss the many considerations to be taken into account when constructing your own. Hensley and East (1989) provided some guidelines, however, to indicate the complexity involved. They state that these tests should

1. Have at least minimally acceptable reliability and validity.
2. Be simple to take and to administer.
3. Have easily understood instructions.
4. Require neither expensive nor extensive equipment.
5. Be reasonable in terms of preparation and administration time.
6. Encourage correct form and be gamelike, but involve only one performer.
7. Be of suitable difficulty (neither too difficult nor too simple).
8. Be meaningful to the performer.
9. Exclude extraneous variables as much as possible.
10. Provide for accurate scoring.
11. Follow specific guidelines if a target is the basis for scoring.
12. Require a sufficient number of trials to obtain a reasonable measure of performance (tests that have accuracy as a principal component require more trials than tests measuring other characteristics).
13. Yield scores that provide for diagnostic interpretation whenever possible.

Although it is probably impossible to meet all of these guidelines in any single test, complying with as many as possible will provide the most valuable measurements. Exhibit 3.4 provides an example of a simple push-up test meeting many of these requirements.

Affective Domain

Of general importance in this domain are assessments of attitudes, states, and traits. Of specific interest is the assessment of these characteristics as they relate to physical performance. For example, many individuals might be con-

Procedures and positioning for a push-up test of upper-body muscular endurance.

exhibit   3.4

1. The subject begins in the up position with arms fully extended and body straight. The hands should be pointed forward and approximately shoulder-width apart (see photoa). Male subjects use the toes as the pivot point. Female subjects should assume the "modified knee push-up" position with the knees bent and touching the floor.

2. The subject lowers his or her body (see photo b) until the chin touches the floor and then returns to the up position by straightening the elbows.

3. A partner should count the number of push-ups performed correctly to exhaustion without stopping.

4. Record the number of correctly performed push-ups. The results can be compared with a norms table.

cerned with the assessment of anxiety or motivation, but the exercise scientist is particularly interested in how these characteristics might affect physical performance and participation.

As with the other two domains, it is not possible here to present in detail the myriad of complex issues associated with developing measuring instruments in the affective domain; rather, an attempt is made to indicate the type and scope of concerns in this area.

Because it is well known that the mind affects the body, the way individuals think and feel has a strong influence on physical performance. This connection is the primary interest of exercise scientists concentrating in this field. Such psychological factors as anxiety, motivation, concentration, personality, confidence, and mental practice are among the most commonly investigated. Another focus has to do with the possibility that the body can affect the mind. For example, many researchers study whether or not sport and physical activity can positively influence mental health through reducing depression and increasing self-worth.

Some of the most intriguing areas of research for the exercise scientist interested in the affective domain include the following:

1. State versus trait measures (state measures are more concerned with the situation at hand and the trait measurements with a more stable characteristic within the individual).

www

Division 47—Exercise and Sport Psychology
www.apa.org/about/division/ div47.html

2. General versus specific measures (whether personality traits should be assessed globally or in the context of specific sport or activity situations).

3. How team members should be selected with regard to assessment of psychological traits.

4. Factors affecting individuals' attitudes toward physical activity and their motivation to participate or not to participate in these types of experiences.

In the past, exercise scientists working in the affective domain probably relied, more than those studying the cognitive or psychomotor domains, on measuring instruments constructed by experts from other fields, rather than developing their own. Today, this is changing as the trend seems to be shifting toward assessment of more specific traits as opposed to relying on general tests. Thus, as with exercise scientists working in the cognitive and psychomotor domains, those working in the affective domain must become increasingly aware of how to recognize when a measuring instrument is accurately assessing the desired characteristics. To do this, it is necessary to understand the two constructs—validity and reliability—discussed earlier.

North American Society for the Psychology of Sport and Physical Activity
www.naspspa.org

MEASUREMENT PURPOSES

Exercise science measurement can be classified in many ways. One possible scheme is to organize measurement according to its intent or purpose. The following presentation represents one of innumerable ways this could be done, and you should notice that there is overlap among these divisions.

For Classification

Assessment of the degree to which individuals possess some attribute allows classification of these individuals into discrete groups. This might be done, for example, to facilitate instruction (ability grouping) or to place subjects into appropriate treatment groups in a research project. A complex subset of this purpose of measurement is the construction of norms. A current interest among exercise scientists is determining the *cut-off points* above which a child is considered to possess enough of various attributes (e.g., strength, flexibility, etc.) to be classified as physically fit in a health-related sense.

For Motivation

Comparison of achievement with norms or standards can stimulate interest and may foster goal-setting behaviors. Although there is some controversy regarding the soundness of using external motivators to encourage learning, there is little doubt that you will pay more attention to the material in this book if you are aware that progress toward certain goals will be measured periodically than if it were not.

For Achievement Assessment

Typically, in a program of instruction or training, a set of objectives or goals is established. Measurement is used as the participants move through the program (called formative evaluation) to assess improvement and progress toward the goals and, usually at the end of the program (called summative evaluation), to assess the final achievement level obtained by each participant. Formative and summative evaluations each have inherent assumptions and concerns that the measurement specialist considers if the assessment results are to be accurate and meaningful. Achievement assessment can also be divided into the use of standardized or authentic methods. *Standardized assessment* typically involves each examinee completing the same task and being scored on how well it is accomplished. *Authentic assessment* takes place in a real-life setting and involves some type of a ranking process of direct, observable behavior.

WWW

Authentic Assessment
*http://gopher.fsu.edu/~jflake/
assess.html*

For Forecasting Potential and Prediction

An exciting and very useful arena for the application of measurement techniques is in forecasting an individual's potential in a future setting (e.g., making the Olympic volleyball team) or in predicting the future based on known tendencies. For example, the exercise epidemiologist may assess cardiovascular endurance measures, physical activity patterns, and other factors to predict your risk of developing cardiovascular disease. This measurement area requires the exercise scientist to develop precise measurement tools and procedures and to use sophisticated statistical techniques.

For Diagnosis

Evaluation of a measurement procedure is often used to determine weaknesses or deficiencies. For example, a cardiologist may administer a treadmill stress test to obtain exercise electrocardiograms to diagnose the presence of or extent of coronary heart disease. If a student is having difficulty learning a particular gymnastics movement, the instructor may use tests to diagnose whether it is a lack of strength, a lack of coordination, or something else that is causing the problem.

For Program Evaluation

At times, it may be necessary to investigate the successful achievement of program objectives. For example, a physical educator may have to assess whether or not the students are receiving adequate physical fitness training. A comparison of the students' fitness test results with the district (or state or national) norms may be in order. Corporate or commercial fitness program directors may decide to measure client success and satisfaction through physical testing and surveys.

For Research

A knowledge of proper measurement techniques is a requirement for anyone seeking to do research in exercise science. In addition, an awareness of the complexities of research design and of statistical treatment of data is required. What may not be as apparent is that exercise science practitioners also need to be equipped with much of this same knowledge to intelligently read, evaluate, and use this research.

HISTORY OF MEASUREMENT

In this country's early years, physical education was very unstructured, and the use of measurement was virtually nonexistent. Not until the second half of the 19th century did formal physical education begin in the United States. As physical education developed, so did an interest in measurement. Many physical education leaders of this period had medical degrees and as youths had been interested in gymnastics—the medical background probably explains their interest in anthropometric measurements. For example, students at Amherst College were periodically given a series of tests centered around anthropometric measures. In 1933, statues of the typical male and female, constructed using a vast number of anthropometric measurements taken and recorded by Dudley Sargent of Harvard University, were displayed at the World's Fair in Chicago.

Measurements were also devised for strength development and athletics during this period. Edward Hitchcock's periodic testing at Amherst involved the measurement of strength. Dudley Sargent also expressed an interest in measuring strength. In fact, he devised a battery of tests that included items intended to measure the strength of the legs, back, grip, arms, and respiratory muscles. This test battery became known as the Intercollegiate Strength Test and was used as a basis for intercollegiate competition. It was later revised by Fred R. Rodgers and later still by C. H. McCloy. Thus, the development and measurement of various strength parameters gradually became integrated with the existing anthropometric measurement programs used in this period.

Because athletic programs, both intramural and intercollegiate, were common at this time, applying measurement techniques to athletics began. For example, in 1890, Luther H. Gulick devised a pentathlon consisting of a rope climb and four track events—the 100-yard dash, hop-skip-jump, running high jump, and shot put.

In the early years of the 20th century, measurement continued to emphasize anthropometrics. Soon, however, a dramatic shift in educational philosophy resulted in sweeping changes in schools' curricula and the methods of instruction. Along with these changes came the realization of the importance of measurement in education. As a result, it became important in physical education to measure many parameters in addition to body structure and strength. In 1902, Dudley Sargent's Universal Test for Speed, Strength, and Endurance was introduced. An interest arose in the circulatory system, as shown by Crampton's 1905 Blood Ptosis Test and the norms for blood pressure and heart rate developed by J. H. McCurdy in 1910. In 1913, the Athletic Badge Tests in baseball, basketball, tennis, and volleyball were devised. These are but a few examples of the diverse areas into which the physical educators of the period were expanding.

By the middle of the 20th century, initial tests had been developed for most of the parameters that are measured in physical education classes today. Many of these initial tests were crude, subjective, and inexact, but they were refined as precision, objectiveness, and test construction methods improved. Most important, advances in the areas of mathematics and statistics made improved measurement techniques possible. Measurement equipment improved with the increase in technological skills.

World War II generated a great concern for physical fitness. The primary emphasis of physical education in the United States swung away from the expanded and varied program to a concentration on physical training. Physical education measurement followed this trend, and measuring physical fitness parameters dominated. The military services established physical fitness parameter tests during this period. Unfortunately, because of the extreme interest in and emphasis on physical fitness measurement during this time, physical education measurement became synonymous with physical fitness testing to a great segment of the U.S. population.

The period after the launching of Sputnik 1 in 1957 marked the beginning of a tremendous emphasis on sciences in U.S. schools. Although generalizations can be misleading, if only one word could be used to describe the greatest single concern of physical education during this period, it would be research. Certainly, research was done in physical education throughout the 20th century, but during this period, the volume of research quite possibly equaled all that had been done previously. The increased research efforts had a tremendous impact on measurements. During this time, most of the measurement techniques and tools now in use were developed, studied, revised, and described in the literature.

Another change that occurred because of the increased emphasis on research was the beginning of specialization within the newly emerging discipline of exercise science. With intense concentration within each subfield of exercise science came improvements in virtually all measurement techniques. Continued technological improvements increased the development of accurate and reliable instruments for measuring many of the new specialized areas of interest.

During recent decades, the march toward specialization has continued. Former physical education departments at many universities have disappeared or evolved into departments with many different names (e.g., Human Performance, Exercise Science, and Integrative Physiology) and foci. Rather than focusing on teaching physical activities, faculty members in these departments study how physical activity affects sleep patterns, the immune system, various diseases, the aging process, brain function, cell structures, and so on.

Changes in measurement practices and techniques now consider how to assess the parameters of interest in these new subfields. The need to measure these attributes of interest led to adopting the instrumentation and procedures used by related disciplines. For example, highly sophisticated computer-assisted performance analyzers, magnetic resonance imaging tests, computerized treadmills, electron microscopes, accurate force platforms, and high-speed digital cameras are some of the newer measurement tools now in use. Technological advances continue to contribute additional measurement possibilities. In a sleep study, for example, the participants swallow a pill that enables the researcher to unobtrusively monitor the subjects' core temperatures during different phases of the experiment.

The amount of knowledge about the effects of physical activity on humans has grown exponentially since 1980, and for the most part, the findings demonstrate a positive relationship between physical activity and health. Ironically, this comes at a time in our history when physical education classes in the nation's school systems have all but disappeared, and we seem on the verge of a national obesity epidemic! From a measurement perspective, this paradox suggests we must increase our efforts to study the sociological and physiological aspects of physical activity. Although we can explain how physical activity affects the sodium transport system inside the body, we know little about why a large part of the population remains sedentary and what techniques can be used to effectively change this lifestyle.

Determining how to measure the amount (frequency, duration, and intensity) of physical activity in which individuals engage is becoming increasingly important. In an article addressing this topic, Morrow (2003) suggests that the measurement of physical activity is gradually supplanting the measurement of physical fitness.

TECHNOLOGY AND RESEARCH TOOLS

T he measurement specialist in exercise science is primarily concerned with the accurate assessment of characteristics related to human performance from the cognitive, psychomotor, and affective domains. Closely related to this focus is expertise in the use of two tools: computers and statistics.

Probably because the computer can efficiently and accurately manipulate numerical data and because the measurement specialist often works with numerical data sets, it is natural for the measurement specialist to become proficient in computer hardware and software use. Whether located in academia, a laboratory setting, or industry, it is very common for the measurement specialist in exercise science to also be a computer expert.

Statistics, a branch of mathematics, has become very important to the exercise science researcher. Statistical tests have a wide variety of applications but primary among them is to determine whether apparent relationships among variables are real or could be due to chance. Although a vast oversimplification, the basic premise in using statistics is to determine the probability of an event occurring if no relationship between the variables of interest actually exists. If that probability is very small, it is deemed evident that the relationship does exist. For example, assume that you randomly place 20 individuals into one of two groups. The 10 individuals assigned to one group are taught to ski using short skis, and the other 10 individuals are taught to ski using conventional-length skis. Assume for purposes of this illustration that all conditions except ski length are identical for both groups.

Following the instructional period, a valid and reliable test of skiing ability is administered to all 20 individuals, with higher test scores indicating a better skiing ability. Assume that the mean score for the short-ski group is 75 and the mean score for the conventional-length-ski group is 71. The question that a statistical test (called an independent *t*-test) could answer in this situation (if all 20 scores are available) is whether 75 is really significantly different from 71. In other words, what is the probability of this event (mean scores of 75 and 71) if there really is no connection between learning to ski with one of these two methods and the individuals' skiing ability as reflected by the test? If the probability of this event is 1 in 100, we might be willing to believe that the two variables (method and skiing proficiency) are, in fact, related and that it is thus better to teach people to ski using short skis. However, if the probability of this event is 50 in 100, we probably would conclude it was just chance that the short-ski group's score was higher than the other group's score.

A vast number of statistical tests were devised over the last 80 years, and each requires certain assumptions to be met if the test is to be employed. The measurement specialist, again because of the connection through numbers, is often attracted to learning about statistics.

This natural connection, along with the software available for computing relatively complex statistical tests, further cements the common venues of measurement, computer, and statistics often found to be of interest to the exercise science measurement specialist. It also should be apparent that knowledge in these areas often makes the measurement specialist a valuable consultant for other exercise scientists.

www

A New View of Statistics
www.sportsci.org/resource/
stats/index.html

www

Statistical Package for
the Social Sciences
www.spss.com

EMPLOYMENT OPPORTUNITIES

In the past, most exercise science measurement specialists found employment in academia. They were most often located in physical education departments; taught measurement, statistics, and computer courses; did their own research in these areas; and served as consultants to department colleagues. For some, this is still the preferred avenue for pursuing their interests and using their abilities. Today, however, exercise science measurement specialists are also being employed elsewhere. Two of the most common areas exist (1) among the many venues that have sprung up with the recent increased awareness of the importance of wellness and physical fitness (e.g., corporate wellness centers and exercise prescription consultants) and (2) in laboratory settings dealing with the same issues, often under the direction of hospitals, corporations, and insurance companies.

It is interesting to note that there are not many institutions of higher education producing exercise science measurement specialists, yet there are many professionals out in the field who serve in this capacity. This has come about primarily through need. Virtually all doctorate programs in exercise science have as a graduation requirement a relatively sophisticated level of exposure to statistics and research design courses, no matter what the area of specialization may be. Many times, this exposure is obtained in graduate-level courses in education, psychology, or other academic disciplines.

When an exercise science department without a resident measurement specialist decides to offer courses in measurement, statistics, computers, research design, and related areas, it is often the faculty member with the most interest in these topics who is asked to teach the courses and who, in the process and over time, becomes the department's measurement specialist.

For the measurement specialist located in an academic setting as a faculty member, the types of activities he or she engages in vary considerably. Of course, the type of institution can range from a community college to a research university. Although the emphasis and amount of time devoted to each activity varies, the primary activities fall into the scholarship, teaching, and service categories.

In the scholarship area, the measurement specialist's activities focus on creating new knowledge and/or applying previously discovered knowledge to new and different situations. For example, a measurement specialist might devise a noninvasive technique for determining muscle fiber type or might develop methods of modifying a measure of muscular strength for one segment of the population for use with a different subset. The types of measurement issues to be studied are virtually limitless. Box 3.1 is an abstract of a research study in the area of measurement in exercise science.

Most curricula in departments of physical education, human performance, or kinesiology contain many courses involving measurement, statistics, research design, and computers. Depending on the institution, teaching duties can range from undergraduate and graduate classes, to running seminar and journal clubs, to directing theses and dissertations.

Service responsibilities take many forms, including work at the institution, state, regional, national, and even international levels. Service in various capacities on committees for institutions and professional organizations (e.g., the Measurement and Evaluation Council of the AAHPERD) is one example. Being an editor or a reviewer for various journals is also a service activity.

WWW

Measurement and Evaluation Council of AAHPERD
www.aahperd.org/aapar/people/councils/ME.cfm

box
3.1

An abstract of a research study in the area of measurement.

Zhu, W., Plowman, S. A., and Park, Y. (2010). A primer-test centered equating method for setting cut-off scores. *Research Quarterly for Exercise and Sport, 81*(4), 400–409.

This study evaluated the use of a new primary field test method based on test equating to address inconsistent classification among field tests. We analyzed students' information on the Progressive Aerobic Cardiovascular Endurance Run (PACER), mile run (MR), and VO_2max from three data sets (college: n = 94; middle school: n = 39; elementary school: n = 96). Using the college and elementary school data, the equivalent relationship between PACER and MR scores was first established by the Kernel equating method. This yielded MR scores derived from PACER (mile run PACER equated [MR PEQ]), which were used to predict maximal oxygen uptake (VO_2max) and classify students according to the FITNESSGRAM® Healthy Fitness Zones™. We compared the results to the predictions and classifications based on measured VO_2max, MR, and PACER-predicted VO_2max and cross-validated the relationships using the middle school data. We found the test conversion to be accurate and that the MR PEQ scores functioned similarly to the original MR scores. Both performed better than the original PACER scores in predicting VO_2max and classifying students. The middle school data generally supported these results. The proposed method is accurate and effective in setting a new field test onto the same scale of a primary field test and determining its cut-off scores.

Acting as a consultant for colleagues and students is another role for the measurement specialist, whether assisting with a research project, writing a grant proposal, or helping with a statistical question. Because the measurement specialist usually is equipped with many tools, he or she is often the "mechanic" of a department's activities.

The measurement specialist located in a corporation, hospital, or business setting generally has two major functions. The first is to act as a consultant to colleagues in the area of measurement and research design, and the second is to act as fund-raiser. Depending on the specific location, the fund-raising could take the form of being the primary investigator or a consultant on a grant application. In some cases, the measurement specialist may concentrate on collecting, organizing, analyzing, and interpreting data collected by others. A laboratory involved with tracking health and disease issues is an example of a setting where data analysis and interpretation are the major activities of the exercise science measurement specialist.

PROMINENT JOURNALS AND RELATED PUBLICATIONS

Because the measurement specialist can deal with a very large variety of assessment issues, it is difficult to restrict the identification of professional journals containing relevant information. The first list includes those journals most likely to contain articles specifically about the measurement process, while the second list includes journals containing articles with content focusing on other areas of the discipline but necessarily containing measurement practices.

PRIMARY JOURNALS

Applied Psychological Measurement

Educational and Psychological Measurement

Journal of Educational Measurement

Journal of Physical Education, Recreation and Dance

Research Quarterly for Exercise and Sport

RELATED PUBLICATIONS

Adapted Physical Activity Quarterly

American Heart Journal

American Journal of Epidemiology

American Journal of Health Promotion

American Journal of Public Health

American Psychologist

Archives of Physical Medicine and Rehabilitation Circulation

Journal of Applied Physiology

Journal of Applied Psychology

Journal of Behavior Medicine

Journal of Chronic Diseases

Journal of Clinical Investigation

Journal of Educational Physiology

Journal of Health Education

Journal of Human Movement Studies

Journal of Occupational Medicine

Journal of Pediatrics

Journal of Sport and Exercise Physiology

Journal of Sport Psychology

Journal of Sports Medicine and Physical Fitness

Journal of Teaching Physical Education

Journal of the American Medical Association

Journal of the American Physical Therapy Association

Medicine and Science in Sports and Exercise

New England Journal of Medicine

Pediatric Exercise Science

Perceptual Motor Skills

Phi Delta Kappan

Sport Psychologist

FUTURE DIRECTIONS

The march toward specialization is continuing unabated. Physical education departments at many universities have disappeared or changed their name and foci. Human Performance, Kinesiology, Exercise Science, and Integrative Physiology are a few of the new titles.

Highly sophisticated computer-assisted performance analyzers, magnetic resonance imaging tests, sophisticated force platforms, and high-speed cameras are just a few examples of tools used by the exercise scientist. Technological advances in measuring devices will continue to further what can be measured as well as the accuracy of the measurements.

Increased attention in the areas of the sociological and psychological aspects of physical activity will be emphasized. We can explain how physical activity affects the sodium transport system inside the body, but we know little about why a large part of the population remains sedentary and what techniques can be used to encourage them to be more physically active. This area should prove fruitful for future investigation.

SUMMARY

The accurate measurement of variables is critical to all disciplines. For exercise scientists to be producers and/or wise consumers of the available information from research, they must be well grounded in measurement practices and techniques.

Two important aspects of measurement are validity and reliability. Validity is the degree to which a test measures what it is intended to measure. Reliability is the extent to which a test consistently yields the same results when repeated under the same conditions. Research in all disciplines requires that tests be valid and reliable.

Measurement practices can be organized according to their purpose (e.g., classification, motivation, achievement assessment, potential and prediction, diagnosis, program evaluation, and research). Within categories, differences exist regarding the precision with which a variable can be measured. The level of measurement can be placed into one of four categories—nominal, ordinal, interval, and ratio—based on the information provided.

study / QUESTIONS

Visit the IES website to study, take notes, and try out the lab for this chapter.

1. Explain and give examples of several uses of measurement in exercise science.
2. What is the difference between measurement and evaluation?
3. Name the four levels of measurement and explain the type of information associated with each.
4. Define the three primary domains of human experience.
5. Explain the importance of the concepts of validity, reliability, and objectivity to the measurement specialist.
6. Give examples of how one might collect evidence for the reliability and validity of the measurement process.
7. What is the basic premise of statistics? Why is it important to measurement specialists?

learning \ ACTIVITIES

1. Go to the Genamics Journal Seek website and look at the category for Measurement in Physical Education and Exercise Science (http://journal seek.net/cgi-bin/journalseek/journalsearch.cgi?field=issn&query=1091-367X). Search for articles covering topics from the chapter. Write abstracts (short summaries) for two articles covering two different subjects.

2. Research via the Internet how measurement is used in exercise science. Write a one- to two-page informative paper. Be sure to include the four levels of measurement.

3. Get involved with a research study in exercise science by observing, volunteering to help, or volunteering to be a participant. Write a brief report describing the role of the exercise scientist, especially as it concerned measurement.

4. Interview a current faculty member in exercise science to discover the role of measurement in his or her research projects. Write a brief report, paying special attention to each phase of the study (e.g., planning, data collection, analysis, and discussion).

suggested / READINGS

Baumgartner, T. A., Jackson, A. S., Mahar, M. T., & Rowe, D. A. (2006). *Measurement for evaluation in physical education and exercise science* (8th ed.). New York: McGraw-Hill.

Bishop, P. (2008). *Measurement and evaluation in physical activity applications.* Scottsdale, AZ: Holcomb Hathaway.

Hensley, L. D., & East, W. B. (1989). Testing and grading in the psychomotor domain. In M. J. Safrit & T. M. Ward (Eds.), *Measurement concepts in physical education and exercise science,* pp. 247–321. Champaign, IL: Human Kinetics.

Morrow, J. R., Jackson, A. W., Disch, J. G., & Mood, D. P. (2011). *Measurement and evaluation in human performance* (4th ed.). Champaign, IL: Human Kinetics.

references

Anderson, L. W., & Krathwohl, D. R. (2001). *A taxonomy for learning, teaching, and assessing.* New York: Addison-Wesley Longman.

Bloom, B. S. (1956). *Taxonomy of educational objectives: Cognitive domain.* New York: McKay.

Harrow, A. J. (1972). *A taxonomy of the psychomotor domain.* New York: McKay.

Hensley, L. D., & East, W. B. (1989). Testing and grading in the psychomotor domain. In M. J. Safrit & T. M. Ward (Eds.), *Measurement concepts in physical education and exercise science,* pp. 247–321. Champaign, IL: Human Kinetics.

Krathwohl, D. R., Bloom, B. S., & Masia, B. A. (1964). *Taxonomy of educational objectives: Handbook II: The affective domain.* New York: McKay.

Morrow, J. (2003). Physical activity not physical fitness assessment. *Measurement News, 7,* 3.

Anatomy in Exercise Science

GLEN O. JOHNSON

INTRODUCTION

Many of us began to study anatomy shortly after we learned our first words. What child has not been asked, "Where is your nose?" or "Where is your ear?" The child then points to the appropriate structure. This is the individual's first lesson in anatomy: learning the names of structures. It must, however, be emphasized that the study of anatomy involves more than just learning the Greek and Latin names of structures, although that is, in the author's opinion, certainly necessary. Where structures are located, their relationship to other structures, their growth, and their basic function are also critically important to students of anatomy and exercise science.

A student's first exposure to anatomy is likely to be a course in gross human anatomy. The method by which gross anatomy is presented or studied can vary. Some courses use the *systemic* method of study. **Systemic anatomy** means that each of the systems of the body is studied independently before moving on to the next system. Typically, the skeletal system is studied first, then the muscular system, nervous system, circulatory system, and the rest of the 11 body systems in various order. The other method of study is **regional anatomy,** which means that everything about a specific region of the body is studied together. In this method, all the bones, muscles, nerves, and vessels of the upper limbs are learned at the same time before moving on to another body area. Beginning courses in anatomy typically use the systemic method, whereas advanced courses, such as those offered in medical schools, usually use the regional method of study. Gross human anatomy is best studied using dissected human cadavers. When cadavers are not available, reasonable knowledge can be obtained by studying animal bodies, such as cats or fetal pigs. Computer simulations of dissection and models are also helpful learning aids when used in conjunction with cadavers.

systemic anatomy ■

regional anatomy ■

DEFINITIONS IN ANATOMY

anatomy ■

The word **anatomy** is from Greek origins and means "to cut" or "to cut up"(*Dorland's Illustrated Medical Dictionary,* 2007). Today we refer to "cut up" as dissection. *Dissection* is the careful cutting up of cadavers (human bodies) to study body structures such as muscles, nerves, and vessels.

Modern textbooks of anatomy, however, define *anatomy* as follows: The study of the parts of the body and their relationship to each other. Anatomy can be broken down into subspecialties of anatomical study. The major subspecialties of anatomy include the following:

gross anatomy ■

Gross anatomy. The study of those body structures, such as the heart and brain, that one can see without the aid of a microscope. The beginning exercise science student will be particularly concerned with the study of gross human anatomy.

histology ■

Histology. The microscopic study of the anatomy of tissues and their cellular basis.

comparative anatomy ■

Comparative anatomy. The comparison of anatomical structures of different animals, both the similarities and differences. For example, how the wing of a bird compares to the arm and forearm of a human.

embryology ■

Embryology. The study of the anatomical changes in tissues from conception to birth.

Developmental anatomy. The study of embryology as well as the anatomical changes that occur from birth to death. This type of anatomy is used in exercise science studies when studying the effect of exercise on growth and development.

■ *developmental anatomy*

Pathological anatomy. The study of the anatomical changes that occur in tissues as a result of disease; for example, lung or vessel diseases (Carola, Harky, & Noback, 1992; *Dorland's,* 2007; Marieb & Mallatt, 1992).

■ *pathological anatomy*

HISTORY OF ANATOMY

As scientists, we must always be ready to ask the most basic (and to some, infuriating) questions. In this case, I can already hear the groans of the students who might be assigned to read this chapter, and I can hear their silent question: Why? Why study the history of anatomy, or any science, or any subject at all? One logical response is that if we do not study history we have no measure of the progress of human beings.

It would not be realistic to present a complete, comprehensive review of the written history of anatomy in this chapter. An attempt will be made to cite some of the major contributors and events in the early development and advancement of anatomical study, recognizing that some individuals and geographical areas will receive reduced coverage or not be mentioned. Interested students are encouraged to use the references at the end of this chapter for more detailed information.

It is also important that students understand that ideas, concepts, and practices develop over long periods of time and that these new ideas, even when correct, are often not readily accepted by the political and religious leaders and scholars of the time period. Dates are presented in this chapter only to emphasize the approximate era when certain advances occurred. The development of anatomical knowledge closely parallels advances in medicine; hence, many important historical figures in anatomy were also famous physicians, or vice versa.

Prescientific Period

Anatomy is one of the basic sciences and can be accurately considered one of the oldest branches of medicine (Knight, 1980). Cave drawings and other archaeological evidence ancient peoples left behind suggest that some knowledge of anatomy was essential for survival (see Exhibit 4.1). Without question, the butchering of animals for meat and other tissues provided these early hunters with practical knowledge about the structures and functions of some organs. Knowing the heart's location and the fact that piercing it was an effective method of killing an animal was certainly important for these hunters' survival.

Prehistoric hunters and foragers were also probably knowledgeable about some aspects of their own bodies. They would recognize which wounds meant death and those that would heal.

The shape of the heart in ancient cave paintings is exactly as it appears today on Valentine's Day with the pointed apex depicting the tip of the ventricles and the two rounded humps depicting the atria (Knight, 1980).

They likely had methods of healing some injuries. There is evidence that 100,000 years ago humans used sharp flint stones to cut out round sections of living human skulls to expose the brain, a process called *trephining* (also trephination). The reasons for trephining are varied. One would be medical;

exhibit / 4.1   Reproduction of a paleolithic cave drawing from Spain showing the heart of a mammoth.

that is, relief of head pain or repair of skull wounds. Another may have to do with ancient religious practices, to satisfy their gods (Hixson, 1966; Lyons & Petrucelli, 1978). Because there are no written records of this prescientific era, we can only speculate on the knowledge and actions of these ancient peoples.

Scientific Period

Traditional Western thought places the beginning of the scientific period, at least regarding anatomy, with the Greeks around 500 BCE (Carola et al., 1992; Persaud, 1984; Singer, 1957), although Homer describes the anatomy of wounds in the *Iliad* in 800 BCE (Lyons & Petrucelli, 1978; Van De Graaff, 1995).

The Greeks, however, undoubtedly obtained some of their concepts regarding the human body from earlier Mesopotamian and Egyptian civilizations. The present country of Iraq contains the Tigris and Euphrates rivers. The fertile land between the two rivers was originally called Mesopotamia and is referred to as the cradle of civilization (Chernow & Vallasi, 1993; Lyons & Petrucelli, 1978; Singer, 1957; Van De Graaff, 1995). Clay models of a sheep's liver have been found (dated around 2000 BCE) in Mesopotamia. Writings on them indicate that they were used more for religious purposes than anatomical study, but they were also important in medicine. For example, in Babylon (an ancient city on the Euphrates River), the liver was considered the seat of life (or guardian of the soul) and was much used in diagnosis. A few records from Mesopotamia describe surgeries that reflect a knowledge of anatomy. Some of these medical procedures are described in the Code of Hammurabi, which was mandated by *Hammurabi,* a great Babylonian king (1792–1750 or 1738–1686 BCE; sources vary).

Egypt

Egypt is west of Mesopotamia. Some ancient Egyptian papyruses thought to be written around 3000–2000 BCE described such maladies as tumors, ulcers, and fractures and treatments such as splinting techniques, suturing, and cauterizing wounds. They also contained the first known mention of the word *brain,* along with a description of the meninges (membranes around the brain) and the gyri (ridges on the surface of the brain). Another papyrus of that period (around 3000 BCE) describes the heart and vessels from it to various parts of the body (Hixson, 1966; Lyons & Petrucelli, 1978; Persaud, 1984). Although anatomically inaccurate with regard to present knowledge, these records indicate a rudimentary understanding of the heart's function.

The Egyptians also practiced embalming and mummification of the body. Mummification, which began around 4000 BCE, was more of religious than medical or anatomical significance, but the process involved intimate knowledge about the body. It is known that they removed most of the brain by inserting a hook through the nostrils. They also removed internal organs such as the liver, lungs, and intestines and stored them in special clay pots. The lids of the pots represented the particular god who was a protector of that body part. The concept of body parts being related to a specific deity or cosmic affiliation continued, as we shall see, long into the Middle Ages.

China, Japan, and India

Chinese religious beliefs (mainly Confucianism) forbade defiling the body; thus, dissection was forbidden and knowledge of organs was obtained only from wounds (Persaud, 1984; Van De Graaff, 1995). However, an ancient Chinese book on anatomy indicates that condemned criminals may have been dissected around 1000 BCE (Knight, 1980). For the most part, however, Chinese physicians were taught only about the surface of the body from models and diagrams (Lyons & Petrucelli, 1978; Persaud, 1984).

The Chinese believed in two basic forces or principles, the yin and the yang, which governed everything from the universe to the human body. With regard to the body, it was believed that balance between these forces was essential for good health (Chewning, 1979; Knight, 1980; Lyons & Petrucelli, 1978; Persaud, 1984). Belief in the yin and yang did not foster a spirit of exploration of the internal body. However, certain aspects of the yin and yang were related to specific body structures, and as a result, acupuncture was developed by the ancient Chinese to attain balance between the forces of yin and yang. Some ancient Chinese, however, knew more than just surface anatomy. In 2600 BCE, Huang Ti, who is considered the father of Chinese medicine, stated that "all the blood of the body is under control of the heart. The heart is in accord with the pulse. The pulse regulates all the blood and the blood current flows in a continuous circle and never stops" (Persaud, 1984). This astounding concept was not confirmed in the Western World until described by *William Harvey* in 1628, 4,200 years later. This emphasizes the importance of communication. If the ancient scientists had had the communication systems of today, advances in anatomy and medicine and all other areas would have occurred at a much accelerated pace, and the credit for specific discoveries would be much different from what we recognize today.

The development of anatomy in Japan mirrored that of China, largely because Japan sent Buddhist monks (in the 6th century) to study anatomy

Because the penalty for adultery in ancient India was to cut off the offender's nose, writings describe detailed plastic surgery techniques to repair the nose (called rhinoplasty), as well as other fairly sophisticated surgeries (Lyons & Petrucelli, 1978; Persaud, 1984).

in China. The Japanese readily adopted these teachings. Later, after some initial association with a few European powers, the Japanese government banned all contact with Western countries in 1603. However, some medical texts (mainly Dutch) with anatomical drawings had already circulated among Japanese physicians, and they contradicted the traditional Chinese models of anatomy that had been used for centuries. Finally, in 1771, a Japanese physician, Genpaku Sugito, was able to observe a dissection and compare the Dutch model with the Chinese concepts. He was disturbed because the dissection proved the errors in the Chinese model. In 1774, Sugito and his colleagues published an anatomy book based on the more correct Dutch anatomical work.

Writings from ancient India indicate that Indians were also contributing to the advance of anatomical and medical knowledge (Lyons & Petrucelli, 1978; Persaud, 1984). Susruta was a well-known Hindu physician who is thought to have lived in the 6th century BCE. Susruta stated that "the surgeon, who wishes to possess the exact knowledge of the science of surgery, should thoroughly examine all parts of the dead body after its proper preparation" (Persaud, 1984). Hindu religious laws, however, banned touching the deceased or using a knife for dissection. Thus, bodies were placed in water until they were soft enough to scrape off skin and other tissues with a broom or scraper to view deeper structures (Knight, 1980; Persaud, 1984).

Greece

The Greeks laid the foundations for the study of science, medicine, and anatomy as well as other disciplines in Western history. The first systematic writings about anatomy were by *Alcmaeon* of Crotona around 500 BCE (Crotona was a Greek colony in southern Italy). From animal dissections, he described the optic nerves and the auditory tube (the auditory tube connects the ear to the throat) (Carola et al., 1992; Lyons & Petrucelli, 1978; Persaud, 1984; Singer, 1957). He also asserted that the brain, not the heart, was where human intelligence was located (Persaud, 1984). Although Alcmaeon may have dissected a human, it is not likely that most of the great Greek scientists/philosophers had, although considerable animal dissection was accomplished (Carola et al., 1992; Persaud, 1984).

Empedocles (493–433 BCE) was from a Greek colony in Sicily (the southern tip of Italy) and lived about the same time as Alcmaeon. Some of his anatomical theories affected anatomical, medical, and scientific thinking for several thousand years. Empedocles taught that the heart was the center of the vascular system (correct), but also that it was the site of and/or distributor of "pneuma" (incorrect). Pneuma was considered to be the "life and soul" of the body. It was thought to be the steamlike substance that could be seen rising from the blood of people or animals slain in the open air. Unfortunately, Empedocles' concept of pneuma and other body functions remained a standard belief for thousands of years (Hixson, 1966; Knight, 1980; Persaud, 1984; Singer, 1957). It is necessary to remember that even though the early anatomists and/or scientists were not always correct, their ideas were important for the next generation of developing scientists.

Hippocrates (460–377 BCE), the Father of Western Medicine, was a Greek physician whose Hippocratic oath is still recited at some medical schools (Carola et al., 1992; Lyons & Petrucelli, 1978; Van De Graaff, 1995). A collection of medical and philosophical writings called the Hippocratic Collection has been attributed to Hippocrates, but evidence indicates he wrote very few of the papers (Knight, 1980; Lyons & Petrucelli, 1978; Persaud, 1984). Hippocrates stated that "anatomy is the foundation of medicine" (Persaud, 1984), but

he never dissected a human body and had little knowledge of internal organs. He described tendons as nerves and thought the brain to do nothing more than secrete mucus, although in the Hippocratic writings the human brain is correctly described as having two identical halves separated by a membrane (Karpovich & Sinning, 1971; McMurrich, 1930; Roche, Heymsfield, & Lohman, 1996; Saunders & O'Malley, 1973).

Hippocrates believed that the mucus secreted by the brain cooled the heart and that the arteries contained nothing but air. In fact, the word *artery* is of Latin and Greek origin meaning "to keep air" or "an air duct." Many ancient scientists and physicians held this concept (Carola et al., 1992; Knight, 1980).

Hippocrates promoted the humoral theory of the body. According to this theory, there were four body humors, each associated with a particular organ. The four humors were blood (with the liver), phlegm (with the lungs), yellow bile (with the gallbladder), and black bile (with the spleen). Hippocrates and others maintained that these four humors must be in balance for a person to be in good health, to some degree a concept similar to the Chinese yin and yang (Nuland, 1995; Persaud, 1984; Singer, 1957; Van De Graaff, 1995).

Unfortunately, the erroneous humoral theory remained a strong force in medicine for some 2,000 years (Lyons & Petrucelli, 1978; Van De Graaff, 1995). While certain of Hippocrates' anatomical concepts were erroneous, he contributed greatly to anatomy and medicine because he believed that diseases are the result of natural causes and not due to the whim of the gods (Carola et al., 1992; Van De Graaff, 1995), a considerable advance.

Although some of the anatomical concepts provided by the Greek scientists, physicians, and anatomists may seem ludicrous and humorous today, their contribution to the advance of knowledge is invaluable. They developed systematic methods of inquiry, were careful observers, and dissected animals. These were the beginnings of the scientific method (Knight, 1980; Singer, 1957).

Aristotle (384–322 BCE), one of the best known of the ancient Greeks, was a scientist and philosopher. He was the son of the physician to King Philip of Macedonia and a student of Plato. He became the tutor for King Philip's son, who is well known historically as Alexander the Great (Lyons & Petrucelli, 1978; Singer, 1957; Van De Graaff, 1995). Aristotle never dissected

a human body, but he dissected many animals (Knight, 1980). Because of his excellent biological descriptions of animals, Aristotle is considered the founder of comparative anatomy, and he also developed ideas concerning organic evolution later praised by Charles Darwin (Knight, 1980; Persaud, 1984; Singer, 1957).

Aristotle was the first to use the term *aorta* (the large artery leaving the left ventricle of the heart), and presented a fairly accurate description of the pathway of the esophagus (Knight, 1980; Singer, 1957). However, his works

Hippocrates stated that "diseases caused by overeating are cured by fasting . . . diseases caused by indolence are cured by exertion . . . and tenseness by relaxation" (Singer, 1957). One might argue that the Father of Western Medicine was also an exercise scientist.

also contained considerable anatomical errors due to the lack of human dissection and the fact that he was more a natural philosopher than anatomist. Aristotle's teacher, Plato, believed the brain to be the seat of intelligence, while Aristotle placed intelligence in the heart. He considered the brain to function only to cool the heart. He also believed that arteries sometimes carried only air and sometimes only blood (Carola et al., 1992; Knight, 1980; Persaud, 1984; Singer, 1957; Van De Graaff, 1995). Despite such errors, Aristotle is considered one of the greatest contributors to anatomy and medicine.

Interestingly, it was Aristotle's philosophy, more than his scientific logic, that influenced biological and anatomical thought for 2,000 years (Knight, 1980; Singer, 1957). One of Aristotle's fascinations was with reproduction, and he believed that the female provided the material substance of the embryo (the soil in which the life grows), but only the male contributed the *psyche*, or actual life, to the organism. Because this psyche is not a material thing, he thus believed that no substance needed to pass from the male to the female. This view of reproduction (in this case human reproduction) is called parthenogenesis (virgin birth). This concept was accepted by many scientists up to the 19th century. Virgin birth is a major belief of Christianity. Thus, many of Aristotle's views were readily accepted by the early Christian Church, whereas many other ancient ideas and writings, although correct, were considered pagan beliefs, not accepted, and often destroyed (Knight, 1980; Persaud, 1984; Singer, 1957).

Alexandria and the Roman Empire

When the Greek cultures of the mainland began to decline, the center of knowledge passed to Alexandria (around 300–250 BCE) in Egypt. Alexandria was founded by Alexander the Great (Aristotle's pupil) and became the center of intellectual pursuits for several centuries (Carola et al., 1992; Persaud, 1984). Anatomical study advanced in the Alexandrian School of Medicine due primarily to the work of two Greek scholars, Herophilus and Erasistratus (Carola et al., 1992; Persaud, 1984; Singer, 1957).

Advances in anatomy were particularly enhanced by the acceptance in Alexandria of human dissection. Although some human dissection had been accomplished in earlier civilizations, the dissections of Herophilus and Erasistratus were probably the first public dissections; that is, viewed by other scholars (Carola et al., 1992; Lyons & Petrucelli, 1978; Persaud, 1984; Singer, 1957). Herophilus was born around 335–300 BCE and is referred to as the Father of Anatomy (Persaud, 1984; Singer, 1957). He is credited with dissecting up to 600 human bodies, which gave him anatomical insights no one before him had obtained. Among other things, Herophilus made the first distinctions between motor and sensory nerves, described the difference between the cerebrum and cerebellum of the brain, and gave detailed descriptions of the liver and uterus. Unlike Aristotle, he correctly maintained that intelligence was located in the brain. His many human dissections probably included some vivisections (dissecting a living person, usually a criminal). Herophilus was a noted teacher and is thought to be one of the first teachers of anatomy and medicine to have female students (Carola et al., 1992; Knight, 1980; Persaud, 1984; Singer, 1957).

Alexandria attracted many famous scholars of the time, including the mathematicians Euclid and Archimedes. Archimedes calculated the value of *pi,* but he is more famous for his principles of buoyancy, which are used in exercise science studies of body composition with underwater weighing (Chernow & Vallasi, 1993; Lyons & Petrucelli, 1978).

Erasistratus (310–250 BCE) was a slightly younger contemporary of Herophilus and is referred to as the Father of Physiology. He noted that the human brain had greater convolutions than animal brains and believed that was the reason for humans' greater intelligence. He studied the heart and described many vessels such as the renal arteries and the vena cavas (the large veins bringing blood back to the heart) but thought that tendons and nerves were the same thing, as did most of the Greek physicians and anatomists.

Erasistratus made significant contributions to knowledge about the heart and circulatory system, but he believed that only veins carried blood and that arteries carried the airlike "vital spirit," much as Empedocles and Hippocrates thought. When he saw people with bleeding arteries, he argued that the injury caused a vacuum and that blood was "sucked into the arteries from veins through very fine intercommunications between the two types of vessels" (Singer, 1957). Far before their discovery, and without knowing it, Erasistratus had perceived the capillary system.

Eventually, Alexandria and its scholarly atmosphere began to decline, and many of the written works stored in the great libraries were destroyed by fanatical Christians or stolen and lost by invading Arabian forces (Knight, 1980). However, the Arabian armies often took many of the libraries' written works with them. Thus, they preserved many of the anatomical papers, particularly those of the Greeks, that would otherwise never have survived. These important records, which were translated from Greek to Arabic, were later returned to European countries and then retranslated from Arabic to Latin (Knight, 1980; Singer, 1957).

The preservation of these writings was critically important because during the Middle Ages, the church forbade studying the human body, as well as any writings concerned with anatomy, and destroyed any materials it found. If the Arabian invaders had not saved these works, they would have been forever lost. Fortunately, these anatomical papers began to appear in Europe during the 13th century, where they helped stimulate a rebirth of anatomical and medical study (Chewning, 1979; Singer, 1957; Van De Graaff, 1995).

The Arabs likewise benefited because their religion strictly forbade dissection and did not even allow pictures of the human body. There were no courses on anatomy in Arabian medical schools at that time. Thus, Arab physicians and scientists, probably at great personal risk, studied and preserved the anatomical works of the Greeks and others (Chewning, 1979; McMurrich, 1930).

With the decline of Alexandria and the advent of the Roman Empire, anatomical and medical knowledge suffered. Dissection was either forbidden or not encouraged. The inquisitiveness, promotion of philosophical theories, and questioning mind-set of the Greeks were no longer prominent. The Romans were practical and wanted what was immediately useful and believed the theoretical pursuits of the Greeks to be relatively unimportant (Knight, 1980; Persaud, 1984; Singer, 1957).

At the height of the Roman Empire, most of the physicians were Greek because the Romans felt that medicine was a lowly profession "fit only for slaves and immigrants" (Knight, 1980). A medical school was started in Rome in 60 BCE by Asclepiades (120–70 BCE), called the Asclepiadic sect in physic

The Asclepiades school recommended exercise-science-like prescriptions such as diet, exercise, massage, and even listening to music. It also used drugs such as opium and wine to treat patients. Asclepiades also rejected Hippocrates' concept of the four humors. However, virtually no advances in anatomy or understanding the human body were made by Asclepiades or the medical school, and unfortunately, the humoral theory remained prominent (Lyons & Petrucelli, 1978).

(Knight, 1980; Lyons & Petrucelli, 1978; Persaud, 1984; Singer, 1957; Van De Graaff, 1995). (The name Asclepiades likely was derived from Aescalapias, who was the Greek god of medicine and a son of Apollo.)

Little advance in anatomy and medicine occurred during this time, because both the Romans and early Christians forbade dissection. The antidissection attitude and general lack of progress in medicine (and other areas) continued for over a thousand years, an era known as the Early Middle Ages or Dark Ages (Singer, 1957; Van De Graaff, 1995).

Two notable individuals from the Roman era had considerable influence on anatomy and medicine: Aulus Celsus, a Roman, and Claudius Galen, a Greek scholar and physician. Celsus wrote eight books (circa 30 BCE–45 CE) on medicine, called *De Re Medicina*. It is suspected that many of his anatomical and medical writings came from the Hippocratic Collection. Celsus described the trachea (windpipe), esophagus, diaphragm, lungs, liver, spleen, and kidneys. His descriptions of surgeries were particularly detailed regarding the skeleton of the extremities. The latter knowledge was likely gained from battlefield physicians. He approved of human dissection but probably never experienced one himself (Karpovich & Sinning, 1971; Knight, 1980; Persaud, 1984; Singer, 1957).

Claudius Galen (129–199 CE), along with Hippocrates, is considered to be the greatest of the early physicians. His influence on medicine was so dominant that, during the Middle Ages (some 1,300 years later), he was called the Prince of Physicians (Knight, 1980; Singer, 1957). His writings on medicine and anatomy were considered virtually infallible for 1,500 years in Western medicine. Because the Catholic church did not allow Galen's anatomical concepts to be criticized, his incorrect ideas persisted and stifled the progress in anatomical study from his death in 201 CE until the Renaissance period of the late Middle Ages. His influence was so dominant that in the 1550s the Royal College of Physicians of London demanded that one of its members retract a statement that described some errors in Galen's work. The accused physician quickly did so (Carola et al., 1992; Knight, 1980; Persaud, 1984; Singer, 1957). The French anatomist Jacobus Sylvius (1478–1555), when faced during dissection with obvious errors in some of Galen's writings, stated that "man must have changed his structure in the course of time, for the teaching of Galen cannot err" (Persaud, 1984).

Galen never dissected a human body, but for a time he served as physician to the gladiators, whose severe wounds allowed him to observe many human anatomical structures. Galen presented descriptions of the skull and vertebral column and the bones of the extremities. He described the difference between arteries and veins and proved that arteries contain blood instead of air, as had been believed since the time of Aristotle (Knight, 1980; Lyons & Petrucelli, 1978; Nuland, 1995; Persaud, 1984).

It is unlikely that any future scientist will dominate any field to the degree of Galen, and we are indebted to him for preserving and describing anatomical and medical knowledge from a time in history that would have otherwise been lost (Persaud, 1984).

The Middle Ages

The Middle Ages is generally accepted to have occurred from the 4th or 5th century CE to the middle of the 15th century. The fall of the Roman Empire, the death of Galen, and the rise of a powerful, tyrannical church considerably impeded the advance of anatomy and other scholarly pursuits. The Early Middle Ages (circa 450–750 CE) is sometimes called the Dark Ages, in part because of the lack of advance in learning during this period.

Western European countries stagnated from the 4th century up to the 11th century. Advances in anatomy and medicine were minimal at best. The powerful and political church forbade dissection; in fact, none had occurred since the Alexandrian period. The prevailing attitude was one of greater concern for what occurred after death, rather than during one's lifetime. Scholars sought "truth" using philosophical or religious concepts, rather than by experimentation or observation. The foundation of knowledge was faith instead of reason (Hixson, 1966; Knight, 1980; McMurrich, 1930; Persaud, 1984).

An interest in astrology developed, and a figure called the zodiacal man became popular (Exhibit 4.2). Different parts of the zodiacal man were related

The zodiacal man from the Middle Ages. Different body parts are related to the stars that were thought to influence a person's health.

exhibit   4.2

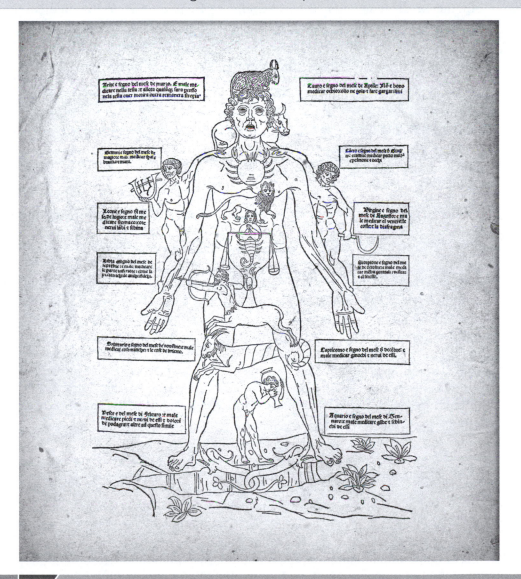

to specific constellations in an attempt to relate body functions and illnesses to the movements of planets, a concept somewhat similar to that of the ancient Egyptians (Chewning, 1979; Knight, 1980; Lyons & Petrucelli, 1978; Persaud, 1984). The carryover regarding astrological predictions about a person's daily life persists and remains a popular (and believable to many) part of today's daily newspapers.

Eventually, society began to slowly change, and during the 12th and 13th centuries new universities emerged in Italy, France, Germany, and England. A renewed interest in anatomy and the study of the body began in these universities. The first medical facility in Europe was established at Bologna in Italy about 1156 (Knight, 1980). Human dissection began to occur; however, the reasons for these dissections were not for learning or the advance of knowledge about the human body. They were done for legal purposes, because the law schools wanted information about how the person died, that is, legal evidence, as in cases of poisoning or knifing. Thus, the technique of dissection was far more important than the study of structures to determine function (Chewning, 1979; Knight, 1980; Singer, 1957).

In the medical schools of the Middle Ages, practitioners of medicine and surgeons were quite different. Medical schools taught medicine to physicians, and most physicians considered surgery beneath their dignity and felt that a detailed knowledge of anatomy was unnecessary. Knowing the position of internal organs was good enough for them. Surgery was done by barbers, bathhouse keepers, and sometimes even executioners (McMurrich, 1930).

The Renaissance

With the rise of the universities, the Middle Ages moved into the Renaissance, a period from the early 14th to the late 16th or early 17th centuries. During this time, major advancements in literature and art and a virtual revolution in science occurred (Chernow & Vallasi, 1993). The invention of the printing press in the 1450s was particularly important because this allowed the anatomical knowledge or theories of a particular scholar or university to spread more easily. The most well-known early anatomy text was written by Mondino de' Luzzi (1276–1326). The book, titled the *Anathomia*, was first published in 1316 but not printed until 1487. It contained no illustrations but became required reading in European medical schools for hundreds of years. Mondino had supervised dissections of executed criminals and accurately described some vessels and heart structures, but he could not bring himself to question Galen's materials; thus, the book continued the attitude that Galen could not be wrong. However, Mondino made detailed descriptions of the dissection process that were useful at the time. As a result, Mondino is called the Restorer of Anatomy (Chewning, 1979; Hixson, 1966; Knight 1980; Persaud, 1984; Singer, 1957).

The increased emphasis on dissection during the Renaissance created a shortage of cadavers. Grave robbing to obtain cadavers became a problem, and some medical students were convicted for it. The main source of bodies for dissection was executed criminals. Because most of these were males, there was little opportunity for dissection and observation of female anatomy, so knowledge about female reproductive organs was scarce (Knight, 1980; Nuland, 1995).

There were many who contributed to anatomy during the Renaissance, but two individuals are particularly noteworthy, one an artist and the other a physician. The artist was Leonardo da Vinci (1422–1519), better known by most as the painter of the *Mona Lisa* and *The Last Supper* (Chernow & Vallasi, 1993). Da Vinci, one of the great geniuses of all time, was also a scientist, inventor, mathematician, astronomer, and philosopher. He dissected many human bodies and produced exquisitely detailed anatomical drawings. He also made many anatomical discoveries and developed technical procedures that enhanced anatomical study. He was the first person to demonstrate the shape of the ventricles (fluid-filled cavities) in the brain by pouring melted wax into them through a hole he had drilled into the brain of an ox. He did this with other body cavities as well. He described **arteriosclerosis** (hardening of the arteries) by comparing the dissected arteries of an old man with those of a young man, along with many other functional anatomical observations.

■ *arteriosclerosis*

Many contemporaries of da Vinci also used dissection to more accurately depict the human form. The physician *Andreas Vesalius* (1514–1564) provided the foundation for modern medicine and revolutionized the study of anatomy. Vesalius was the greatest anatomist of his time and is called the Reformer of Anatomy because he initiated a unique change in the teaching of anatomy. When anatomy and dissection were finally approved as university courses, the professors of anatomy disdained touching a body and sat in elevated high-backed wooden chairs and pointed with a long pole at what they wished their helpers (often local butchers) to cut (origin of the statement "I wouldn't touch that with a 10-foot pole"). The primary intent of these professors was to demonstrate the proper dissecting technique and substantiate what Galen had described.

Vesalius came down from the chair, dismissed the helpers, and did the dissecting himself, all the while lecturing to the students and surrounding audience in a stimulating, challenging manner (Chewning, 1979; Nuland, 1995; Persaud, 1984; Saunders & O'Malley, 1973; Singer, 1957; Van De Graaff, 1995). Like today's students, Vesalius's students probably enjoyed seeing some of the more stuffy professors' stodgy thinking challenged by the intelligent, logical, and charismatic Vesalius. In 1543, at the age of 28, Vesalius published *De Humani Corporis Fabrica (On the Fabric of the Human Body),* often referred to simply as the *Fabrica*. It challenged the long-held beliefs of Galen and was the first accurately illustrated text on human anatomy that also described specific dissection techniques (Nuland, 1995; Persaud, 1984; Saunders & O'Malley, 1973; Singer, 1957). As with most new concepts, Vesalius's teaching methods and the *Fabrica* were not readily accepted by many of the traditional scholars at the time. Exhibit 4.3 shows a drawing of muscles from the *Fabrica* by Vesalius.

According to old Roman law, no deceased pregnant woman could be buried without the fetus first being removed from the womb so it could be baptized. Some knowledge of female anatomy was obtained in this way (Van De Graaff, 1995).

Seventeenth Through Nineteenth Centuries

Following the Renaissance, science in general and anatomy made many advances. The two major advances that occurred during the 17th century were an explanation of how the blood circulates and the development of the microscope (Knight, 1980; Lyons & Petrucelli, 1978; Nuland, 1995; Van De Graaff, 1995). In 1628,

exhibit / 4.3   Diagram of surface muscles from the *Fabrica* by Andreas Vesalius.

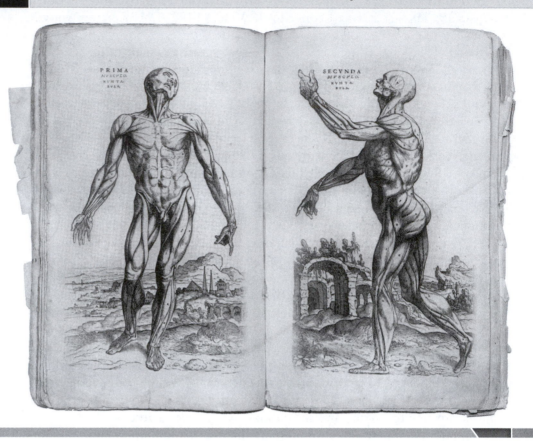

William Harvey (1578–1657), an English anatomist, published a book titled *Anatomical Studies on the Motion of the Heart and Blood in Animals,* in which he described how the blood travels in a circle. Some believe this description to be the greatest anatomical–medical–physiological development of the 17th century (Knight, 1980; Lyons & Petrucelli, 1978; Nuland, 1995).

Harvey's major problem was that he had no way of explaining how blood passed from the smallest arteries to the veins because he had no microscope. Harvey hypothesized that tiny "pores" must exist to connect the arterial–venous system. Thus, he correctly predicted the existence of the capillaries, although he did not perceive their structure as we know it (Lyons & Petrucelli, 1978; Nuland, 1995; Singer, 1957). Today, the basic workings of the heart and circulation and the benefits of exercise to this system are taught to elementary schoolchildren.

We may be astounded, even amused, as to why it took so long for the circulatory system to be described and why this concept was considered a revolution in anatomy and physiology at the time. As scientists, we must always remember that a long-held belief by a society is difficult to change, even when that society is presented with overwhelming evidence refuting previous beliefs. We must also remain cognizant of the fact that small, seemingly insignificant discoveries may eventually lead to a giant leap forward in the understanding of how the human body works.

With the increased emphasis on dissection relating structure to function started by Vesalius's and Harvey's descriptions of the circulation of the blood, advances in anatomy (and medicine) occurred rapidly in the 17th and 18th centuries. A major factor that advanced the study of anatomy was the development of the microscope. In 1665, Robert Hooke (1635–1703), using a primitive microscope, coined the word *cells* to describe the honey-combed appearance of dried cork. Later, a Dutch cloth merchant, Antony van Leeuwenhoek (1632–1723), ground lenses in his spare time and greatly improved the magnification power of microscopes. Van Leeuwenhoek was the first person to describe and measure red blood cells and the striated appearance of skeletal muscle (Knight, 1980; Lyons & Petrucelli, 1978; Nuland, 1995; Van De Graaff, 1995).

Van Leeuwenhoek once ground a tiny lens from one grain of sand (Knight, 1980).

An Italian, Marcello Malpighi (1629–1694), developed techniques for preparing tissues for microscopic study and confirmed the existence of capillaries, which Harvey had hypothesized (Chewning, 1979; Knight, 1980). Considering that 1 cubic millimeter of blood (the size of a large grain of sand) contains 4 to 6 million red blood cells, the discovery of such small entities was an amazing achievement and advancement.

Many other anatomical structures were described during the 17th and 18th centuries by anatomists whose names were subsequently given to the structures that they described, referred to as *eponyms*. The most well-known eponym in the human body is the Achilles tendon. Eponyms are not supposed to be used in present-day anatomy, but some (such as Achilles tendon) will likely remain indefinitely. Exhibit 4.4 presents some still commonly used eponyms along with the modern anatomical name.

During the 19th century, progress in anatomy and understanding the human body was rapid because of improvements in the microscope. A major devel-

Some commonly used eponyms and the appropriate modern anatomical name.

exhibit \ **4.4**

Eponym	Named for:	Appropriate Term
Achilles tendon	Greek warrior in the *Iliad,* whose only vulnerable spot was this tendon.	Calcaneal tendon
Adam's apple	Adam in Christian Bible. Legend states he tried to cough up the "forbidden fruit" and it was trapped in his throat, making it protrude more in men than women. (Actually, men have a larger and differently shaped thyroid cartilage and less fat over it.)	Laryngeal prominence of the thyroid cartilage
Circle of Willis	Thomas Willis (1621–1675). Described the arteries that encircle the base of the brain.	Arterial circle
Eustachian tube	Bartolommeo Eustachio (1524–1574). The tube connecting the middle ear with the throat.	Auditory tube
Fallopian tube	Gabriele Fallopius (1532–1562). Tubes that carry ova (eggs) from the ovaries to the uterus.	Uterine tubes
Graafian follicle	Regnier de Graaf (1641–1673). Structure in the ovary containing the developing egg.	Ovarian follicle
Haversian system and Haversian canal	Clopton Havers (1650–1701). System of canals in bone that carry capillaries and nerves.	Osteon and central canal
Schwann cell	Theodor Schwann (1810–1882). Cell that forms the fatty sheath (myelin) around nerve fibers.	Neurolemmocyte
Wormian bones	Olaus Worm (1588–1654). Extra sutures in some skulls that create islands of bones in the skull; they are not detrimental.	Sutural bones

opment was the cell theory developed by two Germans, M. J. Schleiden and Theodor Schwann in 1838. Schwann (with credit to Schleiden) stated that "cells are organisms and entire animals and plants are aggregates of these organisms arranged according to definite laws" (Hixson, 1966; Knight, 1980; Nuland, 1995). However, Schleiden and Schwann did not know where cells came from.

A row of five red blood cells would about equal the diameter of one period at the end of a sentence (Carola et al., 1992; Chewning, 1979; Knight, 1980).

One thought that they proposed was that the cells came from "spontaneous generation" (i.e., they simply develop), which goes back to the time of Aristotle. In 1858, another German, Rudolf Virchow, published a book titled *Cell Pathology,* in which he correctly described that cells came from other cells (Knight, 1980; Nuland, 1995). Again, we see that what seems so simple today was a revolutionary concept at the time.

In 1858, Henry Gray published the famous *Gray's Anatomy.* This book, which is still in print and contains some of the original illustrations, is probably the most used gross anatomy text of all time and likely remains on the shelf of virtually all anatomists. For many years it was the equivalent of the anatomical bible to physician training, although it is minimally used in most present-day anatomy courses because of improvements in atlases and other medical anatomy texts (Carola et al., 1992; Van De Graaff, 1995).

Twentieth Century to Present Day

Anatomical study has become very specialized, and research about structures is mostly relegated to the cellular and subcellular level. One helpful development in gross anatomy that began in the late 19th century and continues today is the standardization of anatomical nomenclature, so that eponyms (Exhibit 4.4) and/or different terms for the same structure are changed to one name used worldwide. The organization that monitors these and other anatomical interests is called the International Congress of Anatomists (Van De Graaff, 1995).

A dramatic example of gross human anatomy is "Body Worlds," a traveling anatomical exhibition of more than 200 real human bodies preserved using a technique called *plastination* to reveal inner anatomical structures. More than 30 million people have seen a "Body Worlds" exhibit.

Body Worlds
www.bodyworlds.com

TECHNOLOGY AND RESEARCH TOOLS

Today the study of anatomy has reached new heights due to the advanced instrumentation used in diagnosis, teaching, and research techniques. Technological advances increased our understanding of anatomy and how the body works. Future advances will certainly add to this understanding and provide us with better medical care and improved physical performance, along with improved exercise prescriptions.

Electron Microscope and Scanning Electron Microscope

The electron microscope and scanning electron microscope revolutionized our understanding of the cell. These instruments showed that the cells of each tissue were far more complex than imagined by the simple light microscope. Whereas the light microscope can magnify an object about 1,400 times, electron microscopy can magnify to about 10 million times normal. These instruments resulted in the discovery of new cell structures and aided in the understanding of their function, which led to a better understanding of injury and disease and thus new treatments.

Imaging

In addition to microscopy, advances in radiology or medical imaging techniques have also been useful in anatomy. Imaging techniques are important tools in clinical diagnosis, research, and teaching, and their interpretation requires a sound knowledge of anatomy. Following are brief descriptions of medical imaging techniques, all of which are or may be used in exercise science research.

X-rays

X-rays were discovered in 1895 by *Wilhelm Roentgen* (1845–1923). Originally called Roentgen rays, X-rays are short electromagnetic waves. Roentgen called them X-rays because he didn't understand where they came from.

When a part of the body is X-rayed, some of the waves are absorbed by tissues. The amount of absorption depends on the density of the tissue; the more dense the tissue, the more X-rays that are absorbed, causing different exposures on film. X-rays are particularly useful for detecting fractures and locating tumors. Sometimes the patient will swallow or be injected with a contrast medium such as barium before the X-ray is taken. These are called contrast X-rays. For example, in coronary angiography, a dye is injected into the arteries that supply the heart, and an X-ray is taken. Problems in blood flow to heart muscle may then be detected on the film (Carola et al., 1992; Chernow & Vallasi, 1993; *Dorland's*, 2007; Lyons & Petrucelli, 1978; Marieb & Mallatt, 1992; Van De Graaff, 1995).

Computerized tomography (CT scan or CAT scan)

The **CAT scan** utilizes X-rays with computers to obtain three-dimensional transverse (cross) sections of a body part, such as the abdominal cavity. A clinician can obtain "slices" of a particular area and study them separately to detect trauma, blood clots, or tumors (Carola et al., 1992; Marieb & Mallatt, 1992; Van De Graaff, 1995).

■ *CAT scan*

Spiral-CT scans

A spiral-CT scan allows for rapid three-dimensional views of internal organs.

Digital subtraction angiography

A DSA can monitor blood flow through organs like the brain, heart, and lungs. An X-ray is taken prior to and after the patient is given a radiopaque dye. A computer subtracts details common to both images (Martini, Timmons, & Tellitsch, 2003).

Positron emission tomography

PET scans are used to detect metabolic activity (the amount of chemical activity) in organs. In this procedure, a radioactive isotope is added to a substance (such as glucose) and is injected into the bloodstream. The PET scan can detect the rate at which certain tissues absorb the tagged glucose. PET scans are particularly useful in studying brain activity. For example, monitoring

■ *PET scan*

glucose absorption in the brain shows areas damaged by stroke or Alzheimer's disease. PET scans can also be used to study healthy brains because they will identify areas of greatest brain activity when the person performs a specific activity, such as talking or doing a math problem (Carola et al., 1992; Marieb & Mallatt, 1992; Van De Graaff, 1995).

Peripheral quantitative computed tomography

The peripheral quantitative computed tomography (pQCT) is a device that provides cross-sectional images of the arm, forearm, leg, and thigh by calculating the density of human tissues based on the attenuation of X-rays (see Exhibit 4.5). This device helps determine the muscle- and bone-related adaptations to various exercise training and nutritional interventions across the age span.

Magnetic resonance imaging

MRI ■ **MRI** uses a magnetic field 60,000 times stronger than the earth's magnetic fields to produce very clear anatomical pictures in different body planes and to detect areas of diseased tissue. MRI is particularly attractive because it does not use X-rays or radioactive tracer substances. The clarity of MRI sections has even revealed tumors not seen during exploratory surgery (Carola et al., 1992; Marieb & Mallatt, 1992; Van De Graaff, 1995). MRI is now used extensively in research studies by exercise scientists (see Box 4.1). Exhibit 4.6 shows a basic MRI machine.

exhibit / 4.5   A peripheral quantitative computed tomography (pQCT) device.

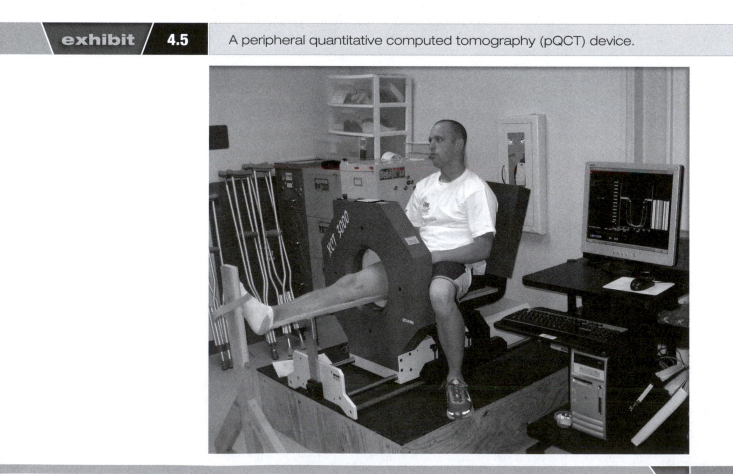

Abstract of an exercise science research study using magnetic resonance imaging (MRI).

Richardson, R. S., Frank, L. R., and Haseler, L. J. (1998). Dynamic knee-extensor and cycle exercise: Functional MRI of muscular activity. *International Journal of Sports Medicine, 19*(3), 182–187.

Repeated studies using human dynamic knee-extensor exercise have reported high mass specific blood flows. These studies suggest that the high perfusion-to-muscle mass ratio can approach 400 ml(-1) x min x 100 g(-1) in the human quadriceps. However, in these studies mass specific blood flows were calculated based on the assumption that the quadriceps are the only muscles involved in the knee-extensor exercise, which is difficult to verify in an *in vivo* human model. Previous validations of this assumption have been performed using electromyography (EMG) and assessments of strain gauge tracings, but neither has been able to completely assess the involvement of all thigh muscles in this exercise. To address this issue four subjects exercised at 90% of their work rate maximum for 2.0–2.5 minutes (45–100 watts) and then a transverse section of the thigh (20 cm proximal to the knee) was studied using proton (1H) transverse relaxation time (T2) weighted magnetic resonance (MR) imaging to distinguish active from non-active muscles by the increased signal intensity (SI). On a separate occasion, measurements following 2.0–2.5 minutes of conventional two-legged cycle ergometry at 90% of maximum work rate (150–400 watts) were made in the same subjects to contrast this traditional "whole leg" exercise with the unique muscle recruitment in dynamic knee-extension. Following knee-extensor exercise there was a clearly visible change in SI and a significant increase in T2 only in the four muscles of the quadriceps (P < 0.05). After bicycle exercise SI changes and T2 revealed a varied muscle use across all muscles. From these MR data it can be concluded that unlike cycle exercise, in which all muscles are recruited to varying extents, single leg knee-extensor exercise is limited to the four muscles of the quadriceps. Thus, the common practice of normalizing blood flow and metabolic data to the quadriceps muscle mass in human knee-extensor exercise studies appears appropriate.

Dual energy X-ray absorptiometry

DXA uses an X-ray with more than one wavelength that passes through a special filter that varies the energy peaks, thus giving greater accuracy for estimating the amount of fat, muscle, and bone tissue. It is currently used in exercise science studies of body composition (Roche, Heymsfield, & Lohman, 1996).

■ *DXA*

Ultrasound imagery sonography

Ultrasound sonography is a noninvasive technique. Sound waves sent into the body are reflected to different degrees by different types of body tissues. These waves cause echoes from which a computer constructs a picture of the tissue. Ultrasound is a very safe procedure and is often used to assess the age and/or health of a developing fetus. It has been used in exercise science research to estimate subcutaneous (under the skin) adipose (fatty) tissue (Carola et al., 1992; Marieb & Mallett, 1992; Roche et al., 1996; Singer, 1957; Van De Graaff, 1995).

■ *ultrasound sonography*

EDUCATIONAL PREPARATION

The anatomy of the human body is an essential course of study for a variety of professional careers. Exercise science students in particular should have a solid preparation in human anatomy combined with other experiences that examine the effect of exercise on body tissues. At major universities and medical schools, where both teaching and research are

exhibit / **4.6** A magnetic resonance imaging (MRI) machine.

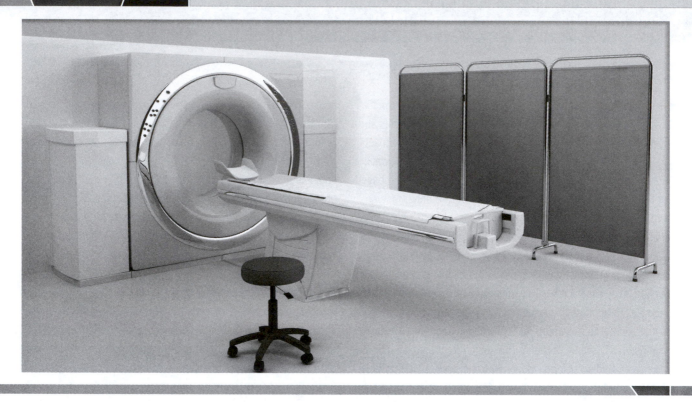

required for employment, a Ph.D. in anatomy is necessary. In some cases, specializing in anatomical studies in exercise science doctoral programs meets this requirement. A master's degree in anatomy or a degree in biology with some emphasis on anatomy is often sufficient to teach certain introductory courses. Requirements may vary, but the author believes that to successfully teach anatomy, a minimum of premedical- or medical-level courses in gross anatomy, neuroanatomy, histology (including electron microscopy), embryology, human physiology, and chemistry through biochemistry is necessary. It is also essential, in the author's opinion, that an anatomy instructor have considerable experience in the dissection of human cadavers.

EMPLOYMENT OPPORTUNITIES

Although it is always difficult to predict future employment opportunities in any field, there will always be a need for teachers of gross and microscopic anatomy at many different levels of sophistication, from medical, dental, and physical therapy schools to one-semester courses in universities, colleges, community colleges, and high schools. Individuals interested in pursuing anatomical studies can obtain further information by writing or calling departments of anatomy at major universities or medical school facilities.

In addition, anatomy is an essential science for many other professions, including medicine, dentistry, physical and occupational therapy, nursing, physical education, and, of course, exercise science. The beginning exercise science student has several career options where a sound background in anatomy will be useful. Some will become certified exercise specialists, designing exercises and leading exercise groups and/or coaching athletes. Others may move on to teaching and research positions at universities or pursue professional degrees in the medical or paramedical fields, including athletic training. In all situations, a firm grasp of basic anatomical concepts is essential.

For exercise specialists, athletic trainers, and coaches, an understanding of bone growth and its reaction to stress, the structure and function of joints and muscles, as well as vessel and nerve pathways, will help them design appropriate exercises, eliminate commonly used but harmful exercises, and understand injury and the repair of tissues.

The exercise science researcher must possess the above knowledge as well as more in-depth insights regarding the structure of cells and tissues and the response of these to different types of exercise stress. For example, we are daily exposed by television and other media to a plethora of exercise devices and/or exercise systems, which more or less guarantee that we will lose weight, gain muscle, or attain super abdominals in "just a few minutes a day." Exercise scientists, by way of their training in anatomy and other sciences, must be credible sources for judging which claims are true and which have no realistic scientific validity. In addition, understanding the relationship of exercise to growth and development, body composition, and the design and improvement of athletic equipment involves a knowledge of anatomy.

Children's sports participation and the appropriate amounts and types of exercise for schools are also important issues for exercise scientists, using their knowledge of anatomy. Children are not just small adults. Exercise and training programs must therefore be designed for them based on an intimate knowledge of a child's anatomy and the variation in growth at different ages. Body composition (basically the relationship of the amount of fat to the amount of lean tissue in the body) and its change during growth and training are other frequently studied areas in exercise science and are important with regard to sports performance and health. Anatomy provides the basis for the study and understanding of these areas. The study of biomechanics, described in Chapter 9, demands a thorough knowledge of anatomy with regard to boney levers, muscle attachments, and the types of movements of which different joints are capable. These few examples, however, merely scratch the surface when addressing the importance of anatomy and how anatomy is used in exercise science. Box 4.2 presents an abstract of a body composition research study.

PROFESSIONAL ASSOCIATIONS

The major professional association for exercise scientists is the American College of Sports Medicine (ACSM), described in other parts of this text. Considerable anatomically related research is presented at ACSM meetings, including assessment of the effects of various types of exercise (or lack of exercise) on body tissues such as muscle, bone, fat, tendons, and ligaments. Such studies may be done on animals or humans using many of the aforementioned devices, such as MRI, DXA, ultrasound, or even anthropometry (measuring external boney structures and skin thickness). Exercise science anatomy specialists may also be members of and contribute research to the American Alliance for Health, Physical Education, Recreation and Dance (AAHPERD) or specific medical specialties. Most anatomists in departments of anatomy belong to the American Association of Anatomists, an organization that conducts worldwide work in imaging, cell biology, genetics, histology, and numerous other areas.

WWW

**American Association
of Anatomists**
www.anatomy.org

box

4.2

Abstract of a body composition research study.

Siatras, T., Skaperda, M., and Mameletzi, D. (2010). Reliability of anthropometric measurements in young male and female artistic gymnasts. *Medical Problems of Performing Artists*, 24(4), 162.

Body dimensions and body composition of children participating in artistic activities, such as gymnastics and many types of dancing, are important factors in performance improvement. The present study aimed to determine the reliability of a series of selected anthropometric measurements in young male and female gymnasts. Segment lengths, body breadths, circumferences, and skinfold thickness were measured in 20 young gymnasts by the same experienced examiner, using portable and easy-to-use instruments. All parameters were measured twice (test–retest) under the same conditions within a week's period. The high intra-class correlation coefficient (ICC) values ranging from 0.87 to 0.99, as well as the low coefficient of variation (CV) values (<5.3%), affirmed that the selected measurements were highly reliable. The technical error of measurement (TEM) values for lengths and breadths were 0.15 to 0.80 cm, for circumferences 0.22 to 1 cm, and for skinfold thickness 0.33 to 0.58 mm. The high test–retest ICC and the low CV and TEM values confirmed the reliability of all anthropometric measurements in young artistic gymnasts. Therefore, these measurements could contribute to further research in this field of investigation, helping to monitor young artistic gymnasts' growth status and identify specific characteristics for increased performance in this sport.

PROMINENT JOURNALS AND RELATED PUBLICATIONS

Considering the whole field of biology and its subspecialties, along with the subspecialties in anatomy described at the beginning of this chapter, it is not realistic to cite all of the journals that publish anatomical research. Instead, a few major anatomical journals are presented, along with some exercise science journals that publish anatomically related research.

PRIMARY JOURNALS

Acta Anatomica

Anatomical Record

Clinical Anatomy

Developmental Dynamics

Journal of Anatomy (published in Great Britain)

Journal of Histochemistry and Cytochemistry

RELATED PUBLICATIONS

International Journal of Sports Biomechanics

Isokinetics and Exercise Science

Journal of Sports Medicine and Physical Fitness

Journal of Strength and Conditioning Research

Medicine and Science in Sports and Exercise

Pediatric Exercise Science

Research Quarterly for Exercise and Sport

FUTURE DIRECTIONS

Without question, there will be future developments of new instruments and advances in current imaging techniques that will add to our knowledge about the human body. The beginning exercise scientist has an exciting future with respect to technological advances that will help us to better understand the human body and how it responds to various forms of exercise stress. Future advances certainly will add to this understanding and provide us with better medical care, improved physical performance, and improved exercise prescriptions.

SUMMARY

Anatomy has a long, controversial history that parallels, to some degree, the history of medicine and, to a lesser degree, the history of exercise science. A well-grounded knowledge of anatomy is crucial for exercise scientists. Without knowledge of the structure of the human body it is difficult to appreciate even the most basic concepts underlying physical activity.

Anatomy has a number of subspecialties including gross anatomy, histology, comparative anatomy, embryology, developmental anatomy, and pathological anatomy. Exercise science students should recognize the importance of these subspecialties to many professions including medicine, dentistry, physical and occupational therapy, and nursing.

Technological advances such as the electron microscope, X-rays, CT scans, PET scans, MRI, DXA, and ultrasonography increased our knowledge of anatomy. Today, these technologies are frequently used in exercise science research, and in the future they will become even more common. The future of anatomy and its contribution to exercise science is an exciting prospect.

study / QUESTIONS

1. Define anatomy.
2. Name and describe the major subdivisions of anatomy.
3. Why is a knowledge of anatomy essential to the exercise scientist?
4. Why is the study of the history of anatomy important?
5. What is the prescientific period? What is meant by the scientific period?
6. Describe the major influence on the study of anatomy in ancient China.
7. What major contributions to anatomy were made by Andreas Vesalius?
8. What was William Harvey's discovery, and why is it considered one of the major anatomical–medical advancements?
9. What causes the different exposures on an X-ray film?
10. What are the differences between a CAT scan, a PET scan, and an MRI?

Visit the IES website to study, take notes, and try out the lab for this chapter.

learning ACTIVITIES

1. Do an Internet search on "anatomy." Choose three subdivisions of anatomy and write a paragraph briefly describing each of them.

2. On the American Association of Anatomists website (www.anatomy. org), research membership in this organization. Write a one-page report listing three of the benefits of membership and describe how you might benefit.

3. Go to the PubMed website (www.ncbi.nlm.nih.gov/pubmed/) to search for "anatomy" articles. Choose three articles and write a paragraph describing their potential impact on anatomy and/or exercise science.

4. Research (using the Internet and/or written sources) the technologies used to study anatomy. Choose three technologies and describe how they have affected knowledge and understanding of anatomy and/or exercise science.

5. Present an example of a research study in exercise science that involves anatomical knowledge.

suggested READINGS

Chung, K. W. (2005). *Gross anatomy* (5th ed.). Philadelphia: Lippincott Williams & Wilkins.

Hall-Craggs, E. C. D. (1986). *Anatomy as a basis for clinical medicine* (2nd ed.). Baltimore: Urban & Schwarzeberg, Inc.

Moore, K. L., & Dalley, A. F. (2005). *Clinically oriented anatomy* (5th ed.). Philadelphia: Lippincott Williams & Wilkins.

references

Body Worlds. www.bodyworlds.com/en/exhibitions/questions_answers.html.

Carola, R., Harky, J. P., & Noback, C. R. (1992). *Human anatomy*. New York: McGraw-Hill.

Chernow, B. A., & Vallasi, G. A. (Eds.). (1993). *The Columbia encyclopedia*. New York: Columbia University Press.

Chewning, E. B. (1979). *Anatomy illustrated*. New York: Simon & Schuster.

Dorland's Illustrated Medical Dictionary (31st ed.) (2007). Philadelphia: W. B. Saunders.

Hixson, J. (1966). *The history of the human body*. New York: Cooper Square Publishers.

Karpovich, P. V., & Sinning, W. C. (1971). *Physiology of muscular activity*. Philadelphia: W. B. Saunders.

Knight, B. (1980). *Discovering the human body*. London: Imprint Books Limited.

Lyons, A., & Petrucelli, R. J. (1978). *Medicine, an illustrated history*. New York: Harry N. Abrams.

Marieb, E. N., & Mallatt, J. (1992). *Human anatomy*. Redwood City, CA: Benjamin/Cummings.

Martini, F. H., Timmons, M. J., & Tallitsch, R. B. (2003). *Human anatomy* (4th ed.). San Francisco: Pearson/Benjamin Cummings.

McMurrich, J. P. (1930). *Leonardo da Vinci, the anatomist*. Baltimore: Williams & Wilkins.

Nuland, S. B. (1995). *Doctors*. New York: Random House.

Persaud, T. V. N. (1984). *Early history of anatomy*. Springfield, IL: Charles C. Thomas.

Roche, A. F., Heymsfield, S. B., & Lohman, T. G. (1996). *Human body composition*. Champaign, IL: Human Kinetics.

Saunders, J. B. de C. M., & O'Malley, C. D. (1973). *The illustrations from the works of Andreas Vesalius of Brussels*. New York: Dover Publications.

Singer, C. (1957). *A short history of anatomy and physiology from the Greeks to Harvey*. New York: Dover Publications.

Van De Graaff, K. M. (1995). *Human anatomy*. Dubuque, IA: William C. Brown.

Exercise Physiology

JOSEPH P. WEIR

DEFINITIONS IN EXERCISE PHYSIOLOGY

E xercise physiology is defined as "the study of how the body, from a functional standpoint, responds, adjusts, and adapts to exercise" (Fox, Bowers, & Foss, 1993), and the exercise physiologist as one who "studies the muscular activity and functional responses and adaptations during exercise" (ACSM, 2010). As is evident from these definitions, the two aspects of exercise physiology that form the core of the discipline are the responses and the adaptations to exercise. A response is distinguished from an adaptation in that a

response ■ **response** is an acute or short-term change (adjustment) in the body that is associated with exercise. For example, as one jogs, the heart rate increases from the

adaptation ■ resting value. In contrast, an **adaptation** to exercise involves a long-term change in the body due to exercise training. For example, highly conditioned runners typically have lower resting heart rates than less-fit individuals. This decrease in resting heart rate (bradycardia) occurs over time as a result of regular exercise training. It is the study of these types of responses and adaptations that provides the scientific basis for the field of exercise physiology.

In addition, exercise physiology has applied aspects, with many people trained to work in a hands-on environment with both healthy and patient populations. The application of the knowledge base of exercise physiology to clinics, health clubs, and athletic conditioning can significantly improve human performance and quality of life.

PROFESSIONAL DUTIES OF AN EXERCISE PHYSIOLOGIST

E xercise physiologists in the broadest sense provide a variety of services in various settings. Clinical exercise physiologists design, implement, and monitor exercise programs for individuals with cardiac, pulmonary, and metabolic disorders (e.g., diabetes). Practitioners in the health and fitness industry perform exercise tests and design exercise programs for the general population in order to improve health, decrease clients' risk for disease, and improve well-being and self-esteem. Researchers study the mechanisms of response and adaptation that occur with exercise as well as the practical aspects of exercise physiology, such as how to maximize the benefits of an exercise intervention.

Most exercise physiologists work in an applied setting; that is, they work with real people in a clinical, athletic, or fitness setting. Nonetheless, researchers are continually adding to the body of knowledge in exercise physiology. Because of this continual information turnover, applied exercise physiologists have the responsibility of staying current with research. Similarly, researchers in exercise physiology have the responsibility of effectively disseminating new information to practitioners.

HISTORY OF EXERCISE PHYSIOLOGY

A lthough the formal study of exercise physiology as a discipline is still relatively new, interest in the physiology of physical activity dates back to the ancient Greeks (Astrand, 1991; Berryman, 1995; Buskirk, 1996, 1992; Costill, 1994; Dill, 1980; Dill, Arlie, & Bock, 1985; Kroll, 1971; McArdle, Katch, & Katch, 2007; Tipton, 1996). Students are strongly encouraged to consult Chapter 1 to develop an appreciation for the rich history that led to modern-day exercise physiology.

PARENT DISCIPLINES OF EXERCISE PHYSIOLOGY

Exercise physiology has two primary parent disciplines: physiology and physical education. Academic training in exercise physiology typically crosses the boundaries of both disciplines. Physiology involves the study of the function of the body. That is, physiology is concerned with how the body works. Physiology itself is based on other disciplines such as anatomy, biochemistry, and cellular biology. Most academic training in exercise physiology focuses on the function of the body from a systems approach; that is, how the organ systems respond and adapt to exercise. Increasing emphasis, however, is being placed on the study of the cellular, molecular, and genetic aspects of exercise (Brooks, 1987; Hagberg et al., 2011; Tipton, 1996). To physiologists, exercise can serve as a stressor, thereby serving as a useful tool to challenge an organism and study its responses and adaptations to the stressor (Brooks, 1987). Indeed, because exercise can provide a potent stimulus to a variety of physiological systems simultaneously (e.g., the muscular, cardiovascular, thermoregulatory, and endocrine systems), it can be a powerful tool to help further the understanding of how the body functions (Brooks, 1994).

The second parent discipline is physical education (Brooks, 1987). To physical educators, the knowledge from the study of exercise physiology can be used to improve health and enhance human performance during physical activity and athletic events. Indeed, as early as the 1890s, exercise physiology was a part of the curricula in some university physical education programs (Buskirk, 1996), and a biological aspect has been a component of physical education since the inception of the field (Kroll, 1971). Currently, most academic programs in exercise physiology are part of departments that are or were affiliated with the applied, professional field of physical education, which now usually involves the preparation of teachers for public and private schools. However, the scope of exercise physiology now extends beyond both physiology and physical education because exercise physiology influences researchers and clinicians in other professions such as medicine, physical therapy, and gerontology. Further discussion of these topics is included later in this chapter.

AREAS OF STUDY IN EXERCISE PHYSIOLOGY

This section presents a brief overview of the different areas of study that are a part of exercise physiology, both basic and applied areas. For simplicity, the areas are covered separately; it should be noted, however, that there is a great deal of overlap. For example, it is difficult to adequately study the control of respiration without considering the nervous system (which controls the respiratory muscles) and the processes of bioenergetics and metabolism (which provide metabolites that influence respiratory control). Similarly, applied areas of study such as gerontology and diabetes involve all of the areas of basic study.

Areas of Basic Study

Cardiovascular system

The cardiovascular system is responsible for the transport of blood, and therefore oxygen and nutrients, to the tissues of the body. Similarly, the cardiovascular system facilitates removal of waste products such as carbon dioxide from the body.

In addition, the cardiovascular system is centrally involved in the dissipation of heat, which is critical during prolonged exercise. The primary components of the cardiovascular system are the heart (see Exhibit 5.1), which pumps the blood, and the arteries and veins (see Exhibit 5.2), which carry the blood to and from the tissues. Clearly, the cardiovascular system's functions are critical during exercise; therefore, a large proportion of study and research in exercise physiology focuses on the responses and adaptations of the cardiovascular system to exercise. Examples of areas of research regarding the cardiovascular system and exercise include the effect of exercise on the structure and function of the blood vessels and the relationship between exercise and the neurological control of the heart.

From a health perspective, the study of the relationships between exercise and the cardiovascular system is critically important because cardiovascular disease is the leading cause of death in the United States (Hoyert et al., 2006).

The primary cardiovascular disease is coronary artery disease, in which **cholesterol** and other blood lipids (fats) build up in the walls of arteries that supply blood to the heart itself. This process of **atherosclerosis** can lead to blockage of a coronary artery and ultimately to a heart attack. Physical activity, habitual exercise, and exercise capacity are associated with decreased risk of morbidity and mortality from cardiovascular disease (Kokkinos & Myers, 2010; Myers et al., 2002; Thompson et al., 2003). Important beneficial effects of exercise on the cardiovascular system include a decrease in resting blood pressure (an important risk factor in cardiovascular disease) and a decrease in blood

- cholesterol
- atherosclerosis

exhibit / 5.1   Basic anatomy of the heart.

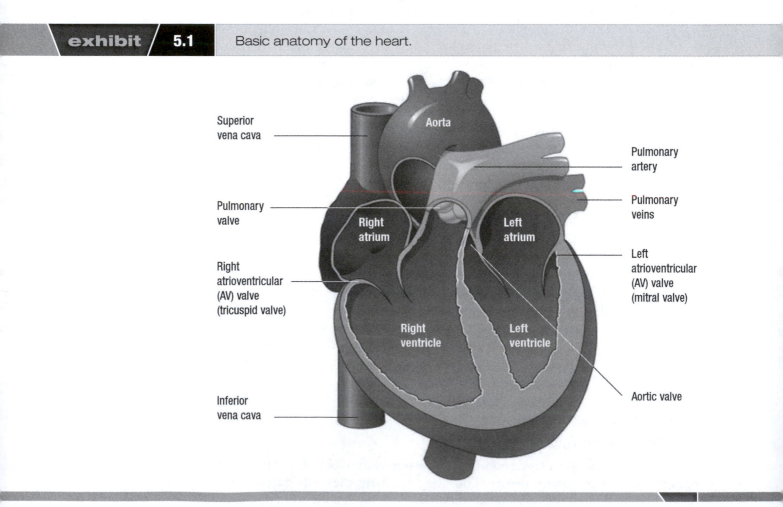

exhibit **5.2**

The one-way valves of the veins. Contraction of the surrounding skeletal muscle aids in the movement of blood toward the heart, and the valves prevent blood from moving away from the heart.

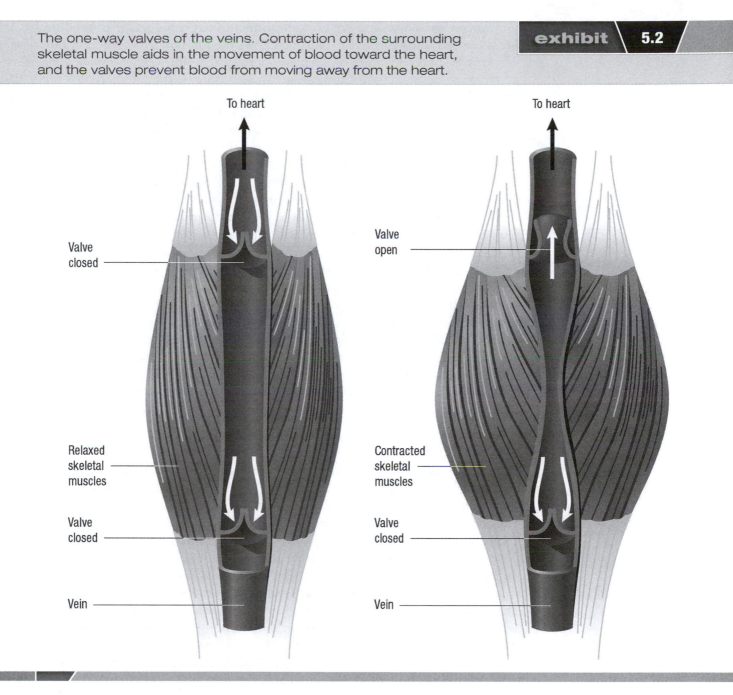

Pulmonary system

The pulmonary system is important for the exchange of oxygen and carbon dioxide between the air and the blood. The primary component of the pulmonary system is the lungs. Exercise places a great deal of stress on the

cholesterol levels (reducing the risk for developing atherosclerosis). Furthermore, exercise is an important component of the cardiac rehabilitation process following a cardiac event such as a heart attack (Leon et al., 2005). Individuals with training in exercise physiology are playing important roles in the research and implementation of exercise programs for the prevention of cardiovascular disease and the rehabilitation of individuals with cardiovascular disease.

pulmonary system as oxygen consumption and carbon dioxide production are increased during exercise, thus increasing the pulmonary ventilation rate. The control and regulation of the pulmonary system during exercise are areas of much research. As with the cardiovascular system, the interplay of exercise and the neurological control of breathing is not completely understood. Surprisingly, most evidence indicates that there are few, if any, adaptations to exercise in the pulmonary system itself in healthy individuals (McArdle et al., 2007). However, adaptations in the musculature that controls breathing are apparent (Housh, Housh, & deVries, 2012). In addition, an interesting area of inquiry is the study of training the inspiratory muscles of ventilation as an intervention to improve exercise performance (Bailey et al., 2010).

From a clinical perspective, exercise is an important component of pulmonary rehabilitation for individuals with diseases such as chronic obstructive pulmonary disease (COPD; includes diseases such as emphysema and asthma), and exercise physiologists may work with physical therapists, respiratory therapists, and pulmonologists as part of the pulmonary rehabilitation team. On the other hand, exercise can induce asthmatic events in some individuals (exercise-induced asthma), and the exact mechanisms of this phenomenon are under study. These events, in which exercise can precipitate airway constriction, shortness of breath, and wheezing, can occur in both asthmatic and nonasthmatic people; however, the incidence is much higher in asthmatics. Obviously, these events can lead to submaximal performance in athletes and likely reduce exercise adherence in nonathletes (Hough & Dec, 1994).

Nervous system

Motor or voluntary. Among the many functions of the nervous system is the control of movement by way of the skeletal muscles, which are under voluntary (and reflex) control. Most of the study of the neural control of movement is considered the domain of motor control and motor learning (see Chapter 10). However, certain areas of inquiry are also of interest to exercise physiologists. Two notable areas are neuromuscular fatigue and neurological adaptations to strength training.

With respect to neuromuscular fatigue, research suggests that under certain conditions the central nervous system (CNS; includes the brain and spinal cord) may play an important role in the development of fatigue (Weir et al., 2006). For example, changes in brain levels of serotonin and dopamine may influence fatigue (Blomstrand, 2006; Davis, Alderson, & Welsh, 2000). In addition, the firing rate of motor units can change during fatigue (Rubinstein & Kamen, 2005), which may be due to an elegant interplay between peripheral receptors and the CNS.

Similarly, strength training may influence the CNS control of muscle activation by changing the number of motor units that the CNS will activate during a contraction and the firing rate of the active muscle (Gabriel, Kamen, & Frost, 2006). Much of the data regarding neurological adaptations to strength training are contradictory, but this remains an important area of study. These areas of study are important to basic researchers in exercise physiology, and new information in these areas may also have implications in the rehabilitation of individuals with neuromuscular disorders.

autonomic nervous
system ■

Autonomic or involuntary. The **autonomic nervous system** is involved in the involuntary control of body functions. The autonomic nervous system has two divisions. The **sympathetic nervous system** becomes active during situations of increased stress, such as during exercise. The **parasympathetic nervous system** is more active during resting conditions. Most notable in exercise physiology is the autonomic control of the cardiovascular system. For example, during exercise an increase in sympathetic activity and a decrease in parasympathetic activity result in an increase in activity of the heart and an increase in blood pressure. In addition, the autonomic nervous system is involved in the redistribution of blood flow away from inactive tissues, such as the gastrointestinal tract, and toward the active tissues during exercise.

- *sympathetic nervous system*
- *parasympathetic nervous system*

Adaptations also occur in the autonomic nervous system following exercise training. For example, the decrease in resting heart rate and heart rate at a submaximal exercise load in trained individuals is believed to be a result, at least in part, of altered autonomic function; that is, elevated parasympathetic activity (Shi et al., 1995; Smith et al., 1989). These adaptations have important clinical implications as a shift in the balance toward sympathetic and away from parasympathetic tone is associated with increased risk of heart attack and sudden death (Chattipakorn, Incharoen, Kanlop, & Chattipakorn, 2007; Tsuji et al., 1994). Therefore, the adaptations in autonomic balance following aerobic exercise training, especially after a first heart attack, may decrease risk.

Recent technological advances allow for the noninvasive assessment of autonomic nervous system function and should further our understanding of the effects of exercise on the autonomic nervous system.

Muscular system

Exercise is about movement, and the muscular system is primarily responsible for creating movement. Therefore, the responses and adaptations of the muscular system to exercise are important parts of exercise physiology. During exercise, many changes take place in skeletal muscle, such as changes in temperature, acidity, and ion concentrations. These changes affect muscle performance and may lead to fatigue. Indeed, the mechanism(s) of muscle fatigue is an important area of inquiry in exercise physiology (MacLaren et al., 1989; Weir et al., 2006). In addition, the adaptations of the muscular system to exercise lead to long-term changes in exercise capability. Depending on the type of exercise, changes in enzyme concentrations, contractile protein content, and vascularization affect the ability of the muscle to perform work. For example, endurance exercise increases concentrations of enzymes in skeletal muscle that are involved in the aerobic production of energy (Gollnick & King, 1969; Holloszy, 1967).

In contrast, strength training is associated with increases in the size of the muscle due to increased synthesis of contractile proteins, with little change in anaerobic enzyme content (Tesch, Komi, & Hakkinen, 1987). These types of adaptations are appropriate for a certain type of activity in that these adaptations will improve muscle performance in the types of activities that stimulated these adaptations. The muscle biopsy procedure has been and continues to be an important tool for studying these adaptations.

Technology such as electromyography (EMG), nuclear magnetic resonance spectroscopy (MRS), and magnetic resonance imaging (MRI) are helping to further our understanding of muscle function with exercise (discussed further in other chapters).

Several neuromuscular conditions, such as multiple sclerosis, postpolio syndrome, and Guillain-Barré syndrome, affect skeletal muscle. The effect of exercise on individuals with these conditions may be important for improving quality of life. Although much of the research is still in its infancy, most studies suggest that appropriately designed exercise programs can benefit those with neuromuscular disorders (Curtis & Weir, 1996; Malek, York, & Weir, 2007). Future research may create new roles for exercise physiologists in the rehabilitation of neuromuscular disease.

Bioenergetics and metabolism

adenosine triphosphate ■ With respect to exercise, the area of bioenergetics and metabolism involves the study of how the body generates energy for muscular work. The energy for exercise, in the form of **adenosine triphosphate (ATP),** is derived from the breakdown of food from the diet. Originally in the form of protein, fat, and carbohydrate, the energy is made available by different enzymatic pathways that break down food and ultimately lead to ATP formation. The specific metabolic pathway used and the associated food broken down for energy are affected by the type of exercise that a person is performing and have implications for the ability of the person to perform that exercise. These are important issues in exercise physiology because they affect decisions that exercise professionals make regarding the type, intensity, and duration of exercise to be prescribed to a client.

The study of whole-body metabolic responses and adaptations to exercise has application to topics such as exercise and obesity because this type of metabolic information can be used to maximize the fat-burning effects of exercise.

Tools that are described later in the chapter, such as indirect calorimetry, muscle biopsy, and magnetic resonance spectroscopy, are used in research to study these processes. Exercise biochemists use muscle biopsy and nuclear magnetic resonance spectroscopy to study the biochemical changes that occur in skeletal muscle during and after exercise. Box 5.1 presents an abstract of a research study that utilized magnetic resonance spectroscopy to examine muscle metabolism at differing intensities during leg exercise. The whole-body metabolic response to

indirect calorimetry ■ exercise is studied with **indirect calorimetry,** which involves the collection and analysis of oxygen and carbon dioxide levels in expired air.

Endocrine system

hormone ■
endocrine gland ■ The endocrine system is the system of **hormones,** which are chemicals released into the blood by certain types of glands called **endocrine glands.** Many hormones are important during exercise and may affect performance. For example, during exercise the hormone called growth hormone increases in concentration in the blood. This hormone is important in regulating blood glucose concentrations. Similarly, other hormones, such as cortisol, epinephrine, and testosterone, increase during exercise. Their effects may be short term in that they affect the body during the exercise bout. Other effects are prolonged and may be important in the long-term adaptation to regular exercise. The effects of exercise training on hormonal responses and the effects of these hormones on the responses and adaptations to acute and chronic exercise are areas of intense study.

Another aspect of exercise endocrinology is the study of exogenous (produced outside the body) hormone supplementation on both short- and long-term exercise. For example, supplemental testosterone and associated anabolic steroids have been used by athletes for many years to enhance performance in athletic events that require strength and power. This is a type of ergogenic aid (discussed later). Although the use of anabolic steroids is against

Abstract of a research study that examined muscle metabolism at differing intensities of exercise.

box

5.1

Jones, A. M., Wilkerson, D. P., DiMenna, F., Fulford, J., & Poole, D. C. (2008). Muscle metabolic responses to exercise above and below the "critical power" assessed using ^{31}P-MRS. *American Journal of Physiology: Regulatory, Integrative and Comparative Physiology, 294*, R585–R593.

We tested the hypothesis that the asymptote of the hyperbolic relationship between work rate and time to exhaustion during muscular exercise, the "critical power" (CP), represents the highest constant work rate that can be sustained without a progressive loss of homeostasis [as assessed using ^{31}P magnetic resonance spectroscopy (MRS) measurements of muscle metabolites]. Six healthy male subjects initially completed single-leg knee-extension exercise at three to four different constant work rates to the limit of tolerance (range 3–18 min) for estimation of the CP (mean ± SD, 20 ± 2 W). Subsequently, the subjects exercised at work rates 10% below CP (<CP) for 20 min and 10% above CP (>CP) for as long as possible, while the metabolic responses in the contracting quadriceps muscle, i.e., phosphorylcreatine concentration ([PCr]), P_i concentration ([P_i]), and pH, were estimated using ^{31}P-MRS. All subjects completed 20 min of <CP exercise without duress, whereas the limit of tolerance during >CP exercise was 14.7 ± 7.1 min. During <CP exercise, stable values for [PCr], [P_i], and pH were attained within 3 min after the onset of exercise, and there were no further significant changes in these variables (end-exercise values = 68 ± 11% of baseline [PCr], 314 ± 216% of baseline [P_i], and pH 7.01 ± 0.03). During >CP exercise, however, [PCr] continued to fall to the point of exhaustion and [P_i] and pH changed precipitously to values that are typically observed at the termination of high-intensity exhaustive exercise (end-exercise values = 26 ± 16% of baseline [PCr], 564 ± 167% of baseline [P_i], and pH 6.87 ± 0.10, all $P < 0.05$ vs. <CP exercise). These data support the hypothesis that the CP represents the highest constant work rate that can be sustained without a progressive depletion of muscle high-energy phosphates and a rapid accumulation of metabolites (i.e., H^+ concentration and [P_i]), which have been associated with the fatigue process.

the rules of most athletic governing bodies and may have detrimental health consequences, the use of such substances may have significant therapeutic effects for those with limited exercise capacity, such as the frail elderly (Bhasin et al., 1996; Sheffield-Moore et al., 2006).

Immune system

The immune system fights off pathogens and infections. The study of the effect of exercise on the immune system is a relatively new phenomenon. Indeed, the first exercise physiology textbook to include a specific chapter on exercise and the immune system was published in 1994 (deVries & Housh, 1994). Currently, the relationship between exercise and the immune system is under intense study; however, much more research is needed to fully understand the implications of exercise on the ability of the body to fight disease. Some evidence indicates that exercise may have a deleterious effect on the immune response under certain conditions, whereas it may enhance the immune response under other conditions (Housh et al., 2012), depending on the immune parameter being measured (Nieman, 1996). Specifically, very intense or exhaustive exercise may result in short-term immunosuppression (deVries & Housh, 1994; Gleeson, 2006; Nieman, 1996). For example, marathon running has been associated with increased incidence of upper respiratory tract infection (Nieman et al., 1990). In contrast, submaximal exercise may result in increases in immune system parameters (Housh et al., 2012). Clearly, more detailed information must be obtained in order for applied exercise physiologists to be able to optimally design exercise programs that enhance rather than suppress immune function.

Skeletal system

The skeletal system serves as a structural framework and provides the lever system by which muscle contraction can lead to movement. In addition, the skeletal system acts as a depot of important minerals such as calcium. Interest in the skeletal system with respect to exercise has largely focused on the effects of exercise, or lack thereof, on bone mass. The importance of this area is reflected in the fact that there is a relationship between bone density and risk of fracture and in the fact that bone mass decreases with time in the elderly (Bailey, Faulkner, & McKay, 1996). In postmenopausal women, the decrease in estrogen production that occurs following menopause is implicated in the development of **osteoporosis.** Exercise may help slow the process of osteoporosis, but the effect may be rather modest (Howe et al., 2011). In addition, weight-bearing exercise prior to the onset of menopause may enhance the development of bone mass so that the effects of menopause on the skeletal system are diminished (Borer, 2005). Individuals with training in exercise physiology may help to design exercise programs that maximize the beneficial effects of exercise on the skeletal system and minimize the deleterious effects.

In younger women, extreme exercise training and excessive weight loss may lead to menstrual dysfunction, hormonal disturbances, and possible deleterious effects on bone mineral density (Arena et al., 1995).

osteoporosis ■

Areas of Applied Study

Microgravity and spaceflight

Spaceflight and the associated microgravity cause a variety of changes in humans, including decreases in muscle and bone mass (Sulzman, 1996) and orthostatic hypotension (low blood pressure upon standing). In addition, decrements in motor function also occur that compromise the ability of astronauts to function effectively, especially upon initial return to Earth. With the potential for more long-term exposure to microgravity (e.g., in an international space station), some of the deleterious effects of microgravity may have significant health and performance implications (Adams, Caiozzo, & Baldwin, 2003). In the case of loss of bone mass, one month of spaceflight results in bone loss that is equal to 1 year of bone loss on Earth in postmenopausal women (Cavanagh, Licata, & Rice, 2005).

Exercise during spaceflight is one countermeasure used to combat these effects. However, under conditions of microgravity, it is difficult to design effective exercise programs, because weight-bearing exercise is not possible. Exercise devices designed specifically for spaceflight have been developed (Convertino, 1996), and future research will need to be performed to take best advantage of these devices. In addition, most early attempts at exercise in microgravity focused on endurance exercise. However, research into exercise countermeasures has involved other types of exercise, most notably resistance exercise (Haus, Carrithers, Carroll, Tesch, & Trappe, 2007; Tesch, Ekberg, Lindquist, & Trieschmann, 2004).

Gerontology

Exercise has great potential to enhance the quality of life of individuals who are elderly and possibly to extend life. Much research is under way to more clearly understand the unique responses and adaptations to exercise in the elderly.

Some of the consequences of the aging process are a decrease in resting metabolic rate, loss of muscle mass, an increase in body fat percentage, and a decline in aerobic capacity (Deschenes, 2004; Evans, 1995; Fleg et al., 2005). These effects are associated with increased incidence of conditions such as cardiovascular disease. Exercise may be a powerful tool to retard these processes (Tanaka & Seals, 2003).

A growing area of study is strength training for the elderly. Although the strength levels of the sedentary elderly have been reported to be quite low, research has shown that the elderly are capable of significantly increasing both muscle size and strength with strength training (Macaluso & De Vito, 2004; Rogers & Evans, 1993). Increased muscle strength makes the performance of the activities of daily living easier, and increased muscle mass may increase metabolism and help in maintaining appropriate body composition (Hunter, McCarthy, & Bamman, 2004). Furthermore, resistance exercise in the elderly appears to have beneficial effects on a variety of indices associated with chronic diseases such as glucose tolerance and triglyceride levels (Hurley, Hanson, & Sheaff, 2011). Although more research is needed, both aerobic and strength training are being utilized by exercise physiologists to improve the quality of life of the elderly.

Spinal cord injury

Every year in the United States approximately 10,000 individuals experience a spinal cord injury (SCI) (Jacobs & Nash, 2004). Depending on the severity and site of the lesion, paralysis can result. Paralysis of both the upper and lower body results in quadriplegia (also called tetraplegia); paralysis of the lower body is referred to as paraplegia. Among the many effects of paralysis, the decrease in physical activity can lead to increases in risk factors for cardiovascular disease (Bauman et al., 1999; Khan et al., 2011).

Although strength training and range of motion exercises are common in the rehabilitation of individuals with SCI, there is great potential for the inclusion of aerobic exercise in the rehabilitation following SCI. Box 5.2 presents an abstract from a research study that examined the effect of exercise in subjects with paraplegia. Individuals with paraplegia can exercise their upper bodies with the use of arm crank ergometers and wheelchair exercise. In addition, functional electrical stimulation (FES) can be used to allow for lower-body aerobic exercise in individuals with SCI (Hettinga & Andrews, 2008; Kirshblum, 2004). This type of intervention has the potential to enable individuals with SCI to experience the beneficial effects of aerobic exercise.

Stroke

In the United States, per year, an estimated 785,000 individuals experience a stroke (Roger et al., 2011). A stroke, or cerebrovascular accident (CVA), occurs as a result of a disruption of blood flow to an area of the brain, resulting in death of the tissue supplied by the now-disrupted blood flow. There are

Abstract of a research study that examined the effect of exercise in subjects with paraplegia.

Wecht, J. M., Marsico, R., Weir, J. P., Spungen, A., Bauman, W., and De Meersman, R. E. (2006). Autonomic recovery from peak arm exercise in fit and unfit individuals with paraplegia. *Medicine and Science in Sports and Exercise, 38*(7), 1223–1228.

INTRODUCTION. Altered autonomic cardiovascular control in persons with paraplegia may reflect peripheral sympathetic denervation caused by the injury or deconditioning due to skeletal muscle paralysis. Parameters of autonomic cardiovascular control may be improved in fit persons with paraplegia similar to effects reported in the noninjured population.

PURPOSE. To determine differences in resting and recovery HR and cardiac autonomic control in fit and unfit individuals with paraplegia.

METHODS. Eighteen healthy males with paraplegia below T6 were studied; nine participated in aerobic exercise conditioning (fit: ≥ 30 min $\bullet$ d^{-1}, ≥ 3 d $\bullet$ wk^{-1}, ≥ 6 months), and nine were sedentary (unfit). Analysis of heart rate variability (HRV) was used to determine spectral power (ln transformed) in the high- (lnHF) and low-frequency (lnLF) bandwidths, and the LF/HF ratio was calculated. Data were collected at baseline (BL) and at 2, 10, 30, 60, and 90 min of recovery from peak arm cycle ergometry.

RESULTS. The relative intensity achieved on the peak exercise test was comparable between the groups (i.e., 88% peak predicted HR). However, peak watts (P < 0.001) and oxygen consumption (P < 0.01) were higher in the fit compared with the unfit group (56 and 51%, respectively). Recovery lnHF was increased (P < 0.05), and recovery lnLF (P < 0.01) and LF/HF (P < 0.05) were reduced in the fit compared with the unfit group. Mean recovery autonomic activity was not different from BL in the fit group. In the unfit group, mean recovery lnHF was reduced, and mean recovery lnLF and LF/HF remained elevated above BL.

CONCLUSION. These data suggest that fit individuals with paraplegia have improved cardiac autonomic control during the postexercise recovery period compared with their unfit counterparts.

a variety of effects of a CVA, and the effects depend on the severity and location of the lesion. Common motor consequences of CVA include hemiparesis and spasticity. **Hemiparesis** is a loss of motor control (including strength) and sensation on one side of the body, whereas **spasticity** is a condition of excessive muscle tone and resistance to stretch. The effects of strength training and aerobic exercise in stroke patients with hemiparesis and spasticity have been studied (Engardt et al., 1995; Macko et al., 2005; Potempa et al., 1995). Indeed, in the past, strength training was avoided in many patients with stroke because of a fear of making certain stroke complications such as spasticity even worse. Although much more research needs to be performed, the rehabilitation of patients with stroke may require increased participation by professionals with training in exercise physiology.

- hemiparesis
- spasticity

Cardiac rehabilitation

The primary tasks of exercise physiologists in cardiac rehabilitation are designing, implementing, and monitoring exercise programs. Functions related to these activities include exercise testing and client education. Exercise testing is useful in diagnosing disease and measuring exercise capacity (Myers, 2005). The diagnosis of cardiac disease is performed under physician supervision and focuses on electrocardiogram (ECG) monitoring, which provides information about blockage in the arteries that supply blood to the heart. However, exercise testing that also incorporates gas exchange measurements (indirect calorimetry) can provide additional valuable clinical information (Balady et al., 2010; Myers, 2005). Determination of exercise capacity is useful in designing exercise programs and monitoring progress. Client education focuses on topics such as self-monitoring of exercise, proper nutrition, stress management, and weight management.

Traditional cardiac rehabilitation programs are separated into three to four phases. Phase I is in-patient (hospital-based) rehabilitation and is usually conducted for patients who have recently experienced a heart attack (called a myocardial infarction), had cardiac surgery, or have been hospitalized for another cardiac condition such as heart failure or peripheral vascular disease. Although exercise physiologists may perform phase I cardiac rehabilitation, it is more typically performed by the nursing staff or physical therapists. Phases II through IV are outpatient services and are more likely to be performed by clinical exercise physiologists than phase I. Phase II occurs from just after discharge from the hospital for up to 12 weeks and involves close supervision, with electrocardiogram monitoring of the patients' exercise sessions. The transition from phase II to III involves less supervision and limited ECG monitoring during exercise. Phase IV is the transition to a commitment to permanent lifestyle changes including regular exercise and a healthful diet.

Although many students think of cardiac rehabilitation as focusing on patients who have had a myocardial infarction or bypass surgery, other cardiovascular conditions are also treated with cardiac rehabilitation. In heart failure, the heart is unable to adequately pump blood through the circulatory system. This may be secondary to a heart attack, but it may also occur from conditions such as damage to the heart valves. The effects of exercise on damaged hearts per se are limited, but exercise tolerance can be significantly increased in these patients, presumably because of adaptations in the skeletal muscle. Peripheral artery disease (PAD) is analogous to atherosclerosis of the arteries supplying blood to the locomotor muscles, such as the calves. A common symptom of PAD is pain and cramping in muscles during tasks such as walking or climbing stairs (Sontheimer, 2006). Exercise training improves exercise tolerance in these patients largely by increasing local muscular endurance in the locomotor muscles.

Pulmonary rehabilitation

The primary purposes of pulmonary rehabilitation are to decrease symptoms, increase function, and reduce health care costs in individuals with respiratory diseases (Nici et al., 2006). Exercise is an important component in the process of pulmonary rehabilitation because one of the primary consequences of pulmonary disease is a decrease in functional abilities (Butcher & Jones, 2006). Exercise and pulmonary rehabilitation can significantly improve quality of life and enhance performance in the activities of daily living. Indeed, pulmonary patients most often initially seek medical attention because of breathlessness during physical exertion. Exercise physiologists perform clinical exercise tests and design and implement exercise programs for these patients.

Exercise testing provides information that is more correlated with functional abilities than even lung-function testing (Bach & Moldover, 1996). The information from clinical exercise testing in the suspected pulmonary patient can be used for diagnostic purposes, to provide information for decision making regarding therapeutic intervention, and to monitor the progress of the rehabilitation.

The primary purpose of exercise training in pulmonary rehabilitation is to increase functional capacity, resulting in an increase in the ability to perform activities of daily living. Of these, increased endurance for walking is essential. Endurance, strength, and flexibility exercises are all components of the rehabilitation process. Endurance exercise training should increase the amount of work that a person can perform without shortness of breath. Because lung disease often leads to weight loss and weakness, strength training exercises increase the ability of patients to do work with less fatigue. Similarly, alterations in posture and mobility that occur as a consequence of pulmonary disease can be corrected or minimized with flexibility training (Barr, 1994). An added benefit of exercise is the component of emotional support (provided by additional human contact), which may also contribute to improvement in patient function (Siebens, 1996).

Body composition and weight control

Obesity is defined as an excess amount of body fat. The current estimate is that approximately 34 percent of U.S. adults are obese, and the incidence has increased over the last 20 years (Flegal et al., 2010). Because obesity has important implications for health, reducing the incidence of obesity is considered an important national health goal. Diseases that are associated with obesity include heart disease, type 2 diabetes, and cancer (Pi-Sunyer, 1993). Epidemiological evidence also indicates that obesity and "overweight" (and also underweight) can lead to an increased risk of illness and/or death (Flegal et al., 2005).

Exercise can facilitate fat loss in a comprehensive weight-management program (Shaw, Gennat, O'Rourke, & Del Mar, 2006; Stiegler & Cunliffe, 2006). However, important questions remain to be answered regarding the most beneficial approach when using exercise in treating obesity. One important consideration is the type of exercise to be used. Aerobic exercise has traditionally been used to burn fat, but the role and effectiveness of resistance exercise needs further study. It has been shown that resistance training helps to maintain lean body weight during weight-loss diets (Ballor et al., 1988) and may increase resting metabolic rate (Ryan et al., 1995). Questions remain regarding the optimal mix of exercise intensity versus exercise duration for facilitating fat loss. Clearly, long-term exercise adherence needs to be a consideration. Gender differences may play an important role in the interaction between exercise and fat loss and need further study.

The effectiveness of physical activity in the prevention of obesity is an important area of inquiry. There are "critical periods" in childhood and adolescence when excessive weight gain will likely influence adult obesity (Daniels et al., 2005). Exercise may be important in preventing obesity during these years and after, especially because obesity at these ages is a significant predictor of obesity in later life. Similarly, as people get older their resting metabolic rate tends to decrease and percent body fat tends to increase. Increasing physical activity may help prevent or slow this process. As can be seen, researchers in exercise physiology have many questions to answer regarding exercise and obesity. Because new information is being reported, applied exercise physiologists in both clinical and health and fitness areas need to stay current in order to adequately serve their clients.

Exercise and diabetes

Diabetes is a disorder of the endocrine system, a system of ductless glands that secretes its products, called hormones, into the blood, which carries them to "target" organs or systems where they have their effects. In healthy individuals, the amount of hormones produced by each gland is carefully balanced. Too much or too little of a certain hormone can have effects throughout the body and cause various endocrine disorders. In the case of diabetes, blood glucose regulation is disrupted due to dysfunction of the body's insulin system. **Insulin** is a hormone secreted from the pancreas and serves to facilitate glucose transport from the blood to the cells. Diabetes is classified as type 1 or type 2. Individuals with type 1 diabetes usually develop the disease in childhood, and almost all require exogenous insulin to supplement pancreatic production. Persons with type 2 diabetes usually develop insulin resistance in later life, and most do not require exogenous insulin (Young, 1995).

■ *diabetes*

■ *insulin*

High fitness levels and high levels of physical activity have been shown to decrease the risk of developing diabetes (Gill & Cooper, 2008; LaMonte, Blair, & Church, 2005); thus, exercise training may help individuals avoid developing type 2 diabetes. For those with diabetes, exercise has been shown to have a beneficial effect on glucose regulation. This effect is in part due to the fact that exercise promotes glucose transport from the blood to muscle cells (Wasserman & Zinman, 1994). Although this effect is largely beneficial, exercise physiologists who work with individuals with insulin-dependent diabetes must be aware of the potential for the combined effects of exercise and exogenous insulin manipulation to result in hypoglycemia (low blood sugar) or hyperglycemia (high blood sugar) (Wasserman & Zinman, 1994). Beyond the effects of exercise on blood glucose regulation per se, exercise can have a beneficial effect on risk factors associated with diabetes, such as obesity, elevated blood cholesterol, and high blood pressure. Because of the high incidence of diabetes, applied exercise physiologists should be aware of all current information regarding exercise and diabetes. The ACSM has specific recommendations for the design of exercise programs for individuals with type 2 diabetes (Colberg et al., 2010).

There are over 19 million diabetics in the United States (Cowie et al., 2006), and complications from diabetes (e.g., heart disease or stroke) are among the major causes of death.

Exercise and pregnancy

There is as yet no conclusive evidence indicating that exercise during pregnancy facilitates the process of labor and delivery; however, a clear benefit of maternal exercise is maternal health and a more rapid return to prepregnancy levels of fitness. Applied exercise physiologists may work with pregnant clients and need to be aware of the exercise modifications necessary for safe and effective exercise during pregnancy.

The effect of exercise on both the mother and the infant has received increased research attention since 1984, when the first guidelines regarding exercise and pregnancy were published by the American College of Obstetrics and Gynecology (ACOG). Two of the primary considerations were the effect of elevation in maternal core temperature on the unborn child and the effects of maternal exercise on fetal blood flow. Because there was relatively little published research at that time, the initial guidelines were conservative in that it was recommended that exercise heart rate not exceed 140 beats per minute and core temperature not exceed 38°C.

Since that time more research and clinical information has accumulated, and the ACOG guidelines were updated (ACOG, 2002). These guidelines encourage physical activity and exercise in pregnant women (including strengthening and flexibility exercises) but provide specific precautions and contraindications for exercise. It has also been noted that exercise may help control gestational diabetes and decrease the risk of preeclampsia (Damm, Breitowicz, & Hegaard, 2007). *ACSM's Guidelines for Exercise Testing and Prescription* (ACSM, 2010) has specific exercise prescription information for exercise during pregnancy.

Muscle soreness and damage

The soreness that occurs 24 to 48 hours following strenuous exercise (especially if it is a new type of exercise) is familiar to all who exercise. This is often referred to as delayed onset muscle soreness (DOMS) (Housh et al., 2012). The specific cause(s) of this soreness is (are) still being investigated, but much evidence suggests that it is associated with muscle damage and is more severe with **eccentric contractions** (contractions in which the muscle actively lengthens, such as when lowering a weight or walking down a hill) than with **concentric contractions** (contractions in which the muscle is shortening, such as when curling a barbell to the chest). Although muscle soreness may be only a nuisance for healthy individuals, for some it may affect exercise adherence. It may also have important health implications for individuals with neuromuscular disease who wish to exercise, because some evidence suggests that muscle damage from overwork may exacerbate some diseases. In addition, muscle soreness is used as a model for the study of mechanisms of injury repair.

eccentric contraction ■

concentric contraction ■

Environmental exercise physiology

Environmental exercise physiology encompasses many aspects. These include issues such as exercise in cold environments and exercise and pollution. In this section, a brief overview of two frequently studied areas, altitude and heat–humidity, will be presented.

Altitude. As one moves from sea level to high altitudes, barometric pressure decreases, which decreases the amount of oxygen that is driven into the blood to bind to **hemoglobin** (hemoglobin is the protein in red blood cells that carries oxygen and carbon dioxide). The decreased oxygen content leads to decreased performance in endurance exercise at the elevated altitude. Prolonged exposure to high altitude, however, results in increased synthesis of hemoglobin and red blood cells. These adaptations increase the oxygen-carrying capacity of the blood and theoretically may improve exercise performance at sea level. One model used in endurance sports is "living high—training low" (Levine & Stray-Gundersen, 2005). In this model, athletes live at high altitude to stimulate red blood cell production, while they train at low altitude so that training is not compromised by hypoxia (the deficiency of oxygen reaching body tissues). Whether the benefits of this model are actually due to increases in red blood cells is an open debate (Gore & Hopkins, 2005).

hemoglobin ■

Altitude exposure also poses health risks and unique problems for those who exercise. For example, mountain climbers must perform work at altitudes that may lead to mountain sickness and even death. Therefore, the study of physiological adaptations to altitude and the consequences of associated exercise is an important area of research. Projects such as Operation Everest II (Sutton, Maher, & Houston, 1983), in which a hypobaric chamber allowed for the simulation of high altitude, have made important contributions to our understanding of these issues.

Heat and humidity. Thermal adjustments comprise a very important aspect of exercise in a hot and/or humid environment, where exercise without adequate thermal adjustments can lead to serious health consequences, including death. In general, the most important heat-dissipating mechanism during exercise is sweating. The evaporation of sweat from the skin results in a transfer of heat from the skin to the environment, resulting in cooling. This process, however, can lead to a loss of body water and electrolytes (e.g., sodium). Therefore, both the increase in body temperature and the effect of the water and electrolyte loss can affect performance and lead to medical problems such as heat stroke. Humidity is an especially important problem because high humidity minimizes the amount of sweat that can evaporate; thus, sweat is wasted.

Research by exercise physiologists led to important recommendations regarding exercise in the heat, fluid replacement, and prevention of heat illnesses with exercise (Armstrong et al., 2007; Sawka et al., 2007). Current areas of research focus on issues such as the proper method of fluid replacement during exercise in the heat (ACSM, 2010). Many sports drinks are commercially available, and many have been developed in part from research conducted by exercise physiologists. More recently, it was recognized that drinking too much fluid during exercise can lead to hyponatremia (decreased concentration of sodium in the blood), a potentially life-threatening condition (Hsieh et al., 2002).

Ergogenic aids

In athletic competition, the difference between winning and losing can be small. Because of this, athletes and coaches will try many things in order to gain a competitive advantage. The term **ergogenic aid** refers to any substance, device, or treatment that can or is believed to improve athletic performance. In contrast, **ergolytic** refers to practices that can impair performance. Many nutritional products and practices (e.g., carbohydrate loading) are used to gain a competitive advantage. Some techniques can be beneficial, but most don't work. Drugs such as amphetamines and anabolic steroids are used illegally and may have dangerous side effects. Other aids can be mechanical, such as knee wraps in power lifting.

A large amount of research in exercise physiology has been conducted to evaluate the efficacy of different ergogenic aids. The research into ergogenic aids is important not only for the immediate effect of the data on athletic practices but also because examination of these issues can provide insight into the limiting processes and mechanisms involved in human performance. In addition, because ergogenic aids are an important issue in athletic competition, applied exercise physiologists need to be up to date on the efficacy, safety, and ethical issues surrounding ergogenic aids that may be used by clients. Of special concern are the potential health consequences of some ergogenic aids. A few of these aids are discussed next.

Anabolic steroids are synthetically developed cholesterol-based drugs that resemble naturally occurring hormones such as testosterone and have anabolic (growth-promoting) and androgenic (masculinizing) effects (ACSM, 1984).

■ *ergogenic aid*

■ *ergolytic*

At the 2008 Olympics, Michael Phelps beat Milorad Čavić by 1/100th of a second in the men's 100 meter butterfly.

■ *anabolic steroids*

Because testosterone is involved in skeletal muscle development, among other functions, anabolic steroids are used by athletes primarily to facilitate strength and power development. Therefore, they are most frequently used in sports such as weight lifting, throwing events in track and field, and football (Hoberman & Yesalis, 1995; Yesalis & Bahrke, 1995). Although the research data are equivocal, the general consensus is that anabolic steroids do seem to be effective in this regard. However, illegal use of anabolic steroids can have significant legal implications. In addition, as noted earlier, their use is against the rules of almost all athletic governing bodies. Moreover, many health consequences are associated with the use of these drugs.

Caffeine is a drug commonly found in coffee, tea, chocolate, and many carbonated soft drinks. It also appears to be effective as an ergogenic aid (Tarnopolsky, 2010). Caffeine can affect arousal levels and alter metabolism. The main beneficial effect is in endurance activities (Tarnopolsky, 2010). The influence of caffeine on strength and power events seems to be minimal (Williams, 1991).

creatine supplementation ■   An ergogenic aid receiving much attention since the mid-1990s is **creatine supplementation.** Creatine phosphate is involved in ATP restoration in skeletal muscle, and research shows that creatine supplementation can increase intramuscular concentrations of both free creatine and creatine phosphate (Tarnopolsky, 2010; Terjung et al., 2000). Creatine supplementation has also been shown to enhance performance and recovery from high-intensity exercise, which may also lead to more productive training sessions. Strength and power athletes are the primary beneficiaries of creatine supplementation. The effects of creatine may also occur via effects on gene expression (Willoughby & Rosene, 2001, 2003).

Sodium bicarbonate, an alkalizing substance (neutralizes acids), has been studied for use as an ergogenic aid because increased acidity is one possible mechanism of muscle fatigue. Sodium bicarbonate is used to buffer acids during exercise and delay fatigue. Research suggests that this procedure may be beneficial for high-intensity, large muscle mass activities where a large increase in acidity would be expected (Requena et al., 2005). However, side effects include gastrointestinal distress.

blood doping ■   **Blood doping** refers to two techniques used to increase red blood cell content to enhance endurance performance. One technique involves the infusion of red blood cells, either from a sample taken at an earlier time from the same subject or from another donor. The second technique involves administration of a drug called erythropoietin (EPO), which stimulates red blood cell production by the bone marrow. Research generally shows that blood doping may enhance endurance performance, but both techniques violate current International Olympic Committee rules and can have negative health consequences (Joyner, 2003). Use of EPO has led to scandals in sporting events such as the Tour de France (Joyner, 2003).

Pediatric exercise physiology

Pediatric exercise physiology is concerned with children and adolescents. Clearly, this area of exercise physiology has a direct bearing on the field of physical education. This is especially true considering the relatively poor state of physical fitness in American youth. In addition, the topic of pediatric exercise physiology has important clinical and health implications. As with adults, clinical exercise testing in children is used in the diagnosis of cardiovascular and pulmonary disease (Tomassoni, 1996). The growth of the area of pediatric exercise physiology is evidenced by the publication of *Pediatric Exercise*

Science, which was first published in 1989. Because most of the subdisciplines addressed previously have application to pediatric exercise physiology, in this section we address only a few select areas.

The relationship between bone mineral density and physical activity in children has important implications for the prevention of the loss of bone mass in later years. Most bone mass is laid down during childhood and adolescence, with peak bone mass occurring at about 30 years of age (Bailey et al., 1996). Vigorous weight-bearing exercise appears to increase bone growth during these years, which may be protective during adulthood. In contrast, poor diet, menstrual irregularities, and lack of physical activity may minimize the development of bone tissue and result in increased risk of fracture in later life.

Strength training for children and adolescents also may pose unique risks. In addition, the question of whether children can increase their strength with resistance training has received considerable examination. With respect to risks, because the growth plates at the ends of long bones are fragile and damage to these growth plates can affect growth, safety is of paramount concern. Although reports of growth plate injuries with strength training are rare, conservative guidelines were developed and can be found in the position paper by the National Strength and Conditioning Association (Faigenbaum et al., 2009). In general, children are to avoid "weight lifting"; that is, children should not attempt to lift as much as they can. Rather, strength training can be used to help improve strength levels. Research evaluating the use of strength training in children has generally shown that children can increase strength levels with resistance training, but the amount of change in muscle mass is limited until after puberty, at which time the endocrine system develops to the point that adequate hormone concentrations exist to support muscle mass development (Blimkie, 1992).

The effect of exercise on the rate and amount of growth in children and adolescents has important implications for the prescription of exercise in children. Exercise provides conflicting signals for growth in children. On the one hand, the increased metabolic demands of physical activity can potentially divert nutrients away from growth processes. On the other hand, exercise stimulates endocrine responses that facilitate growth (Borer, 1995). Comparing growth in active versus sedentary subjects is problematic due to selection bias; that is, any differences in growth and development between active and less-active subjects may be due to a tendency for individuals with a specific body type to gravitate toward certain activities and athletic pursuits. Malina (1994), in a review of growth and maturation data in young athletes, concluded that most athletic training did not affect these processes in the long term. However, inadequate nutritional support, as may be associated with sports like wrestling and gymnastics, may have effects (Roemmich, Richmond, & Rogol, 2001). Clearly, female gymnastics is associated with short stature and delayed menarche (time of first menstruation), but the factors driving these observations (e.g., selection bias, stress, nutrition, training) are difficult to untangle (Thomis et al., 2005). In wrestling, where "making weight" is common in young athletes, the data indicate that growth patterns are similar between wrestlers and nonathletes (Housh et al., 1993; Roemmich & Sinning, 1997).

Exercise and human immunodeficiency virus

Human immunodeficiency virus (HIV) is the virus that causes AIDS (acquired immune deficiency syndrome). It is believed that HIV attacks specific types of immune cells, which ultimately leads to decreases in the ability of the body to fight infection. There is no cure, but important strides are being made with respect to increasing both the life span and quality of life for individuals who are HIV positive.

Of interest here is the relationship between exercise and HIV. Exercise appears to have beneficial effects for individuals with HIV (Hand, Lyerly, Jaggers, & Dudgeon, 2009; O'Brien, Nixon, Tynan, & Glazier, 2010). For example, strength training may help maintain muscle mass, which may help to slow down the loss in lean body mass associated with AIDS wasting (Lawless, Jackson, & Greenleaf, 1995). Aerobic exercise will similarly improve cardio-respiratory endurance and quality of life. As noted previously regarding exercise and immunology, however, exercise also has the potential to be immunosuppressive. Nonetheless, to date the limited number of studies that examined exercise and HIV showed that exercise is safe (Hand et al., 2009).

TECHNOLOGY AND RESEARCH TOOLS

T he tools used by exercise physiologists for conducting research are numerous, and a comprehensive review is beyond the scope of this chapter. However, this section presents a brief outline of some common tools, with emphasis placed on noninvasive techniques.

Treadmills and Ergometers

The treadmill and cycle ergometer are the basic tools used by exercise physiologists to induce exercise in research subjects. The treadmill is very common in the United States (see Exhibit 5.3), where walking and jogging are familiar

| exhibit | 5.3 | Exercise test on a treadmill. |

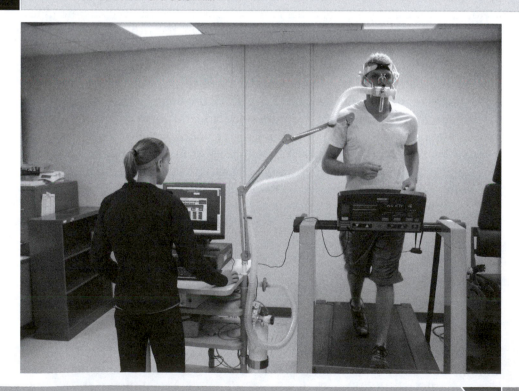

forms of exercise. In Europe, where bicycling is more common, the use of cycle ergometers is more prevalent (see Exhibit 5.4). However, both devices are used frequently.

With treadmills, the intensity of exercise is controlled by manipulating the speed of the treadmill belt and the grade of the treadmill (i.e., the steepness of the slope). The disadvantage of the treadmill is that it is difficult to precisely measure the exact work output by a subject because of differences in mechanical efficiency between people. In contrast, because cycle ergometers support the subject's body weight, the work by the subject is just a function of the resistance of the machine. Most cycle ergometers have resistance applied by a friction belt. When the exercise intensity is to be increased, the resistance by the belt is increased. However, the pedal rate affects the intensity of the exercise; therefore, subjects must maintain a constant pedal rate. More expensive electronically braked cycle ergometers use an electromagnet to provide resistance. These devices have the advantage of allowing the power output of the subject to be manipulated independent of pedal rate, so subjects can choose the pedal rate that is most comfortable for them.

Although less common than either the treadmill or the cycle ergometer, other types of ergometers, such as those for arm cranking, allow for exercise testing with modes of exercise other than running or cycling. The arm-crank ergometer is a modified cycle ergometer for which the arms are used to "pedal" the device. These devices are important for exercise testing and training of individuals such as those with paraplegia who are unable to use the lower body. Sports physiology laboratories may have access to sport-specific ergometers, such as rowing ergometers, cross-country skiing ergometers, and swim flumes. In the training and testing of high-level athletes, these devices provide information that is more specific to the types of events in which the athletes will be competing (Thoden, 1991).

Exercise test on a Monark cycle ergometer. **exhibit** **5.4**

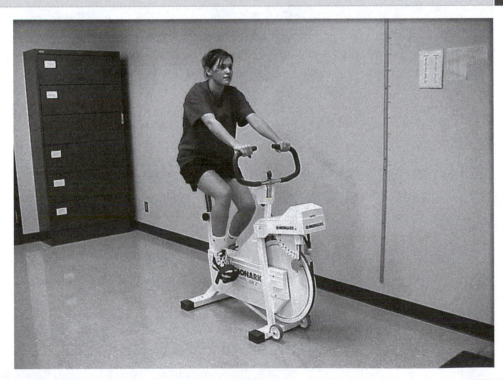

Metabolic Measurements

Probably the most common physiologic measurement in exercise physiology is the determination of oxygen consumption and carbon dioxide production for the purpose of measuring metabolic activity using indirect calorimetry. This is most often performed during exercise on a treadmill or cycle ergometer. These measurements, obtained by collecting and analyzing expired gases from the lungs, allow for the determination of a variety of factors, including the amount of energy (calories) used during an activity, the relative amount of fat versus carbohydrate burned, and the fitness status of a given individual.

$\dot{V}O_2\ max$ ■ The maximal rate of oxygen consumption, or $\dot{V}O_2$ **max,** is the primary standard for determining aerobic fitness. Prior to the development of fast and inexpensive computers, performance of these metabolic measurements was labor intensive and time-consuming. Currently, however, computerized and automated metabolic carts (see Exhibit 5.5) allow metabolic exercise tests to be performed quickly and with fewer technicians.

| **exhibit** / **5.5** | A metabolic (met) cart. |

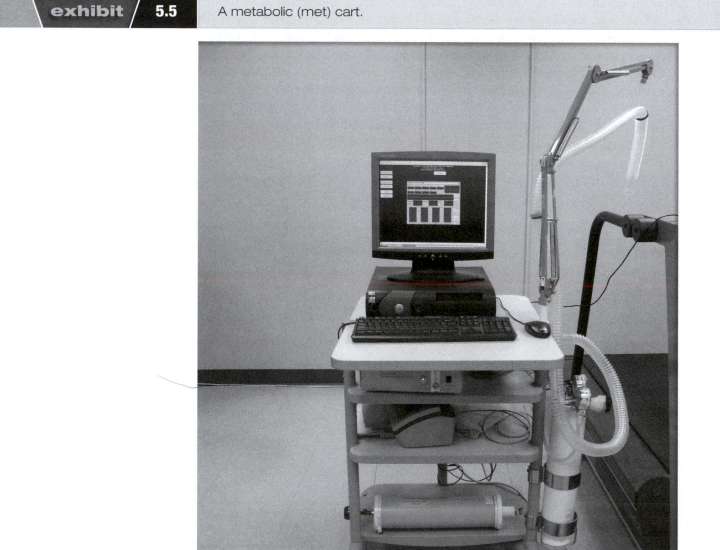

Body Composition Assessment

Measurement of body composition is an important tool for studying the effects of various exercise and/or dietary interventions. The most common model of body composition is the two-component model, which divides the body into fat weight and fat-free weight components. The fat-free weight component includes tissues such as muscle, bone, and various organs. The fat weight component is primarily adipose tissue (fat tissue) but also includes some neurological tissue. Newer multicomponent models further delineate body composition components into smaller subcomponents. These approaches are likely to improve measurement of body composition, especially for different racial groups (Heyward, 1996).

The practical utility of body composition assessment is that it facilitates the design of exercise and dietary programs for fat loss. Body composition data are used to set fat-loss goals for clients. In addition, continued measurement of body composition allows for the monitoring of progress over time.

Hydrostatic weighing, or underwater weighing, is the primary gold standard for assessing body composition. New technology such as dual-energy X-ray absorptiometry (DXA; also used to study bone mineral content) is expanding the assessment of body composition and may displace underwater weighing as the gold standard. Other techniques, such as the use of skinfold calipers, bioelectrical impedance analysis (BIA), and near infrared reactance (NIR), provide predictions of what a person's body composition would be if assessed with underwater weighing. These latter techniques, while less accurate than underwater weighing, do allow for more convenient and therefore widespread use of body composition assessment (Heyward, 1996). Air displacement plethysmography assesses body composition using logic similar to that of hydrostatic weighing (calculation of body density by determining body volume and mass). The validity and reliability of the technique appear acceptable (Lee & Gallagher, 2008). Newer approaches include techniques based on MRI and computerized tomography (CT) (Lee & Gallagher, 2008).

Muscle Biopsy

The muscle biopsy procedure has been in use since the 1960s and can be traced to Bergstrom (1962). In this procedure, a needle is inserted into the belly of a muscle, and a small piece of tissue is removed. From this procedure, an exercise physiologist can make a variety of observations. For example, comparison of pre- versus post-exercise biopsy samples has been used to study substrate utilization and metabolite accumulation during exercise. In addition, the muscle biopsy procedure is a technique by which muscle fiber type percentages can be determined in humans. The three primary fiber types in human skeletal muscle are **slow-twitch oxidative (SO)**, **fast-twitch oxidative glycolytic (FOG)**, and **fast-twitch glycolytic (FG)** (Peter et al., 1972). These fiber types have also been called type I, type IIa, and type IIb, or Beta/slow, type IIa, and type IIx, respectively. The names SO, FOG, and FG, however, provide descriptive information about the characteristics and functioning of the various fiber types, while type I, IIa, and IIb do not. For example, from the names, we know that SO fibers are slow-twitch and favor oxidative (aerobic; with oxygen) energy production, while FG fibers are fast-twitch and favor glycolytic anaerobic (anaerobic; without oxygen) energy production.

- slow-twitch oxidative (SO)
- fast-twitch oxidative glycolytic (FOG)
- fast-twitch glycolytic (FG)

Research employing muscle biopsies has led to many advances in our understanding of the physiology of exercise. Because of its invasive nature, however, use of the procedure requires extensive training, which limits its use to a relatively small number of research laboratories.

Electromyography

electromyography ■   **Electromyography** involves the measurement of muscle electrical activity. Because the stimulus for a muscle to contract is electrical, the measurement of this electrical activity provides information regarding the activation of the skeletal muscles involved during exercise. In general, there are two types of EMG measurement procedures. Intramuscular EMG involves placing recording electrodes into the belly of the muscle itself, most typically in the form of a needle electrode. This common clinical tool is used for the diagnosis of neuromuscular diseases, but it also has some utility in studying exercise. More common, however, is the use of surface electrodes to record the EMG signal. Surface EMG provides information about the relative strength of a muscle contraction because, in general, the larger the amount of muscle activated, the larger the amount of electrical activity produced. Changes in the amount of electrical activity recorded have been used to study the neurological effects of strength training (Gabriel et al., 2006; Moritani & deVries, 1979). In addition, as a muscle fatigues, there occur changes in the EMG signal that provide insight into the rate of fatigue of the muscle as well as the mechanisms of fatigue (Dimitrova & Dimitrov, 2003).

Magnetic Resonance Imaging and Nuclear Magnetic Resonance Spectroscopy

Magnetic resonance technology has been a tool used for studying muscles and exercise since the early 1980s. Both magnetic resonance imaging and nuclear magnetic resonance spectroscopy (MRS) are based on the application of strong magnetic fields to the tissue of interest. MRI has been used to examine changes in muscle size following strength training, because the MRI images offer advantages over ultrasound and CT scans in visualizing muscle tissue and other soft tissues (Housh, Housh, Johnson, & Chu, 1992). Two other applications involve the use of MRI to study body composition and activation patterns of skeletal muscle during different tasks. For body composition, a series of cross-sectional scans can be made from head to toe. This allows for the assessment of not only the amount of fat versus lean tissue but also the distribution of fat in different areas of the body, most notably in the abdominal cavity versus under the skin (subcutaneous). This is important because intra-abdominal fat appears to be more related to disease risk than does subcutaneous fat. Although the use of MRI for this purpose is likely to be limited to research, data derived using these procedures may significantly improve our understanding of exercise, diet, and obesity.

With respect to muscle activation, changes in the contrast of MRI images of skeletal muscle are indicative of activation of the muscle. Future research with MRI may reveal important new information regarding muscle activation during exercise.

In contrast to MRI, MRS does not involve imaging of the tissues under study per se; rather, it allows for the noninvasive measurement of muscle substrates and metabolites so that changes that occur during an exercise bout can be monitored. This facilitates investigations of muscle fatigue and is being used in research studies that previously would have required subjects to undergo muscle biopsy. Another potential use is for the noninvasive determination of muscle fiber type. The primary disadvantage of both MRI and MRS is the cost associated with their use. Because of the expense, the use of these technologies to study exercise physiology will likely be limited to relatively few laboratories (Kent-Braun, Miller, & Weiner, 1995).

EDUCATIONAL PREPARATION

A cademic programs in exercise physiology vary to some degree in their requirements and course content (see Chapter 1). Another complication is that there is no set standard for the amount of education required to become an exercise physiologist; that is, an individual is not required to obtain a bachelor's, master's, or doctoral degree in exercise physiology to call himself or herself an exercise physiologist. Similarly, there is no consensus about what every exercise physiologist should know. For example, some academic programs heavily stress clinical aspects of exercise physiology in which students are trained to work in clinical environments such as cardiac rehabilitation and pulmonary rehabilitation. Other academic programs prepare students for research careers. In both cases, undergraduate and graduate programs are offered.

Undergraduate

Courses in exercise physiology have long been a part of the curriculum for undergraduate physical education majors. Intensive study of exercise physiology at the undergraduate level is a more recent phenomenon. Most undergraduate degrees related to exercise physiology are not exercise physiology degrees per se; rather, they are more likely to be degrees in exercise science. This more generic title allows for a broad emphasis in which exercise physiology is integrated with other areas of study, such as biomechanics and motor learning. Although an undergraduate degree may be sufficient for many purposes, it is often the case that these degrees are preparatory for more advanced training at the graduate level or in professional school.

As preparation for the core courses in the degree, mathematics and basic science courses such as chemistry, physics, and general physiology are helpful and may be required. In addition, for those individuals who wish to pursue graduate training or who will apply for professional school (e.g., medicine or physical therapy), these courses are often requirements for application to the various programs.

Core courses in the degree program will typically include one or more courses in exercise physiology itself, with emphasis on the basic areas of study outlined in this chapter. Additional courses at the undergraduate level may include emphasis on nutrition, cardiovascular exercise physiology, exercise biochemistry, exercise testing, and exercise prescription. With respect to exercise testing, these courses often provide hands-on experiences in conducting exercise tests for both fitness evaluation and clinical evaluation. Similarly, exercise prescription courses provide theoretical and practical information regarding the design and implementation of individualized exercise programs for both healthy individuals and those with conditions such as cardiovascular disease.

Graduate

Graduate programs in exercise physiology tend to be more specialized than undergraduate programs. Indeed, differences between institutions for similarly titled programs can be quite large. Outlined next are some characteristics of different types of graduate programs at both the master's and doctoral levels. For those interested in pursuing graduate training in exercise physiology, it is advisable to research the specific programs of interest carefully to ensure that the chosen program fits the student's specific needs and goals.

Master's

At the master's level, many programs emphasize training in clinical exercise physiology. Courses in these programs tend to focus on advanced training in exercise testing and exercise prescription. Specialized training often includes in-depth analysis of exercise electrocardiograms, study of the effect of cardiovascular medications on exercise, study of the effect of exercise on cardiovascular disease, and designing of exercise programs for those with cardiovascular disease. Many clinical exercise physiology programs do not require the completion of a thesis project. At the other end of the spectrum, some master's programs focus on preparation for doctoral training and place very little emphasis on clinical training. These programs tend to place an increased emphasis on basic science and perhaps statistics and research design.

Doctoral

Doctoral education provides advanced training with a focus on developing research skills. The two most common degrees in exercise physiology are the doctor of philosophy (Ph.D.) and the doctor of education (Ed.D.). In general, the Ph.D. degree emphasizes training in research, while the Ed.D. degree, as the title suggests, tends to place more emphasis on training in education. Traditionally, the Ed.D. degree tends to require more formal course work than the Ph.D., while the scientific rigor of the Ph.D. dissertation is expected to be higher than that for the Ed.D. degree. It is often the case, however, that there is little difference in the two degrees, and many fine educators hold Ph.D. degrees, while a number of outstanding researchers have an Ed.D.

During the training for the doctoral degree, the course work typically includes courses in exercise physiology, but many courses are taken outside the primary department. For example, training in statistical procedures often occurs through statistics departments or other departments with statistical specialists, such as psychology or educational psychology. Advanced basic science courses such as endocrinology, immunology, and neurophysiology are taught in biology departments or through affiliated allied health and/or medical schools.

The culminating step in the doctoral degree is the completion of a dissertation. Traditionally, the dissertation project is the first independent research project by the doctoral candidate. The process involves developing a dissertation proposal, completing the data collection and analysis, writing the document, and finally defending the dissertation before a faculty committee.

Exercise Physiology as Part of a Preprofessional School Degree

Courses in exercise physiology can also be important in preparing for admission to various professional programs, such as physical therapy, medicine, chiropractic, and others.

Physical therapy

Physical therapists are primarily involved in the rehabilitation of patients following injury and disease. As part of the treatment process, physical therapists are often involved in the design of exercise programs to increase cardiovascular fitness, muscular strength, and flexibility (American Physical Therapy Association, 1995). Therefore, expertise in exercise physiology can be of great benefit to many physical therapists.

Today, all physical therapy academic programs are required to be at the postbaccalaureate level; that is, upon completion, the graduate will have at least a master's degree, and most programs now offer a clinical doctorate degree in physical therapy (DPT). The academic programs do not typically require that an applicant receive his or her undergraduate degree in a specific major for admission; however, most require broad training in the sciences (biology, chemistry, and physics) and have specific requirements for the humanities. Many of these requirements overlap with requirements for exercise science and, combined with the overlap in content area, make training in exercise science an appealing choice in preparation for admission to physical therapy school.

Medicine

Admission to both allopathic (grants the medical doctor, M.D., degree) and osteopathic (grants the doctor of osteopathy, D.O., degree) medical schools requires high-level performance in basic science courses at the undergraduate level. As with physical therapy, many of the courses required for admission to medical school are also prerequisites for many courses in exercise physiology. More important, training in exercise physiology may be very useful to practicing physicians. Therefore, an undergraduate degree with emphasis in exercise science, along with the appropriate premedical requirements, is an attractive option for those seeking admission to medical school.

Chiropractic

In general, the admission requirements for chiropractic schools are similar to those of medical schools. Therefore, as with the M.D. and D.O. programs, undergraduate training in exercise physiology is an appealing approach for those who wish to pursue the D.C. degree.

Other preprofessional opportunities

A strong background in the basic sciences as well as exercise physiology provides a foundation for other professional schools, such as dentistry, physician's assistant, and optometry.

CERTIFICATIONS

Unlike physical therapists, nurses, physicians, and other health professionals, no license is required to practice exercise physiology. However, professional organizations, such as the ACSM and the NSCA, offer certifications in related areas.

American College of Sports Medicine

The ACSM began certification in 1975 and thousands have received certifications since then. Currently, the ACSM has two certification categories, each with two levels.

The Health Fitness Certifications include the ACSM Certified Personal Trainer and the ACSM Certified Health Fitness Specialist. Both certifications are designed for individuals who will provide exercise services to apparently healthy clients and low-risk individuals who are cleared to exercise.

The second category of ACSM certifications includes the Clinical Certifications. As the name suggests, these certifications are designed for those who will work in clinical environments such as cardiac and pulmonary rehabilitation. The first level, the ACSM Certified Clinical Exercise Specialist, requires a minimum of a bachelor's degree and a specified number of hours of clinical experience in order to sit for the exam. The highest level of clinical certification is the ACSM Registered Clinical Exercise Physiologist. Among other requirements, to take the exam one must have at least a master's degree in exercise physiology (or similar degree) and at least 600 hours of clinical experience.

Specific requirements and competencies are described in detail in various ACSM publications, such as *ACSM's Guidelines for Exercise Testing and Prescription* (ACSM, 2010), and on its website. Certification examinations in both tracks are administered online.

ACSM Certifications
www.acsm.org/certification/

National Strength and Conditioning Association

The NSCA began a certification in 1985 called the Certified Strength and Conditioning Specialist (CSCS). To sit for the CSCS examination, a minimum of a bachelor's degree (or senior-level standing at an accredited institution) and CPR certification are required. The focus of the examination is on the design and implementation of strength training programs for application to sports conditioning. The examination includes questions on both the scientific and practical–applied aspects of strength and conditioning training.

The NSCA has also instituted another certification track for those individuals who are or will be personal fitness trainers. This is called the NSCA Certified Personal Trainer certification (NSCA CPT).

Information on both of the NSCA's certifications is available on its website.

NSCA Certifications
www.nsca-cc.org

EMPLOYMENT OPPORTUNITIES

Clinics

Exercise physiologists have been working in clinical settings for many years, and the two most common areas of clinical exercise physiology, cardiac and pulmonary rehabilitation, were addressed previously in this chapter.

The education required for expertise in clinical exercise physiology is not standardized. At the very minimum, a bachelor's degree in exercise science or a related discipline with specialized course work in clinical topics of exercise physiology, such as exercise testing and electrocardiography, is important. A master's degree is often necessary. Hands-on experience, often gained from an internship as part of an academic program, is very helpful, as is one of the ACSM's clinical certifications. The AACVPR website (see p. 115) has information about job openings in cardiac and pulmonary rehabilitation.

One important task of a clinical exercise physiologist is to perform clinical exercise testing. Currently, clinical exercise testing (stress testing) is used primarily for assessing individuals with suspected or diagnosed cardiovascular or pulmonary disease. The general approach is to stress the client with a progressive exercise test so that indications of disease, severity of disease, and exercise capacity can be determined; *progressive* in this context means that the exercise intensity starts at a low level and increases over time until the subject can no longer continue or signs and symptoms develop such that stopping the test is warranted. Unless an orthopedic or neurological condition prevents lower-body exercise, testing is usually performed with a treadmill or, less often, a cycle ergometer.

Clinical exercise testing always includes electrocardiographic monitoring and may, but does not always, include metabolic measurements by indirect calorimetry. ECG monitoring is important for client safety but is also used as a diagnostic tool for assessing coronary artery disease. The diagnostic utility comes from the fact that heart size and occlusion of coronary arteries due to atherosclerosis result in specific alterations in ECG signals. These effects may not show up at rest, but because exercise places stress on the heart, coronary artery occlusion will become evident during exercise and result in these changes in the ECG. Similarly, pulmonary dysfunction may not be fully exhibited with resting pulmonary measurements, whereas ventilatory and metabolic changes during exercise testing can provide diagnostic information (Jones, 1988). For both cardiac and pulmonary disease, impairments in peak workload attained during exercise, low maximal oxygen consumption, abnormalities in blood pressure response, and other information from the exercise test, considered in context with other diagnostic information, can be useful in the diagnostic process.

In addition, the exercise testing data provide information regarding the severity and progression of disease and can be used to monitor the effects of interventions such as exercise training. With respect to exercise, data such as maximal oxygen consumption, heart-rate response to different exercise intensities, and ventilatory responses to the exercise test are used to design the exercise program for the client. Finally, exercise test data are used to predict outcomes and survival in patients.

Health and Fitness Venues

For those with training in exercise physiology, there appear to be two primary types of positions in the health and fitness industry: one is to work in a private health club, YMCA/YWCA, or corporation-based center, and the other is to serve as a personal trainer. Employment in health clubs involves tasks such as providing fitness evaluations, designing exercise programs, and educating members about exercise, nutrition, and health. Personal trainers are often employed through a health club, but many are entrepreneurs who contract their services to clients on an individual basis. Regardless of the route of employment, personal trainers design exercise programs for their clients and then supervise the clients' individual exercise sessions.

Sports Conditioning Venues

The area of sports physiology, a subdiscipline of exercise physiology, emphasizes the study and application of exercise physiology to the improvement of athletic performance. Most coaches have historically been involved in the design and implementation of exercise and conditioning programs to improve the performance of their athletes. A strong knowledge base in sports physiology is clearly helpful in this regard.

More recently, the emergence of the personal trainer has led to many individuals serving as one-on-one conditioning coaches for some athletes, especially for individual sports such as distance running and cycling. As with many personal trainer situations, these types of positions are often entrepreneurial in that the trainers contract their services individually with their clients. At colleges, universities, and many large high schools, full- or part-time strength and conditioning coaches develop the conditioning programs for the athletes in many different sports. These types of positions require knowledge in not only sports physiology but also in other areas of exercise science (e.g., biomechanics and sports nutrition).

PROFESSIONAL ASSOCIATIONS

American College of Sports Medicine (ACSM)

ACSM
www.acsm.org

As mentioned previously, the ACSM has grown to become the leading organization in the world dedicated to the disciplines associated with exercise science and sports medicine. Its membership has grown from an initial 11 founding members to over 20,000 today. The ACSM has 12 regional chapters that hold their own meetings and programs. The annual national meeting grows almost every year and attracts several thousand participants each year. The national meeting includes lectures, tutorials, colloquia, and research presentations addressing all areas of exercise science and sports medicine.

American Physiological Society (APS)

APS
www.the-aps.org

The APS is an organization of scientists who specialize in the physiological sciences. Regular membership is restricted to those who conduct original research in physiology; however, other membership categories, such as student membership, are available.

American Alliance for Health, Physical Education, Recreation and Dance (AAHPERD)

AAHPERD
www.aahperd.org

AAHPERD is the primary professional organization for individuals in physical education and related disciplines. Because of the ties between exercise physiology and physical education, many exercise physiologists have AAHPERD membership and are active in the organization. However, because of AAHPERD's primary focus on teaching at the kindergarten through 12th-grade levels, the activity level of exercise physiologists in this organization is less than in the ACSM and APS.

National Strength and Conditioning Association

The NSCA was started in 1978 and was originally called the National Strength Coaches Association, which reflects its roots as an organization for individuals who work as strength and conditioning coaches, often at the collegiate or professional level. Since that time the organization has grown in size and scope and attracts members from the health and fitness industry and from competitive athletics.

American Association of Cardiovascular and Pulmonary Rehabilitation (AACVPR)

The AACVPR is an organization of physicians, nurses, exercise physiologists, and other health care professionals who specialize in cardiac and pulmonary rehabilitation. Student memberships are available.

WWW

AACVPR
www.aacvpr.org

PROMINENT JOURNALS AND RELATED PUBLICATIONS

The *American Journal of Physiology* was an important venue for exercise physiology research in the first half of the 1900s. Although this is still an important source of exercise-physiology-related research, the publication of *Journal of Applied Physiology* in 1948 was a significant event in that it became and remains a primary outlet for research in exercise physiology. European researchers also made use of *Internationale Zeitschrift für angewandte Physiologie einschlieslich Arbeitsphysiologie* (currently *European Journal of Applied Physiology*) and *Acta Physiologica Scandinavia*. In 1969, the ACSM began publishing *Medicine and Science in Sports* (currently *Medicine and Science in Sports and Exercise*), which has grown into another primary journal for research in exercise physiology and is the official journal of the ACSM. This journal publishes research in exercise physiology and other areas of exercise science and sports medicine. In addition, the ACSM also publishes *Exercise and Sport Sciences Reviews,* a quarterly publication that contains timely review articles by leading researchers.

Other professional organizations also publish journals with articles of interest to exercise physiologists. The APS publishes several different journals, one of which is *Journal of Applied Physiology*. As mentioned, this is a primary journal for original research in exercise physiology. In addition, *American Journal of Physiology* regularly publishes original research in exercise physiology. Other publications of the APS include *Journal of Neurophysiology, Physiological Reviews, News in the Physiological Sciences, The Physiologist,* and *Advances in Physiology Education.* AAHPERD's research journal, *Research Quarterly for Exercise and Sport,* has historically published and continues to publish research in exercise physiology. The NSCA publishes two journals, *Strength and Conditioning* and *Journal of Strength and Conditioning Research,* which as the name suggests, is a research journal in which original investigations that have application to strength training and conditioning are published. *Strength and Conditioning* publishes reviews and opinion articles with more direct application to the strength and conditioning professionals. The official journal of the AACVPR is *Journal of Cardiopulmonary Rehabilitation,* which publishes research articles addressing issues of cardiac and pulmonary rehabilitation.

As an indication of the growth of the field of exercise physiology, more than 25 scientific journals frequently publish research in exercise physiology. These include:

PRIMARY JOURNALS

Acta Physiologica Scandinavia
Applied Physiology, Nutrition, and Metabolism
British Journal of Sports Medicine
European Journal of Applied Physiology
International Journal of Sports Medicine
Journal of Applied Physiology
Journal of Physiology
Journal of Sports Medicine and Physical Fitness
Journal of Strength and Conditioning Research
Medicine and Science in Sports and Exercise
Pediatric Exercise Science
Pflügers Archives: European Journal of Physiology
Sports Medicine

RELATED PUBLICATIONS

American Heart Journal
American Journal of Clinical Nutrition
American Journal of Physical Medicine and Rehabilitation
American Journal of Sports Medicine
Archives of Physical Medicine and Rehabilitation
Circulation
Ergonomics
International Journal of Sports Nutrition and Exercise Metabolism
Journal of the International Society of Sports Nutrition
Journal of Orthopaedic and Sports Physical Therapy
Muscle and Nerve
Physical Therapy

FUTURE DIRECTIONS

Two trends in the population will likely significantly influence exercise physiology and exercise physiologists: (1) the dramatic increased incidence of obesity (and associated type 2 diabetes) and (2) the aging of the baby boom generation. Therefore, it seems likely that obesity, diabetes, and gerontology will continue to grab a larger share of attention in exercise physiology curricula and practice. Applied exercise physiologists would be well served by looking at these trends as opportunities to expand their practice and sphere of influence.

With respect to research, cutting-edge exercise physiology research must employ one of two approaches to take advantage of technological innovations. The first approach is the melding of genetics and molecular biology into the study of integrative exercise physiology. For example, specific genes that are associated with high-level exercise performance have been identified. Understanding how these genes and their products affect exercise performance at the organism level will be a key goal of future research. Second, advances in noninvasive measurement technology and sophisticated digital signal processing techniques will be increasingly employed by scientists to explore responses and adaptations to exercise. Therefore, increased training in bioengineering, software development, and mathematics will be expected of future exercise physiology researchers.

Finally, as the technical sophistication and medical importance of exercise physiology increases, it seems likely that academic exercise physiology will continue to drift away from its roots in physical education and move closer to physiology, biology, and medicine.

SUMMARY

Exercise physiology is the study of how the body responds, adjusts, and adapts to exercise. The knowledge base of exercise physiology is applicable to many settings, including clinics, laboratories, and health clubs. It is important for exercise science students to study the principles of exercise physiology and to be able to utilize this knowledge base to improve human performance and quality of life. For example, a track coach may use the principles of exercise physiology to design training programs for athletes that will enable them to improve their running times, whereas a fitness instructor may use the principles of exercise physiology to design exercise programs for the elderly that will make the performance of the activities of daily living easier. The area of exercise physiology has applications in a number of areas of exercise science.

study / QUESTIONS

1. Distinguish between a response and an adaptation to exercise. Provide examples of each.
2. Explain why the study of the cardiovascular system is of prime importance in the study of exercise physiology.
3. Define ergogenic aid and provide examples of different ergogenic aids, describing their potential uses and dangers.
4. Explain the importance of the study of exercise and the skeletal system.
5. Describe the phases of cardiac rehabilitation programs.
6. Define obesity, and outline current areas of study in exercise physiology related to obesity.
7. Outline the advantages and disadvantages of treadmill versus cycle ergometer exercise modes.
8. Explain the difficulty in defining an exercise physiologist.
9. Describe the process of clinical exercise testing, and explain its uses.
10. Explain the relationships among exercise physiology, physiology, and physical education.

Visit the IES website to study, take notes, and try out the lab for this chapter.

learning ACTIVITIES

1. Go to the NSCA website (www.nsca-lift.org/). Find information on the NSCA national conference and the NSCA Personal Trainers' conference. List the dates and locations of these conferences. Choose two sessions from each conference that relate to exercise physiology and write a two- to three-sentence summary for each session.

2. Go to the AAHPERD website (www.aahperd.org/index.cfm). Describe the membership options and benefits as they relate to you.

3. Visit the websites for the ACSM Certified Health Fitness Specialist certification and the NSCA Certified Personal Trainer certification. Compare the requirements for the two certifications.

suggested READINGS

Astrand, P. O., Rodahl, K., Dahl, H. A., & Stromme, S. (2003). *Textbook of work physiology: Physiological bases of exercise* (4th ed.). Champaign, IL: Human Kinetics.

Brooks, G. A., Fahey, T. D., & Baldwin, K. (2005). *Exercise physiology: Human bioenergetics and its applications* (4th ed.). Boston: McGraw-Hill.

Wilmore, J. H., & Costill, D. L. (2004). *Physiology of sport and exercise* (3rd ed.). Champaign, IL: Human Kinetics.

references

ACOG committee opinion. (2002, January). Exercise during pregnancy and the postpartum period. *International Journal of Gynecology and Obstetrics, 77*(1), 79–81.

Adams, G. R., Caiozzo, V. J., & Baldwin, K. M. (2003). Skeletal muscle unweighting: Spaceflight and ground-based models. *Journal of Applied Physiology, 95*(6), 2185–2201.

American College of Sports Medicine. (2010). *ACSM's guidelines for exercise testing and prescription* (8th ed.). Baltimore, MD: Williams & Wilkins.

American College of Sports Medicine Position Stand (1984). The use of anabolic-androgenic steroids in sports. *Sports Medicine Bulletin, 19*, 13–18.

American Physical Therapy Association. (1995). A guide to physical therapist practice, volume l: A description of patient management. *Physical Therapy, 75*, 709–748.

Arena, B., Maffulli, N., Maffulli, F., & Morleo, M. A. (1995). Reproductive hormones and menstrual changes with exercise in female athletes. *Sports Medicine, 19*, 278–287.

Armstrong, L. E., Casa, D. J., Millard-Stafford, M., Moran, D. S., Pyne, S. W., & Roberts, W. O. (2007). American College of Sports Medicine position stand. Exertional heat illness during training and competition. *Medicine and Science in Sports and Exercise, 39*(3), 556–572.

Astrand, P.-O. (1991). Influence of Scandinavian scientists in exercise physiology. *Scandinavian Journal of Medicine and Science in Sports, 1*, 3–9.

Bach, J. R., & Moldover, J. R. (1996). Cardiovascular, pulmonary, and cancer rehabilitation. 2. Pulmonary rehabilitation. *Archives of Physical Medicine and Rehabilitation, 77*, S45–S51.

Bailey, D. A., Faulkner, R. A., & McKay, H. A. (1996). Growth, physical activity, and bone mineral acquisition. *Exercise Sport Science Review, 24*, 233–266.

Bailey, S. J., Romer, L. M., Kelly, J., Wilkerson, D. P., DiMenna, F. J., & Jones, A. M. (2010). Inspiratory muscle training enhances pulmonary O2 uptake kinetics and high-intensity exercise tolerance in humans. *Journal of Applied Physiology, 109*, 457–468.

Balady, G. J., et al. on behalf of the American Heart Association Exercise, Cardiac Rehabilitation, and Prevention Committee of the Council on Clinical Cardiology (2010). Clinician's guide to cardiopulmonary exercise testing in adults. A scientific statement from the American Heart Association. *Circulation, 122*, 191–225.

Ballor, D. L., Katch, V. L., Becque, M. D., & Marks, C. R. (1988). Resistance weight training during caloric restriction enhances lean body weight maintenance. *American Journal of Clinical Nutrition, 47,* 19–25.

Barr, R. N. (1994). Pulmonary rehabilitation. In E. A. Hillegass & H. S. Sadowsky (Eds.), *Essentials of cardiopulmonary physical therapy.* Philadelphia: W. B. Saunders Company.

Bauman, W. A., Kahn, N. N., Grimm, D. R., & Spungen, A. M. (1999). Risk factors for atherogenesis and cardiovascular autonomic function in persons with spinal cord injury. *Spinal Cord, 37*(9), 601–616.

Bergstrom, J. (1962). Muscle electrolytes in man. *Scandinavian Journal of Clinical Lab Investigations, 68*(Suppl), 1–110.

Berryman, J. W. (1995). *Out of many, one: A history of the American College of Sports Medicine.* Champaign, IL: Human Kinetics.

Bhasin, S., Storer, T. W., Berman, N., Callegari, C., Clevenger, B., Phillips, J., Bunell, T. J., Tricker, R., Shirazi, A., & Casaburi, R. (1996). The effects of supraphysiologic doses of testosterone on muscle size and strength in normal men. *New England Journal of Medicine, 335,* 1–7.

Blimkie, C. J. R. (1992). Resistance training during pre- and early puberty: Efficacy, trainability, mechanisms, and persistence. *Canadian Journal of Sports Medicine, 17,* 264–279.

Blomstrand, E. (2006). A role for branched-chain amino acids in reducing central fatigue. *Journal of Nutrition, 136*(2), 544S–547S.

Borer, K. T. (1995). The effects of exercise on growth. *Sports Medicine, 20,* 375–397.

Borer, K. T. (2005). Physical activity in the prevention and amelioration of osteoporosis in women: Interaction of mechanical, hormonal and dietary factors. *Sports Medicine, 35*(9), 779–830.

Brooks, G. A. (1987). The exercise physiology paradigm in contemporary biology: To molbiol or not to molbiol—that is the question. *Quest, 39,* 231–242.

Brooks, G. A. (1994). 40 years of progress: Basic exercise physiology. In *40th Anniversary Lectures,* Indianapolis, IN: American College of Sports Medicine.

Buskirk, E. R. (1992). From Harvard to Minnesota: Keys to our history. *Exercise and Sport Sciences Review, 20,* 1–26.

Buskirk, E. R. (1996). Exercise physiology. Part I. Early history in the United States. In J. D. Massengale & R. A. Swanson (Eds.), *History of exercise and sport science,* pp. 367–396. Champaign, IL: Human Kinetics.

Butcher, S. J., & Jones, R. L. (2006). The impact of exercise training intensity on change in physiological function in patients with chronic obstructive pulmonary disease. *Sports Medicine, 36*(4), 307–325.

Cavanagh, P. R., Licata, A. A., & Rice, A. J. (2005). Exercise and pharmacological countermeasures for bone loss during long-duration space flight. *Gravity and Space Biology Bulletin, 18*(2), 39–58.

Chattipakorn, N., Incharoen, T., Kanlop, N., & Chattipakorn, S. (2007). Heart rate variability in myocardial infarction and heart failure. *International Journal of Cardiology, 120*(3), 289–290.

Colberg, S. R., Albright, A. L., Blissmer, B. J., Braun, B., Chasen-Tabor, L., Fernhall, B., Regensteiner, J. G., Rubin, R. R., & Sigal, R. J. (2010). Exercise and type 2 diabetes: American College of Sports Medicine and the American Diabetes Association: Joint position statement. Exercise and type 2 diabetes. *Medicine and Science in Sports and Exercise, 42*(12), 2282–2303.

Convertino, V. A. (1996). Exercise as a countermeasure for physiological adaptation to prolonged spaceflight. *Medicine and Science in Sports and Exercise, 28,* 999–1014.

Costill, D. L. (1994). 40 years of progress: Applied exercise physiology. In *40th Anniversary Lectures,* Indianapolis, IN: American College of Sports Medicine.

Cowie, C. C., Rust, K. F., Byrd-Holt, D. D., Eberhardt, M. S., Flegal, K. M., Engelgau, M. M., et al. (2006). Prevalence of diabetes and impaired fasting glucose in adults in the U.S. population: National health and nutrition examination survey 1999–2002. *Diabetes Care, 29*(6), 1263–1268.

Curtis, C. L., & Weir, J. P. (1996). Overview of exercise responses in healthy and impaired states. *Neurology Report, 20,* 13–19.

Damm, P., Breitowicz, B., & Hegaard, H. (2007). Exercise, pregnancy, and insulin sensitivity—what is new? *Applied Physiology, Nutrition, and Metabolism, 32,* 537–540.

Daniels, S. R., Arnett, D. K., Eckel, R. H., Gidding, S. S., Hayman, L. L., Kumanyika, S., et al. (2005). Overweight in children and adolescents: Pathophysiology, consequences, prevention, and treatment. *Circulation, 111*(15), 1999–2012.

Davis, J. M., Alderson, N. L., & Welsh, R. S. (2000). Serotonin and central nervous system fatigue: Nutritional considerations. *American Journal of Clinical Nutrition, 72*(2 Suppl), 573S–578S.

Deschenes, M. R. (2004). Effects of aging on muscle fibre type and size. *Sports Medicine, 34*(12), 809–824.

deVries, H. A., & Housh, T. J. (1994). *Physiology of exercise for physical education, athletics, and exercise science* (5th ed.). Dubuque, IA: W. C. Brown.

Dill, D., Arlie, B., & Bock, V. (1985). Pioneer in sports medicine. *Medicine and Science in Sports and Exercise, 17,* 401–404.

Dill, D. B. (1980). Historical review of exercise physiology science. In W. R. Johnson & E. R. Buskirk (Eds.), *Structural and physiological aspects of exercise and sport,* pp. 37–41. Princeton, NJ: Princeton Book Company.

Dimitrova, N. A., & Dimitrov, G. V. (2003). Interpretation of EMG changes with fatigue: Facts, pitfalls, and fallacies. *Journal of Electromyography and Kinesiology, 13*(1), 13–36.

Engardt, M., Knutsson, E., Jonsson, M., & Sternhag, M. (1995). Dynamic muscle strength training in stroke patients: Effects on knee extensor torque, electromyographic activity, and motor function. *Archives of Physical Medicine and Rehabilitation, 76,* 419–425.

Evans, W. J. (1995). What is sarcopenia? *Journal of Gerontology, 50A*(Special Issue), 58.

Faigenbaum, A. D., Kraemer, W. J., Blimkie, C. J., Jeffreys, I., Micheli, L. J., Nitka, M., & Rowland, T. W. (2009).

Youth resistance training: updated position statement paper from the National Strength and Conditioning Association. *Journal of Strength and Conditioning Research, 23*(5 Suppl), S60–S79.

Fleg, J. L., Morrell, C. H., Bos, A. G., Brant, L. J., Talbot, L. A., Wright, J. G., et al. (2005). Accelerated longitudinal decline of aerobic capacity in healthy older adults. *Circulation, 112*(5), 674–682.

Flegal, K. M., Carroll, M. D., Ogden, C. L., & Curtin, L. R. (2010). Prevalence and trends in obesity among US adults, 1999–2008. *Journal of the American Medical Association, 303*(3), 235–241.

Flegal, K. M., Graubard, B. I., Williamson, D. F., & Gail, M. H. (2005). Excess deaths associated with underweight, overweight, and obesity. *Journal of the American Medical Association, 293*(15), 1861–1867.

Fox, E. L., Bowers, R. W., & Foss, M. L. (1993). *The physiological basis for exercise and sport* (5th ed.). Dubuque, IA: W. C. Brown.

Gabriel, D. A., Kamen, G., & Frost, G. (2006). Neural adaptations to resistive exercise: Mechanisms and recommendations for training practices. *Sports Medicine, 36*(2), 133–149.

Gill, J. M. R., & Cooper, A. R. (2008). Physical activity and prevention of type 2 diabetes mellitus. *Sports Medicine, 38*(10), 807–824.

Gleeson, M. (2006). Can nutrition limit exercise-induced immunodepression? *Nutrition Reviews, 64*(3), 119–131.

Gollnick, P. D., & King, D. (1969). Effects of exercise and training on mitochondria of rat skeletal muscle. *American Journal of Physiology, 216*, 1502–1509.

Gore, C. J., & Hopkins, W. G. (2005). Counterpoint: Positive effects of intermittent hypoxia (live high:train low) on exercise performance are not mediated primarily by augmented red cell volume. *Journal of Applied Physiology, 99*(5), 2055–2057; discussion 2057–2058.

Hagberg, J. M., Rankinen, T., Loos, R. J., Perusse, L., Roth, S. M., Wolfarth, B., & Bouchard C. (2011). Advances in exercise, fitness, and performance genomics in 2010. *Medicine and Science in Sports and Exercise, 43*(5), 743–752.

Hand, G. A., Lyerly, G. W., Jaggers, J. R., & Dudgeon, W. D. (2009). Impact of aerobic and resistance exercise on the health of HIV-infected persons. *American Journal of Lifestyle Medicine, 3*(6): 489-499.

Haus, J. M., Carrithers, J. A., Carroll, C. C., Tesch, P. A., & Trappe, T. A. (2007). Contractile and connective tissue protein content of human muscle: Effects of 35 and 90 days of simulated microgravity and exercise countermeasures. *American Journal of Physiology, 293*(4), R1722–1727.

Hettinga, D. M. & Andrews, B. J. (2008). Oxygen consumption during functional electrical stimulation-assisted exercise in persons with spinal cord injury: Implications for fitness and health. *Sports Medicine, 38*, 825–838.

Heyward, V. H. (1996). Evaluation of body composition. Current issues. *Sports Medicine, 22*, 146–156.

Hoberman, J. M., & Yesalis, C. E. (1995, February). The history of synthetic testosterone. *Scientific American,* 76–81.

Holloszy, J. (1967). Effects of exercise on mitochondrial oxygen uptake and respiratory enzyme activity in skeletal muscle. *Journal of Biological Chemistry, 242*, 2278–2282.

Hough, D. O., & Dec, K. L. (1994). Exercise-induced asthma and anaphylaxis. *Sports Medicine, 18*, 162–172.

Housh, D. J., Housh, T. J., Johnson, G. O., & Chu, W. (1992). Hypertrophic response to unilateral concentric isokinetic resistance training. *Journal of Applied Physiology, 73*, 65–70.

Housh, T. J., Housh, D. J., & deVries, H. A. (2012). *Applied exercise and sport physiology* (3rd ed.). Scottsdale, AZ: Holcomb Hathaway.

Housh, T. J., Johnson, G. O., Stout, J., & Housh, D. J. (1993). Anthropometric growth patterns of high school wrestlers. *Medicine and Science in Sports and Exercise, 25*, 1141–1150.

Howe, T. E., Shea, B., Dawson, L. J., Downie, F., Murray, A., Ross, C., Harbour, R. T., Caldwell, L. M., & Creed, G. (2011). Exercise for preventing and treating osteoporosis in postmenopausal women. Cochrane Database of Systematic Reviews, Jul. 6(7): CD000333.

Hoyert, D. L., Heron, M. P., Murphy, S. L., & Kung, H. C. (2006). Deaths: Final data for 2003. *National Vital Statistics Reports, 54*(13), 1–120.

Hsieh, M., Roth, R., Davis, D. L., Larrabee, H., & Callaway, C. W. (2002). Hyponatremia in runners requiring on-site medical treatment at a single marathon. *Medicine and Science in Sports and Exercise, 34*(2), 185–189.

Hunter, G. R., McCarthy, J. P., & Bamman, M. M. (2004). Effects of resistance training on older adults. *Sports Medicine, 34*(5), 329–348.

Hurley, B. F., Hanson, E. D., & Sheaff, A. K. (2011). Strength training as a countermeasure to aging muscle and chronic disease. *Sports Medicine, 41*(4), 289–306.

Jacobs, P. L., & Nash, M. S. (2004). Exercise recommendations for individuals with spinal cord injury. *Sports Medicine, 34*(11), 727–751.

Jones, A. M., Wilkerson, D. P., DiMenna, F., Fulford, J., & Poole, D. C. (2008). Muscle metabolic responses to exercise above and below the "critical power" assessed using ^{31}P-MRS. *American Journal of Physiology: Regulatory, Integrative and Comparative Physiology, 294*, R585-R593.

Jones, N. L. (1988). *Clinical exercise testing* (3rd ed.). Philadelphia: W. B. Saunders.

Joyner, M. J. (2003). VO$_2$ max, blood doping, and erythropoietin. *British Journal of Sports Medicine, 37*(3), 190–191.

Kearny, J. T. (1996, June). Training the Olympic athlete. *Scientific American,* 52–63.

Kent-Braun, J. A., Miller, R. G., & Weiner, M. W. (1995). Human skeletal muscle metabolism in health and disease: Utility of magnetic resonance spectroscopy. *Exercise and Sport Sciences Review, 23*, 305–347.

Khan, B., Bauman, W. A., Sinha, A. K., & Kahn, N. N. (2011). Non-conventional hemostatic risk factors for coronary heart disease in individuals with spinal cord injury. *Spinal Cord, 49*(8), 858–866.

Kirshblum, S. (2004). New rehabilitation interventions in spinal cord injury. *Journal of Spinal Cord Medicine, 27*(4), 342–350.

Kokkinos, P., & Myers, J. (2010). Exercise and physical activity. Clinical outcomes and applications. *Circulation, 122*, 1637–1648.

Kroll, W. P. (1971). *Perspectives in physical education.* New York: Academic Press.

LaMonte, M. J., Blair, S. N., & Church, T. S. (2005). Physical activity and diabetes prevention. *Journal of Applied Physiology, 99*(3), 1205–1213.

Lawless, D., Jackson, C. G. R., & Greenleaf, J. E. (1995). Exercise and human immunodeficiency virus (HIV-1) infection. *Sports Medicine, 19*, 235–239.

Lee, S. Y., & Gallagher, D. (2008). Assessment methods in human body composition. *Current Opinion in Clinical Nutrition and Metabolic Care, 11*(5), 566–572.

Leon, A. S., Franklin, B. A., Costa, F., Balady, G. J., Berra, K. A., Stewart, K. J., et al. (2005). Cardiac rehabilitation and secondary prevention of coronary heart disease: An American Heart Association scientific statement from the Council on Clinical Cardiology (subcommittee on exercise, cardiac rehabilitation, and prevention) and the Council on Nutrition, Physical Activity, and Metabolism (subcommittee on physical activity), in collaboration with the American Association of Cardiovascular and Pulmonary Rehabilitation. *Circulation, 111*(3), 369–376.

Levine, B. D., & Stray-Gundersen, J. (2005). Point: Positive effects of intermittent hypoxia (live high:train low) on exercise performance are mediated primarily by augmented red cell volume. *Journal of Applied Physiology, 99*(5), 2053–2055.

Macaluso, A., & De Vito, G. (2004). Muscle strength, power and adaptations to resistance training in older people. *European Journal of Applied Physiology, 91*(4), 450–472.

Macko, R. F., Ivey, F. M., Forrester, L. W., Hanley, D., Sorkin, J. D., Katzel, L. I., et al. (2005). Treadmill exercise rehabilitation improves ambulatory function and cardiovascular fitness in patients with chronic stroke: A randomized, controlled trial. *Stroke, 36*(10), 2206–2211.

MacLaren, D. P. M., Gibson, H., Parry-Billings, M., & Edwards, R. H. T. (1989). A review of metabolic and physiological factors in fatigue. *Exercise and Sport Sciences Review, 17*, 29–66.

Malek, M. H., York, A. M., & Weir, J. P. (2007). Resistance training for special populations. In T. J. Chandler & L. E. Brown (Eds.), *Conditioning for strength and human performance.* Philadelphia: Lippincott Williams & Wilkins.

Malina, R. M. (1994). Physical growth and biological maturation of young athletes. *Exercise and Sport Sciences Review, 22*, 389–433.

McArdle, W. D., Katch, F. L., & Katch, V. L. (2007). *Exercise physiology: Energy, nutrition and human performance* (5th ed.). Philadelphia: Lippincott Williams & Wilkins.

Moritani, T., & deVries, H. A. (1979). Neural factors versus hypertrophy in the time course of muscle strength gain. *American Journal of Physical Medicine, 58*, 115–130.

Myers, J. (2005). Applications of cardiopulmonary exercise testing in the management of cardiovascular and pulmonary disease. *International Journal of Sports Medicine, 26*(Suppl 1), S49–55.

Myers, J., Prakash, M., Froelicher, V., Do, D., Partington, S., & Atwood, J. E. (2002). Exercise capacity and mortality among men referred for exercise testing. *New England Journal of Medicine, 346*(11), 793–801.

Nici, L., Donner, C., Wouters, E., Zuwallack, R., Ambrosino, N., Bourbeau, J., et al. (2006). American Thoracic Society/European Respiratory Society statement on pulmonary rehabilitation. *American Journal of Respiratory and Critical Care Medicine, 173*(12), 1390–1413.

Nieman, D. C. (1996). The immune response to prolonged cardiorespiratory exercise. *American Journal of Sports Medicine, 24*, S-98–103.

Nieman, D. C., Johanssen, L. M., Lee, J. W., et al. (1990). Infectious episodes in runners before and after the Los Angeles Marathon. *Journal of Sports Medicine and Physical Fitness, 30*, 316–328.

O'Brien, K., Nixon, S., Tynan, A. M., & Glazier, R. (2010). Aerobic exercise interventions for adults living with HIV/AIDS. *Cochrane Database of Systematic Reviews, Aug. 4*, (8); CD001796.

Peter, J. B., Barnard, R. J., Edgerton, V. R., Gillespie, C. A., & Stempel, K. E. (1972). Metabolic profiles of three fiber types of skeletal muscle in guinea pigs and rabbits. *Biochemistry, 11*, 2627–2633.

Pi-Sunyer, F. X. (1993). Medical hazards of obesity. *Annals of Internal Medicine, 119*, 655–660.

Potempa, K., Lopez, M., Braun, L. T., Szidon, J. P., Fogg, L., & Tincknell, T. (1995). Physiological outcomes of aerobic exercise training in hemiparetic stroke patients. *Stroke, 26*, 101–105.

Requena, B., Zabala, M., Padial, P., & Feriche, B. (2005). Sodium bicarbonate and sodium citrate: Ergogenic aids? *Journal of Strength and Conditioning Research, 19*(1), 213–224.

Roemmich, J. N., Richmond, R. J., & Rogol, A. D. (2001). Consequences of sport training during puberty. *Journal of Endocrinological Investigation, 24*(9), 708–715.

Roemmich, J. N., & Sinning, W. E. (1997). Weight loss and wrestling training: Effects on nutrition, growth, maturation, body composition, and strength. *Journal of Applied Physiology, 82*(6), 1751–1759.

Rogers, M. A., & Evans, W. J. (1993). Changes in skeletal muscle with aging: Effects of exercise training. *Exercise and Sport Sciences Review, 21*, 65–102.

Roger, V. L., et al. on behalf of the American Heart Association Statistics Committee and Stroke Statistics Subcommittee. (2011). Heart disease and stroke statistics – 2011 update. A report from the American Heart Association. *Circulation, 123*, e18–e209.

Rubinstein, S., & Kamen, G. (2005). Decreases in motor unit firing rate during sustained maximal-effort contractions in young and older adults. *Journal of Electromyography and Kinesiology, 15*(6), 536–543.

Ryan, A. S., Pratley, R. E., Elahi, D., & Goldberg, A. P. (1995). Resistive training increases fat-free mass and maintains RMR despite weight loss in postmenopausal women. *Journal of Applied Physiology, 79,* 818–823.

Sawka, M. N., Burke, L. M., Eichner, E. R., Manghan, R. J., Montain, S. J., & Stachenfeld, N. S. (2007). American College of Sports Medicine position stand. Exercise and fluid replacement. 39(2), 377–390.

Shaw, K., Gennat, H., O'Rourke, P., & Del Mar, C. (2006). Exercise for overweight or obesity. Cochrane Database of Systematic Reviews, 4, CD003817.

Sheffield-Moore, M., Paddon-Jones, D., Casperson, S. L., Gilkison, C., Volpi, E., Wolf, S. E., et al. (2006). Androgen therapy induces muscle protein anabolism in older women. *Journal of Clinical Endocrinology and Metabolism, 91*(10), 3844–3849.

Shi, X., Stevens, G. H. J., Foresman, B. H., Stern, S. A., & Raven, P. B. (1995). Autonomic nervous system control of the heart: Endurance exercise training. *Medicine and Science in Sports and Exercise, 27,* 1406–1413.

Siebens, H. (1996). The role of exercise in the rehabilitation of patients with chronic obstructive pulmonary disease. *Physical Medicine Rehabilitation Clinics of North America, 7,* 299–313.

Smith, H. L., Hudson, D. L., Graitzer, H. M., & Raven, P. B. (1989). Exercise training bradycardia: The role of autonomic balance. *Medicine and Science in Sports and Exercise, 21,* 40–44.

Sontheimer, D. L. (2006). Peripheral vascular disease: Diagnosis and treatment. *American Family Physician, 73*(11), 1971–1976.

Stiegler, P., & Cunliffe, A. (2006). The role of diet and exercise for the maintenance of fat-free mass and resting metabolic rate during weight loss. *Sports Medicine, 36*(3), 239–262.

Sulzman, F. M. (1996). Overview. *Journal of Applied Physiology, 81,* 3–6.

Sutton, J. R., Maher, J. T., & Houston, C. S. (1983). Operation Everest II. *Progress in Clinical and Biological Research, 136,* 221–233.

Tanaka, H., & Seals, D. R. (2003). Invited review: Dynamic exercise performance in masters athletes: Insight into the effects of primary human aging on physiological functional capacity. *Journal of Applied Physiology, 95*(5), 2152–2162.

Tarnopolsky, M. A. (2010). Caffeine and creatine use in sport. *Annals of Nutrition and Metabolism, 57* (Suppl 2), 1–8.

Terjung, R. L., Clarkson, P., Eichner, E. R., Greenhaff, P. L., Hespel, P. J., Israel, R. G., et al. (2000). American College of Sports Medicine roundtable. The physiological and health effects of oral creatine supplementation. *Medicine and Science in Sports and Exercise, 32*(3), 706–717.

Tesch, P. A., Komi, P. V., & Hakkinen, K. (1987). Enzymatic adaptations consequent to long-term strength training. *International Journal of Sports Medicine, 8,* 66–69.

Thoden, J. S. (1991). Testing aerobic power. In J. D. MacDougall, H. A. Wenger, & H. J. Green (Eds.), *Physiological testing of the high-performance athlete.* Champaign, IL: Human Kinetics.

Thomis, M., Claessens, A. L., Lefevre, J., Philippaerts, R., Beunen, G. P., & Malina, R. M. (2005). Adolescent growth spurts in female gymnasts. *Journal of Pediatrics, 146*(2), 239–244.

Thompson, P. D., Buchner, D., Pina, I. L., Balady, G. J., Williams, M. A., Marcus, B. H., et al. (2003). Exercise and physical activity in the prevention and treatment of atherosclerotic cardiovascular disease: A statement from the Council on Clinical Cardiology (subcommittee on exercise, rehabilitation, and prevention) and the Council on Nutrition, Physical Activity, and Metabolism (subcommittee on physical activity). *Circulation, 107*(24), 3109–3116.

Tipton, C. M. (1996). Exercise physiology. Part II. A contemporary historical perspective. In J. D. Massengale & R. A. Swanson (Eds.), *History of exercise and sport science.* Champaign, IL: Human Kinetics.

Tomassoni, T. L. (1996). Introduction: The role of exercise in the diagnosis and management of chronic disease in children and youth. *Medicine and Science in Sports and Exercise, 28,* 403–405.

Tsuji, H., Venditti, F. J., Manders, E. S., Evans, J. C., Larson, M. G., Feldman, C. L., & Levy, D. (1994). Reduced heart rate variability and mortality risk in an elderly cohort. The Framingham Heart Study. *Circulation, 90,* 878–883.

Wasserman, D. H., & Zinman, B. (1994). Exercise in individuals with IDDM. *Diabetes Care, 17,* 924–937.

Wecht, J. M., Marsico, R., Weir, J. P., Spungen, A. M., Bauman, W. A., & De Meersman, R. E. (2006). Autonomic recovery from peak arm exercise in fit and unfit individuals with paraplegia. *Medicine and Science in Sports and Exercise, 38*(7), 1223–1228.

Weir, J. P., Beck, T. W., Cramer, J. T., & Housh, T. J. (2006). Is fatigue all in your head? A critical review of the central governor model. *British Journal of Sports Medicine, 40*(7), 573–586; discussion 586.

Williams, J. H. (1991). Caffeine, neuromuscular function and high-intensity exercise performance. *Journal of Sports Medicine and Physical Fitness, 31,* 481–489.

Willoughby, D. S., & Rosene, J. (2001). Effects of oral creatine and resistance training on myosin heavy chain expression. *Medicine and Science in Sports and Exercise, 33*(10), 1674–1681.

Willoughby, D. S., & Rosene, J. M. (2003). Effects of oral creatine and resistance training on myogenic regulatory factor expression. *Medicine and Science in Sports and Exercise, 35*(6), 923–929.

Yesalis, C. E., & Bahrke, M. S. (1995). Anabolic–androgenic steroids. Current issues. *Sports Medicine, 19,* 326–340.

Young, J. C. (1995). Exercise prescription for individuals with metabolic disorders. Practical considerations. *Sports Medicine, 19,* 43–54.

Exercise Epidemiology

TRAVIS W. BECK

exercise epidemiology   ■

DEFINITION OF EPIDEMIOLOGY

Exercise epidemiology has been defined as the study of "factors associated with participation in a specific behavior—that is, physical activity—and how this behavior relates to the probability of disease or injury" (Dishman, Washburn, & Heath, 2004, p. 14). Thus, a central tenet of exercise epidemiology is the fact that participation in regular physical activity affects one's risk of developing certain diseases. For example, some of the early studies in exercise epidemiology found that individuals in manual labor occupations (e.g., railroad workers, bus conductors, dock workers) were less susceptible to coronary heart disease (CHD) than those who had a more sedentary occupation (e.g., office clerks, telephone operators). These investigations laid the foundation for future studies that examined the relationship between physical activity and other diseases such as diabetes, osteoporosis, and cancer.

A secondary component of exercise epidemiology involves the study of physical activity levels in certain populations and the various factors that are associated with participation in physical activity. This line of study was developed after it was established that regular physical activity was inversely related to the risk of developing specific chronic diseases. Thus, exercise epidemiology evolved as a subdiscipline of exercise science for the purpose of studying the relationship between exercise and the risk for various diseases.

ACTIVITIES OF EXERCISE EPIDEMIOLOGISTS

Exercise epidemiologists are primarily concerned with studying who exercises; what they do; and when, where, and why they do so. They seek answers to such questions as "To what extent are individuals within a particular society or culture physically active?" and "In which physical activities are individuals most likely to engage?" They may also study variations in physical activity patterns across certain groups based on race, age, sex, socioeconomic status, and so forth; why certain individuals are physically active, while others are not; and the links among physical activity, various diseases, and mortality. This information is important so "health care professionals can target specific populations of people for intervention, and highlight public consequences of current behavioral trends" (Lox, Ginis, & Petruzzello, 2006, p. 28).

HISTORY OF EXERCISE EPIDEMIOLOGY

The origins of exercise epidemiology date back to the Ancient Greeks, who recommended vigorous physical exercise as treatments for improving mental health and overcoming physical illness (Dishman et al., 2004). In the mid-1600s, gymnastics was advocated by the Swiss pharmacologist Joseph Duchesne for improving digestion, strengthening the heart and joints, and improving the circulation of blood in the lungs. Exercise was also supported by various scientists and physicians in the 1700s and 1800s. One primary contributor to the development of exercise epidemiology was Thomas K. Cureton, who performed some of the first research studies that examined the relationship between physical activity and health. Many of Dr. Cureton's students continued this line of research, thereby developing the foundation for exercise epidemiology.

The first research studies in exercise epidemiology focused on the relationship between CHD and physical activity. Morris et al. (1953), Paffenbarger and Hale (1975), and Slattery and Jacobs (1988) found that individuals involved in occupations that required a large amount of physical activity were less susceptible to CHD than those with a more sedentary occupation. These investigations led to several large, population-based studies that examined the relationship between physical activity and CHD—the Framingham Heart Study (Kannel & Sorlie, 1979) and the Tecumseh Community Health Study (Francis, 1961). These investigations were landmark studies in exercise epidemiology and provided the basis for much of the current work that examines the relationship between physical activity and the risk for various diseases such as cancer, type 2 diabetes, osteoarthritis, osteoporosis, and obesity.

AREAS OF STUDY IN EXERCISE EPIDEMIOLOGY

Cardiovascular Disease

Cardiovascular disease (CVD) alone accounts for approximately 20 percent of all deaths each year worldwide, and the numbers and percentages of deaths are projected to increase at unprecedented rates (Dishman et al., 2004; World Health Organization, 2012). In the United States, CVD has been the number one killer every year since 1900 (except 1918, the year of the great influenza epidemic), with an estimated economic cost of approximately $300 billion annually. Between 2012 and 2030, total direct medical costs of CVD are projected to triple, from $300 billion to $834 billion (American Heart Association, 2012). Thus, the fact that physical activity is associated with a decreased risk for CVD is extremely important from both a preventative and an economic standpoint. Most studies have found that expending about 1000 kcal per week with physical activity resulted in a 20 to 30 percent reduction in mortality risk for CVD, with additional risk reduction for activity-related energy expenditures greater than 1000 kcal per week (Lee & Skerrett, 2001). Perhaps the most prevalent form of CVD is CHD. Generally speaking, CVD is any disease that affects the cardiovascular system. CHD, however, is a type of CVD that involves atherosclerosis of the arteries that supply blood to the heart. Atherosclerosis is characterized by deposits of fatty plaques on the inner linings of arteries, thereby compromising blood flow to the tissues they supply. One of the most important factors influencing the development of atherosclerosis is the ratio of low-density lipoproteins and high-density lipoproteins (LDLs and HDLs, respectively) in the bloodstream. Specifically, high LDL levels increase the rate of atherosclerosis, while high HDL levels decrease it. Physical activity is also associated with increased HDL levels, thereby reducing development of atherosclerosis and CHD.

■ *cardiovascular disease*

Reducing the risk of developing CVD does not necessarily require strenuous exercise. Research has found that significant health benefits can be attained through moderate-intensity exercise (i.e., 40 to 70 percent of maximum capacity) performed on most days of the week (Durstine & Thompson, 2000).

Cerebrovascular Disease and Stroke

A **cerebrovascular disease** is any disease resulting from the obstructive effects of atherosclerosis in the arteries that supply blood to the brain. A **stroke** is the loss or impairment of bodily function resulting from injury or death of brain cells after insufficient blood supply. Most strokes occur due to the

■ *cerebrovascular disease*
■ *stroke*

development of a thrombosis (clotting in a vessel), stenosis (narrowing of the artery), or embolism (occlusion of a vessel by a circulating clot or atheroma) (Dishman et al., 2004). Strokes are a fairly common killer in the United States; they represent the third leading cause of death, behind CHD and cancer (Dishman et al., 2004). Physical inactivity is considered a secondary risk factor for a stroke (Kohl, 2001), and several studies (Sacco et al., 1998; Salonen, Puska, & Tuomilehto, 1982; Shinton & Sagar, 1993) found that the overall cerebrovascular disease risk was inversely related to the amount of regular physical activity performed by the study participants. Although the mechanism underlying an increased risk for stroke with inactivity is unclear, physical activity is inversely related to such factors as hypertension and obesity, both of which are primary risk factors for a stroke. It is also important to note that the cause of a stroke is often related to the atherosclerosis that occurs in CHD. Thus, any factor that reduces the risk for CHD (such as physical activity) may also be useful for decreasing the risk of a stroke.

Hypertension

hypertension ■ **Hypertension** is persistently high arterial blood pressure, which either may have no known cause (*essential hypertension*) or may be associated with other primary diseases (*secondary hypertension*). Blood pressure is determined by the total volume of blood in the cardiovascular system (see Chapter 5), the rate of blood flow, and the diameter of the vessels in which the blood is traveling. Of these factors, vessel diameter is by far the most important in determining blood pressure, although hypertension can result from an abnormal elevation of any factor that influences resistance to blood flow. Resistance to blood flow in the cardiovascular system is often referred to as the *total peripheral resistance* (TPR). The TPR is particularly important because it has been suggested that a regular exercise program can decrease resting blood pressure by reducing basal cardiac output and/or TPR (Fletcher & Bulpitt, 1994). In addition, results from at least one study suggest that exercise does not necessarily have to be of a high intensity to reduce blood pressure (Fagard, 2001). Specifically, Fagard (2001) reports that individuals who regularly performed exercise at intensities between 40 and 70 percent of aerobic capacity demonstrated fewer incidences of hypertension than inactive individuals. Thus, regular manual labor tasks, such as yard or garden work, can be of significant benefit in reducing blood pressure in hypertensive individuals.

Diabetes

As discussed in Chapter 5, diabetes is a chronic disease caused by a deficiency in the production of insulin or in the use of insulin to transport glucose from the blood into other tissues, thereby resulting in excess glucose in the blood (i.e., hyperglycemia). There are two primary types of diabetes: type 1, also known as insulin-dependent or juvenile diabetes, and type 2, also known as non–insulin-

type 1 diabetes ■ dependent diabetes. **Type 1 diabetes** typically develops during childhood and adolescence and is characterized by a failure of the pancreas to produce insulin.

type 2 diabetes ■ **Type 2 diabetes** is much more common than type 1 and occurs due to insulin insensitivity. Thus, although type 2 diabetics are usually capable of producing adequate amounts of insulin, their cells do not respond normally to it. Although type 1 diabetics can certainly benefit from regular physical activity, exercise does little to prevent or completely cure the disease. On the other hand, type 2 diabetes is preventable by diet, weight loss, and physical activity (Dishman et al., 2004). Specifically, development of type 2 diabetes is almost always linked with some degree of impaired glucose tolerance. The most effective way to reduce the progression of impaired glucose tolerance into type 2 diabetes is through weight loss by diet and increased physical activity. Although the mechanisms underlying type 2 diabetes have not been fully identified, physical activity probably reduces the risk of developing the disease by promoting fat loss and by increasing insulin sensitivity. Specifically, individuals with a high fat mass typically have a decreased insulin sensitivity. Therefore, activities that promote improvements in body composition, such as diet and exercise, are also beneficial in reducing the risk for type 2 diabetes. In addition, research has shown that exercise promotes the uptake of glucose from the bloodstream independent of insulin (Holloszy & Hansen, 1996). Thus, regular exercise can be very beneficial for type 2 diabetics because it helps lower blood glucose without the need for insulin. Box 6.1 is an abstract of a research study that examined the relationships among physical activity, sedentary behavior, and the metabolic syndrome.

Osteoporosis

Osteoporosis is a disease characterized by abnormally low bone mass and deterioration of bone tissue that leads to an increased risk of fractures. There

■ *osteoporosis*

---

box 6.1

Abstract of a research study that examined the relationships among physical activity, sedentary behavior, and the metabolic syndrome.

Hsu, Y. W., Belcher, B. R., Ventura, E. E., Byrd-Williams, C. E., Weigensberg, M. J., Davis, J. N., McClain, A. D., Goran, M. I., & Spruijt-Metz, D. (2011). Physical activity, sedentary behavior, and the metabolic syndrome in minority youth. *Medicine and Science in Sports and Exercise, 439*(12), 2307–2313.

PURPOSE: This study aimed to determine the associations among physical activity, sedentary behavior, and the metabolic syndrome (MetS) in Latino and African American youth using both subjective and objective measures of activity levels.

METHODS: Cross-sectional data from 105 participants from three pediatric obesity studies that share a core set of methods and measures (Latino 74%, female 75%, mean age = 13 ± 3 yr) were used. Measures included moderate-to-vigorous physical activity and sedentary behavior by accelerometry and 3-Day Physical Activity Recall (3DPAR), fat and lean tissue mass by BodPod™, fasting glucose, lipids, blood pressure, and waist circumference. Associations between physical activity, sedentary behavior, and MetS were examined using ANCOVA, Pearson correlations, partial correlations, and logistic regressions with adjustments for age, sex, ethnicity, fat and lean mass, and pubertal Tanner stage.

RESULTS: Accelerometry data showed that greater time engaging in moderate-to-vigorous physical activity was related to lower odds of the MetS (odds ratio = 0.49, 95% confidence interval = 0.25–0.98), independent of sedentary behavior and covariates, and inversely correlated with fasting glucose ($r = -0.21$, $P = 0.03$) and systolic blood pressure ($r = -0.25$, $P = 0.01$), adjusting for covariates. Data from the 3DPAR showed that higher levels of sedentary behavior were related to higher odds of the MetS (odds ratio = 4.44, 95% confidence interval = 1.33–14.79), independent of moderate-to-vigorous physical activity and covariates, negatively correlated with HDL-cholesterol ($r = -0.21$, $P = 0.04$) and positively correlated [with] systolic blood pressure ($r = 0.26$, $P = 0.009$), adjusting for covariates.

CONCLUSIONS: Future interventions aiming to improve metabolic health in youth should target both the promotion of physical activity and the reduction of sedentary behavior. Subjective and objective measures should be used in conjunction to better capture activity behaviors.

are two main types of osteoporosis: (1) primary osteoporosis, which includes both age-related and postmenopausal bone loss, and (2) secondary osteoporosis, which is bone loss caused by another disease that is independent of age or menopause. Although there may be some situations where physical activity is useful in treating secondary osteoporosis, regular exercise has a more pronounced effect on primary osteoporosis. Specifically, physical activity is particularly important for increasing peak bone mass during adolescence and young adulthood and for decreasing bone loss during aging. In addition, even though primary osteoporosis can occur in men, it is most prominent in women after menopause. Estrogen, which has a protective effect on bone tissue, undergoes a decrease in production during menopause. Thus, reduced estrogen levels after menopause typically result in greater breakdown of bone tissue and decreased bone mass. Physical activity levels typically decrease with age, thereby compounding the problem and further increasing the risk of osteoporosis. Numerous studies, however, found that weight-bearing exercises (e.g., walking, jogging, resistance training) promote increases in bone mineral density (Dembo & McCormick, 2000; Van Loan, 1998). Thus, exercise is often recommended as a preventative measure for osteoporosis as well as for reducing or stopping bone loss in postmenopausal women.

Cancer

cancer ▪ **Cancer** refers to a group of related diseases that result from the uncontrolled growth and spread of abnormal cells. Approximately 50 percent of men and 33 percent of women in the United States will develop some form of cancer in their lifetime. Although there are many different types of cancer, all forms occur in two general phases: (1) initiation and (2) promotion. During the *initiation phase,* normal cells are changed into potentially harmful cells by damage from mutational factors. During the *promotion phase,* however, tumor growth is stimulated by other agents, such as hormones. Over 80 percent of the studies that examined the influence of physical activity on the risk of cancer found that regular exercise has a protective effect, particularly for reducing the risk of colon cancer. Most of these investigations suggested that physical activity decreases the gastrointestinal transit time of foods, thereby reducing potential carcinogen contact with the lining of the colon. It also has been hypothesized that physical activity may reduce the risk of cancer by changing prostaglandin levels in the body (Shephard, 1995, 1996). Specifically, elevated prostaglandin E2 levels have been associated with decreased gut motility (capability of movement) and increased colon cell growth. Martinez et al. (1999), however, found that individuals who regularly exercised had lower prostaglandin E2 levels than those who were not as physically active. Thus, although more studies need to be done, there are several potential mechanisms by which exercise could reduce the risk of cancer. Box 6.2 provides an abstract of a research study that examined the effects of resistance training in lung cancer patients.

Mental Health

Approximately $150 billion is spent each year on mental health in the United States. Depression is one of the most common mental health problems, and it is estimated that 50 percent of the suicide deaths in the

box

6.2

Abstract of a research study that examined the effects of resistance training in lung cancer patients

Peddle-McIntyre, C. J., Bell, G., Fenton, D., McCargar, L., Courneya, K. S. (2012, Jan.). Feasibility and preliminary efficacy of progressive resistance exercise training in lung cancer survivors. *Lung Cancer, 75*(1), 126–132.

Lung cancer survivors exhibit poor functional capacity, physical functioning, and quality of life (QoL). Here, we report the feasibility and preliminary efficacy of a progressive resistance exercise training (PRET) intervention in post-treatment lung cancer survivors. Seventeen post-treatment lung cancer survivors (10 female), with a mean age of 67 (range 50–85), mean BMI of 25, and diagnosed with non–small cell lung cancer (94%) were recruited in Edmonton, Canada, between August 2009 and August 2010 to undergo PRET. The primary outcomes focused on feasibility including eligibility and recruitment rate, loss to follow-up, measurement completion, exercise adherence, and program evaluation. Secondary outcomes addressed preliminary efficacy and included changes in muscular strength (1 repetition maximum), muscular endurance (repetitions at 70% of 1 repetition maximum), body composition (DXA scan), physical functioning (6-minute-walk-test, up-and-go, sit-to-stand, arm curls), and patient-reported outcomes including QoL (SF-36, FACT-L), fatigue (FACT-F), dyspnea (MRCD), and patient-rated function (LLFI). Forty of 389 lung cancer survivors were eligible (10%) and 17 of the 40 (43%) were recruited. Over 80% of participants were able to complete all testing; two participants were lost to follow-up, and the median adherence rate was 96% (range: 25–100%). Ratings of testing burden were low (i.e., less than two out of seven for all items), and trial evaluation was high (i.e., greater than six out of seven for all measures). Paired *t*-tests showed significant increases in muscular strength ($p < .001$), muscular endurance ($p < .001$), six-minute walk distance ($p < .001$), up-and-go time ($p < .05$), number of arm curls ($p < .001$), and number of chair stands ($p < .001$). There were no significant changes in body composition or patient-reported outcomes. PRET is a feasible intervention with potential health benefits for a small proportion of lung cancer survivors in the post-treatment setting.

United States each year can be attributed to depression (Dishman et al., 2004). Although there are many different causes of depressive disorders, it has been suggested that depression may result from imbalances in neurotransmitters. Specifically, depression is linked with the dysfunction of the noradrenergic and serotonergic systems in the brain. The most common treatments for depression are medication, psychotherapy, or a combination of the two. Studies, however, found that exercise may be helpful in preventing depression (Dunn, Trivedi, & O'Neal, 2001; Stephens, 1988). For example, Stephens (1988) reported that a survey of nearly 7,000 Americans between 25 and 74 years of age indicated that individuals who performed little or no exercise reported more symptoms of depression than those who regularly participated in physical activity. In addition, a survey of 22,000 Canadians, ages 10 years and older, indicated that inactive people reported more symptoms related to negative moods than those who were moderately active or very active (Stephens, 1988).

It also has been suggested that exercise may be useful for treating depression. Specifically, physical activity was associated with improvements in self-ratings of depression that were similar to those from psychotherapy and drug treatment. The clinical effects of exercise, however, last longer than the effects of drugs (Babyak et al., 2000). Thus, in some cases, exercise is not only cheaper but also a more effective long-term treatment for depression than drugs and/or psychotherapy.

RESEARCH METHODOLOGIES

Incidence Rates

incidence rate ■

One of the most important measurements in exercise epidemiology is the incidence rate. An **incidence rate** is the frequency or number of events that occur over a defined time period, divided by the average size of the population at risk. There are three general categories of incidence rates: crude, specific, and standardized. *Crude rates* are based on a total population without considering any of the population characteristics such as the distribution of age, sex, or ethnicity. Thus, in some cases, crude rates are misleading. For example, it is inappropriate to compare crude breast cancer rates in two populations where the sex distribution varied greatly, because one population could simply have more women. One technique that can be used to overcome this drawback is to divide the population into subgroups and then calculate a specific rate. A *specific rate* involves computing the incidence rate for each subgroup of the population (e.g., for each age group, sex group, or ethnicity group). Although specific rates often allow for more valid comparisons than crude rates, the procedure can be somewhat cumbersome to perform, and the results are often difficult to interpret, particularly when numerous subgroups must be compared. An alternative to the specific rate, however, is the standardized rate. *Standardized rates* are crude rates that have been statistically adjusted to control for the effect of a population characteristic such as age or sex. This procedure can usually be performed with statistical software packages and allows incidence rates to be compared without the bias introduced by differences in such factors as age, ethnicity, or sex.

Cross-Sectional Surveys

cross-sectional surveys ■

Cross-sectional surveys measure risk factors and the presence or absence of a disease at the same time. Although these studies are relatively inexpensive, they cannot determine potential cause-and-effect relationships. For example, the results of a cross-sectional survey might indicate that low levels of physical activity are positively correlated with several CVD risk factors. The cross-sectional survey cannot, however, determine whether the low physical activity or the high risk factors came first. Thus, it is inappropriate to conclude that low levels of physical activity caused the CVD risk factors. Cross-sectional surveys are typically used to generate hypotheses regarding relationships between risk factors and diseases. They can also be used, however, to assess the prevalence of risk factors in a specific population. For example, one of the most common types of cross-sectional surveys is an ecological study, which examines the frequency of a particular risk factor and then compares this frequency with an outcome measure in a specific geographic location. This information can be very useful when describing the geographic distribution of various risk factors.

Case-Control Studies

case-control studies ■

Case-control studies use subjects who are selected based on the presence of the disease being investigated and then matched with controls—subjects who do not have the disease. Comparisons are then made between the two groups (cases and controls) for frequency of past exposure to potential risk factors for the disease. One of the most common uses of the case-control study is to examine the relationship between physical activity and various forms of cancer. For example, researchers select a sample of subjects who have some type of cancer.

Each subject is then matched for age and residence location with a control subject. The researchers then gather information from both the case and control subjects regarding the amount of physical activity they perform and other risk factors for cancer (e.g., smoking, alcohol use). After gathering all of the necessary information, the data from both groups are analyzed to determine whether a relationship exists between physical activity and the risk of cancer.

One of the disadvantages of the case-control study technique is that it is often difficult to find a representative control group. Thus, researchers often have to use multiple control groups to improve the probability of obtaining a representative group. Another disadvantage of the case-control study is *recall bias,* meaning that individuals who have experienced a disease such as cancer may think more about why they have the disease than healthy individuals, thereby making them more likely to avoid acknowledging potential risk factors. Furthermore, case-control studies allow for the investigation of only one disease outcome at a time. Despite these disadvantages, case-control studies are relatively quick and inexpensive. They also require a fairly small number of subjects and allow for the investigation of multiple risk factors at the same time. Thus, case-control studies are very useful for the initial development and testing of hypotheses to determine whether a more time-consuming study is needed.

Prospective Cohort Studies

A **prospective cohort study** is a study in which the subjects are randomly selected from a defined population (i.e., a cohort), and baseline information is collected regarding potential risk factors for the disease of interest. The subjects are then followed over time to track the incidence of the disease. Prospective cohort studies are usually very costly and much more time-consuming than either a cross-sectional survey or a case-control study. In addition, they can assess the effects only of those risk factors that are measured at the beginning of the study (i.e., baseline). The primary advantage of the prospective cohort study, however, is that the risk profile is established before the outcome is assessed. In addition, data collection can be controlled as the study is being performed. This allows the investigator to assess changes in risk factors over time, classify disease end points, and study multiple disease outcomes, some of which may not have been planned at the beginning of the study. Perhaps the most important advantage, however, is that it allows for an estimation of the true absolute risk of developing a disease.

■ *prospective cohort study*

Randomized Controlled Trial

The **randomized controlled trial** is considered the gold standard for testing a research hypothesis, because it gives the researcher more control than any of the other research designs. In a randomized controlled trial, the subjects are randomly assigned to either an experimental group or a placebo group. The experimental group subjects receive the intervention being studied (e.g., a drug, an exercise program, a nutritional supplement), while the placebo group receives a placebo. Both groups are tested before and after the intervention to determine whether the intervention had an effect when compared with the placebo. Thus, the most important factor is that the subjects are randomly assigned to the experimental and placebo groups. Randomization ensures that both groups possess similar characteristics. Thus, any differences noted between the two groups for any particular factor can be attributed only to the intervention being studied.

■ *randomized controlled trial*

There are also several drawbacks, however, to using the randomized controlled trial. For example, the study's subjects must agree to participate without knowing whether they will be in the experimental or the placebo group. Thus, randomized controlled trials are often conducted in a double-blind fashion, in which neither the subjects nor the investigators know the group assignments until after all the data have been collected. Another disadvantage is that it is often conducted with a very selective sample of subjects. Thus, in some cases, it is difficult to generalize the study's results to other populations. Furthermore, there are some research questions in exercise epidemiology that cannot be answered using a randomized controlled trial. For example, it would be extremely difficult to use a randomized controlled trial to determine which characteristics of an exercise program (e.g., exercise modality, frequency, intensity, or duration) are most important for reducing the incidence of CHD. This research focus is too broad—a randomized controlled trial is usually designed to answer a very specific question.

It is important to note that the questions that exercise epidemiology studies attempt to answer are often open-ended and require the measurement of multiple outcome variables. Thus, in some cases, prospective cohort studies or case-control studies are better suited for exercise epidemiology research questions, even though the randomized controlled trial is the gold standard.

TECHNOLOGY AND RESEARCH TOOLS

Unlike most areas of exercise science that rely heavily on the use of equipment (e.g., metabolic carts, skinfold calipers, isokinetic dynamometers) to measure physiological variables, in exercise epidemiology data is usually acquired through surveys and surveillance systems. Surveys are typically used to determine the prevalence of physical activity in a particular population. A **surveillance system,** however, involves conducting the same survey in a population every year for an extended time period to measure trends in physical activity. For example, the Behavioral Risk Factor Surveillance System (BRFSS) was the first such system used to estimate and monitor physical activity in the United States. The BRFSS uses a population-based telephone survey to estimate national and state trends in physical activity, obesity rates, and fruit and vegetable consumption (Dishman et al., 2004). Other examples are the National Health Interview Survey (NHIS) and Youth Risk Behavior Surveillance System (YRBSS).

Most survey systems generate large amounts of data that must be stored, organized, and analyzed. These tasks are usually handled by using statistical software packages such as SPSS (Statistical Package for the Social Sciences).

One technological advancement of note has been the development of exercise-based video gaming software. Video gaming has become very popular, particularly for children and teens. For both of these groups the risk of developing type 2 diabetes and obesity is growing; thus, any method that can be used to promote physical activity among them is important in preventing these diseases. Devices such as the Nintendo Wii, Kinect for Xbox 360, and PlayStation 3 all support a variety of games that call for varying levels of physical activity. Some games involve dancing or simple step aerobic activity; some mimic sports such as tennis, golf, and baseball; while others incorporate traditional exercise equipment such as cycle ergometers and stair climbers. In

surveillance system ■

SPSS Predictive Analytics Software
http://www-01.ibm.com/ software/analytics/spss

addition to home use, such systems can be used in physical education, physical therapy, research, and other settings.

EMPLOYMENT OPPORTUNITIES

In earlier times, most professionals in exercise epidemiology were employed in a college or university setting, where they taught courses in exercise epidemiology and conducted research in their area(s) of interest. Increased growth in the area of exercise epidemiology has created more employment opportunities in colleges and universities, as well as in nationally funded organizations such as the U.S. Department of Health and Human Services and the Centers for Disease Control and Prevention (CDC). Furthermore, individuals employed in health-related fitness settings are indirectly involved in exercise epidemiology. Personal trainers, YMCA directors, health club owners, strength and conditioning specialists, and physicians are all responsible for promoting physical activity. Thus, making a contribution to the field of exercise epidemiology does not require employment in a college or university setting.

CERTIFICATION

The American College of Sports Medicine (ACSM) offers a number of clinical- and specialty-based certifications available for those interested in pursuing a career in exercise epidemiology. These certifications include the following:

CLINICAL CERTIFICATIONS

Certified Clinical Exercise Specialist (CES)

Registered Clinical Exercise Physiologist (RCEP)

SPECIALTY CERTIFICATIONS

Certified Cancer Exercise Trainer (CET)

Certified Inclusive Fitness Trainer (CIFT)

Physical Activity in Public Health Specialist (PAPHS)

Each of these certifications has specific requirements for licensure, and those interested should visit ACSM's website (www.acsm.org) for more information.

PROFESSIONAL ASSOCIATIONS

The International Epidemiological Association (IEA)

The International Corresponding Club, as the IEA was first called, was founded in 1954 by John Pemberton of Great Britain and Harold N. Willard of the United States, with the advice and help of the late Robert Cruickshank. The first formal meeting took place at the Ciba Foundation in London in June 1956. The Association's goals are to facilitate communication among those engaged in research and teaching in epidemiology throughout the world and to engage in the development and use of epidemiological methods in all fields of health, including social, community, and preventive medicine and health services administration. These goals are achieved by holding scientific meetings and seminars; publishing journals, reports, monographs,

IEA
www.IEAWEB.org

transactions, and books; and networking among members. An international quarterly journal of epidemiology, *International Journal of Epidemiology,* was developed in 1971. The journal has proved to be a valuable function of the IEA and has enhanced the reputation and contribution of epidemiology.

American Heart Association (AHA)

The AHA was founded in 1924 to share research in cardiology and promote future studies in the field. In the early years, the AHA's primary goal was to educate the public about the dangers of heart disease. Today, the AHA publishes five scientific journals that are recognized as the premier publications in the areas of cardiovascular disease and stroke: *Arteriosclerosis, Thrombosis, and Vascular Biology; Circulation Research; Hypertension; Stroke;* and *Circulation.* The AHA also holds numerous conferences that address current research topics related to the cardiovascular system (e.g., hypertension, arteriosclerosis, atherosclerosis, pulmonary circulation, cerebrovascular disease, and stroke).

AHA
www.heart.org

American Diabetes Association (ADA)

The ADA was founded in 1940 to promote diabetes research and educate the general public regarding the etiology of diabetes and how the disease could be prevented and treated. The ADA publishes four scientific journals—*Diabetes, Diabetes Care, Clinical Diabetes,* and *Diabetes Spectrum*—that contain research articles addressing the pathophysiology of diabetes, new developments in diabetes treatments, and the important medical/legal issues involved in diabetes care. The ADA also publishes *DOC News,* which provides practical information for health care professionals regarding current issues in diabetes *(D),* obesity *(O),* and cardiovascular disease *(C).*

ADA
www.diabetes.org

American Cancer Society (ACS)

The ACS was established in 1913 as the American Society for the Control of Cancer (ASCC). Initially, the society's primary purpose was to increase public awareness of cancer and promote cancer research. The ACS has grown rapidly since that time and is now considered the worldwide leader in promoting cancer research and disseminating cancer information to the general public. The ACS publishes three scientific journals: *CA: A Cancer Journal for Clinicians, Cancer,* and *Cancer Cytopathology. CA: A Cancer Journal for Clinicians* is the primary journal and contains review articles of interest to oncologists, primary care physicians, nurses, and other allied health professionals interested in cancer prevention. *Cancer* and *Cancer Cytopathology* publish original research articles regarding the prevention, detection, diagnosis, and cure of cancer. The ACS also actively supports all areas of cancer research, providing approximately $108 million in research grants annually.

ACS
www.cancer.org

PROMINENT JOURNALS AND RELATED PUBLICATIONS

PRIMARY JOURNALS

American Journal of Epidemiology

International Journal of Epidemiology

Journal of Applied Physiology

Journal of Chronic Diseases
Journal of Clinical Epidemiology
Medicine and Science in Sports and Exercise

RELATED PUBLICATIONS

American Journal of Cardiology
American Journal of Clinical Nutrition
American Journal of Medicine
Atherosclerosis
CA: A Cancer Journal for Clinicians
Cancer
Cancer Cytopathology
Circulation
Circulation Research
Clinical Diabetes
Diabetes
Diabetes Care
Diabetes Spectrum
Hypertension
Journal of Hypertension
Journal of the American Medical Association
New England Journal of Medicine
Preventive Medicine
Stroke
The Physician and Sportsmedicine

FUTURE DIRECTIONS

Although it is a relatively new discipline in the exercise science field, exercise epidemiology is growing, and the number and breadth of employment opportunities will grow as the field continues to develop. One of the most significant areas of growth is in examining the factors that underlie childhood obesity. According to the Centers for Disease Control and Prevention (CDC, 2011),

> Childhood obesity has more than tripled in the past 30 years. The percentage of children aged 6–11 years in the United States who were obese increased from 7% in 1980 to nearly 20% in 2008. Similarly, the percentage of adolescents aged 12–19 years who were obese increased from 5% to 18% over the same period. In 2008, more than one third of children and adolescents were overweight or obese. Children and adolescents who are obese are likely to be obese as adults and are therefore more at risk for adult health problems such as heart disease, type 2 diabetes, stroke, several types of cancer, and osteoarthritis.

Obesity is most prevalent among lower income and minority groups, where it can affect as much as 50 percent of the population. Because there are relatively few drugs available to treat obesity, additional emphasis is placed

metabolic syndrome X ■

on physical activity as a measure for preventing/treating obesity. As indicated above, it is also important to note that obesity is often linked with other diseases. The simultaneous occurrence of diabetes, hypertension, and hyperlipidemia is defined as **metabolic syndrome X.** Metabolic syndrome X is, in turn, a major risk factor for CHD and cardiovascular mortality.

Another area that will be important in future exercise epidemiology research is the investigation of factors involved with all-cause mortality. *All-cause mortality* refers to deaths from all known factors. The United States has one of the lowest average life expectancies (approximately 74.3 years for men and 79.5 years for women) of developed countries (Dishman et al., 2004). Although a longer life expectancy does not necessarily ensure more years of good health, research has shown that increased levels of physical activity are associated with longer life spans (Lee & Skerrett, 2001). Specifically, the all-cause mortality risk is approximately 20 to 30 percent lower for those who expend at least 1000 kcal per week in physical activity (Dishman et al., 2004). Thus, future studies will be very useful in examining those characteristics of an exercise program (e.g., mode, intensity, frequency, duration) that are most important for increasing life span.

SUMMARY

Exercise epidemiology is the study of how physical activity relates to the probability of disease or injury. Many of the early studies in exercise epidemiology found that individuals with manual labor occupations were less susceptible to CHD than those who had a more sedentary occupation. These investigations laid the foundation for future studies examining the relationship between physical activity and other diseases such as diabetes, osteoporosis, and cancer. Exercise epidemiology evolved as a subdiscipline of exercise science for the purpose of studying the relationship between exercise and the risk for various diseases. There are several different areas of study in exercise epidemiology, including cardiovascular disease, cerebrovascular disease and stroke, hypertension, diabetes, osteoporosis, cancer, and mental health. Research conducted in each of these areas examines the link between physical activity and the risk for disease. There are various types of research methods used in exercise epidemiology, including incidence rates, cross-sectional surveys, case-control studies, prospective cohort studies, and randomized controlled trials. Of these, the randomized controlled trial is considered the gold standard for testing a research hypothesis, because it gives the researcher more control than the other research designs.

Perhaps the most significant area of growth in exercise epidemiology is in the study of childhood obesity. Childhood obesity is often linked with other diseases—diabetes, hypertension, and hyperlipidemia.

study / QUESTIONS

Visit the IES website to study, take notes, and try out the lab for this chapter.

1. Define exercise epidemiology and list some of the chronic diseases that are studied.

2. What is CVD, and why is it one of the most studied areas in exercise epidemiology?

3. Can hypertension be treated with an exercise program? If so, what are the proposed mechanisms for exercise-related decreases in blood pressure?

4. Describe the differences between type 1 (insulin-dependent) diabetes and type 2 (non–insulin-dependent) diabetes.

5. Which type of osteoporosis does physical activity have the largest impact on, and what is the mechanism for this effect?

6. Is physical activity an effective treatment for depression? If so, does it have any advantages over other treatments such as drugs and psychotherapy?

7. What is an incidence rate and what are the three general types of incidence rates?

8. What are the disadvantages of a cross-sectional survey?

9. Why is the randomized controlled trial considered the gold standard for testing a research hypothesis, and how is a randomized controlled trial conducted?

10. Why do the research tools used in exercise epidemiology differ from those used in most areas of exercise science?

11. What is the most common measurement tool in exercise epidemiology?

12. Most exercise epidemiology professionals are employed in a university or college setting. Describe some other occupations that contribute directly or indirectly to exercise epidemiology.

learning ACTIVITIES

1. Go to the CDC website and access the "Heart Disease" topic (www.cdc.gov/heartdisease). Use the links to gather information on the risk factors for cardiovascular disease and any recommendations for the standardization or improvement of the measurement of these factors. Use this information to write a one- to two-page paper.

2. Go to the ADA website (www.diabetes.org). Select "Diabetes Basics," then select "Risk Test". Follow the directions to determine your personal risk for diabetes. When you're finished, look at your results and the "Lower Your Risk Factsheet." Write a short summary of your 30-year risk assessment, including any recommendations for lifestyle changes.

3. Go to the ACSM website (www.acsm.org). Search for "hypertension." Write an abstract on ACSM's *Exercise and Hypertension Position Stand*.

4. Search the Internet to discover the spectrum of research being conducted in the area of osteoporosis. Write a brief synopsis of what you find.

suggested READINGS

Cyr, N. M. (2003). *Health promotion, disease prevention, and exercise epidemiology*. Lanham, MD: University Press of America.

Dishman, R. K., Washburn, R. A., & Heath, G. W. (2004). *Physical activity epidemiology*. Champaign, IL: Human Kinetics.

Gormley, J., & Hussey, J. (Eds.) (2005). *Exercise therapy: Prevention and treatment of disease*. Malden, MA: Blackwell.

references

American Heart Association (2012). Heart disease and stroke statistics: 2012 update. Retrieved from http://circ.ahajournals.org/content/early/2011/12/15/CIR.0b013e31823ac046

Babyak, M. A., Blumenthal, J. A., Herman, S., Khatri, P., Doraiswamy, P. M., Moore, K. A., Craighead, W. E., Baldewicz, T. T., & Krishnan, K. R. (2000). Exercise treatment for major depression: Maintenance of therapeutic benefit at 10 months. *Psychosomatic Medicine, 62*(5), 633–638.

CDC (2011). Health effects of childhood obesity (updated Sept. 2011). Retrieved from http://www.cdc.gov/healthyyouth/obesity/facts.htm

Dembo, L., & McCormick, K. M. (2000). Exercise prescription to prevent osteoporosis. *ACSM's Health and Fitness Journal, 4*, 32–38.

Dishman, R. K., Washburn, R. A., & Heath, G. W. (2004). *Physical activity epidemiology.* Champaign, IL: Human Kinetics.

Dunn, A. L., Trivedi, M. H., & O'Neal, H. A. (2001). Physical activity dose-response effects on outcomes of depression and anxiety. *Medicine and Science in Sports and Exercise, 33* (Suppl. 6), S587–S597.

Durstine, J. L., & Thompson, R. W. (2000). Exercise modulates blood lipids and lipoproteins, a great explanation and exercise plan. *ACSM's Health and Fitness Journal, 4*, 7–12.

Fagard, R. H. (2001). Exercise characteristics and the blood pressure response to dynamic physical training. *Medicine and Science in Sports and Exercise, 33* (Suppl. 6), S484–S492.

Fletcher, A., & Bulpitt, C. (1994). Epidemiology of hypertension in the elderly. *Journal of Hypertension, 12* (Suppl. 6), S3–S5.

Francis, T., Jr. (1961). Aspects of the Tecumseh Study. *Public Health Reports, 76*, 963–966.

Holloszy, J. O., & Hansen, P. A. (1996). Regulation of glucose transport into skeletal muscle. *Reviews of Physiology, Biochemistry, and Pharmacology, 128*, 99–193.

Kannel, W. B., & Sorlie, P. (1979). Some health benefits of physical activity: The Framingham Study. *Archives of Internal Medicine, 139*, 857–861.

Kohl, H. W., III. (2001). Physical activity and cardiovascular disease: Evidence for a dose response. *Medicine and Science in Sports and Exercise, 33* (Suppl. 6), S472–S483.

Lee, I. M., & Skerrett, P. J. (2001). Physical activity and all-cause mortality: What is the dose-response relation? *Medicine and Science in Sports and Exercise, 33* (Suppl. 6), S459–S471.

Lox, C. L., Martin Ginis, K. A., & Petruzzello, S. J. (2006). *The psychology of exercise: Integrating theory and practice.* Scottsdale, AZ: Holcomb Hathaway.

Martinez, M. E., Heddens, D., Earnest, D. L., Bogert, C. L., Roe, D., Einspahr, J., Marshall, J. R., & Alberts, D. S. (1999). Physical activity, body mass index, and prostaglandin E2 levels in rectal mucosa. *Journal of the National Cancer Institute, 91*, 950–953.

Morris, J. N., Heady, J. A., Raffle, P. A. B., Roberts, C. G., & Parks, J. W. (1953). Coronary heart disease and physical activity of work. *Lancet, 2*, 1053–1057, 1111–1120.

National Center for Health Statistics. (2005). *Heath, United States, 2005.* Washington, DC: U.S. Government Printing Office.

Paffenbarger, R. S., Jr., & Hale, W. E. (1975). Work activity and coronary heart disease mortality. *New England Journal of Medicine, 292*, 545–550.

Sacco, R., Gan, R., Boden-Albala, B., Lin, F., Kargman, D., Hauser, A., Shea, S., & Paik, M. (1998). Leisure-time physical activity and ischemic stroke: The Northern Manhattan Stroke Study. *Stroke, 29*, 380–387.

Salonen, J. T., Puska, P., & Tuomilehto, J. (1982). Physical activity and risk of myocardial infarction, cerebral stroke, and death: A longitudinal study in Eastern Finland. *American Journal of Epidemiology, 115*, 526–537.

Shephard, R. J. (1995). Exercise and cancer: Linkages with obesity. *International Journal of Obesity, 19*, S62–S68.

Shephard, R. J. (1996). Exercise and cancer: Linkages with obesity. *Critical Reviews in Food Science and Nutrition, 36*, 321–339.

Shinton, R., & Sagar, G. (1993). Lifelong exercise and stroke. *British Medical Journal, 307*, 231–234.

Slattery, M. L., & Jacobs, Jr., D. R. (1988). Physical fitness and cardiovascular disease mortality: The U.S. Railroad Study. *American Journal of Epidemiology, 127*, 571–580.

Stephens, T. (1988). Physical activity and mental health in the United States and Canada: Evidence from four population surveys. *Preventive Medicine, 17*, 35–47.

Van Loan, M. D. (1998). What makes good bones? Factors affecting bone health. *ACSM's Health and Fitness Journal, 2*, 27–34.

World Health Organization (2012). Cardiovascular disease: The atlas of heart disease and stroke. Retrieved from http://www.who.int/cardiovascular_diseases/resources/atlas/en/

Athletic Training

KYLE T. EBERSOLE • RONALD E. PFEIFFER

DEFINITION OF AN ATHLETIC TRAINER

According to the **Board of Certification (BOC)** for the practice of athletic trainer, **athletic trainers (ATs)** are "healthcare professionals who collaborate with physicians to optimize activity and participation of patients and clients" (BOC, 2011). The practice of athletic training includes a wide array of knowledge and skills encompassing the prevention, examination, diagnosis, treatment, and rehabilitation of acute, subacute, and chronic neuromuscular conditions involving impairment, functional limitations, and disabilities.

The scope of the practice of athletic training is defined within the *Athletic Training Educational Competencies (Competencies)* and the *Role Delineation Study (RDS)*. The Competencies were established by the National Athletic Trainers' Association (**NATA**), whereas the RDS was conducted and published by the BOC. Both documents are generally revised every 5 years to ensure that they reflect the most current best-practice guidelines for ATs. The 5th edition of the Competencies and the 6th edition of the RDS were published in 2010.

PROFESSIONAL RESPONSIBILITIES OF THE ATHLETIC TRAINER

Employment settings for an athletic trainer include high schools, colleges and universities, professional sports teams, hospitals, rehabilitation clinics, physician offices, corporate and industrial settings, the military, and the performing arts (see Exhibit 7.1). Regardless of the employment setting, the practice of athletic training by an AT is informed and guided by the practice domains identified by the RDS and by state practice acts and regulations. ATs work under the direction of physicians, as prescribed by state licensure statutes. The 6th edition of the RDS identifies the following five practice domains (BOC, 2010):

1. Injury/illness prevention and wellness protection
2. Clinical evaluation and diagnosis
3. Immediate and emergency care
4. Treatment and rehabilitation
5. Organizational and professional health and well-being

The relative amount of time spent in each practice domain will vary according to the employment setting. For example, a typical day for an athletic trainer employed in a traditional high school or collegiate setting will likely include activities within each practice domain, whereas an AT employed as a physician extender may spend a majority of the day providing services associated with evaluation, treatment, and rehabilitation.

HISTORY OF ATHLETIC TRAINING

Historical records indicate that some of the earliest known athletic trainers were associated with the athletes of the ancient Greek civilization. In those days the athletic trainers were known as *paidotribi,* meaning "youth, or boy, rubbers" (Arnheim & Prentice, 1993). Although it is doubtful that these early athletic trainers provided much more than simple massages and basic nutritional advice to their athletes, they were no doubt greatly appreciated. The "modern" version of the athletic trainer first evolved in asso-

exhibit 7.1

Typical athletic training rooms.

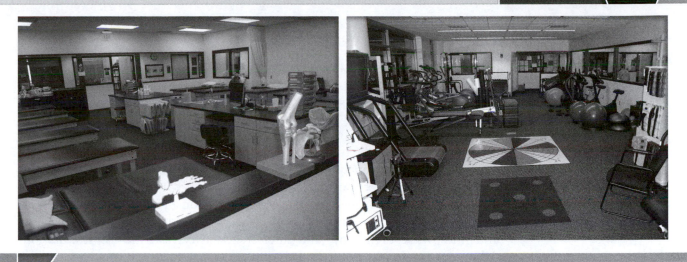

ciation with the growth of intercollegiate athletes in the late 19th and early 20th centuries in the United States. As sports programs grew in size, it was inevitable that the numbers of injuries would increase as well. This is particularly true in the sport of tackle football, where safety equipment was extremely crude and offered little protection from the forces of the game. As intercollegiate athletic programs grew in popularity during the first half of the 20th century, there was parallel growth in the numbers of athletic trainers associated with these programs. Because no formal professional education programs for athletic trainers existed, much of their knowledge was learned on the job and borrowed from the medical community.

The need for a professional association for athletic trainers became apparent during the 1940s, when a number of regional athletic training associates began to meet on a regular basis. Thus, the stage was set for the establishment of a professional association of athletic trainers at the national level. On June 24–25, 1950, the first national meeting of athletic trainers was held in Kansas City, Missouri, and the National Athletic Trainers' Association was formed. This first meeting was attended by 101 athletic trainers from across the United States (O'Shea, 1980). The following year, the first organized meeting of the newly formed association was held on June 22–24, again in Kansas City, Missouri (O'Shea, 1980).

Five years later, NATA approved the publication of its professional journal, *The Journal of the National Athletic Trainers' Association*, which was published quarterly, and is now called *Journal of Athletic Training*. Many changes occurred in both NATA and the profession of athletic training during the next several decades, as several committees were formed to oversee such functions as professional education, certification, and membership.

On June 21, 1967, the American Medical Association (AMA) first recognized the role of the athletic trainer as an important part of an athlete's health care team. In essence, the AMA recognized that the AT formed an extremely valuable link between the athlete, coach, and physician. On June 22, 1990, the AMA's Council on Medical Education (CME) formally recognized athletic training as an allied health profession. This major milestone was achieved by NATA-PEC chairman Dr. Robert Behnke, former chairman Dr. Gary Delforge, NATA vice president Dr. John Schrader, NATA executive director Alan A. Smith, and a small group of other NATA members. AMA recognition brought with it a significant amount of prestige for the athletic training profession.

TECHNOLOGY AND TOOLS

The modern sports medicine clinic is typically equipped with an array of exercise machines, both isokinetic and isotonic. State-of-the-art isokinetic machines such as Cybex and Biodex (see Exhibit 7.2) are highly sophisticated rehabilitation devices that typically include computer hardware and software used to both assess and record patient progress.

electrotherapeutic ▪
devices

In addition, athletic trainers receive extensive training in the proper application of **electrotherapeutic devices**—machines that use electrical energy in the treatment of disease or injury. Those commonly used by athletic trainers include transcutaneous electrical nerve stimulation (TENS), ultrasound, galvanic stimulators, neuromuscular electrical stimulation (NMES), shortwave and microwave diathermy, and interferential electrical muscle stimulation. All of these devices can be used during the injury recovery process. Athletic trainers receive formal education in the proper application and protocols used in exercise rehabilitation and reconditioning.

EDUCATIONAL PREPARATION

ATEP ▪

Students interested in becoming Certified Athletic Trainers (ATCs) must earn a degree requiring courses from an accredited athletic training curriculum. Athletic training education programs (**ATEP**) are commonly housed in Kinesiology or Exercise Science departments, as the basic science and movement science preparation of Kinesiology and Exercise Science degree programs provide a strong foundation for the athletic training–specific clinical

exhibit / **7.2** Biodex isokinetic dynamometer.

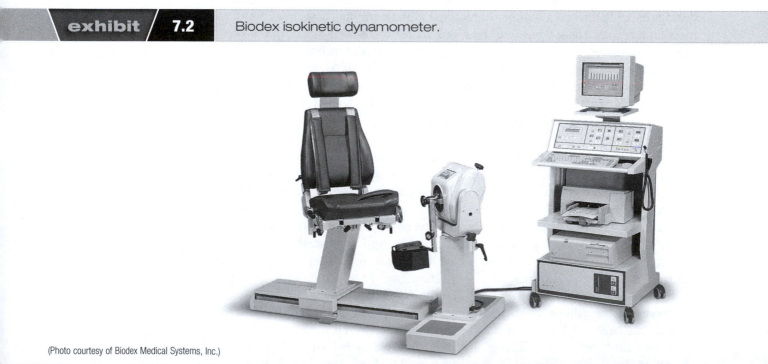

(Photo courtesy of Biodex Medical Systems, Inc.)

courses. Athletic training is an academic major or graduate equivalent major program that is accredited by the Commission on Accreditation of Athletic Training Education (**CAATE**). The current minimum entry point into the profession of athletic training is at the baccalaureate level; however, the number of entry-level master's degree programs is growing. By 2014–2015, all accredited ATEPs must lead to a degree in athletic training (NATA, 2009). Upon completion of a CAATE-accredited ATEP, students are eligible to obtain national certification granted by the independent BOC.

■ *CAATE*

CAATE
www.caate.net

Accreditation of Programs

During the late 1960s, the "professional advancement committee," a subcommittee of NATA, began developing guidelines for the structure of future academic programs in athletic training. It was determined that NATA would grant approved curriculum status to programs meeting the minimum requirements. In 1969, only two schools met the requirements for NATA approval of their curricula in athletic training—the University of New Mexico and Mankato State College (O'Shea, 1980). Interest in such programs was quick to develop, however, and by 1979, there were 23 NATA-approved undergraduate curricula.

AMA recognition of athletic training as an allied health profession in 1990 signaled a transition in the professional education of athletic trainers. Effective in 1993, all entry-level athletic training programs were evaluated by the AMA's Committee on Allied Health Education and Accreditation (CAHEA) instead of using NATA education subcommittee guidelines. Professional accreditation by an "outside" agency, the AMA, was a major step in the professional advancement of athletic training. CAHEA was ultimately replaced by another accreditation body known as the Committee on Accreditation of Allied Health Education Programs (**CAAHEP**), which worked in harmony with the Joint Review Committee–Athletic Training (**JRC–AT**) of NATA until the summer of 2006, when yet another milestone in education program accreditation was achieved with the formation of the CAATE. The JRC–AT determined that self-accreditation via CAATE will best position the athletic training profession with other allied health professions. CAATE is sponsored by the American Academy of Pediatrics, the American Orthopaedic Society for Sports Medicine, and NATA.

■ *CAAHEP*
■ *JRC–AT*

CAATE now accredits all undergraduate entry-level athletic training education programs. At the time of this writing, there were approximately 350 CAATE accredited professional entry-level programs in the United States. (A complete list of CAATE-accredited programs can be found on its website.) Accreditation ensures that all educational programs deliver a quality program based on the:

- *Educational Competencies* established by NATA
- *Role Delineation Study and Standards of Practice* established by the BOC
- *Standards for Accreditation* established by CAATE

Entry-Level Education

Entry-level athletic training education uses a competency-based educational model in both classroom and clinical settings. The competencies for students in athletic training include specific knowledge and skills organized into eight domains of clinical practice:

1. Evidence-based practice
2. Prevention and health promotion
3. Clinical examination and diagnosis
4. Acute care of injury and illness
5. Therapeutic interventions
6. Psychosocial strategies and referral
7. Health care administration
8. Professional development and responsibility

The 5th edition of the Competencies included a reorganization of the clinical proficiencies resulting in removing the proficiencies from each domain of practice and creating a separate section for all proficiencies. This new section, Clinical Integrated Proficiencies (CIPs), is designed to be a measure of real-life application. Programs are encouraged to assess student performance of CIPs on actual patients when possible. If this is not possible, standardized/simulated patients or scenarios are typically used to measure student proficiency.

Subject areas

The eight domains of practice must be incorporated into the ATEP via classroom and clinical instruction components. Current CAATE standards do not require specific courses; rather, general subject matter areas are required and must be established in the program. ATEPs, however, are given considerable flexibility to develop and implement a program based on the unique aspects of each institution. Here are the subject matter areas required for ATEPs:

The Facts About Certified Athletic Trainers and NATA
www.nata.org/athletic-training

BASIC AND APPLIED SCIENCES

- Human anatomy
- Human physiology
- Chemistry
- Biology
- Physics
- Statistics and research design
- Exercise physiology
- Kinesiology/biomechanics

PROFESSIONAL CONTENT

- Risk management and injury prevention
- Pathology of injuries and illnesses
- Orthopedic clinical examination and diagnosis
- Medical conditions and disabilities
- Acute care of injuries and illnesses
- Therapeutic modalities
- Rehabilitation conditioning, rehabilitative exercise
- Pharmacology
- Psychosocial intervention and referral
- Nutritional aspects of injuries and illnesses
- Health care administration

Clinical Education

Athletic training students are required to participate in a minimum of two years of academic **clinical education.** These experiences must be organized to provide meaningful hands-on experiences associated with a variety of different patient populations defined but not limited to gender, varying levels of risk, utilization of protective equipment, and general medical conditions that address the continuum of care. Clinical experiences provide students with opportunities to practice under the direct supervision of qualified clinical instructors (i.e., ATCs or other credentialed health care professionals). Clinical experiences must occur in the context of patient care in a variety of settings. All clinical instruction that involves an assessment of the students' mastery of the competencies must be provided by an approved clinical instructor (ACI). In many cases, athletic training students will gain experience with high school and collegiate populations and in unique and exciting settings such as a physician's office or an industrial clinical environment. In addition, athletic training students are often provided with opportunities to view surgeries, learn from a variety of health care professionals, and learn many of the essential administrative tasks required for the successful operation of an athletic training facility. For many students, the clinical education component of the ATEP is the most rewarding and interesting.

■ *clinical education*

Graduate Education

Two types of graduate education programs in athletic training are offered in the United States: CAATE-accredited entry-level master's degree programs and NATA-accredited post-certification graduate programs. Accredited entry-level graduate programs are designed for those students who have an undergraduate degree in a field other than athletic training. Requirements in the Competencies are identical to those of the CAATE-accredited undergraduate programs, including the two-year minimum clinical education requirement. As of December 2011, there were 25 CAATE-accredited entry-level master's programs. A complete list of such programs is available at the CAATE website.

Entry-Level Graduate Programs in Athletic Training
www.caate.net

NATA-accredited post-certification programs are designed for those students who possess an undergraduate degree in athletic training and are interested in earning an advanced degree. Most of these programs offer a master's degree, although doctoral degrees are also available at some programs. As of December 2011, there were 15 NATA-accredited post-professional graduate programs. A complete list of such programs is available at the NATA website.

Post-Professional Graduate Education Programs
http://www.nata.org/education/ educational-programs/ accredited-programs

BOC CERTIFICATION

December 31, 1969, was a historic date in the profession: This was the date of the first NATA certification examination. Prior to this date, no form of standardized examination existed for the purposes of establishing a minimal competency level for the entry-level athletic trainer. In 1970, a formal NATA certification committee (later the Board of Certification) was established to oversee the examination process.

The first NATA certification examination was developed with the help of the Professional Examination Service (PES) of the American Public Health Association.

History of the BOC Examination

The first certification examination, given in 1969, was designed to verify what were considered to be the cognitive and psychomotor skills necessary for an athletic trainer. The test consisted of both a written and an oral/practical component. With the inception of the certification exam, all currently practicing athletic trainers were grandfathered (automatically certified); only those individuals wishing to enter the profession were required to sit for the examination.

In 1973, the following general requirements were established by NATA in order to sit for the certification examination:

1. College graduate with a teaching license
2. Work under a NATA-certified trainer
   a. Approved curricula (2 years)
   b. Physical therapy degree (2 years)
   c. Apprenticeship (2 years)
3. One-year NATA membership prior to examination

BOC Examination Eligibility Today

Since the early days of the NATA certification examination, the profession of athletic training has changed significantly in virtually all aspects of the field. Although most of the entry-level jobs in the 1970s were in the high school and collegiate settings, this shifted to a new venue in the 1980s: the sports medicine clinic. In addition, the educational requirements evolved, placing more emphasis on specialized course work, requiring more structure in the practical hours, and eliminating the teaching certificate requirement. Thus, the certification examination process also has been modified significantly to better reflect changes in the profession.

The headquarters for the BOC are currently located in Omaha, Nebraska, where a full-time staff provides a number of certification and continuing education services to athletic trainers. The BOC is a member of the National Organization of Competency Assurance (NOCA), located in Washington, DC.

Several major structural changes that took place during the 1980s had a significant impact on the certification testing process. The certification committee formally separated from NATA in 1989 to become an independent, incorporated certification body, the Board of Certification. This change was viewed as an important step in improving the professional status and recognition of the certification examination process.

A new professional testing agency was brought into the process in an effort to make the examination as up to date as possible. Currently, CASTLE® Worldwide, Inc., of Morrisville, North Carolina, is charged with developing and administering the BOC certification examination.

The test itself was modified significantly and now consists of three major components: written questions, practical/oral exam, and written simulation. These three components are designed to test candidates on their mastery of the essential cognitive skills, clinical proficiencies, and psychomotor skills that have been identified as necessary for the entry-level AT. The BOC presently requires the following in order to qualify as a candidate for the BOC certification examination:

1. Endorsement of the exam application by the recognized program director of the CAATE-accredited program.

2. Proof of current certification in emergency cardiac care (ECC). Must include adult and pediatric CPR, airway obstruction, second rescuer CPR, AED, and barrier devices.

The BOC provides a detailed description of the certification examination application process, including application criteria and specific requirements, in the "BOC Exam Candidate Handbook," available by visiting the BOC website.

BOC Exam Candidate Qualifications and Handbook
www.bocatc.org

BOC Examination Format

Until 2007, the BOC examination format consisted of three components: (1) 150 written multiple-choice questions, (2) an oral practical administered by two ATCs, and (3) a written simulation designed to evaluate the candidate's real-life decision-making skills. In June 2007, the BOC moved to an online examination format, which is now the only format for the exam.

The current BOC certification exam consists of 175 scored and unscored (experimental) questions delivered in a combination of the following formats:

1. Multiple-choice items
2. Stand-alone "alternative" items such as drag and drop, text-based simulation, multi-select, and hot spot
3. Focused testlets that consist of a scenario followed by five key/critical questions related to that scenario

The BOC examination is offered three times annually at various locations throughout the United States. In the event a candidate does not pass the examination, he or she has one year to retake and pass the exam.

Candidates taking the exam will not know which questions are scored and unscored (experimental). A total of 4 hours is allotted to complete the exam. All 175 test items are presented in one part, and candidates have the ability to move forward or backward throughout the entire exam.

Certification is granted, and a BOC certification number is awarded upon successful completion of the BOC examination and submission of all required documentation. At that time, a candidate is legally allowed to claim the credential of ATC.

BOC Recertification Requirements

Successful completion of the BOC certification exam is the start of a career-long commitment to continuing education. In order to maintain a current and active Certified Athletic Trainer credential, all ATs must fulfill the recertification requirements. As of December 2011, the BOC is implementing a process that will end the staggered recertification process and move to a 2-year reporting cycle with common expiration dates for all ATs.

The current recertification requirements include:

- Adherence to the BOC *Standards of Professional Practice*
- Submission of the BOC Annual Recertification Fee
- Maintenance of emergency cardiac care
- Completion of *continuing education units (CEUs)*

A significant component of recertification is the completion of continuing education (CE). According to the BOC, the CE requirements are designed to ensure that the BOC ATC continues to:

- Stay on the cutting edge in the field of athletic training
- Obtain current professional development information
- Explore new knowledge in specific content areas
- Master new athletic training–related skills and techniques
- Expand approaches to effective athletic training
- Further develop professional judgment
- Conduct professional practice in an ethical and appropriate manner

The current 3-year recertification process requires the completion of 75 CEUs every 3 years. As of January 2014, ATs will be required to report 50 CEUs every 2 years. The required number of CEUs must meet the minimum categorical requirements established by the BOC. The current CEU categories include:

- Category A (BOC-approved provider programs) includes events such as workshops, seminars, conferences, or home study courses.
- Category B (professional development) includes activities such as professional speaking engagements, presentation of research at a conference, and authorship of a research publication, a textbook, or multimedia material.
- Category C (post-certification college/university coursework) includes completion of courses that reflect one or more of the practice domains as identified in the current RDS.
- Category D (individualized options) encompasses activities such as online learning and educational programs and professionally relevant, but not BOC-approved, seminars, conferences, and/or workshops.

To receive credit for a CEU, an AT must utilize the online CE reporting system at the BOC website. This online system allows ATs to record and submit all CE activities. Evidence of completing and earning specific CEU's must be kept on file by the AT in the event of an audit by the BOC.

STATE REGULATION OF ATHLETIC TRAINERS

Although having a well-established process for professional certification ensures the general public of some level of quality control (minimum level of competence) for anyone claiming to be an AT, it does little with respect to defining the specific procedures and/or services that can be performed and the population that can legally be treated. This is due to the fact that the professional standards and scope of practice in the medical and allied health professions are virtually always regulated at the state level. The end result of legislative action is usually a "practice act" that defines a profession in terms of who may legally claim to be a member of the profession, what services may legally be provided, and to whom the services may be provided. The specific mechanism is most often a state license or registration that is typically monitored, either directly or indirectly, by the Board of Medicine in each state.

According to Rello (1996),

state licensure not only ensures that only those credentialed may refer to themselves as ATs (ATCs), it also provides guidance as to where and how the

AT may practice, by placing limitations on approved settings, clarifying proper medical supervision, and restricting client population. For example, ATCs should not be caring for stroke patients in a hospital but should be allowed to care for athletes in a sports medicine clinic.

Getting such legislation enacted is a complex and often expensive process, both in monetary terms and in time; however, practicing athletic trainers, regardless of professional setting, stand to benefit from having such state regulation in place. Virtually all other medical and allied health professionals, including medical doctors, nurses, physical therapists, occupational therapists, dentists, and others, operate under such statutes.

To date, 48 states have enacted some form of licensure regulation governing the practice of athletic training. As of December 2011, the states of Alaska and California remained the only states that do not regulate the practice of athletic training. Compliance with state regulatory requirements is mandatory, and the only avenue to legal athletic training practice. Contact information for the various state regulatory agencies can be found on the BOC website.

EMPLOYMENT OPPORTUNITIES

Today, ATs continue to work in the traditional setting of secondary schools, colleges/universities, and professional sports; however, new employment opportunities are being created in emerging practices in such areas as hospital and clinical, industrial/occupational, military, performing arts, physician extender, and law enforcement. According to the 2011 NATA salary survey (NATA, 2011a), the national average for a full-time AT position is $51,483, which is up from $44,235 in 2008.

Clinical

ATs form an important component of the health care team in hospitals and clinics and in orthopedic, family, pediatric, physiatry, and sports medicine office practices. Although the job responsibilities vary, ATs working in these settings provide services that ultimately improve productivity, patient outcomes, and satisfaction. The role of ATs as **physician extenders** has become increasingly popular as many physicians are choosing to hire athletic trainers as a part of their staff and utilize the unique skills of an AT in triage, taking patient histories, performing evaluations, providing instruction on exercise prescriptions, overseeing rehabilitation and general patient education, and fabricating foot orthotics.

■ *physician extenders*

Another common job in the clinical setting is the contracted AT. In this role, the AT is often contracted out to a high school to provide athletic training services for a portion of each day or week. The remaining time is spent in the clinic providing athletic training services.

According to the September 2011 NATA employment statistics (NATA, 2011a), almost 26 percent (7,788) of the certified NATA members are employed in the clinical setting. An additional 2.3 percent (686) are employed in a traditional hospital setting. The 2011 NATA salary survey (NATA, 2011b) indicated that the national average salary for an AT in the clinical setting ranged from $41,791 (contracted AT) to $83,214 (clinical administration position).

Industrial, Commercial, and Fitness Clubs

Employment in the industrial, commercial, and fitness club settings includes athletic training personnel working in in-house health/fitness facilities or on-site clinics. Some positions involve working in the area of ergonomics—tailoring the worksite to prevent injuries. The 2011 NATA salary survey (NATA, 2011b) indicated that the national average salary for an AT in the commercial setting ranged from $44,252 to $61,837.

Secondary Schools

Secondary schools (high schools and middle schools) continue to be a source of employment for a significant number of athletic trainers. The teacher/athletic trainer provides classroom instruction during the day and serves as the AT in the afternoons and evenings. This option is the most common because it allows the administration to fill a need in the classroom as well as provide athletic training services to the student-athletes. Available data suggest that the majority of athletic trainers who graduate with a teaching degree are credentialed in either physical education or health education (Curtis, 1995).

Some schools may hire a full-time athletic trainer with no teaching assignments, so that the AT has more time to provide training services to the student-athletes. Most school administrators, however, cannot justify the expense of hiring a full-time athletic trainer. In 1998, the AMA recommended that ATCs be available to all schools with athletics programs. Further support for the role of ATs in secondary schools came in a 2007 public statement from the American Academy of Family Physicians stating that a BOC-certified AT is an important component of a high school athletic program and should be employed whenever possible by secondary schools.

The potential employment market in secondary schools is tremendous, and the need is considerable when one considers the millions of student-athletes who participate in interscholastic sports annually. According to the September 2011 NATA employment statistics (NATA, 2011b), almost 16 percent (4,748) of the certified NATA members are employed in the secondary school setting. ATs employed in school settings typically enjoy a great deal of autonomy and can serve as physician extenders for the team physician. The future looks bright for continued growth in athletic training positions within the secondary schools, as more schools find ways to provide the funds necessary to employ these highly trained and qualified health care professionals. According to the 2011 NATA salary survey (NATA, 2011b), the average salary for a secondary school AT is $52,935 in public high schools and $51,483 in private high schools.

Colleges and Universities

For many aspiring athletic trainers, the dream job is working with an intercollegiate athletic program. The college/university positions take several forms, ranging from a full-time head or assistant athletic trainer to an AT with some teaching responsibilities. According to the September 2011 NATA employment statistics (NATA, 2011b), almost 23 percent (6,751) of the certified NATA members are employed in the college/university setting. The growth and stability of collegiate athletics suggest that this employment setting will remain an important practice setting for ATs.

The salary for an AT in this setting can vary based on whether the AT is a member of the professional clinical staff with service and/or teaching responsibilities or a member of the ATEP faculty with research expectations. In addition, salaries can vary between 2-year institutions and 4-year institutions. According to the 2011 NATA salary survey (NATA, 2011b), the national average salary for an AT position in the college and university setting ranged from $45,842 to $66,252.

Professional Sport

For many students in athletic training, the lure of professional sports is most compelling. The prospect of providing health care for multimillion-dollar, high-profile athletes seems almost too good to be true. Unfortunately, the fact is that because of the money involved in professional sports, especially in football, baseball, and basketball, the number of these positions is very limited. For example, a typical NFL team will employ only three athletic trainers, while professional baseball and basketball teams typically employ two or less.

In professional sport, a great deal of pressure is placed not only on the athletes to perform but also on the support staff, including athletic trainers, to keep the athletes healthy and able to play. Therefore, the hours are long, and the amount of travel is considerable, especially with baseball and basketball teams that have long seasons and a large number of road games. According to the September 2011 NATA employment statistics (NATA, 2011b), only 2.8 percent (845) of the certified NATA members are employed in the professional sport setting. The 2011 NATA salary survey (NATA, 2011b) indicated that the national average salary for an AT in the professional sport setting ranged from $51,451 to $128,438.

Performing Arts

ATs have been providing services within the performing arts for more than 25 years. Though in 2011, fewer than 1 percent of NATA-certified members were employed in this sector (NATA, 2011a), the performing arts represent an emerging field due to the growth of the industry and evolving hiring practices of the various performing arts companies. Entertainment venues and groups (for example, Disney World, Cirque du Soleil, Blue Man Group, and some ballet companies) use an athletic training program to keep their performers in peak condition. The 2011 NATA salary survey (NATA, 2011b) indicated that the national average salary for an AT in the performing arts setting was $68,207.

Military and Law Enforcement

Another small but emerging employment opportunity for ATs is developing within the military and law enforcement. In recent years, ATs have been hired by the various Armed Forces to assist in the health and welfare of active duty soldiers and their dependents. In most cases, the ATs are hired as independent contractors or part of the civil service system. ATs are also being employed in law enforcement to help employees maintain top health and performance. The unique aspects of this emerging employment sector make it difficult to predict growth potential, but at this time fewer than 1 percent of NATA-certified members are employed in this setting. The 2011 NATA salary survey (NATA, 2011b) indicated that the national average salary for an AT in the military setting was $58,282 and $68,000 in law enforcement.

PROFESSIONAL ASSOCIATIONS

National Athletic Trainers' Association (NATA)

www

NATA
www.nata.org

NATA's mission statement reads as follows: "The mission of the National Athletic Trainers' Association is to enhance the quality of health care provided by ATCs and to advance the athletic training profession" (NATA, 2009).

NATA has over 37,000 members. NATA offers several types of membership: Certified, Associate, Student, and Noncertified International. NATA membership details can be obtained by visiting the NATA website.

NATA's national office, located in Dallas, Texas, coordinates a variety of membership services, including marketing, publications, governmental relations, continuing education, management, research and education foundation, placement, conventions/meetings/exhibits, and accounting. The national office is staffed by a number of full-time personnel.

NATA has established professional liaisons with many organizations, including the following: Academy of Sports Dentistry, American Academy of Family Physicians, American Academy of Orthopaedic Surgeons (AAOS), American Academy of Pediatrics, American College of Sports Medicine (ACSM), Athletic Equipment Managers' Association (AEMA), American Optometric Association's Sport Vision Section (AOA), American Orthopaedic Society for Sports Medicine (AOSSM), American Osteopathic Academy of Sports Medicine, American Physical Therapy Association, American Physical Therapy Association: Sports Physical Therapy Section, American Public Health Association, National Collegiate Athletic Association (NCAA), and National Strength and Conditioning Association (NSCA).

NATA Research and Education Foundation

In keeping with its mission statement, in 1991 NATA established the Research and Education Foundation (NATA Foundation, 2011). The NATA Foundation is the only non-profit organization completely dedicated to advancing the profession of athletic training by supporting research and education. Basic science research and research providing patient outcomes are vital to establishing evidence for best-practice guidelines within athletic training.

The NATA Foundation awards research grants; as of December 2009, 198 grants totaling $2,889,234 had been awarded. The NATA Foundation also funds educational scholarships at the undergraduate and graduate levels. The number of scholarships varies annually (typically from 50 to 75); at this time the value of each scholarship is $2,300 (NATA Foundation, 2011).

Regional and State Associations

In addition to NATA, 10 district athletic trainers' associations exist that are independent of and yet aligned with NATA and its priorities. Each of the

10 districts represents a specific area of the United States, and the districts are further divided into individual state associations. Each of the 10 districts develops an independent mission and agenda and elects a district director. The 10 district directors constitute the NATA Board of Directors. Links to district and state websites are available on the NATA site.

PROMINENT JOURNALS AND RELATED PUBLICATIONS

NATA publishes a quarterly professional journal, *Journal of Athletic Training*, and a monthly news magazine, *NATA News*. The *Journal of Athletic Training* regularly features a variety of scientific, clinical, and pedagogically based research manuscripts. A sample abstract is shown in Box 7.1. Both publications are provided to NATA members as a member benefit.

Professional journals related to athletic training include the following:

American Journal of Sports Medicine

Athletic Therapy Today

Journal of Orthopedic and Sports Physical Therapy

Journal of Sports Medicine and Physical Fitness

Journal of Sports Rehabilitation

Journal of Strength and Conditioning Research

Medicine and Science in Sports and Exercise

Sports Health

Sports Medicine

FUTURE DIRECTIONS

Predicting future trends relative to almost any profession, especially in the health care field, is at best a nebulous endeavor. What is known is that the major areas of employment for entry-level athletic trainers appear to continue to be colleges/universities, various clinical settings, and secondary schools. Of these, the school settings continue to have the greatest potential for future growth, as the majority of the nation's middle and high schools still do not employ full-time athletic trainers.

Athletic training students should recognize that many high schools may prefer that the athletic trainer be able to teach at least a partial load and also serve as the AT. Thus, athletic training students should consider earning teaching credentials in fields that are in high demand (e.g., math, science, or English) while also completing their athletic training studies.

Changes in the health care system within this country have resulted in major changes in how health care services are delivered. While new models of health care delivery are being developed, one current model that seems to favor the AT is the physician extender paradigm. A major factor that will contribute to more athletic trainers becoming physician extenders will be an increased willingness on the part of health insurance companies to reimburse for the services provided by athletic trainers. This is already beginning to occur in isolated regions across the country, and it is anticipated that this trend will grow as the value of athletic trainers in the health care setting becomes better recognized.

Abstract of a research study that measured the effect of fatigue on electromechanical efficiency.

box
7.1

Ebersole, K. T., & Malek, D. M. (2008). Fatigue and the electromechanical efficiency of the vastus medialis and vastus lateralis muscles. *Journal of Athletic Training, 43,* 152–156.

CONTEXT: The relationship between the amplitudes of the mechanomyographic (MMG) and electromyographic (EMG) signals has been used to examine the "electromechanical efficiency" (EME) in normal and diseased muscle. EME may have application in better understanding the neuromuscular relationship between the vastus medialis (VM) and vastus lateralis (VL).

OBJECTIVE: To examine the EME of the VM and VL during a fatiguing task.

DESIGN: Repeated measures.

SETTING: Research Laboratory

PATIENTS OR OTHER PARTICIPANTS: Ten healthy males (23.2 ± 1.2 yrs) with no history of knee pathology.

INTERVENTIONS: Seventy-five consecutive, maximal concentric isokinetic leg extensions at a velocity of 180^{o-1}.

MAIN OUTCOMES MEASURES: Bipolar surface EMG electrode arrangements were placed over the VM and VL with an MMG contact sensor placed adjacent to the superior EMG electrode on each muscle. MMG and EMG amplitude values (root mean squares) were calculated for each of the 75 repetitions and normalized to the highest value from the 75 repetitions. EME was expressed as the ratio of the log transformed normalized MMG amplitude to the normalized EMG amplitude. For each muscle, the linear relationship for the normalized group, mean EME was determined across the 75 repetitions.

RESULTS: Linear regression indicated decreases in torque ($R^2 = .96$), VM EME ($R^2 = .73$), and VL EME ($R^2 = .73$). The slopes for VM and VL EME were not different ($P > 0.10$).

CONCLUSIONS: The similarities in the fatigue-induced decreases in EME for the VM and VL suggested symmetry was present between the muscles in the electrical and mechanical responses to repeated, maximal muscle actions. EME measurements may provide unique insight into the influence of fatigue on the contractile properties of skeletal muscle including alterations that occur to the intrinsic electrical and mechanical components. EME may be useful in assessing and quantifying clinically relevant asymmetries in VM and VL function in those with knee injuries.

SUMMARY

Athletic training is practiced by athletic trainers who are highly educated and multi-skilled health care professionals. ATs collaborate with physicians to provide care to optimize activity and participation of patients and clients of all ages. The practice of athletic training is guided by the RDS, which has identified five practice domains: (1) injury/illness prevention and wellness protection, (2) clinical evaluation and diagnosis, (3) immediate and emergency care, (4) treatment and rehabilitation, and (5) organizational and professional health and well-being. ATs work in a variety of practice settings; these include the traditional settings of secondary schools, colleges/universities, and professional sports as well as the emerging sectors such as hospital and clinical, industrial/occupational, military, law enforcement, performing arts, and physician extenders. The practice of athletic training is licensed or regulated in 48 states. The future of the athletic training profession is quite strong as a growing number of organizations hire ATs to optimize patient and client outcomes and as research continues to provide evidence to support the efficacy of the practice of athletic training.

study / QUESTIONS

1. The scope of the practice of athletic training is defined within the _____ and the _____.

2. Once certified, athletic trainers must continue their education by earning a minimum of _____ continuing education units every _____ years.

3. What organization is responsible for accrediting athletic training education programs?

4. When did the AMA Council on Medical Education formally recognize athletic training as an allied health profession?

5. Describe the current BOC examination format.

6. Describe the four continuing education categories as set forth by the BOC and list a specific activity from each category.

7. Briefly describe types of athletic training positions that can be created within the public school setting.

Visit the IES website to study, take notes, and try out the lab for this chapter.

learning \ ACTIVITIES

1. Go to the NATA website (www.nata.org). Research how to become a certified athletic trainer. Write a brief summary of the process.

2. Use the information on the NATA website to write a one-page summary of the organization's history.

3. Research (using the Internet and/or written sources) RICE (rest, ice, compression, and elevation). Create a brief PowerPoint presentation to inform others. You should have a minimum of eight slides, including title and bibliography.

4. Search online for "Athletic Trainer" jobs. Briefly describe the variety of jobs available.

5. Visit the Board of Certification website (www.bocatc.org) and click on the "Sample Exam Questions" link. Try the practice exam. Were you surprised by what you knew or didn't know? Did this information increase or decrease your interest in athletic training?

suggested / READINGS

Arnheim, D. D., & Prentice, W. E. (2006). *Arnheim's principles of athletic training* (12th ed.). New York: McGraw-Hill.

Berry, D. C., Miller, M. G., & Berry, L. M. (2011). *Athletic & orthopedic injury assessment: A case study approach.* Scottsdale, AZ: Holcomb Hathaway.

Berry, D. C., Miller, M. G., & Berry, L. M. (2011). *Athletic & orthopedic injury assessment: Case responses and interpretations.* Scottsdale, AZ: Holcomb Hathaway.

Pfeiffer, R. P., & Mangus, B. C. (2005). *Concepts of athletic training* (4th ed.). Boston: Jones & Bartlett.

references

Anderson, M. K., Parr, G. P., & Hall, S. J. (2009). *Foundations of athletic training* (4th ed.). Philadelphia: Lippincott Williams & Wilkins.

Arnheim, D. D., & Prentice, W. E. (1993). *Principles of athletic training* (8th ed.). St. Louis: Mosby.

Board of Certification (2011). About. Available at www.bocatc.org.

Board of Certification (2010). *The 2009 Athletic Trainer Role Delineation Study*. Omaha, NE: Stephen B. Johnson.

Curtis, N. C. (1995). Teacher certification among athletic training students. *Journal of Athletic Training, 30,* 349–351.

NATA (2009). Athletic Training Education Overview. Available at http://www.nata.org/sites/default/files/education-overview.pdf

NATA (2010). *Athletic Training Education Competencies* (5th ed.). Available at http://www.caate.net.

NATA (2011a). Information About Athletic Training. Available at http://www.nata.org/athletic-training.

NATA (2011b, Nov. 11). Athletic training salaries on the rise according to latest survey. *NATA News*, 12–14.

NATA Foundation (2011). Summary of Funded Research. Available at http://www.natafoundation.org/research/grants/grant-recipient-and-publication-listing.

O'Shea, M. E. (1980). *A history of the National Athletic Trainers Association* (2nd ed.). Greenville, NC: NATA.

Rello, M. N. (1996). The importance of state regulation to the promulgation of the athletic training profession. *Journal of Athletic Training, 31,* 160–164.

Exercise and Sport Nutrition

JOAN M. ECKERSON

DEFINITIONS IN NUTRITION

nutrition ■

dietetics ■

T he role of nutrition in health and sports performance has gained importance primarily through increased knowledge of exercise physiology. **Nutrition** is the science of food and is generally described as the sum total of the processes involved in the intake and utilization of food, including the ingestion, digestion, absorption, and metabolism of food. **Dietetics** is the science of applying food and nutrition to health and disease; therefore, individuals who receive training to become experts in food and nutrition are commonly referred to as *dietitians*.

Dietitians work in a variety of settings, including health care facilities, corporate wellness programs, universities and schools, business and industry, community and public health, research, government agencies, the military, and private practice (Academy of Nutrition and Dietetics website). Although job responsibilities vary depending on the working environment, the primary role of most dietitians is to supervise food service operations and meal planning for their clients, promote healthy eating habits through education, and prevent and treat chronic diseases, such as coronary heart disease (CHD) and diabetes, by recommending dietary modifications (Exhibit 8.1). Depending

www

Academy of Nutrition & Dietetics
*www.eatright.org/Health
Professionals/content.aspx?id=6858*

exhibit / 8.1 ChooseMyPlate.gov includes information for consumers and professionals to build a healthier diet and reduce the risk for diet-related chronic disease.

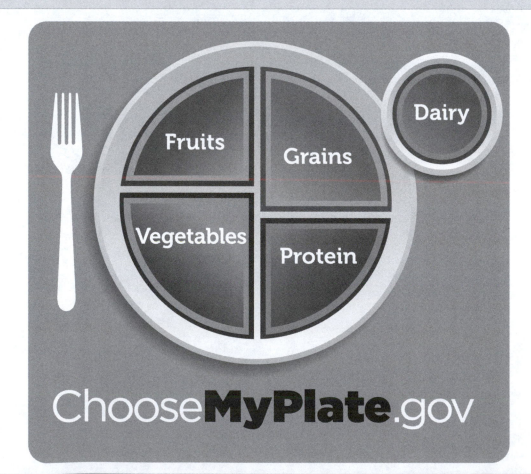

on their interests, many dietitians earn additional specializations to become clinical dietitians, consultant dietitians, management dietitians, and sports dietitians. Exercise or sport nutrition is a relatively new specialty area in the field of nutrition that integrates the principles of nutrition and physical activity as they relate to the enhancement of sports performance or the prevention of chronic disease and is the primary focus of this chapter.

HISTORY OF THE STUDY OF NUTRITION

T o provide a comprehensive historical perspective of the many facets of nutrition that relate to athletic performance and health and disease is beyond the scope of this chapter. Therefore, this section primarily reflects on those aspects of nutrition that have made a significant contribution to the knowledge base in exercise physiology.

Nutrition science developed in the 20th century, with its roots in medicine, physiology, and the biological sciences. However, dietetics and interest in diet may be traced back to the ancient Egyptians, Greeks, and Romans. More than 2,300 years ago, Egyptian physicians perceived that some of their patients were suffering from a lack of proper nutrition and prescribed enemas and nutritional clysters (injection of fluids into tissue spaces, the rectum, or abdominal cavity). Greek physicians adopted these same practices and administered rectal clysters, which included wine, whey, and milk (Brooks & Kearns, 1996).

The term *nutrition* in its various forms in the English language originated sometime between the 15th and 16th centuries.

Although the importance of nutrition was first realized thousands of years ago, it was not officially recognized as an independent discipline until April 11, 1933, with the founding of the American Institute of Nutrition (AIN). Until the formation of AIN, there was no organization specifically devoted to the study of nutrition science (Todhunter, 1983). Today, this organization is known as the American Society for Nutrition.

Early nutrition research focused on identifying all of the essential nutrients and the dietary requirements for each nutrient. In addition, it was necessary to determine the distribution of each nutrient in various foods in order to define a nutritionally adequate diet or analyze a diet and determine whether it was nutritionally balanced (Hegsted, 1985).

Although the Nutrition Laboratory at the Carnegie Institute in Washington, D.C., was created in 1904 to study nutrition and energy **metabolism**, the real impact of laboratory research in exercise physiology and exercise and sport nutrition occurred in 1927 with the creation of the Harvard Fatigue Laboratory under the direction of David Bruce Dill. Although the laboratory closed in 1947, the research conducted there in the areas of metabolism, environmental physiology, physical fitness, and nutrition formed the foundation for research in modern laboratories of exercise physiology (McCardle, Katch, & Katch, 2010).

■ *metabolism*

Ancel Keys, a biochemist and physiologist associated with the Harvard Fatigue Laboratory, conducted what is now considered classical research in nutrition and semi-starvation at the Laboratory of Physical Hygiene at the University of Minnesota in the late 1930s. Based on requests from the U.S. Army, Keys and his colleagues conducted experiments to develop high-calorie, nonperishable foods that could be used in the field by soldiers. Their research resulted in the Keys, or K-rations, which were widely used in World War II and continued to be used until replaced by the MRE (Meal, Ready-to-Eat) in the early 1980s (Buskirk, 1992). Keys also envisioned the impact that the war would have on worldwide starvation and realized that experimental data on the effects of starvation were needed. His concern led to the classic Minnesota Starvation Study, which was a comprehensive evaluation of the physiological effects of starvation and the recovery that followed. The results of this study were published in the two-volume work *The Biology of Human Starvation* in 1950 (Keys et al., 1950). Studies on starvation continued into the 1950s and contributed to a better understanding of moderate periods of semi-starvation; however, none were as comprehensive as the classic Minnesota Starvation Study (Buskirk, 1992).

Epidemiological studies (see Chapter 6), which examine the distribution of disease in a large population, were also important in the development of nutrition, particularly as it relates to chronic disease. Two major studies were the Public Health Service's Framingham Heart Study and the Harvard Alumni Study. The Framingham Heart Study began in 1948 in Framingham, Massachusetts, to determine health behaviors associated with the development of cardiovascular disease. Over 5,200 subjects were examined during the study's first 4 years, to obtain information regarding their physical activity, lifestyle habits (e.g., smoking, alcohol use, diet), and several parameters of health, including blood pressure, body weight, lung function, cholesterol levels, glucose intolerance, and an assessment of atherosclerosis. The original cohort has been reexamined every 2 years since 1948, and the study now includes five additional groups of participants, including an offspring cohort, a third-generation cohort, a new offspring spouse cohort, and Omni generation 1 and 2 cohorts. Information obtained from these participants over the past 64 years has been instrumental in identifying the lifestyle behaviors (risk factors) and genetic patterns associated with the development of CHD, and it has also resulted in the publication of over 1,200 research papers (www.framinghamheartstudy.org).

The Harvard Alumni Study is an ongoing longitudinal study of men who entered Harvard University as undergraduates between 1916 and 1950. The study was initiated in 1962 and, like the Framingham Heart Study, has also resulted in numerous publications that identified risk factors associated with CHD. The study results were used to develop national recommendations for physical activity and diet that reduce the risk of developing chronic disease.

As previously mentioned, the association between diet and sports performance can be traced back thousands of years; however, it is only within approximately the last 50 years that a true science developed, which complements the increase in interest and understanding of exercise physiology. Although the role that carbohydrate plays in maintaining adequate stores of muscle and liver glycogen and its importance during prolonged exercise had been studied as early as 1919 (Courtice & Douglas, 1935; Krogh & Lindhard, 1919), a major revelation in the development of sports nutrition occurred in the 1960s with the reintroduction of the muscle biopsy technique. During this time, several prominent investigators from Sweden used this technique to determine glycogen depletion rates at various exercise intensities and durations (McCardle et al., 2010). The discovery of the fatigue-delaying effects of carbohydrate eventually led Astrand (1967) to recommend a 7-day dietary technique to supersaturate the muscles with carbohydrates (classic **carbohydrate loading**). This protocol was modified in the 1970s when it was found that eating a high-carbohydrate diet and tapering exercise 2 to 3 days

carbohydrate loading ■

before the event was just as effective for maximizing glycogen storage and delaying fatigue (Sherman et al., 1981).

Fluid balance during exercise has received considerable attention over the past 40 years by a number of investigators, thanks to the commercial producers of sports drinks. In 1988, the Gatorade Company created the Gatorade Sports Science Institute (GSSI) to encourage and disseminate education, service, and research in sports nutrition as well as other aspects of exercise science. The GSSI currently serves approximately 110,000 members in more than 145 countries all over the world. Commercial producers of sports drinks and organizations such as the GSSI have provided research funding for studies that examine the effects of water, electrolyte, and carbohydrate balance during prolonged exercise. The results of such studies have helped establish guidelines for fluid replacement during exercise that help to prevent fluid and electrolyte imbalances and enhance performance, determine the role of gastric emptying and intestinal absorption as potential limiting factors in maintaining fluid balance, and formulate rehydration beverages that meet the fluid, sodium, and carbohydrate needs of exercise.

Because of a greater understanding of exercise physiology and human metabolism, as well as technological advances, hundreds of nutrients and cellular compounds have been developed, each with specific applications for improving performance. Although much research has been performed to evaluate the effectiveness of these compounds and nutritional supplements, many questions remain. Ergogenic aids currently receiving attention include creatine monohydrate; beta-alanine; caffeine; different types of amino acids and proteins, including whey protein; HMB (beta-hydroxy beta methylbutyrate); and milk as a post-exercise nutrition recovery drink.

www Gatorade Sports Science Institute
www.gssiweb.com

FOCUS POINT

Probably one of the most widely known sports drinks is Gatorade™, which was developed by a University of Florida research team to help prevent dehydration and improve performance. The drink was first tested on University of Florida Gator football players in 1965 and was shown to delay fatigue and prevent heat-related illness.

Many significant contributions have been made to further the science of nutrition and form a firm foundation for future research. The study of nutrition will continue to evolve as new knowledge is obtained regarding the effects of nutrients on human physiology and performance and with the discovery of nutritive agents that may play a role in health and disease.

Box 8.1 is an abstract of a research study on the effect of fat-free milk on body composition and strength.

PARENT AND RELATED DISCIPLINES

Biology and chemistry serve as the foundation for understanding almost every aspect of nutrition, exercise, and health. Biology is the science of life and living things. Chemistry is the science that studies the structure and composition of matter: the solids, liquids, and gases that are the basic building blocks of our universe. Biochemistry is the chemistry of living things, the science of the chemical changes associated with the vital processes of plants and animals.

Dietetics and **food science** are interrelated disciplines in that they both involve the study of food. Traditionally, however, dietetics has been associated with the study of foods in health and disease, whereas food science uses principles of biological and physical sciences to study the nature of foods, the causes of food deterioration, and the principles underlying the processing and

■ *food science*

Abstract of a research study on the effect of fat-free milk on body composition and strength.

box
8.1

Josse, A. R., Tang, J. E., Tarnopolsky, M. A., & Phillips, S. M. (2010). Body composition and strength changes in women with mild and resistance exercise. *Medicine & Science in Sports & Exercise, 42*(6), 1122–1130.

PURPOSE: We aimed to determine whether women consuming fat-free milk versus isoenergetic carbohydrate after resistance exercise would see augmented gains in lean mass and reductions in fat mass similar to what we observed in young men.

METHODS: Young women were randomized to drink either fat-free milk (MILK: n = 10; age (mean ± SD) = 23.2 ± 2.8 yr; BMI = 26.2 ± 4.2 kg • m^{-2}) or isoenergetic carbohydrate (CON: n = 10; age = 22.4 ± 2.4 yr; BMI = 25.2 ± 3.8 kg • m^{-2}) immediately after and 1 h after exercise (2 × 500 mL). Subjects exercised 5 d • wk^{-1} for 12 wk. Body composition changes were measured by dual-energy x-ray absorptiometry, and subjects' strength and fasting blood were measured before and after training.

RESULTS: CON gained weight after training (CON: +0.86 ± 0.4 kg, $P < 0.05$; MILK: +0.50 ± 0.4 kg, $P = 0.29$). Lean mass increased with training in both groups ($P < 0.01$), with a greater net gain in MILK versus CON (1.9 ± 0.2 vs 1.1 ± 0.2 kg, respectively, $P < 0.01$). Fat mass decreased with training in MILK only (−1.6 ± 0.4 kg, $P < 0.01$; CON: −0.3 ± 0.3 kg, $P = 0.41$). Isotonic strength increased more in MILK than CON ($P < 0.05$) for some exercises. Serum 25-hydroxyvitamin D increased in both groups but to a greater extent in MILK than CON (+6.5 ± 1.1 vs +2.8 ± 1.3 nM, respectively, $P < 0.05$), and parathyroid hormone decreased only in MILK (−1.2 ± 0.2 pM, $P < 0.01$).

CONCLUSIONS: Heavy, whole-body resistance exercise with the consumption of milk versus carbohydrate in the early post exercise period resulted in greater muscle mass accretion, strength gains, fat mass loss, and a possible reduction in bone turnover in women after 12 wk. Our results, similar to those in men, highlight that milk is an effective drink to support favorable body composition changes in women with resistance training.

preparation of food. Pharmacology, which is the study of drugs, their origin, nature, properties, and effects on living things, is also an important discipline to consider, because drugs may have a significant effect on performance or health due to alterations in nutritional status. In addition, some nutrients may act as **nutraceuticals,** a term used to describe nutrients that exhibit druglike properties when taken in appropriate dosages.

nutraceuticals ■

AREAS OF STUDY IN NUTRITION

Sport-Related Aspects

Although genetic endowment is an important factor when considering the potential for success in an athletic event or sport, the athlete's nutritional status may also exert a significant impact on performance. True athletic potential may not be attained if the athlete has insufficient fuel stores or lacks the nutrients that are necessary for optimal performance. Inadequate intakes of nutrients, electrolytes, and water can hinder athletic performance. Conversely, excessive intakes of some nutrients may impair athletic performance by disrupting normal physiological processes or by leading to undesirable changes in body composition (Williams, 2009).

The use of the muscle biopsy technique was instrumental in establishing the role of diet and exercise on muscle **glycogen** depletion and repletion and led to effective applications of specific dietary techniques, such as carbohydrate loading, to enhance athletic performance.

glycogen ■

Carbohydrate intake and performance

All biological functions require energy; therefore, the use of dietary manipulation to determine how the body uses and stores energy for biological work has been, and continues to be, a major research interest. As early as 1939, Christensen and Hansen first examined the effects of dietary manipulation on exercise performance, and today it is well known that the availability of carbohydrates to muscles is a limiting factor in prolonged exercise of moderate intensities (Costill, 1994).

Protein intake and performance

Determining the amounts and quality of protein necessary to build muscle size and strength is an area of research that is of considerable interest to athletes, trainers, and coaches. Athletes, particularly strength athletes such as weight lifters and bodybuilders, routinely consume large amounts of protein in the belief that these diets enhance performance. In addition, wide varieties of commercially available protein supplements claim to enhance muscle strength and size by stimulating protein synthesis through enhanced absorption and/or inhibition of protein breakdown.

Protein requirements are greater for athletes and physically active individuals than for the general population. The current recommended dietary intake (RDI) for protein is based on the **recommended dietary allowances** (RDAs) and is 0.8 g/kg body weight (BW) (0.36 g/lb). However, in a recently published joint position stand by the American College of Sports Medicine (ACSM), American Dietetics Association, and Dieticians of Canada, it was recommended that strength athletes ingest approximately 1.2–1.7 g • kgBW^{-1} and endurance athletes ingest 1.2–1.4 g • kgBW^{-1} of protein each day (Rodriguez, Di Marco, & Langley, 2009). Although these values may serve as guidelines for athletes, current studies suggest that relying on recommendations for a given amount of protein per day may be too simplistic. Tipton and Wolfe (2004) suggest that the metabolic response of protein intake is dependent on several other factors, including timing of ingestion relative to exercise and its intake with other nutrients, the composition of amino acids, and the type of protein ingested.

■ *recommended dietary allowances*

Athletes view protein powders as a cost-effective and convenient source of additional dietary protein, and the demand for these products equates to millions of dollars for commercial suppliers of protein supplements. Some companies claim improved or faster absorption over dietary proteins and decreased protein catabolism using their "secret formula" of amino acid mixtures. However, only a limited number of well-controlled laboratory studies have been performed to support or contradict these manufacturers' claims.

Current research suggests that the *timing* of protein intake following exercise is more important than the quantity ingested for increasing protein synthesis and does not require the purchase of expensive over-the-counter supplements (Borsheim et al., 2002; Tipton et al., 2004). For example, Elliott et al. (2006) recently reported that the ingestion of either whole milk or fat-free milk 1 hour after a leg resistance exercise routine stimulated muscle protein synthesis, with whole milk having a greater effect. Karp et al. (2006) report that chocolate milk is an effective recovery aid when ingested between two exhaustive bouts of exercise.

Fat intake and performance

Fat represents a major source of energy for working muscles, particularly at low intensities, and training enhances the muscle's ability to utilize free fatty acids (FFAs) as an energy source during exercise. The use of dietary fat as a means to enhance athletic performance has received a considerable amount of research attention and has resulted in mixed findings. For example, Jacobs et al. (2004) reported that a short-term (about 10 days) high-fat diet resulted in significant increases in fat oxidation and reduced carbohydrate oxidation without negatively impacting high-intensity time trial performance, and Lambert et al. (2001) found that a 10-day high-fat diet followed by 3 days of carbohydrate loading significantly improved cycling time trial performance by 1.4 minutes. Other studies also suggest that highly trained endurance athletes tolerate short-term high-fat diets better than untrained individuals (Erlenbusch et al., 2005; Yeo et al., 2011) and that endurance training blunts the potential deleterious effects of high-fat diets on mitochondrial efficiency (Edwards et al., 2011). However, the metabolic adaptations that occur following a high-fat diet, including glycogen sparing and enhanced FFA oxidation, do not always translate to enhanced performance, since studies also show that both acute (Okano, Sato, Takumi, & Sugawara, 1996; Okano, Sato, & Yoshihisa, 1998) and chronic high-fat diets (Burke et al., 2000; Fleming et al., 2003; Havemann et al., 2006) have negative effects on exercise performance. Although consuming a high-fat diet is not recommended for reasons of health, more research is warranted regarding its effect on exercise performance in physically active individuals.

Vitamin and mineral intake and performance

Vitamins and minerals do not provide a direct source of energy, but they do serve as essential links and regulators in the chain of metabolic reactions within cells and, therefore, help release the energy trapped inside carbohydrates, fats, and proteins. Although vitamin supplementation is not usually necessary, many athletes believe it is essential for athletic success and, therefore, consume vitamins with the hope of improving performance. Manufacturers of vitamin supplements are aware of athletes' perceptions regarding vitamins and suggest through their advertising that their products do, indeed, enhance performance. Although the general consensus is that vitamin supplementation does not significantly enhance either anaerobic or aerobic exercise performance,

Most athletes, as well as the general population, receive the RDA for vitamins in their daily diets and there is therefore little need for concern regarding vitamin deficiency, even for athletes in sports that require low body weights (Williams, 2009). Mineral deficiencies, however, are of greater concern.

research is incomplete, especially with regard to the dosages that would be necessary for enhanced performance, effects of megadoses, time of administration, and use of different forms of vitamins (Williams, 2009).

antioxidant ■ **Antioxidant** vitamins, such as vitamins E, C, and beta-carotene, have received a great deal of attention in recent years because of their ability to protect the body from oxidative, free-radical–mediated damage. Free radicals are oxygen molecules with an unpaired electron, making them highly reactive, and are naturally produced through cellular metabolism. Free radicals destroy cells by attacking the cellular membrane and have been linked to aging, cancer, CHD, and other chronic diseases. Fortunately, a considerable amount of protection exists in the body in the form of antioxidants (e.g., vitamins E and C) and certain enzymes (e.g., glutathione peroxidase, catalase, and superoxide dismutase), which react directly with free radicals to reduce their reactivity and thus help to protect cells (Ji, 2002). Vitamin D is an important fat-soluble vitamin involved in several physiological functions, including calcium absorption, but it is difficult to get in adequate amounts unless the diet is high in fatty fish such as trout and salmon. In fact, vitamin D deficiency is very common in athletes as well as the general population, particularly during the winter months (Cannell et al., 2009; Holick, 2007). The Dietary Reference Intake (DRI) for vitamin D for men and women between the ages of 19 and 70 is 600 IU per day. However, because vitamin D deficiency can impair athletic performance and most athletes are vitamin D deficient, many sports nutrition and health professionals recommend at least 1,000–2,000 IU per day.

FOCUS POINT

Osteoporosis is commonly associated with old age; however, there is a growing concern among investigators regarding disordered calcium metabolism in young female athletes involved in endurance and weight-control sports such as long distance running, dance, and gymnastics (Williams, 2009).

Minerals are essential to human body structure and function. Most research has been devoted to the role of mineral nutrition in health and disease, including both epidemiological and laboratory research. However, increasing numbers of studies have utilized athletes to determine the effect of mineral nutrition on performance and the effect of exercise on mineral metabolism (Exhibit 8.2). Several major dietary concerns of female athletes are linked to mineral deficiencies, particularly calcium and iron. The female athlete triad comprises three entities that are interrelated: disordered eating, amenorrhea, and osteoporosis. Many female athletes have unhealthy or inadequate dietary practices that can lead to amenorrhea (absence of menstrual cycles) and increase their risk for premature osteoporosis.

Gymnasts on very-low-calorie diets may be at risk for mineral deficiencies, such as calcium and iron.   **exhibit** 8.2

The importance of iron for oxygen transport via hemoglobin and endurance exercise has been well documented. Female endurance athletes, in particular, frequently exhibit low levels of hemoglobin and sports anemia. Iron supplementation to anemic persons (including athletes) has been shown to improve hemoglobin concentration, red blood cell count, maximal oxygen consumption, maximal work times to exhaustion, heart-rate responses, and performance time (McCardle et al., 2010). The effects of iron supplementation on athletic performance need to be explored; however, a few studies have shown that iron supplementation improves the iron status of athletes (Friedmann, Weller, Mairbauri, & Bartsch, 2001; Pitsis et al., 2004). Much more research is needed to fully determine the effects of iron supplementation as well as the effects of other micro- and macrominerals for both athletes and the general population.

Water, electrolytes, and physical performance

Normal body function depends on a balance between water and electrolytes. Electrolytes are substances that, when in solution, conduct a current. Some electrolytes, important for normal biological function, include sodium, potassium, chloride, and calcium. Of all the nutrients, water is the most important to physically active individuals and is one of the few that may have beneficial effects on performance when used in supplemental amounts before or during exercise (Williams, 2009). The effects of exercise on normal fluid balance and the role of water in body temperature regulation have been major areas of research focus. For example, researchers have identified how environmental heat and cold and dehydration and hypohydration affect physical performance and have established guidelines regarding the maintenance of water balance during exercise (Exhibit 8.3). Research has also provided guidelines for fluid and electrolyte replacement after different types of exercise and under different types of environmental conditions (Williams, 2009).

Ergogenic aids

Although the dietary intake of nutrients such as water and carbohydrates can be manipulated to enhance performance, most exercise and health professionals consider ergogenic aids to be any agent or practice that improves performance. During the past century, a considerable number of substances have been studied for their potential ergogenic effect. Few, however, have been shown to delay the onset of fatigue and/or to be of practical value for improving performance. Although there has been a great deal of controversy regarding the effectiveness of a large number of ergogenic aids, those receiving the most attention include caffeine, creatine, and different types of amino acids. (See Chapter 5 for a more detailed discussion of ergogenic aids.)

Application to injury rehabilitation and sports medicine

An extensive amount of laboratory research and clinical work has been performed regarding the therapeutic use of nutrients for healing. The applications of this research resulted in recommended combinations of nutrients that enhance the healing of sports injuries and other musculoskeletal conditions. Research has shown that specific nutrients, proteases (enzymes that

exhibit 8.3

Water and hydration play a critical role in regulating and sustaining the body during exercise.

break down proteins) in particular, can accelerate healing rates and shorten recovery to full function for sports injuries such as bruises, strains, sprains, lacerations, and fractures. Nutrient combinations for these types of injuries include multiple vitamins and minerals, multiple antioxidants, and multiple proteases. Although nutrients should not necessarily be used as replacements for drugs or medical care, they may have the potential to significantly affect healing and return the athlete to competition sooner than traditional rehabilitation programs (Brown & Phillips, 2010; Kavalukas & Barbul, 2011).

Health-Related Aspects

Epidemiological, animal, clinical, and metabolic research has established that diet and physical activity play important roles in health promotion and disease prevention. Clinical studies, in particular, show a possible synergistic effect of diet and exercise in the prevention and treatment of **hyperlipidemia** (an elevated level of lipids in the blood), hypertension, diabetes, and osteoporosis. However, the mechanisms of action and optimal diet and exercise prescription needed for benefit have not been clearly illustrated. Current evidence suggests that individuals with higher levels of reported physical activity and diets lower in fat have lower mortality risk than their unfit, sedentary peers (LaMonte & Blair, 2006; Xu et al., 2006).

■ *hyperlipidemia*

   Box 8.2 is an abstract of a health-related research study regarding vitamin D deficiency.

Abstract of a health-related research study regarding vitamin D deficiency.

box 8.2

Forrest, K. Y. Z., & Stuhldreher, W. L. (2011). Prevalence and correlates of vitamin D deficiency in US adults. *Nutrition Research, 31*(1), 48–54.

Mounting evidence suggests that vitamin D deficiency could be linked to several chronic diseases, including cardiovascular disease and cancer. The purpose of this study was to examine the prevalence of vitamin D deficiency and its correlates to test the hypothesis that vitamin D deficiency was common in the U.S. population, especially in certain minority groups. The National Health and Nutrition Examination Survey 2005 to 2006 data were analyzed for vitamin D levels in adult participants (N = 4,495). Vitamin D deficiency was defined as a serum 25-hydroxyvitamin D concentrations ≤ 20 ng/mL (50 nmol/L). The overall prevalence rate of vitamin D deficiency was 41.6%, with the highest rate seen in blacks (82.1%), followed by Hispanics (69.2%). Vitamin D deficiency was significantly more common among those who had no college education, were obese, with a poor health status, hypertension, low high-density lipoprotein cholesterol level, or not consuming milk daily (all $P < .001$). Multivariate analyses showed that being from a non-white race, not college educated, obese, having low high-density lipoprotein cholesterol, poor health, and no daily milk consumption were all significantly, independently associated with vitamin D deficiency (all $P < .05$). In summary, vitamin D deficiency was common in the U.S. population, especially among blacks and Hispanics. Given that vitamin D deficiency is linked to some of the important risk factors of leading causes of death in the United States, it is important that health professionals are aware of this connection and offer dietary and other intervention strategies to correct vitamin D deficiency, especially in minority groups.

Coronary heart disease

Coronary heart disease (CHD) remains the leading cause of death in the United States and is a major contributor to disability, lost productivity, and medical costs (Roger et al., 2011). This disease begins in childhood and progresses over time, resulting in atherosclerotic plaques on the walls of the coronary arteries, thus reducing blood flow to the heart. Risk factors include elevated levels of total and low-density lipoprotein (LDL) cholesterol, reduced levels of high-density lipoprotein (HDL) cholesterol, hypertension, smoking, physical inactivity, diabetes, and obesity, particularly when characterized by excessive abdominal fat (android-type obesity).

The mechanisms underlying their preventive effect are not fully understood, but both diet and exercise affect several risk factors and are believed to influence both atherogenic (plaque-forming) and thrombotic (blood-clotting) processes.

Clinical research has also shown a relationship between calcium and osteoporosis and dietary fat and certain types of cancers. Future research will continue to examine the relationships among nutrition, health, and disease to better understand their interaction. In addition, ethnic and cultural factors are now being recognized for their importance in influencing diet quality and metabolic responses to diet. The roles of nonnutrients in foods such as **phytochemicals** (chemical substances found in plants that possess medicinal properties that help prevent chronic disease) and of the overall variety in the diet are also being examined for effects on health.

phytochemicals ■

Nutrigenomics

Chronic diseases, such as CHD and diabetes, result from a contribution of several genes and their interactions with the environment, and many genes are also regulated by nutrients associated with a particular diet, which may contribute to the development of several disease states (Ghosh, Skinner, & Laing, 2007; Kaput, 2007). The recent completion of the Human Genome and International Haplotype (HapMap) Projects, as well as scientific advances in molecular biology, have resulted in the development of powerful tools that have helped provide a growing understanding of how nutrients can alter an individual's gene expression and explain why individuals differ in metabolism of foods at the molecular level (Kaput, 2007). The study of the interaction of nutrients with the human genome is called nutritional genomics, or **nutrigenomics**, and has paved the way for *personalized nutrition* in which a health care professional may eventually have the tools to specifically tailor dietary interventions that promote health and prevent disease, based on the genetic profile of an individual. In addition, nutrigenomics may help explain why some individuals respond better to a particular dietary intervention than others and may also lead to the development of new genotype-dependent foods that could help manage or prevent a variety of chronic diseases (Ravi Subbiah, 2007).

■ *nutrigenomics*

Obesity

As stated previously, obesity is a major health concern in the United States and other industrialized nations. Results from the 2007–2008 National Health and Nutrition Examination Survey (NHANES) estimated that 68 percent of adults in the United States, age 20–74 were either overweight (body mass index $\geqslant 25$) or obese (body mass index $\geqslant 30$) (Flegal, Carroll, Ogden, & Curtin, 2010). Therefore, studies regarding the development of fat substitutes, weight-loss drugs, fat patterning, and nutrients that offer health benefits will continue to be a focal point for research.

TECHNOLOGY AND RESEARCH TOOLS

Muscle Biopsy Technique

It is well known that the availability of carbohydrates to muscles is a limiting factor for prolonged, moderately intense exercise. The use of the muscle biopsy technique was instrumental to researchers in establishing the role of diet and exercise on muscle glycogen depletion and repletion and has led to effective applications of specific dietary techniques to enhance both high-intensity and endurance activities. The technique involves removing a very small piece of tissue from the belly of the muscle for analysis. After the area from which the biopsy is taken is deadened with a local anesthetic, a small incision is made through the skin and subcutaneous tissue with a scalpel, and a hollow needle is inserted into the muscle belly. A small plunger is pushed through the center of the needle, and a tissue sample is extracted. Biochemical assays may then be performed to determine the muscle's glycogen content and other factors related to substrate utilization (Wilmore & Costill, 2008).

Blood and Urine Analyses

To evaluate the effect of nutritional or pharmacological substances on exercise-induced muscle damage and performance, researchers measure markers of protein degradation such as the amino acid 3-methylhistidine, end products of lipid peroxidation such as malondialdehyde, or serum enzymes that leak from the muscle, including creatine kinase and lactate dehydrogenase (Williams, 2009). In addition, the influence of different supplements, diet, and exercise on metabolic hormones such as insulin, glucagon, testosterone, cortisol, and growth hormone may also be determined through blood analyses. Blood and urine analyses may also be used to examine the effects of diet and exercise intervention programs in the development, prevention, and treatment of certain metabolic diseases, such as diabetes and hyperlipidemia.

Calorimetry

bomb calorimeter ■
calorimetry ■

To determine the energy value of food, researchers use instruments called **bomb calorimeters.** Bomb calorimeters operate on the principle of direct **calorimetry,** in which food is completely burned and a measurement is taken of the heat that is released. In bomb calorimetry, food is placed inside a sealed chamber filled with oxygen. An electrical current moving through a fuse at the top of the chamber ignites the food–oxygen mixture, and the food literally explodes. As the food burns, the heat (energy) released is absorbed by a layer of water surrounding the bomb (Exhibit 8.4). Because the calorimeter is fully insulated from the external environment, a measured increase in water temperature directly reflects the amount of heat liberated during oxidation of the food nutrient (McCardle et al., 2010).

Metabolic Measurements

Direct calorimetry may also be used in humans to measure the amount of energy that the body uses at rest and during exercise. When using direct calorimetry, a person is placed inside an insulated chamber, and the heat released is calculated

exhibit / **8.4**   A bomb calorimeter.

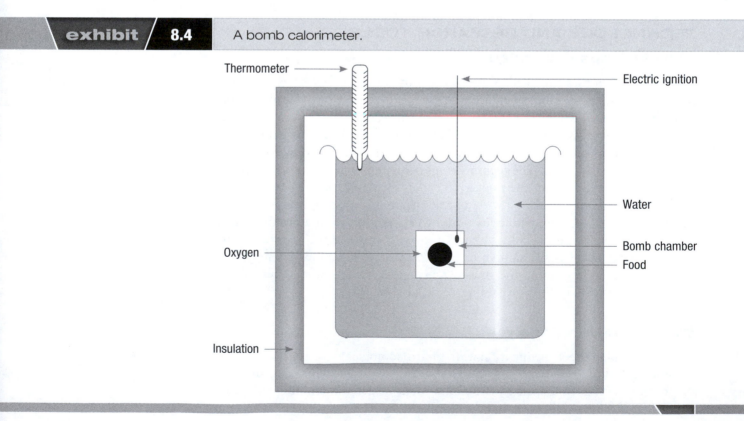

by measuring the increase in the temperature of a layer of water surrounding the chamber. This method is similar to the bomb calorimeter used to measure the energy value of food. A **kilocalorie** is defined as the amount of heat necessary to raise the temperature of 1 liter of water 1° Celsius. Therefore, by measuring the temperature of the water surrounding the direct calorimeter before and after the activity, the number of kilocalories used can be determined. Other heat-measuring devices have been developed over the years, including airflow calorimeters, which measure heat production by monitoring the temperature change in airflow through an insulated space, and gradient layer calorimetry, which measures body heat through a sheet of insulating material worn by a subject (McCardle et al., 2010). However, because of its expense and complexity, direct calorimetry is rarely used to determine energy expenditure; instead, researchers use indirect calorimetry.

■ *kilocalorie*

When using indirect calorimetry, a technician measures the exchange of respiratory gases, because there is a predictable relationship between the body's use of energy and its use of oxygen or production of carbon dioxide (CO_2). Instruments used to measure respiratory gases (gas analyzers) are widely available and much less expensive than direct calorimeters. These instruments can be mounted on carts and rolled up to a treadmill. Alternatively, portable models may be carried in backpacks for measurements while a person is engaged in sports activities.

Measurements obtained from indirect calorimetry provide for the determination of a variety of factors, including **basal metabolic rate (BMR),** the amount of energy (kilocalories) used during an activity, and the type of food (carbohydrate, fat, or protein) being used to supply the energy.

Another approach to indirect calorimetry involves the use of isotopes, such as hydrogen 2 (deuterium, or ^2H), as tracers that may be followed in the body. *Isotopes* are elements with an atypical atomic weight and may be radioactive (radioisotopes) or nonradioactive (stable isotopes). The use of doubly labeled water is a common tracer technique to monitor energy expenditure. In this technique, the subject consumes a known quantity of water labeled with two isotopes ($^2H_2{}^{18}O$), thus the term *doubly labeled water*. The deuterium (^2H) diffuses through the water content of the body, while the oxygen 18 (^{18}O) diffuses through both the water and bicarbonate stores. The rate at which the two isotopes leave the body is then measured by determining their presence in a series of blood, urine, or saliva samples. These turnover rates are then used to calculate how much CO_2 is produced, and this value is converted to energy expenditure using calorimetric equations (McCardle et al., 2010).

■ *basal metabolic rate*

Because isotope turnover is relatively slow, this technique is not used for measurements of acute exercise metabolism. However, because of its accuracy and the low amount of risk involved to the subject, this technique is well suited for determining day-to-day energy expenditure.

Dietary Recall and Analysis

To determine whether an individual is meeting his or her recommended dietary allowances for essential nutrients, nutritionists require individuals to keep a record of the food that they eat over several days and then use computer software programs to analyze the nutritional content of their diet. With this information, the nutritionist can determine total daily energy expenditure, discover where deficiencies or excesses are occurring, and make recommendations for changes in the individual's diet.

Body Composition Assessment

Assessing body composition, particularly an individual's percentage of body fat (% fat), is an important tool for monitoring the effects of various dietary and exercise intervention programs and for examining the distribution of fat in the body. There are many laboratory and field techniques used to estimate % fat.

densitometry ■ **Densitometry** provides a measure of body density (mass/volume) and is one of the most common laboratory techniques for assessing body composition. The mass of the body is easily determined from an accurate scale. Body volume can be obtained by several different techniques, but the most common is hydrostatic (or underwater) weighing, in which the individual is weighed while totally immersed in water (Exhibit 8.5). The difference between the person's scale weight and underwater weight, when corrected for water density and the residual volume of the lungs, equals the body's volume. Body density is then converted to % fat using standard regression equations (McCardle et al., 2010).

Other laboratory methods for assessing body composition include radiography, magnetic resonance imaging, hydrometry (for measuring total body water), photon absorptiometry, total body electrical conductivity, air displacement plethysmography, and dual-energy X-ray absorptiometry. Most laboratory techniques are time-consuming, complex, and expensive and are therefore not well suited for mass body composition screening.

Field techniques for assessing body composition are more accessible than laboratory techniques because the equipment is less expensive, more portable, and convenient to use for mass body composition testing. Field techniques provide reasonably accurate estimates of body composition and are based on a criterion

exhibit / 8.5   Underwater weighing is an accurate laboratory technique for determining body composition characteristics.

exhibit 8.6

Body composition testing using skinfold measurements.

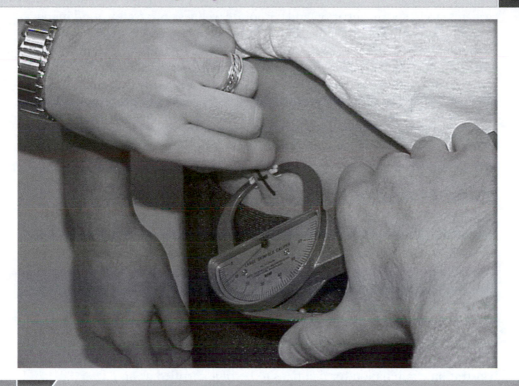

method such as densitometry or hydrometry. The most widely applied field technique involves measuring an individual's skinfold thickness with a caliper at one or more sites on the body to obtain a sum of skinfolds (Exhibit 8.6). The sum of skinfolds is used, in turn, to estimate body density or % fat using regression equations. Other commonly used field techniques include bioelectrical impedance analysis, which provides an estimate of body composition from a measure of total body resistance, and near-infrared interactance, which is based on the principles of light absorption and reflection using near-infrared spectroscopy. At the present time, however, most research does not support the use of near-infrared interactance as a valid technique to assess body composition, and it is therefore not recommended.

EDUCATIONAL PREPARATION

Whether individuals choose to pursue a career in the field of dietetics or sport and exercise nutrition, they will find academic programs available to help them prepare for these professions.

Dietetics

As stated previously, dietetics is the science of applying food and nutrition to health and disease. A dietitian is a highly qualified professional recognized as an expert on food and nutrition. A dietetic technician is trained in food and nutrition and is an integral part of health care and food service management teams. Individuals interested in dietetics can become either a registered dietitian (RD) or a dietetic technician, registered (DTR). The letters RD and DTR indi-

www

Academy of Nutrition and Dietetics
www.eatright.org/Health Professionals

cate that an individual has completed a specialized program of education and training. Dietetic professionals work in a variety of settings, including health care, research, sports nutrition and corporate wellness programs, food management and preparation, the government, and private practice. Many of the jobs in the field of nutrition require an RD or a DTR credential. The **Academy of Nutrition and Dietetics** (formerly known as the American Dietetic Association) is the world's largest organization of food and nutrition professionals and is an excellent resource for individuals interested in becoming an RD or a DTR. The Academy annually publishes a comprehensive list of colleges and universities that offer a didactic program in dietetics (DPD), courses leading to registration as a dietetic technician, and accredited internship programs.

Academy of Nutrition and Dietetics ■

Academic preparation of RDs

There are two primary avenues of academic preparation to become an RD—a coordinated program or a didactic program. A coordinated program (CP) is a bachelor's or master's degree program that integrates classroom instruction with a minimum of 1,200 hours of supervised practical experience and is accredited by the Commission on Accreditation for Dietetics Education (CADE). The purpose of the CADE is to establish and enforce standards of education for the preparation of dietetics professionals and to accredit or approve those dietetics education programs that comply with the academic standards (see the Academy of Nutrition and Dietetics website). Graduates of coordinated programs are eligible to take the registration examination for dietitians to become certified as an RD.

A DPD is an academic program that has been accredited by the CADE, culminating in a minimum of a bachelor's degree. Upon graduation from a DPD, students become eligible to apply to participate in a supervised practice program by completing a CADE-accredited dietetic internship (DI), which must be completed before a student can become eligible to take the registered examination to become an RD. Dietetic internships provide a minimum of 1,200 hours of supervised practice, and most appointments are awarded on a competitive basis through a computer matching process. The DI is typically completed in 8 to 24 months, depending on the availability of a part-time schedule or requirement for graduate credit, with longer internships associated with master's programs (see the Academy of Nutrition and Dietetics website).

Although the two pathways sound very similar, the primary difference is that a CP is an accredited bachelor's or master's degree program that *combines* both classroom instruction and 1,200 hours of a supervised practice program, whereas a DPD is an accredited program and requires that specific course work and a minimum of a bachelor's degree (i.e., the didactic portion) be completed first, followed by the completion of a DI (L. Young, personal communication, November 2011).

www

Academy of Nutrition and Dietetics Accredited Education Programs for DTR and RD

www.eatright.org/BecomeanRD orDTR/content.aspx?id=8156

Academic preparation of DTPs

The dietetic technician program (DTP) is a 2-year program accredited by the CADE that combines didactic instruction with a minimum of 450 hours of supervised practice experience and culminates in an associate's degree. Exhibit 8.7 shows the educational pathway to become eligible to take the RD exam following high school. Those contemplating a second degree or a career change may already have completed a college degree but will need to complete additional schooling.

The Academy of Nutrition and Dietetics educational pathway for high school graduates.

exhibit   8.7

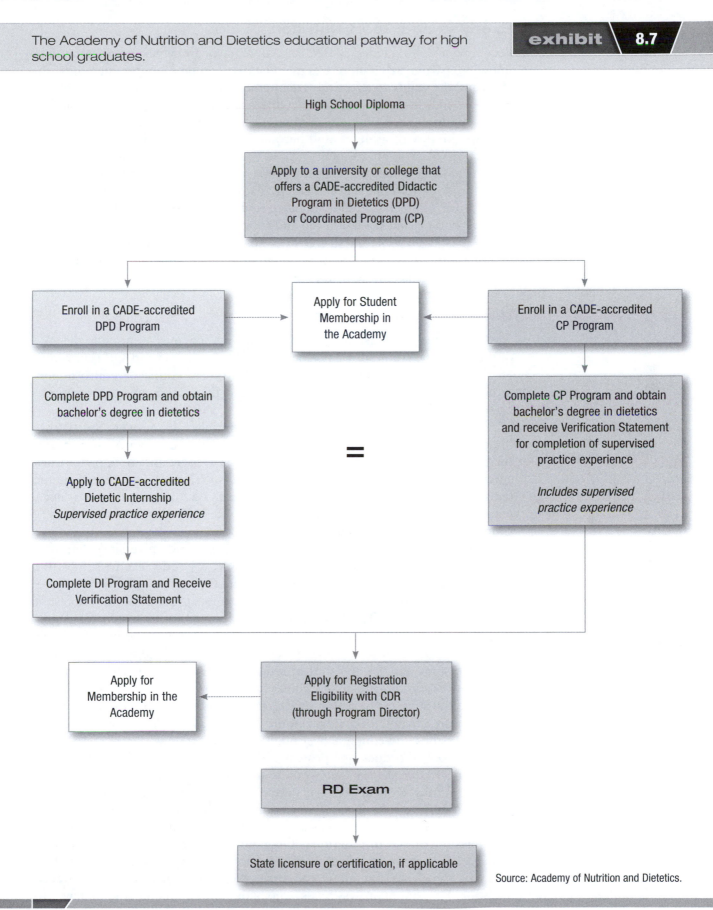

Source: Academy of Nutrition and Dietetics.

Exercise and Sport Nutrition

Becoming a well-qualified sports dietician requires an extensive background in nutrition, particularly as it relates to athletic performance, experience with athletes, and the ability to effectively communicate with both coaches and athletes. The best and, perhaps, most marketable strategy for securing a position as a sports dietitian is to obtain a minimum of a bachelor's degree, gain experience working with athletes, and become certified as an RD (*sports RD*) via a DPD or CP program at an accredited university or college, as described in the previous section of this chapter. While many positions in the field of sport nutrition do require the RD credential as a qualification for employment, it is possible for non-certified individuals to find jobs in exercise and sports nutrition, depending on their education and experience. For example, an individual with a master's or doctoral degree in exercise science or human nutrition with certifications, licensure, and/or relevant experience would be well-qualified for many positions in the field of sports nutrition.

Undergraduate programs

Science courses (such as biology, physiology, and chemistry) provide the core of the academic studies for a person interested in exercise and sport nutrition. Math, English, sociology, psychology, and business courses are also important. Many people combine nutrition courses with those in exercise science to broaden their educational base.

Because it is difficult to gain direct experience from every sport, it is important to read scientific literature, popular sport magazines, and sports-related newsletters to be aware of current issues in sport nutrition, better learn specifics of the sport, understand the demands of training, and appreciate the stress of competition. Experience with physically active people and athletes may be achieved by volunteering nutrition services to high school or university sports teams, youth sports leagues, or club sports.

If a person is interested in searching for colleges and universities that offer degrees in nutrition and/or exercise physiology, a good place to start is the reference collection at a university library. The *College Blue Book* and *Index of Majors* are two resources commonly used to locate programs of interest at different universities. The Internet is also a good place to search for degree programs that meet an individual's personal needs. Once the list of schools has been narrowed down, the next step is to contact the admissions office at the universities and ask the staff to send materials and a university bulletin. Many university libraries and/or counseling centers also subscribe to databases that allow students to search by degrees and other criteria. CollegeSource® Online is an example of a subscription database available at several colleges and universities and contains over 60,000 school catalogs.

A person who does not possess a desire to attend graduate school or obtain the RD credential but would like to be more marketable following graduation may wish to consider becoming a licensed nutrition therapist or becoming certified through organizations such as ACSM or the National Strength and Conditioning Association (NSCA) (see Chapter 5). The Medical Commission of the International Olympic Committee (IOC) also offers a distance-learning postgraduate-level program in Sport and Exercise Nutrition on a part-time basis that takes two years to complete. The program is designed for sports nutrition professionals who work with athletes and coaches to

www
CollegeSource
www.collegesource.org

enhance their knowledge in nutrition. Applicants must have a university degree or equivalent in nutrition or dietetics, the biological sciences (i.e., physiology, exercise science, biology, biochemistry), or medicine and, upon successful completion of the program, graduate with the IOC Committee's Diploma in Sports Nutrition. For more information, visit the IOC website.

WWW

International Olympic Committee
www.sportsoracle.com/ioc/

Graduate programs

Large numbers of colleges and universities offer graduate programs in exercise science and/or nutrition. Most programs require certain prerequisites before acceptance is granted; therefore, it is important to establish some professional goals before graduating with a bachelor's degree. Admission requirements for graduate school at most universities require an earned bachelor's degree in a related discipline, a grade point average of 3.0 or higher, and satisfactory Graduate Record Examination (GRE) scores. The graduate school selected should offer a program that meets the individual's career goals. For example, if a person is interested in becoming an RD, it is important to find a university that offers a master's program in dietetics that has been accredited by the Academy of Nutrition and Dietetics. The curriculum for a master's or doctoral degree in nutrition generally has a strong foundation in biological sciences, chemistry, clinical nutrition, nutrition education, and nutrition research. However, if a person is interested in exercise and nutrition or sport nutrition, then a program that combines aspects of both disciplines is more appropriate. Universities offering these types of graduate programs are often interdisciplinary programs; that is, they are offered through a collaborative effort between the department of nutrition or food science and the department of kinesiology, physical education, or exercise science. The master of science degree (M.S.) in Exercise and Sports Nutrition at Texas Woman's University and the M.S. in Nutrition and Exercise at the University of Nebraska–Lincoln are examples of such programs. Other departments combine the two disciplines, such as the Department of Nutrition, Food, and Exercise Sciences at Florida State University, which offers an M.S. in food and nutrition with a specialization in sport nutrition.

Relatively few programs specifically offer a doctoral degree in exercise nutrition. Typically, a degree is obtained in either exercise physiology or nutrition. However, most doctoral programs allow a person to tailor a program through elective courses and thus meet his or her professional goals. Admission requirements generally require an earned M.S. degree with the completion of a thesis; that is, a major research project. A thesis is often required as a prerequisite for programs that culminate in a doctor of philosophy (Ph.D.) degree, because the focus of these programs is to prepare students to perform research, analyze data, and competently evaluate research conducted by their peers. Doctoral programs in both exercise physiology and nutrition typically require 40+ credit hours beyond a master's degree.

CERTIFICATION

Dietetics

RD is a legally protected professional designation. As mentioned, achieving the RD credential requires at least a bachelor's degree from an accredited U.S. college or university and completion of specific course work and a supervised practice program that has been accredited by the Commission on Accreditation for Dietetics Education of the Academy of Nutrition and Dietetics. In addition, it requires successful completion of a national credentialing examination. The Commission on Dietetic Registration (CDR) is the credentialing agency for the Academy.

Graduates of a DTP are eligible to take the registration examination for dietetic technicians to become certified as a DTR. Once an individual becomes an RD or a DTR, he or she must maintain registration status through participation in and reporting of continuing education activities to the CDR (Academy of Nutrition and Dietetics website). Examples of activities that meet these requirements include attending local or national meetings related to dietetics, publishing articles in peer-reviewed journals, and participating in educational workshops.

Sport Nutrition Certifications

A number of specialty certifications are available through the Academy of Nutrition and Dietetics that are accredited by the Commission on Dietetic Registration including Board Certified Specialist in Gerontological Nutrition, Renal Nutrition, Pediatric Nutrition, or Oncology Nutrition, and the Certified Specialist in Sport Dietetics (CSSD) (www.cdrnet.org). To be eligible to become a CSSD, an individual must be certified as an RD for a minimum of 2 years and acquire 1,500 hours of specialty practice within a 5-year period. Upon successful completion of the exam, the individual may then use the designation "RD, CSSD" in his or her title. Currently, RDs working at the United States Olympic Training Center and those working with military combat units are required to have the CSSD certification.

CISSN
www.sportsnutritionsociety.org

The International Society of Sports Nutrition (ISSN) offers two certifications in sports nutrition: the CISSN, or Certified Sports Nutritionist from the ISSN, and the Sports Nutrition Specialist (SNS). The SNS focuses primarily on the applied aspects of sports nutrition and is intended for individuals who may not have a formal 4-year college degree. The primary purpose of the SNS is to provide personal trainers and other fitness professionals with a working knowledge of sports nutrition and supplementation strategies. The CISSN is more advanced and requires a 4-year degree in exercise science, kinesiology, nutrition, or related biological science but does not require an RD credential. Successful completion of the CISSN exam indicates that an individual possesses a fundamental understanding of the role that nutrition plays in the acute and chronic response to exercise, but it does not allow that person to provide education or to consult in the area of medical nutrition. In addition, the CISSN is not a form of licensure and is currently not an accredited certification. See the ISSN website for more information.

LICENSURE

The Academy of Nutrition and Dietetics encourages dietitians to pursue licensure in their state of residence. The purpose of licensure is to ensure that only qualified, trained professionals provide nutrition counseling to individuals seeking nutrition care or advice. Nonlicensed dietetics professionals who practice nutrition counseling or therapy may be subject to prosecution. States with certification laws restrict the use of titles such as dietitian or nutritionist to persons meeting specific requirements. Eligibility to take a licensing exam varies from state to state. Some states require an RD credential, whereas others allow individuals with a bachelor's, master's, or doctoral degree in Human Nutrition or a related field to take the licensing exam. Currently, 46 states confer some form of licensure under titles such as licensed medical nutrition therapist (LMNT), certified nutritionist (CN), and licensed dietitian (LD), depending on the state in which licensure is obtained (see the Academy of Nutrition and Dietetics website). Because each state's licensure program is different, interested individuals should contact the licensure division affiliated with their State Department of Health.

Commission on Dietetic Registration
www.cdrnet.org/certifications/licensure/index.cfm

EMPLOYMENT OPPORTUNITIES

Dietetics

According to the U.S. Bureau of Labor Statistics, employment for dietitians is expected to grow at a pace comparable to that of other professional occupations, particularly in the areas of residential health care facilities, nursing homes, and physician clinics. The job market for dietetic technicians, however, is expected to grow at a rapid pace over the next several years.

Clinical dietitians have important roles as members of medical teams in hospitals, nursing homes, health maintenance organizations (HMOs), and other health care facilities. They work with doctors, nurses, and therapists to speed recovery following illness or injury and set goals for long-term health. Community dietitians are primarily employed in public and home health agencies; daycare centers; health and recreation clubs; and government-funded programs that feed and counsel families, the elderly, pregnant women, children, and disabled or underprivileged individuals.

Dietetic professionals work in a variety of settings, including clinical health care, education, research, food management, fitness, and private practice.

Dietitians involved in the business world work in food- and nutrition-related industries. Their primary responsibilities include product development, sales, marketing, advertising, public relations, and purchasing. Management dietitians play a key role wherever food is served and work mainly in health care institutions, schools, cafeterias, and restaurants, where they are responsible for such things as personnel management, menu planning, budgeting, and purchasing.

Consultant dietitians may work full- or part-time in their own private practice or under contract within a health care facility. Consultant dietitians in private practice typically perform nutrition screening and counseling for their own clients and those referred to them by a physician. They offer advice on weight loss, cholesterol reduction, and a variety of other diet-related concerns.

Academy of Nutrition and Dietetics
www.eatright.org/BecomeanRD orDTR/content.aspx?id=8129

Dietitians who are educators work in colleges, universities, and community or technical schools and teach future doctors, nurses, exercise physiologists, dietitians, and dietetic technicians the complex science of foods and nutrition. Research dietitians work in major universities and medical centers, government agencies, and food and pharmaceutical companies and conduct investigations to answer critical nutrition questions and find alternative foods or dietary recommendations for the public (Exhibit 8.9).

According to the 2009 Dietetics Compensation and Benefits Survey, one-half of all registered dietitians who have been employed full-time in dietetics

Research dietitians conduct studies to answer important nutrition questions and provide dietary recommendations for the public.

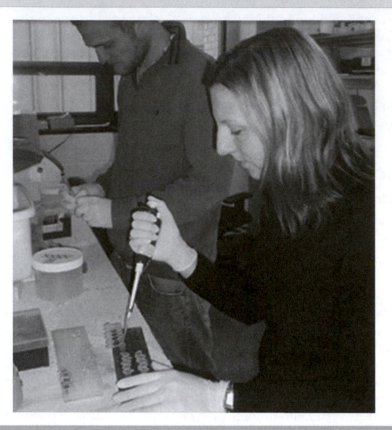

for less than 4 years report annual incomes between $43,400 and $62,200. Registered dietitians in private practice, management, and business may earn salaries in excess of $86,000. Salary levels vary with the geographical location, years of experience, scope of responsibility, and supply of applicants.

A dietetic technician works independently or in partnership with an RD in many of the same settings described above. In clinical settings, technicians assess clients' nutritional statuses and assist in the development, implementation, and review of nutrition care plans. As part of food service management teams, dietetic technicians help to supervise food production and monitor the quality of food service in schools, daycare centers, correctional facilities, restaurants, corporations, nursing homes, and hospitals. Dietetic technicians who are interested in health and wellness teach nutrition classes at health clubs, weight-management clinics, and community wellness centers.

The salary levels for DTRs vary with geographical location and the range of responsibilities for the position. Most DTRs with 1 to 4 years of experience report annual incomes between $30,800 and $43,100.

Exercise and Sport Nutrition

Exercise nutrition, as an independent discipline, is practiced in many different settings by individuals with a wide variety of educational backgrounds and a subspecialization in nutrition. Primary employment is usually teaching and/or performing research at a college or university, acting as a sports dietitian for athletic teams, consulting within a private practice, working in cardiac rehabilitation in a hospital, or working in a corporate wellness or fitness center or health club.

Teaching and research

A teaching position within a college or university typically requires at least a master's degree; however, a doctoral degree is often preferred, especially at large institutions (Exhibit 8.10). Certification as an RD may or may not be a requirement, depending on the department in which one is employed. For example, teaching a nutrition course as a faculty member in a department of exercise science or department of kinesiology does not necessarily require certification. It does, however, require a strong background in nutrition principles as they relate to health and human performance. In contrast, certification may be a requirement for individuals teaching courses in a department of food science or department of dietetics that offers curricula accredited by the CADE of the Academy of Nutrition and Dietetics and prepares students to take the exam to become an RD.

In addition to teaching and advising students, full-time faculty members at colleges and universities are expected to be active in research and/or other scholarly activity and perform university and community service. Appointments typically range from 9 to 12 months, and entry-level salary is often commensurate with experience, typically ranging from $50,000 to $75,000.

Teaching and performing research at a college or university typically requires a minimum of a master's degree.

exhibit   8.10

Exercise and sport nutrition specialists

Many athletic departments in colleges and universities realize the value of the sports dietician in providing both clinical nutrition services to athletes and nutrition education programs to teams, coaches, and trainers. Sports dieticians at small colleges and mid-major universities typically work on a part-time basis as consultants. However, large NCAA Division I universities, which have several athletic programs and are self-supportive with large operating budgets, have at least one full-time sports dietician who is responsible for such things as training, meal planning, and nutrition education.

Full-time sports dieticians typically work long hours, 6 to 7 days per week for 12 months. With the possible exception of the summer months, it is not uncommon for a sports dietician to work 10 to 12 hours per day. Although at any given time during an academic year at least one sport is in season, the responsibilities of the sports dietician may vary, depending on whether a team is in-season or off-season. During the off-season, athletes generally participate in intensive training to elicit desirable changes in body composition and engage in activities that enhance strength, speed, and power. The sports dietician's role includes monitoring the athletes' exercise programs, diets, and lifestyles to ensure that the athletes reach their off-season performance goals. It is during the off-season that education is stressed and goals and objectives from a dietary standpoint, including fueling strategies, are formulated. Body composition testing, as well as analyses of the athletes' diets, may be performed to determine where nutrient deficiencies or excesses are occurring. Workshops and/or presentations on eating disorders, proper weight gain, or weight loss are examples of educational programs provided by the sports dietician. During the summer months, when athletes are no longer dining at the training table, it is not uncommon for the sports dietician to take athletes to the supermarket to teach them how to shop nutritiously or to provide counseling regarding food preparation and proper food storage.

During the in-season, the primary goal of the athlete is to maintain any changes that he or she made during the off-season with regard to performance, eating behaviors, and body composition. To ensure that athletes eat healthily on road trips and have foods available that are familiar to them, the sports dietician often contacts the hotels where the athletes will be staying and restaurants at which the team will be stopping, to plan menus and pre-order meals.

The minimum amount of education required for employment as a sports dietician at a major university is a bachelor's degree in dietetics or a related discipline and an RD certification. Experience with athletes is also valuable. Many undergraduate students gain experience volunteering nutrition services to high school or university sport teams, a local running club, Little Leagues, or sports clubs. A sports RD employed full-time at a major university could expect a starting salary ranging from $45,000 to $65,000 (L. Remmers, personal communication, November 2011).

Sports dieticians in college and university athletic departments work closely with personnel from the campus dining facilities, both in- and off-season, to review and plan menus for the training table and to determine whether dining hours can be expanded to meet the athletes' busy schedules.

Nutrition consultants

Many professional teams employ a sports RD either full-time or on a part-time consulting basis. Although the sports dieticians employed by professional teams have similar responsibilities, the job description for these individuals varies with the team's goals and needs during particular times of the season. For example, a sports dietician for a professional team may come in 1 day per week for 6 to 8 hours during the off-season to provide educational programs on topics such as ergogenic aids, protein, fat, and meal planning for the athletes as part of their training regimen. During this time, players are encouraged to ask questions, and the dietician often works one-on-one with the athletes, performing dietary recall and analysis, counseling them on proper weight-gain and weight-loss techniques, accompanying athletes to the supermarket to teach them how to shop and read labels, and providing cooking demonstrations and sample menus that are nutritious and low in fat.

At training camp, the dietician works with the food service facilities at the local college where the team practices to review and design menus that provide plenty of carbohydrates, lean proteins, and foods low in fat. Millions of dollars are spent by these organizations on food, so it is important to the management that the members of the team eat at the training table, rather than visit a fast-food restaurant after practice. To make sure that players do, in fact, take advantage of the training table, a wide variety of foods is available, including regional favorites, because players come from all parts of the country. During the in-season, the dietician works with the caterers who provide lunches at the stadium during practice to make sure that training-table food is served. The dietician also works with airlines and hotels to provide a training-table menu and proper pregame meals to the players when they travel.

Consultants who work with professional teams are registered dietitians who typically charge anywhere from $800 to $1,600 per day for their services. In addition to working with their respective teams, many also work with individuals as private consultants; lecture at area high schools, universities, and business corporations; and provide nutrition counseling at cardiac rehabilitation facilities.

Cardiac rehabilitation

Registered dietitians who work in cardiac rehabilitation facilities typically work as a team with nurses and exercise specialists to educate patients about the synergistic effect of exercise and nutrition as it relates to primary and secondary prevention of cardiovascular disease. The responsibilities of the clinical dietitian include providing one-on-one nutrition counseling, lipid management, cooking demonstrations using low-fat and low-sodium foods and recipe modification, and teaching patient education classes on topics such as risk-factor modification and weight management. An RD serving as a clinical nutrition manager or director of a cardiovascular disease prevention program typically earns an annual salary between $48,000 and $65,000 (R. Frickel, personal communication, November 2011).

Corporate fitness and health clubs

Employment in a corporate or community fitness or wellness facility or commercial health club typically requires a bachelor's degree in exercise science with a strong emphasis in nutrition. Job responsibilities include personal training, teaching exercise classes, health promotion, nutrition education, fitness testing, and health screening for the risk of developing CHD. In addition to nutrition education, professionals in the corporate fitness setting may assist in the planning and implementation of meals served in the company cafeteria.

Entry-level, full-time salaries typically range from $24,000 to $32,100, depending on the geographical location. Certifications through the ACSM (Certified Health Fitness Specialist), the NSCA (Certified Personal Trainer; Certified Strength and Conditioning Specialist), or the Academy of Nutrition and Dietetics (RD, DTR) may increase marketability and result in a higher starting salary.

PROFESSIONAL ASSOCIATIONS

Academy of Nutrition and Dietetics

Academy of Nutrition and Dietetics
www.eatright.org

Founded as the American Dietetic Association in 1917, the Academy of Nutrition and Dietetics (the Academy) is now the world's largest organization of food and nutrition specialists. The aim of the Academy is to influence the public's food choice and nutritional status. Membership includes dietitians, dietetic technicians, and others who hold bachelor's and advanced degrees in nutrition and dietetics. For more information on the Academy visit its website.

Sports, Cardiovascular, and Wellness Nutritionists (SCAN)

SCAN
www.scandpg.org

SCAN is one of the largest dietetic practice groups within the Academy of Nutrition and Dietetics. To become a member of SCAN, individuals must be a certified RD or DTR and have expertise in the role of nutrition in one or more of the following areas: sports performance, cardiovascular health, wellness and weight management, and the prevention and treatment of disordered eating and eating disorders. One of SCAN's primary goals is to provide sound nutrition information to athletes, health and fitness professionals, the media, and regulatory agencies. To learn more about SCAN, visit its website.

International Society of Sports Nutrition (ISSN)

ISSN
www.sportsnutritionsociety.org

Formed more recently, ISSN is an academic society dedicated solely to sport nutrition. In contrast with SCAN, membership does not require certification as an RD or a DTR and includes exercise physiologists, strength and conditioning professionals, personal trainers, and nutritionists interested in sports and exercise.

Other Related Organizations

UNITED STATES GOVERNMENT AGENCIES

Centers for Disease Control and Prevention
(800) 232-4636
www.cdc.gov

Center for Nutrition Policy and Promotion
(703) 305-7600
www.cnpp.usda.gov

Consumer Information Center
(719) 295-2675
www.publications.usa.gov/USAPubs.php

Food and Drug Administration
(888) 463-6332
www.fda.gov

Food and Nutrition Information Center
National Agricultural Library
(301) 504-5755
www.nal.usda.gov

PROFESSIONAL AND SERVICE ORGANIZATIONS

American College of Sports Medicine
(317) 637-9200
www.acsm.org

American Heart Association, National Center
(800) 242-8721
www.americanheart.org

American Society for Nutrition
(301) 634-7050
www.nutrition.org

Gatorade Sports Science Institute
(800) 616-4774
www.gssiweb.com

USDA Center for Nutrition Policy and Promotion
www.choosemyplate.gov

National Dairy Council
(312) 240-2880
www.nationaldairycouncil.org

National Strength and Conditioning Association
(800) 815-6826
www.nsca-lift.org

PROMINENT JOURNALS AND RELATED PUBLICATIONS

PRIMARY JOURNALS

American Journal of Clinical Nutrition

Food Technology

International Journal of Obesity

International Journal of Sport Nutrition and Exercise Metabolism

Journal of Food Science

Journal of Nutrition

Journal of Nutrition Education and Behavior

Journal of Strength and Conditioning Research

Journal of the Academy of Nutrition and Dietetics (formerly Journal of the American Dietetic Association)

Journal of the American College of Nutrition

Journal of the American Medical Association

Journal of the International Society of Sports Nutrition

Medicine and Science in Sports and Exercise

Nutrition and Metabolism

Nutrition Journal

Nutrition Reviews

RELATED PUBLICATIONS

Nutrition Review
www.nutritionreview.org

Medline Plus—Dietary Supplements
www.nlm.nih.gov/medlineplus/dietarysupplements.html

Harvard Medical School Health Letter
www.health.harvard.edu/newsletters/Harvard_Health_Letter

Tufts University Health and Nutrition Letter
www.tuftshealthletter.com

University of California at Berkeley Wellness Letter
(800) 829-9170
www.wellnessletter.com

FUTURE DIRECTIONS

Although the number of full-time positions for sports dietitians is growing, private consulting is one area that holds considerable promise for the future. In this case, the individual essentially creates his or her own position and may work with athletes as well as individuals interested in weight management and personal wellness (Fink, Mikesky, & Burgoon, 2012). Given the rising rates of obesity among the U.S. population, nutrition professionals will play important roles in disease management and prevention and health promotion.

In terms of research, childhood obesity is increasing at a rapid rate; therefore, future studies will likely focus on nutrition and education intervention programs to improve clinical outcomes, including type 2 diabetes. Because of the growing number of older adults in the United States, nutrition research will also be an important component for personal health care management in this population.

Another emerging area in nutrition research discussed earlier in this chapter is nutrigenomics, which some experts believe will eventually impact all dietetics professionals (DeBusk, 2005). The Human Genome and HapMap Projects have been the primary catalysts for this rapidly developing field. As previously mentioned, the term *nutrigenomics* itself refers to the effects that bioactive compounds in food may have on cell biology and gene expression. If these compounds are isolated, they could be used as dietary supplements and in the development of functional foods to prevent disease and promote good health.

By creating associations among nutrients, genes, and disease, scientists will be able to develop dietary therapeutic interventions and guidelines based on genetic predisposition (DeBusk, 2005; Kaput, 2007).

Scientists interested in sports nutrition will continue to explore the effects of dietary manipulation and ergogenic aids on exercise performance and body composition. The issue of nutrient timing for optimal recovery from exercise will likely continue to receive much research attention, particularly as it relates to the types and amounts of protein that are ingested prior to, during, and following both aerobic and anaerobic exercise.

Because knowledge in sport nutrition is always changing and evolving, it will be important for nutrition and dietetics professionals to keep current with the ever-expanding research and job opportunities that may result from such research, including nutrigenomics. Therefore, joining professional organizations, reading peer-reviewed journals, attending conferences, and participating in continuing education programs are all ways that individuals can remain current with the most up-to-date information.

SUMMARY

Exercise and sport nutrition is an area of study that integrates the principles of nutrition and physical activity as they relate to performance or the prevention of disease. A number of employment opportunities are available, including teaching and research positions in colleges and universities as well as specialist or consultant positions for colleges, universities, amateur and professional teams, corporate fitness facilities, and community health clubs. Because of the recent growing interest in nutritional agents to enhance general health and supplements to enhance athletic performance, the area of exercise and sport nutrition is a rapidly expanding subdiscipline of exercise science.

study / QUESTIONS

1. What organization was founded in 1933 and helped nutrition to be recognized as an independent discipline?

2. Name the classic comprehensive study Ancel Keys conducted to evaluate the physiological effects of starvation and recovery from starvation.

3. Sports nutritionists require a strong background in nutrition and what other area of exercise science?

4. Describe three research tools used to study health- and exercise-related aspects of nutrition and explain what types of studies could be performed using each technology.

5. Describe the two primary avenues of academic preparation for becoming a registered dietitian.

6. Explain the differences between dietetics, food science, and exercise nutrition and describe what types of jobs are available in each discipline.

7. Determine your professional goals for a career in exercise nutrition and develop a course of study designed to meet those goals: desired degree(s) and courses needed, certifications, and the like. If you are interested in an area other than nutrition, write about how nutrition will impact your field.

Visit the IES website to study, take notes, and try out the lab for this chapter.

learning ACTIVITIES

1. Go to the Academy of Nutrition and Dietetics website (www.eatright.org). Write a brief description of the Academy and identify its goals or initiatives.
2. Go to the American Society for Nutrition (ASN) website (www.nutrition.org). What are the benefits and expenses of a student membership?
3. What does the Gatorade Sports Science Institute (GSSI) have to offer a sports nutritionist? Go to the GSSI website (www.gssiweb.com), find three articles from the Sport Science Library, and then summarize them.

suggested READINGS

Campbell, B., & Spano, M. (Eds.) (2011). *NSCA's guide to sport and exercise nutrition.* Champaign, IL: Human Kinetics.

Clark, N. (2008). *Sports nutrition guidebook* (4th ed.). Champaign, IL: Human Kinetics.

Dunford, M. (2006). *Sports nutrition: a practice manual for professionals* (4th ed.). Chicago, IL: American Dietetics Association.

Dunford, M. (2010). *Fundamentals of sport and exercise nutrition.* Champaign, IL: Human Kinetics.

Greenwood, M., Kalman, D. S., & Antonio, J. (Eds.) (2008). *Nutritional supplements in sports and exercise.* Totowa, NJ: Human Press.

Watson, R., Gerald, J., & Preedy, V. (2011). *Nutrients, dietary supplements, and nutriceuticals: Cost analysis versus clinical benefits.* SpringerLink eBook (www.springerlink.com).

references

Astrand, P. O. (1967). Diet and athletic performance. *Fed. Proc., 26,* 1772–1777.

Borsheim, E., Tipton, K. D., Wolf, S. E., & Wolfe, R. R. (2002). Essential amino acids and muscle protein recovery from resistance exercise. *American Journal of Physiology, Endocrinology and Metabolism, 283*(4), E648–E657.

Brooks, S., & Kearns, P. (1996). Enteral and parental nutrition. In E. E. Ziegler & L. J. Filer, Jr. (Eds.), *Present knowledge in nutrition* (7th ed., p. 530). Washington, DC: ILSI Press.

Brown, K., & Phillips, T. (2010). Nutrition and wound healing. *Clinics in Dermatology, 28,* 432–439.

Burke, L., Angus, D., Cox, G., Cummings, N., Febbraio, M., et al. (2000). Effect of fat adaptation and carbohydrate restoration on metabolism and performance during prolonged cycling. *Journal of Applied Physiology, 89,* 2413–2421.

Buskirk, E. R. (1992). From Harvard to Minnesota: Keys to our history. In J. O. Holloszy (Ed.), *Exercise and sports science reviews* (Vol. 20, pp. 1–26).

Cannell, J., Hollis, B., Sorenson, M., Taft, T., & Anderson, J. (2009). Athletic performance and vitamin D. *Medicine and Science in Sports and Exercise, 41*(5), 1102–1110.

Costill, D. L. (1994). Applied exercise physiology. In *American College of Sports Medicine—40th anniversary lectures,* pp. 69–79. Indianapolis, IN: American College of Sports Medicine.

Courtice, F. C., & Douglas, C. G. (1935). The effect of prolonged muscular exercise on the metabolism. *Proc. Roy. Soc., London, 119,* 381–383.

DeBusk, R. M. (2005). Nutrigenomics and the future of dietetics. *Nutrition & Dietetics, 62*(2/3), 63–65.

Edwards, L., Holloway, C., Murray, A., Knight, N., Carter, E., et al. (2011). Endurance exercise training blunts the deleterious effect of high-fat feeding on whole body efficiency. *American Journal of Physiology: Regulatory, Integrative, and Comparative Physiology, 301,* R320–R326.

Elliott, T. A., Cree, M. G., Sanford, A. P., Wolfe, R. R., & Tipton, K. D. (2006). Milk ingestion stimulates net muscle protein synthesis following resistance exercise. *Medicine and Science in Sports and Exercise, 38*(4), 667–674.

Erlenbusch, M., Haub, M., Munoz, K., MacConnie, S., & Stillwell, B. (2005). Effect of high-fat or high-carbohydrate diets on endurance exercise: A meta-analysis. *International Journal of Sport Nutrition and Exercise Metabolism, 15*, 1–14.

Fink, H. H., Mikesky, A. E., & Burgoon, L. A. (2012). *Practical applications in sports nutrition*. Boston: Jones & Bartlett.

Flegal, K., Carroll, M., Ogden, C., & Curtin, L. (2010). Prevalence and trends in obesity among US adults, 1999–2008. *Journal of the American Medical Association, 303*(3), 235–241.

Fleming, J., Sharman, M., Avery, N., Love, D., Gomez, A., et al. (2003). Endurance capacity and high-intensity exercise performance responses to a high-fat diet. *International Journal of Sport Nutrition and Exercise Metabolism, 13*, 466–478.

Friedmann, B., Weller, E., Mairbauri, H., & Bartsch, P. (2001). Effects of iron repletion on blood volume and performance capacity in young athletes. *Medicine and Science in Sports and Exercise, 33*(5), 741–746.

Ghosh, D., Skinner, M., & Laing, W. (2007). Pharmogenomics and nutrigenomics: Synergies and differences. *European Journal of Clinical Nutrition, 61*, 567–574.

Havemann, L., West, S., Goedecke, J., Macdonald, I., St. Clair Gibson, A., et al. (2006). Fat adaptation followed by carbohydrate-loading compromises high intensity sprint performance. *Journal of Applied Physiology, 100*, 194–202.

Hegsted, D. M. (1985). Nutrition: The changing scene. *Nutrition Reviews, 43*, 357–367.

Holick, M. (2007). Vitamin D deficiency. *New England Journal of Medicine, 357*, 266–281.

Jacobs, K. A., Paul, D. R., Geor, R. J., Hinchcliff, K. W., & Sherman, W. M. (2004). Dietary composition influences short-term endurance training-induced adaptations of substrate partitioning during exercise. *International Journal of Sport Nutrition and Exercise Metabolism, 14*(1), 38–61.

Ji, L. (2002). Exercise-induced modulation of antioxidant defense. *New York Academy of Science, 959*, 82–92.

Kaput, J. (2007). Nutrigenomics—2006 update. *Clinical Chemistry and Laboratory Medicine, 45*, 279–287.

Karp, J. R., Johnston, J. D., Tecklenburg, S., Mickleburg, T. D., Fly, A. D., & Stager, J. M. (2006). Chocolate milk as a post-exercise recovery aid. *International Journal of Sport Nutrition and Exercise Metabolism, 16*, 78–91.

Kavalukas, S., & Barbul, A. (2011). Nutrition and wound healing: An update. *Plastic and Reconstructive Surgery, 127*(Suppl.), 38S–43S.

Keys, A., Brozek, J., Henschel, A., Mickelsen, O., & Taylor, H. (1950). *The biology of human starvation*, Vols. I & II. Minneapolis: University of Minnesota Press.

Krogh, A., & Lindhard, J. (1919). The relative value of fats and carbohydrates as sources of muscular energy. *Biochemical Journal, 14*, 290–294.

Lambert, E. V., et al. (2001). High-fat diet versus habitual diet prior to carbohydrate loading: Effects on exercise metabolism and cycling performance. *International Journal of Sport Nutrition and Exercise Metabolism, 11*, 209–225.

LaMonte, M. J., & Blair, S. N. (2006). Physical activity, cardiorespiratory fitness, and adiposity: Contributions to disease risk. *Current Opinion in Clinical Nutrition and Metabolic Care, 9*(5), 540–546.

McCardle, W. D., Katch, F. I., & Katch, V. L. (2010). *Exercise physiology: Energy, nutrition, and human performance* (7th ed.). Baltimore: Lippincott Williams & Wilkins.

Okano, G., Sato, Y., Takumi, Y., & Sugawara, M. (1996). Effect of 4 h pre-exercise high carbohydrate and high fat meal ingestion on endurance performance and metabolism. *International Journal of Sports Medicine, 17*, 530–534.

Okano, G., Sato, Y., & Yoshihisa, M. (1998). Effect of elevated blood FFA levels on endurance performance after a single fat meal ingestion. *Medicine and Science in Sports and Exercise, 30*(5), 763–768.

Pitsis, G. C., Fallon, K. E., Fallon, S. K., & Fazakerley, R. (2004). Response of soluble transferring receptor and iron-related parameters to iron supplementation in elite, iron-depleted, nonanemic female athletes. *Clinical Journal of Sport Medicine, 14*(5), 300–304.

Ravi Subbiah, M. (2007). Nutrigenics and nutraceuticals: The next wave riding on personalized medicine. *Translational Research, 149*, 55–61.

Rodriguez, N., Di Marco, N., & Langley, S. (2009). Position of the ADA, Dietitians of Canada, and the American College of Sports Medicine: Nutrition and athletic performance. *Journal of the American Dietetic Association. 109*(3), 509–527.

Roger, V., Go, A., Lloyd-Jones, D., Adams, R., Barry, J., et al. (2011). Heart disease and stroke statistics—2011 update: A report from the American Heart Association, *Circulation, 123*, e18–e209.

Sherman, W. M., Costill, D. L., Fink, W. J., & Miller, J. M. (1981). Effects of exercise-diet manipulation on muscle glycogen and its subsequent utilization during performance. *International Journal of Sports Medicine, 2*, 1–15.

Tipton, K. D., Elliott, T. A., Cree, M. G., Wolf, S. E., Sanford, A. P., & Wolfe, R. R. (2004). Ingestion of casein and whey proteins result in muscle anabolism after resistance exercise. *Medicine and Science in Sports and Exercise, 36*(12), 2073–2081.

Tipton, K. D., & Wolfe, R. R. (2004). Protein and amino acids for athletes. *Journal of Sports Sciences, 22*(1), 65–79.

Todhunter, E. N. (1983). Reflections on nutrition history. *Journal of Nutrition, 113*, 1681–1685.

Williams, M. H. (2009). *Nutrition for health, fitness, and sport* (9th ed.). New York: McGraw-Hill.

Wilmore, J. H., & Costill, D. L. (2008). *Physiology of sports and exercise* (4th ed.). Champaign, IL: Human Kinetics.

Xu, J., Eilat-Adar, S., Loria, C., Goldbourt, U., Howard, B. V., Fabsitz, R. R., et al. (2006). Dietary fat intake and risk of coronary heart disease: The Strong Heart Study. *American Journal of Clinical Nutrition, 84*(4), 894–902.

Yeo, W., Carey, A., Burke, L., Spriet, S., & Hawley, J. (2011). Fat adaptation in well-trained athletes: Effects on cell metabolism. *Applied Physiology, Nutrition, and Metabolism, 36*, 12–22.

Biomechanics

NICHOLAS STERGIOU, DANIEL L. BLANKE,
SARA A. MYERS, AND KA-CHUN SIU

DEFINITIONS IN BIOMECHANICS

biomechanics ■

Biomechanics is a discipline. A discipline deals with understanding, predicting, and explaining phenomena within a content domain, and **biomechanics** is the study of the human body in motion. By applying principles from mechanics and engineering, biomechanists are able to study the forces that act on the body and the effects they produce (Bates, 1991). Hay (1973) describes biomechanics as the science that examines forces acting on and within a biological structure and the effects produced by such forces, whereas Alt (1967) describes biomechanics as the science that investigates the effect of internal and external forces on human and animal bodies in movement and at rest. Each of these definitions describes the essential relationship between humans and mechanics found in biomechanics.

Kinesiology, the parent discipline of biomechanics, is a science that investigates movement. It can be divided into the mechanical and anatomical aspects of human movement. The mechanical aspects can be further subdivided into statics and dynamics. **Statics** is a branch of mechanics that investigates bodies, masses, and forces at rest or in equilibrium. **Dynamics** investigates bodies, masses, and forces in motion. Dynamics consists of temporal analysis, kinematics, and kinetics. **Temporal analysis** uses time as the sole basis for analysis. **Kinematics** investigates motion without reference to masses or forces. **Kinetics** investigates the actions of forces in producing or changing the motion of masses.

statics ■
dynamics ■

temporal analysis ■
kinematics ■
kinetics ■

In the United States, the use of mathematical and mechanical principles to study human movement was initially called kinesiology; in Europe, it was called biomechanics (Nelson, 1980). Although there has been considerable controversy over the years as to the correct name for this area of study, it seems to have been settled with biomechanics as the most accepted term worldwide.

In biomechanics, movement is studied in order to understand the underlying mechanisms involved in the movement or in the acquisition and regulation of skill. The uniqueness of biomechanics as an area of study evolves not from the unique body of knowledge but from the questions that are asked relative to understanding human movement (Bates, 1991). Techniques and methods from other scientific disciplines, such as physics and engineering, are used to examine human movement. In this way, biomechanics involves mechanical measurements used in conjunction with biological interpretations (Higgins, 1985). Thus, biomechanics is a key area of study within the realm of exercise science.

The study of movement involves explaining and understanding the structural and functional mechanisms underlying human performance, in all its presentations, from fundamental motor skills to demanding exercise. Higgins (1977) proposed that skill is a movement that allows the organism to respond or act effectively within the environment and to integrate past and present. To become skillful requires mastery of the redundant degrees of freedom (Bernstein, 1967). These degrees of freedom or constraints are morphological (having to do with the body's structure), biomechanical, environmental, and task specific (Higgins, 1977). The study of these constraints is required in order to explain and understand the underlying mechanisms of movement. Thus, movement must be approached from an interdisciplinary perspective. Movement, as a very broad phenomenon, appears in many different forms: play, dance, sport, work, and daily living activities. This is why a biomechanist cannot study meaningful questions without adequate preparation in such areas as anatomy, motor control, physics, exercise physiology, and engineering.

HISTORY OF BIOMECHANICS

The history of biomechanics can be traced back to the ancient Greeks. According to Nigg and Herzog (1994), the contribution to biomechanics during the period 700 BCE to 200 CE included the distinction between facts and fiction in the discipline, development of mechanical and mathematical models, development of anatomical models, and the first attempt to examine the human body biomechanically.

Aristotle (384–322 BCE) was the first to examine and write about complex movements such as running and walking. He said, "The animal that moves makes its change of position by pressing against that which is beneath it. Hence, athletes jump farther if they have the weights in their hands than if they have not, and runners run faster if they swing their arms, for in extension of the arms there is a kind of leaning upon the hands and wrists" (Nigg & Herzog, 1994). Archimedes (287–212 BCE) was the first to examine floating bodies and their movements in the water.

Hippocrates (460–377 BCE), the Father of Western Medicine, advocated that humans should base observations on and draw conclusions from only what was perceived through the senses. Galen (131–201) was the physician of the gladiators. He developed anatomical descriptions and the present-day terminology in use in certain biological fields. During the Renaissance, Leonardo da Vinci (1452–1519) examined the structure and function of the human body in a variety of movements. The contribution of the Renaissance period of 1450 to 1527 to biomechanics included the awakening of science, the foundation of modern anatomy and physiology, and an early examination of movement and muscle action (Nigg & Herzog, 1994). In the modern era, another group of scientists contributed to the growth of biomechanics. Galileo Galilei (1564–1642) studied the action of falling bodies and laid the basis for the mechanical analysis of movement.

Alfonso Borelli (1608–1679), a student of Galileo, examined muscular movement and mechanical principles. His work *De Motu Animalium* is

The famous story in which Galileo is said to have dropped a weight from the Leaning Tower of Pisa is false. The actual experiment was done by Simon Stevin, several years before Galileo's work.

the first biomechanical "textbook," in which he combined the sciences of mathematics, physics, and anatomy. Isaac Newton (1642–1727) developed his famous mechanical laws and was the founder of calculus, statics, and dynamics. Contributions to biomechanics during this time period included Newtonian mechanics, which provided a theory for mechanical analysis, as well as an improvement in science through development of the process of theory and experimentation (Nigg & Herzog, 1994).

During the 19th century, contributions to biomechanics included the foundation of electromyography, the development of measuring techniques to examine the kinematics and kinetics of movement, and the beginning of the use of engineering principles in biomechanical analysis (Nigg & Herzog, 1994). The Weber brothers (around 1836) investigated the influence of gravity on limb movements in walking and running and were the first to study the path of the center of gravity during movement. Eadweard Muybridge (1830–1894) was the first to develop cinematographical serial pictures to study animals (horses) and humans. Étienne Jules Marey (1830–1904) used various photographic methods to examine movement.

During the 20th century, biomechanics became an academic discipline with graduate programs and faculty positions; biomechanical research influenced

Christian Wilhelm Braune (1831–1892) and Otto Fischer (1861–1917) were the founders of the scientific method of studying human movement, which resulted in the development of the prosthesis.

applications in industrial, medical, and other practical areas; and biomechanics evolved as a necessary discipline-based method in the study of human and animal movement (Nigg & Herzog, 1994). During this time period, Jules Amar (1879–1935) summarized the physical and physiological aspects related to industrial work. His book, *The Human Motor,* was translated into English in 1920 and set the standards for human engineering in the United States and Europe. Nicholas Bernstein (1896–1966) examined walking, running, and jumping. He laid the foundation for the study of motor control and coordination. A. V. Hill (1886–1977) investigated efficiency and energy cost in human movement, and in 1931, W. O. Fenn published the first biomechanical works in the exercise and sport science literature, a cinematographical analysis of sprint running (Fenn, 1929, 1931).

In the 1960s, the term *biomechanics* began appearing with more frequency in the literature, and biomechanics finally became a graduate specialization, first at Pennsylvania State University and then at the University of Indiana. Richard Nelson developed a laboratory for biomechanical research at Penn State in 1966, and it was the first that was identified with the term *biomechanics* (Atwater, 1980). His initial graduates were Doris Miller and Charles Dillman. Following his graduation, Charles Dillman went to the University of Illinois to establish a biomechanics program. John Cooper developed a similar laboratory at the University of Indiana in 1967. The first graduate of this program was Barry Bates, who later developed the biomechanics program at the University of Oregon. From these pioneer programs and their graduates, many programs around the country were developed. Others who made tremendous contributions to the development of biomechanics programs around the nation were James Hay (University of Iowa), Stanley Plagenhoef (University of Massachusetts), and Carol Widule (Purdue University).

In the United States, the first North American meeting in biomechanics was organized by John Cooper at Indiana University in 1970 (Cooper, 1971).

The period from 1966 to the present has been an era of great growth in biomechanics. It includes the development of a number of new societies, journals, and professional meetings, such as the First International Seminar on Biomechanics, which was held in Zurich, Switzerland, in 1967 (Wilkerson, 1997), and the origination of the *Journal of Biomechanics* in 1968.

In 1973, the Fourth International Seminar on Biomechanics was held at Penn State University (Bates, 1974). This marked the foundation of the International Society of Biomechanics (ISB). In 1975, the Fifth International Seminar on Bio-mechanics in Jyvaskyla, Finland, marked the conceptualization of the American Society of Biomechanics (ASB), which was founded the following year in Chicago, Illinois. This society includes members from physical education, medicine, ergonomics, biology, and engineering (Wilkerson, 1997).

Another important meeting was held in 1977 at the University of Illinois: the first national conference on teaching kinesiology. At this conference, the differences between the terms *biomechanics* and *kinesiology* were discussed at length. Kinesiology was found to vary from a name of a course to a title of a college department (Dillman & Sears, 1978). It was also found that in the United States, the use of mathematical and mechanical principles to study human movement was initially called kinesiology, whereas in Europe it was called biomechanics (Nelson, 1980). *Kinesiology* was defined as the parent discipline of biomechanics and generally of the science that investigates movement. *Biomechanics* was defined as a discipline for the study of forces that act on the body and the effects they produce.

In 1982, the International Society of Biomechanics in Sport (ISBS) was founded in San Diego, California (Terauds, 1982). More recently, an international electronic mail communication list with the name BIOMCH-L (Biomechanics-List) was established at the University of Calgary, Canada, to help biomechanists from all over the world exchange ideas, problems, information, and the like (Bogert & Gielo-Perczak, 1992). Finally, in 1989, the Academy of Physical Education was renamed the Academy of Kinesiology and Physical Education, because kinesiology was defined as the overall science of human movement (Charles, 1994). As a result, in 1993, the Kinesiology Academy of the American Alliance for Health, Physical Education, Recreation and Dance (AAHPERD), which was representing the biomechanics section, was renamed the Biomechanics Academy to more clearly identify its role (Wilkerson, 1997).

Exhibit 9.1 summarizes important events in the history of biomechanics.

Important dates in biomechanics.   **exhibit** 9.1

DATE	EVENT
384–322 BCE	Aristotle examined and wrote about complex movements such as running and walking.
1452–1519	Leonardo da Vinci examined the function of the human body.
1608–1679	Alfonso Borelli wrote the first biomechanical text, *De Motu Animalium*.
1642–1727	Sir Isaac Newton developed calculus and his mechanical laws.
1830–1894	Eadweard Muybridge developed cinematographical serial pictures to study animals and humans.
1920	Jules Amar's book, *The Human Motor,* was translated into English.
1931	W. O. Fenn published about the cinematographical analysis of sprint running.
1966	Richard Nelson developed the first laboratory for biomechanical research at Penn State.
1967	First International Seminar on Biomechanics, Zurich, Switzerland.
1968	Origination of the *Journal of Biomechanics.*
1973	Founding of the International Society of Biomechanics.
1976	Founding of the American Society of Biomechanics.
1982	Founding of the International Society of Biomechanics in Sports.
1993	The Kinesiology Academy of AAHPERD was renamed the Biomechanics Academy of AAHPERD.

AREAS OF STUDY IN BIOMECHANICS

U sing similar techniques and instruments, biomechanists work in a variety of areas. Each of these areas can be identified and the type of research described. The five areas discussed here are developmental biomechanics, biomechanics of exercise and sports, rehabilitative biomechanics, occupational biomechanics, and forensic biomechanics.

Developmental Biomechanics

Biomechanical research in human development focuses on evaluating essential movement patterns across the life span. Individuals of different ages are examined while performing a variety of daily-living motor skills. The activities can then be quantified, described, and analyzed. Biomechanical analysis is specifically important in quantifying the developmental motor skills and movement patterns such as walking, kicking, jumping, throwing, and catching. This research resulted in the description of a typical activity pattern for each age group. This pattern can then be compared to an individual's performance to determine his or her level of ability at any age. This type of analysis has also been performed for a variety of other activities of daily living across the life span, including ascending and descending stairs, raising from and lowering to a different level (such as a chair or bed), lifting and carrying objects, pushing and pulling objects, and working with short- and long-handled implements. Again, evaluations and quantification of each type of activity at a variety of age levels allowed comparisons to be made between age levels and made it possible to evaluate an individual's skill or ability in a specific activity at a particular age.

For example, biomechanics experts have used high-speed camera systems and force platforms to capture and analyze slight movement changes in young children. Based on this information, biomechanists objectively examine movements such as body sway during sitting and standing, and/or the range of motion at the joints during walking. These results are then shared with pediatricians and pediatric physical therapists to accurately evaluate developmental motor milestones during infancy and childhood. In particular, such objective biomechanical measurements are used to evaluate therapies for children with developmental movement disorders (e.g., global developmental delay, cerebral palsy, Down syndrome).

Another example is biomechanical research focused on the aging process. Through the developmental process, aging is the ultimate and inevitable stage. Activity levels and working capacity are diminished in older adults. Physiological and motor performance, such as reaction time, movement time, muscle strength, and flexibility, are also reduced with age. Biomechanical analysis is commonly used to assess movement changes in older adults in order to identify the causes of slips, trips, and falls that the elderly population experiences. In addition, biomechanists strive to develop biotechnology that can improve the quality of life for the elderly, prevent injury, and quantify the best treatment approaches for restoring diminished balance and other motor abilities.

Biomechanics of Exercise and Sport

Biomechanical research in the area of exercise and sport has focused on postures and movement patterns that minimize the risk of injury during physical activity and improve performance. Among the contributions of biomechanics are the development of exercise machines for improving strength, endurance, flexibility, and speed; the development of new exercise modes, such as plyometrics and isokinetics, to improve performance; the design of exercise and sports equipment to minimize injuries; and the development of exercise and sport techniques to optimize performance.

The design of sport footwear is an example of the use of biomechanics to improve performance and reduce injury. Until the beginning of the 1970s, changes in the design of sport shoes were based on the subjective observations of athletes and coaches. Because the movements of the lower extremities were too fast to be evaluated with the naked eye or even standard film cameras, a new technology needed to be developed. A welcome invention was high-speed cinematography. Sixteen-millimeter film taken at high speed could be displayed at normal speed or evaluated frame by frame for a detailed examination of the movement of the foot and leg during contact with the ground while walking or running. Today, advanced digital video camera systems are used to capture movements in sports that are extremely fast, such as the golf swing and the baseball pitch.

Among the contributions of biomechanics are the development of exercise machines for improving strength, endurance, flexibility, and speed; the development of new exercise modes, such as plyometrics and isokinetics, to improve performance; the design of exercise and sports equipment to minimize injuries; and the development of exercise and sports techniques to optimize performance.

The amount of force that is applied to a surface or an individual during a sport activity is also important to the biomechanist. To determine this force, biomechanists developed special scales, known as **force platforms** (Exhibit 9.2), that can measure the impact forces between the shoe and the ground. By measuring these forces, we know today that the foot and the shoe must absorb two to three times the body's weight with each running step.

■ *force platform*

Force platforms.

exhibit 9.2

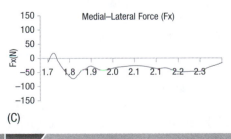

(A)

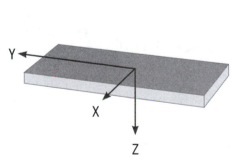

(B)

(A) A force platform (Kistler Instrument Corp., Amherst, New York) is used to measure the forces between the shoe and the ground.

(B) A typical force platform can measure forces in three dimensions (X, Y, and Z).

(C) Typical force profiles are shown in X-dimension (medial–lateral force), Y-dimension (anterior–posterior force), and Z-dimension (vertical force).

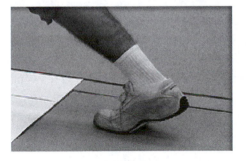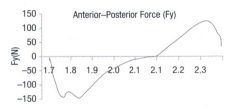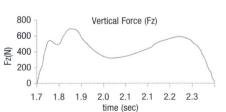

(C)

Another recently developed device is an insole (see page 204) that can be worn in a shoe under the foot, where it measures the pressure between the shoe and the foot. With this device, biomechanists can determine the extent that each part of the insole plays in a specific activity. This information can then be used to determine which bones will sustain most of the load while the foot is in contact with the ground. Knowing the amount of force that each bone receives allows the sport shoe manufacturer to adjust the amount of support and cushion in the shoe to best support the foot and reduce the chance of injury.

Currently, most of the biomechanical shoe research is directed toward the cushioning and stability of the sport shoe. Some other important considerations in shoe design are the flexibility and density of the sole as well as the weight, durability, and breatheability of the upper part of the shoe. Using the techniques previously described, biomechanists analyze the demands of a specific sport (e.g., basketball or volleyball) in relation to the shoes that are designed for that sport. This research has dramatically improved the design of all sport shoes.

Examples of biomechanists' involvement with the development of exercise equipment for improving strength and endurance can be found in stair-stepping machines and exercise bicycles. Biomechanists evaluated posture and the ability to produce force, while reducing the potential for injury, on each of these devices. The result has been the evolution of both the stair-stepping machine and the exercise bicycle. These devices are now more comfortable and easier to use, while still providing safe and effective resistance for improving strength and endurance.

Biomechanists also have been involved in the development and testing of protective devices (e.g., eyeguards and football helmets and pads) and in the development and testing of sport equipment (e.g., golf clubs, ice skates, and tennis racquets). These devices help athletes improve performance.

An example of the use of biomechanics to improve sport performance can be found in the golf-swing analysis now available from many professionals who teach golf. With a high-speed video camera and speed-measuring device, the golf instructor can determine a player's position and movement throughout the golf swing. The speed and path of the golf club head, as well as the speed and path of the ball after contact, can also be determined. These data provide the instructor with the information necessary to describe the player's actions that result in the path of the golf ball. By adjusting the player's actions, the instructor can alter the path of the ball and perhaps improve performance. This type of analysis can be helpful to the beginner as well as the highly skilled player.

Rehabilitative Biomechanics

Biomechanical research also focused on studying the movement patterns of injured and disabled people. Biomechanists analyze the movement changes after injury and determine the specific movement abnormality. This information is crucial for clinicians, especially physical therapists and athletic trainers, when developing an appropriate rehabilitation protocol for individuals to relearn the motor skills after an injury.

Biomechanical research in the area of rehabilitative biomechanics led to the development of sound exercises and exercise machines to train injured individuals back to pre-injury functioning; the development of supplement devices such as canes, crutches, walkers, and orthotics; and the development of substitution devices such as prostheses and wheelchairs. By using objective biomechanical measurements obtained through equipment such as goniometers and force transducers, biomechanists can determine the effectiveness of those devices and provide professional opinions to help physicians and therapists improve their usage.

An example of rehabilitative biomechanics is the study of the effects of peripheral arterial disease (PAD) on gait patterns (Chen et al., 2006; Huisinga, Piponos, Stergiou, & Johanning, 2010). PAD is a progressive disease that limits patients' ambulation due to intermittent pain in the leg muscles and cramping pain induced by movement (i.e., walking). Rehabilitative biomechanists can determine specific abnormalities in the joint movement patterns of the patients' legs. Then the effect of pharmacotherapy, conservative treatment, and surgical treatment can be evaluated by biomechanically monitoring these abnormalities. Multiple sclerosis patients are another population that can benefit from rehabilitative biomechanics. A progressive neurological disorder that results in a high incidence of gait disturbance, multiple sclerosis can be studied with biomechanics to determine specific gait impairments and to develop rehabilitation techniques that address the problems identified (Wurdeman, Huisinga, Filipi, & Stergiou, 2010).

Occupational Biomechanics

Biomechanical research often focuses on providing a safer and more efficient environment for the worker. The development of better safety equipment (e.g., helmets, shin guards, footwear) for protecting the body from the effects of falling or colliding with other objects is an important area of biomechanical research. In addition, the development of safer or more mechanically efficient tools, improvement in the design of transportation modules (e.g., airplanes, spacecrafts, trains, boats, automobiles), and decreased occupational injury are major contributions by biomechanists to various work environments.

As with other areas of biomechanical inquiry, biomechanists are also involved with legal cases involving industrial design and safety. For example, a biomechanist was asked to determine the factors that contributed to two nail-gun accidents. The issues assessed included the adequacy of the design relative to human performance capabilities, expected use patterns, and the use and effect of warnings. The adequacy of machine design relative to safety when cleaning and operating the nail-gun was also a concern. Site and product examination, coupled with an analysis of human perceptions and expectations, suggested that the design was unsafe and a contributing cause of the accidents.

Product liability is another area in which biomechanists are asked to testify. Product evaluation and design effects on a performance injury are common issues in this area. For example, a woman playing softball severely injured her ankle when she slid while wearing an improperly designed shoe. The analysis demonstrated within a reasonable degree of biomechanical probability that the specific injuries were caused by the improper shoe design even though the slide was properly executed. In another case, the possible causes of a knee injury while playing golf were evaluated to determine the likelihood that poorly designed shoes were the cause (see www.hpwbiomechanics.com).

To reduce the incidence of occupational injury, biomechanists objectively evaluate working performance and develop optimal environments. For example, biomechanists have examined proficiency in robotic assistive surgery by measuring the joint range of motion and the muscle activation of the surgeons' upper extremities during surgical procedures (Judkins, Oleynikov, & Stergiou,

2009; Narazaki, Oleynikov, & Stergiou, 2006). These biomechanical measurements were used to develop an advanced surgical training program that optimizes surgeons' performance and minimizes tissue injury in a variety of surgical operations.

Forensic Biomechanics

Biomechanical research in this area is related to questions that arise in legal situations. Forensic biomechanists are invited to analyze evidence, clarify some of the most important issues, and facilitate the decisions of the jury. In most cases, biomechanists provide forensic investigations, technical reports, and expert testimony for a broad range of human performance-related incidents involving personal injury. The work of an expert witness always involves a human element or component interacting with various aspects of the environment. Most accidents typically involve an initial perceptual component, some form of expectation, and an action, which typically results in a biomechanical consequence. Also, there is often a need to match the resulting injuries with the actions.

For example, a biomechanist was asked to determine which of two occupants involved in a fatal auto accident was driving. Vehicle and site inspection data and an evaluation of the occupants' injuries were incorporated in the analysis to show that the driver was likely to be thrown from the auto during the accident's progress. In another case, an analysis and evaluation was done to determine the potential effects of lap belt and shoulder harness restraint systems on the injuries suffered by a passenger in an auto accident. Various forces on the spine were calculated to demonstrate the differential effects of the restraint systems and body positions. A number of cases involving low-speed, rear-end impacts were also evaluated. Such case evaluations typically use a computer simulation program that estimates movement and forces of the head and neck. Investigations of the possible causes of auto accidents involving unexpected acceleration, which involves the human elements of perception and expectation regarding the function of the gas and brake pedals, also have been done. In addition, biomechanical analyses were conducted on the system designs to determine their adequacy (www.hpwbiomechanics.com).

In another case, the biomechanist was asked to determine the possible causes of a fall while descending a stairway. The primary issue for investigation was whether small deviations in riser heights and tread slopes could sufficiently alter performance such that a fall resulted. The biomechanical evaluation, however, suggested the fall resulted from other factors. Evaluations also have been done to determine whether poorly designed and constructed shoes can cause a slip-and-fall accident. The ensuing site and product examination verified that the shoe construction was such that, over time, deterioration took place, resulting in a hazardous product when worn on selected surfaces. A fall from a kitchen stool being used on a linoleum surface was also investigated. A biomechanical evaluation of the stool–surface system showed that a typical movement by the user was sufficient to cause the stool to slide, resulting in the fall.

TECHNOLOGY AND RESEARCH TOOLS

 iomechanists use many pieces of equipment to measure and record time, motion, and force. These devices are essential for the biomechanist to collect and analyze human movement (Rodgers & Cavanagh, 1984).

To record time and motion, timing devices (e.g., watches, digital clocks) and motion image recording methods and devices (e.g., cinematography, videography, digital imaging, magnetic resonance imaging, goniometers) are used to provide temporal and kinematic data. Temporal and kinematic data can also be combined with force measurements quantified by force platforms, pressure insoles, accelerometers, and electromyography to obtain kinetic data such as joint movements and powers. Furthermore, this information can be integrated with modeling and simulation techniques to predict performance.

When body movement is captured by the motion recording device, the recorded images of reflective skin markers are converted into spatial coordinates (see Exhibit 9.3A). From the coordinates of the digitized markers, the displacements, velocities, and accelerations of each recorded moving body segment can be calculated (Exhibit 9.3B). **Motion recording devices** use optical lenses to capture body motion and provide permanent recorded images of movement that can be evaluated with more precision than perception with the naked eye alone (Exhibit 9.4). The human eye operates at a speed of only 12 frames per second. Therefore, many activities, such as the contact of the foot with the ground while running, happen so quickly that they must be analyzed by specialized equipment that can capture the activity in many more frames per second. In this way, a biomechanist can more precisely analyze such things as foot injuries that may occur while running.

■ *motion recording devices*

Photographs provide permanent still images of one instant in a performance that can then be analyzed and described. A photograph can also be used to record the location of equipment used to collect research data. A 35-mm camera with a variable focal length lens and adjustable shutter speed and aperture provides the most flexibility when photographing a performance or the data collection environment.

Capturing body movement.	**exhibit** 9.3

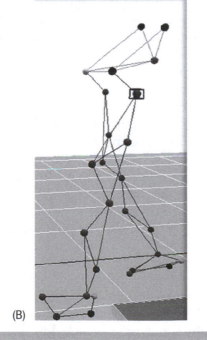

(A)   (B)

(A) Reflective skin markers are placed in various anatomical positions. (B) Body segment locations are calculated as a model by using the information gathered with the reflective skin markers.

exhibit / 9.4   Optical recording devices in a biomechanics laboratory, such as high-speed digital optoelectronic cameras provide permanent recorded digital images for evaluation.

Photo courtesy of Motion Analysis Corp., Santa Rosa, California.

cinematography ■   **Cinematography** provides a sequence of images that can be displayed as a motion picture or be viewed one by one. Filming can be done at nearly any speed, from less than one frame per second to more than five million frames per second. Filming at high frame rates allows motion that is too fast to see with the naked eye to be captured and viewed in slow motion or as individual images. Although rarely used today, the 16-millimeter film cameras used in cinematography with variable focal length lenses and adjustable shutter speeds and apertures, capable of adjustable frame rates of up to 500 frames per second, provide the most flexibility in data collection.

videography ■   **Videography** also provides a sequence of images that can be displayed as a motion picture or viewed individually. Videography has most of the features of cinematography, with the convenience of instant viewing and the ability to reuse the recording. The most common video cameras and recorders capture images at 30 frames per second using variable focal length lenses and adjustable shutter speeds and apertures. Today, video cameras have evolved into high-speed digital optoelectronic systems that directly capture the digital images of movement described by the trajectories of reflective skin markers (see Exhibit 9.3A). The digital trajectories of the markers are then directly stored into a computer hard drive.

Thus, videotapes are no longer needed in a digital optoelectronic motion capture system. Today's motion capture systems are mostly of two types: passive and active systems. Passive motion capture systems use markers coated with a reflective material to reflect light from the cameras. Active motion capture systems use active markers with light-emitting diodes (LEDs); rather than reflecting light back to the camera, the active makers are powered to emit their own light and their relative positions are tracked by illuminating the LEDs (see Exhibit 9.5).

For a more comprehensive biomechanics analysis, a motion capture system can be used with other equipment, such as an instrumented treadmill (discussed later; refer to Exhibit 9.11) to evaluate both kinematics and kinetics during walking. Motion of the leg can be captured by either an active or a passive marker of a motion capture system, while forces from the ground can be measured and captured by the force plate embedded in the instrumented treadmill. By combining the kinematic data from the motion capture system with kinetic data from the instrumented treadmill, the neuromuscular responses and their contributions in the form of joint movements and powers can be evaluated during walking.

Magnetic resonance imaging (MRI) provides a computer-generated two-dimensional image of any body part (discussed in earlier chapters). After the two-dimensional image is acquired, it is manipulated so that it can be viewed on a video monitor and reconstructed into a three-dimensional image. MRI provides a noninvasive means of viewing the structures under the skin. This allows for a better evaluation of an injury or a muscle adaptation to training.

Goniometers provide kinematic data on joint positioning. They are used to measure static positions of limb segments with respect to a joint axis (Exhibit 9.6). An *electrogoniometer* is a goniometer with a *potentiometer* (variable resistor) at its axis of rotation. The electrogoniometer provides an indication of joint position during movement and can be calibrated to determine speed of movement. The device is most often attached to the body with the axis of the potentiometer aligned with the long axis of segments. The electrogoniometer provides an output voltage, proportional to the joint angle, that can be measured, scaled, and recorded. This information can be used to assess flexibility for diagnosis, rehabilitation, and exercise prescription.

When kinematic data of movement are measured, they can be combined with data from force platforms, pressure insoles, accelerometers, and **electromyography (EMG)** to provide even more details regarding body motion.

Dynamography provides kinetic or force data. An example of a dynamographic device is a force platform with built-in force transducers that provide electrical signals proportional to the components of force acting on it. A transducer is a measuring device that converts one form of energy into another. An electrical displacement transducer, for example, converts kinetic energy from movement into electrical energy. Force transducers used in a force platform are usually either strain gauges, which change their electrical resistance with strain, or piezoelectric elements, which generate a charge when stressed. The electrical energy can then be measured and recorded as an indication of the

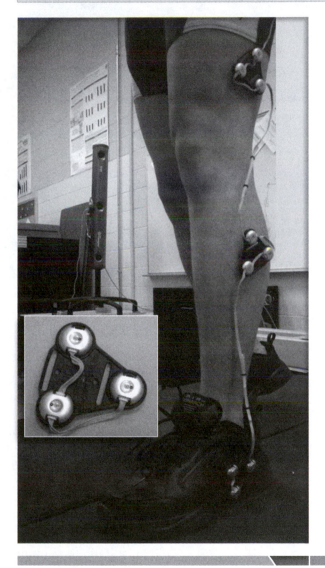

exhibit	9.5

An active motion capture system in a biomechanics laboratory tracks the relative position of the markers by illuminating LEDs. Three LEDs are attached on a rigid body (see insert at bottom left).

Photo courtesy of Northern Digital, Inc., Ontario, Canada.

- *magnetic resonance imaging*
- *goniometer*
- *electromyography*
- *dynamography*

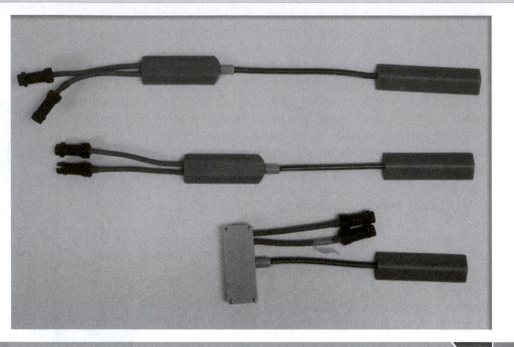

Photo courtesy of Biometrics Ltd, Gwent, UK.

amount of force inserted. The most common use of a force platform is to measure the three orthogonal components of ground reaction forces (GRFs) in vertical (Fz), anterior–posterior (Fy), and medial–lateral (Fx) between the foot and the floor during locomotor activities (refer back to Exhibit 9.2). Force platforms can be used to assess the forces generated during contact with the ground in a variety of activities such as running, walking, jumping, landing, and hopping.

pressure insole ∎   Another example of a dynamographic device is a **pressure insole.** The pressure insole consists of a matrix of elements that are small-force transducers of a known area (see Exhibit 9.7). If the area is sufficiently small, the force on each element can be considered uniformly distributed, and thus, an estimate of pressure is available. This device gives more information concerning pressure distribution under the foot than a force platform because the pressure acting on individual anatomical foot regions can be measured, rather than just the resultant force acting on an entire region; for example, the whole foot. This information is especially important in shoe design, diabetic foot evaluation, and pathological gait.

accelerometer ∎   An **accelerometer** is an electronic device that measures acceleration forces (see Exhibit 9.8). It usually consists of an inertial mass that exerts a force against an element, such as a beam, whose resulting strain is then measured. Because we know from Newton that force is the product of mass and acceleration (the change in how fast an object is moving), and that mass is a constant, we can estimate forces if we know accelerations. Therefore, accelerometers are used when other force measurement devices cannot be. For example, it is very difficult to use a force platform on a treadmill; however, an accelerometer can provide information about the forces generated during treadmill running.

Pressure distribution under a foot can be measured by a pressure insole. The pressure insole consists of a matrix of small-force transducers (top left of the figure).

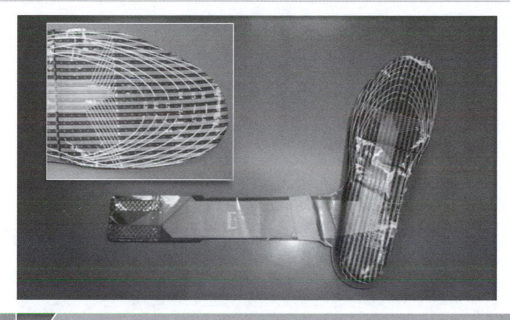

Photo courtesy of Tekscan, Inc., South Boston, MA.

Motion acceleration can be measured by an accelerometer.

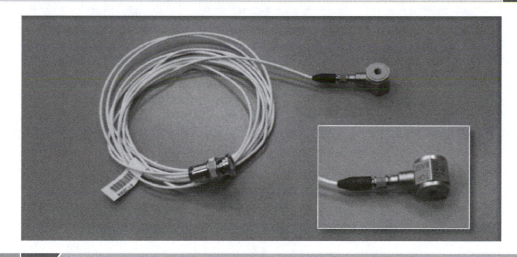

Photo courtesy of PCB Piezotronics, Inc., Depew, NY.

As mentioned in Chapter 5, electromyography provides data on muscle activity (see Exhibit 9.9). An electromyograph records electrical changes that occur in a muscle during or immediately before contraction. This electrical activity can be captured, amplified, filtered, and recorded as an indication of muscle activity during a performance.

Modeling and **simulations** provide a prediction of kinematic and kinetic data. These techniques are used to provide insight into specific activities or events. For example, muscles can be modeled as springs and bones as rigid

■ *modeling*
■ *simulation*

Muscle activity can be measured by surface EMG. This EMG system consists of 16 electrodes; one of them is shown at the bottom left of the figure.

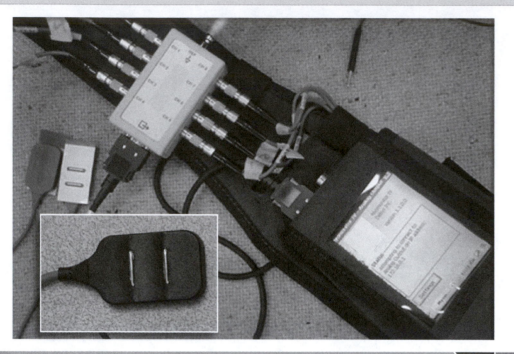

Photo courtesy of Delsys Inc., Boston, MA.

bodies and then internal forces can be predicted. Such information can be valuable for estimating forces, such as those acting at the lower back during lifting. To fully understand the mechanism of human movement, more complex and sophisticated biomechanical instruments are now being utilized in biomechanics laboratories. For example, staircases (Exhibit 9.10) and treadmills (Exhibit 9.11) instrumented with force platforms provide biomechanists unique abilities to investigate stair negotiation and generation of forces during locomotion, respectively.

instrumented staircase ■   An **instrumented staircase** typically is equipped with multiple force platforms. For example, in Exhibit 9.10, a force platform is embedded under the first three steps, and an additional force platform is connected to the handrail structure. An instrumented staircase can accurately measure the amount of force applied on each step during stair ascent and descent and can detect the usage of handrails during stair negotiation. Combining the force (kinetic) data from the instrumented staircase with kinematic data from motion recording devices, the neuromuscular responses and their contributions in the form of joint movements and powers can be estimated. In this fashion biomechanists can fully understand the mechanism of human stair negotiation and help physicians and therapists to develop strategies for patients to regain their ability to climb stairs.

instrumented treadmill ■   An **instrumented treadmill** has force platforms embedded below the belt. In Exhibit 9.11, a custom split-belt instrumented treadmill has two large force platforms under its dual belt design. It can allow biomechanists to measure the amount of force applied while walking or running on the treadmill. An additional unique feature of this device is its split-belt

A custom instrumented staircase with multiple force platforms.

exhibit 9.10

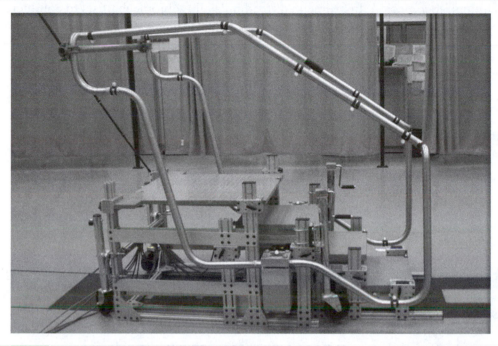

The amount of force during locomotion can be measured by a split-belt instrumented treadmill.

exhibit 9.11

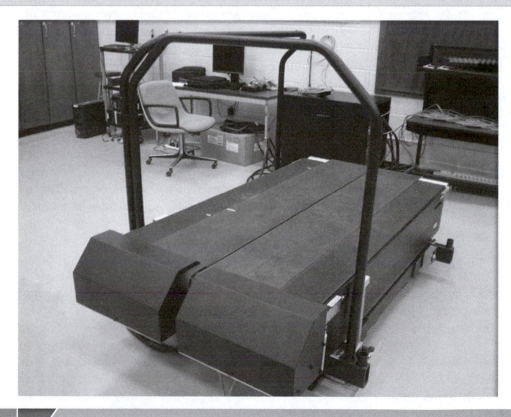

Photo courtesy of Bertec Corporation, Columbus, OH.

design, which can provide a different speed for each belt or even two different directions. It creates a more challenging environment for studying human locomotion. Instrumented treadmills allow biomechanists to conduct advanced biomechanical research study, such as locomotion adaptation and asymmetrical walking.

computerized dynamic posturography ■ **Computerized dynamic posturography** is used to measure the control of posture and balance in upright stance. To study balance, biomechanists can use a device such as the SMART Balance Master (Exhibit 9.12) to measure body sway in a standing position. This sophisticated instrument provides different research protocols that allow biomechanists to study the contribution of different sensory systems (visual, vestibular, and somatosensory) in maintaining postural stability. The embedded force platform with rotation and translation capabilities provides either a stable or unstable support surface and measures the amount of force exerted by the participant. The movable visual surround provides an additional complexity and challenge for participants regarding how they can maintain their postural stability in a stable or dynamic visual environment.

exhibit / 9.12

Body sway can be measured by the SMART Balance Master.

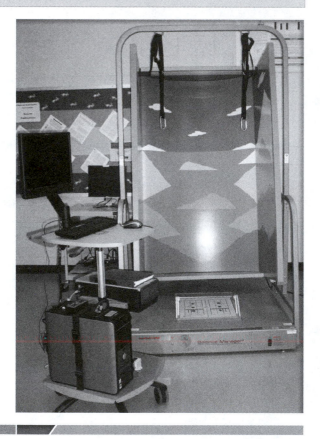

Photo courtesy of NeuroCom, a division of Natus; Clackamas, OR.

EDUCATIONAL PREPARATION

B ecause of the diversity of the areas related to the field of biomechanics, a broad range of knowledge is required to be successful. For example, the entrance requirements for the doctoral program in biomechanics at the University of Calgary include course work in mechanics (statics and dynamics), mathematics (calculus, linear algebra, and differential equations), computers (competence in one language), measuring techniques (force measuring systems, accelerometers, electromyography, videography, goniometers), and gross anatomy and mechanical properties of human tissues (bone, cartilage, joints, tendons, muscles). Course requirements for entry into the doctoral program at the University of Nebraska at Omaha include study in the areas of mathematics, computer science, physics, and motor control and learning.

Although the general course requirements for entry into a doctoral program in biomechanics and those required to complete a doctoral program are similar from one university to another, the courses and activities are specific to each university. The courses are often tied to the focus of the research being conducted at the particular university's biomechanics laboratory. Because biomechanics is a broad and diverse field, there should be variety in the training of the individuals working in the field. The training for someone working in rehabilitative biomechanics will be distinctly different from that of someone working in sport biomechanics or industrial biomechanics. Therefore, if there is a question about who is the best trained in the field, the answer is it depends on the job requirements.

EMPLOYMENT OPPORTUNITIES

Employment opportunities in biomechanics are extremely varied as a result of the great variety of applications related to biomechanics. The opportunities can be arbitrarily classified into academic, postdoctoral, research and graduate assistant, and industry and government positions. An indication of the type and great quantity of the positions available can be found at the Biomechanics website.

Biomechanics
www.uni-essen.de/~qpd800/
WSITECOPY.html

PROFESSIONAL ASSOCIATIONS

Several professional associations in the field of biomechanics allow biomechanists to meet and discuss specific topical areas. For more information about these organizations, visit their respective websites.

The American Society of Biomechanics (ASB) was founded in 1977 and has about 500 members today. The purpose of ASB is to provide a forum for the exchange of information and ideas among researchers. The society is affiliated with the *Journal of Biomechanics*. Meetings are held on an annual basis throughout the United States.

ASB
www.asbweb.org

The Canadian Society of Biomechanics (CSB) was founded in 1973. Its purpose is similar to the ASB's; however, the CSB has successfully expanded internationally, as evidenced by the large participation of international scientists. The meetings are held biannually.

CSB
www.csb-scb.com

The International Society of Biomechanics (ISB) was founded in 1973 and has about 1,000 members today. The purpose of the ISB is to promote the study of all areas of biomechanics at the international level, although special emphasis is given to the biomechanics of human movement. The ISB meetings are held on a biannual basis.

ISB
www.isbweb.org/

The International Society of Biomechanics in Sports (ISBS) was set up to provide a forum for the exchange of ideas between sport biomechanics researchers, coaches, and teachers; to bridge the gap between researchers and practitioners; and to gather and disseminate information and materials on biomechanics in sports. The first meeting took place in 1982, and a constitution was developed by 1983. Meetings are held on an annual basis.

ISBS
www.isbs.org/

PROMINENT JOURNALS AND RELATED PUBLICATIONS

Because of the breadth of scientific inquiry in the field of biomechanics, several journals publish articles related to the field. Those in which scientific articles are most commonly found follow.

PRIMARY JOURNALS

Clinical Biomechanics

Journal of Applied Biomechanics

Journal of Biomechanics

RELATED PUBLICATIONS

American Journal of Sports Medicine

British Journal of Sports Medicine

Ergonomics

Foot and Ankle International

Gait & Posture

Human Factors

Human Movement Science

International Journal of Sports Medicine

Journal of Bone and Joint Surgery

Journal of Electromyography and Kinesiology

Journal of Human Movement Studies

Journal of Orthopaedic and Sports Physical Therapy

Journal of Orthopaedic Research

Journal of Sports Medicine and Physical Fitness

Journal of Strength and Conditioning Research

Journal of the American Podiatric Medical Association

Medicine & Science in Sport & Exercise

Medicine, Exercise, Nutrition and Health

Physical Therapy

Research Quarterly for Exercise and Sport

Strength and Conditioning Research

www

BIOMCH-L
*http://biomch-l.isbweb.org/
forum.php*

The BIOMCH-L newsgroup is an e-mail discussion group for biomechanics and human and animal movement science. To subscribe, and for more information on the resources available on BIOMCH-L, visit the site at left.

Boxes 9.1 and 9.2 are typical abstracts presented at the American Society of Biomechanics scientific conference.

FUTURE DIRECTIONS

In the future, biomechanics will be applied across many professional domains to understand fundamental movement in sports, exercise, medicine, robotics, biology, gaming, and occupational science. Applications of biomechanical analysis utilizing various measurements and tools will examine human movement from infants to elderly and from healthy to pathological populations. New and innovative analyses in biomechanics—for example, nonlinear analysis for human movement variability (Stergiou, 2004)—have been developed to study human performance. By using advanced mathematical algorithms, biomechanists can understand human movement variability in a nonlinear fashion. Such approaches will expand our understanding of human movement in many biomechanical applications, especially in clinical areas.

Biomechanics will also be combined with other disciplines in exercise science to provide a complete picture of how biomechanics influences human movement (Hamill, 2007). One such example is the interaction of biomechanics and exercise physiology in the physiological cost of running. Interestingly, runners' preferred speed represents the most efficient speed, as noted by the lowest oxygen consumption. Running faster or slower than the preferred speed results in increases in oxygen consumption (Hamill, 2007). Integrating multiple disciplines within exercise science will make the study of biomechanics

An abstract presented at the American Society of Biomechanics.

Myers, S. A., Johanning, J. M., Pipinos, I. I., & Stergiou, N. (2010). Gait variability patterns are altered in healthy young individuals during the acute reperfusion phase of ischemia-reperfusion. *Journal of Surgical Research, 164*(1), 6-12.

INTRODUCTION

Peripheral arterial disease (PAD) is a localized manifestation of systemic atherosclerosis, affecting the leg arteries and resulting in significantly reduced blood to the lower extremities. PAD affects eight to twelve million individuals in the US, with the majority of these being elderly[1]. Intermittent claudication, a cramping pain occurring in the lower extremity muscles with physical activity and relieved with rest, is the most common symptom of PAD. PAD has been shown to lead to poor health outcomes, immobility, physical dependence, and an increased risk for falling. Previous research in our laboratory indicates that PAD patients have altered gait variability patterns prior to the onset of claudication pain[2]. However, the specific mechanisms that contribute to these alterations in PAD patients are unclear. Potential mechanisms include insufficient blood flow, underlying neural and muscular abnormalities of the lower extremity, and systemic co-morbidities[3]. Therefore, our study sought to isolate and determine the impact of reduced blood flow on gait parameters by evaluating lower extremity gait variability before and after induced lower extremity vascular occlusion in healthy younger and older individuals. We hypothesized that a decrease in blood flow would result in significant gait variability alterations compared to baseline gait. Additionally, we hypothesize that age would augment the changes in gait variability following the vascular occlusion.

METHODS

Thirty healthy young subjects (Age: 22.8 ± 4.2 years) and 28 healthy older subjects (Age: 60.2 ± 8.2 years) walked on a treadmill while kinematics (60 Hz) were recorded using a Motion Analysis system. Participants walked at their self-selected speed for 3 minutes (Baseline). Next, vascular occlusion was induced by thigh cuffs placed bilaterally on the upper thighs and inflated to 200 mmHg for three minutes while subjects were standing. After three minutes of occlusion, the thigh cuffs were removed and the subjects immediately began walking on the treadmill (Post Occlusion). Relative joint angles of the ankle, knee, and hip were calculated for thirty strides from the Baseline and Post Occlusion conditions. Gait variability was assessed from the unfiltered joint angles using the largest Lyapunov exponent (LyE) and approximate entropy (ApEn). The LyE is a measure of the rate of divergence of neighbored state-space trajectories and it estimates the sensitivity of the locomotor system to perturbations. The ApEn quantifies the regularity or predictability of a time series. The Chaos Data Analyzer[4] was used to calculate the LyE. ApEn was computed using algorithms written by Pincus[5] implemented in Matlab. Gait variability was compared using a 2 X 2 ANOVA (Groups: Younger vs. Older, Conditions: Baseline vs. Post Occlusion). When a significant interaction was identified, independent t-tests were used for post-hoc analysis to identify significant differences between the group/condition combinations.

RESULTS AND DISCUSSION

There was a significant effect of condition for all variables tested. Specifically, the LyE and ApEn values were significantly higher Post Occlusion compared to the Baseline condition. There was also a significant effect of group, with the ApEn at the hip being significantly higher in the older group. Additionally, there was a significant interaction for the ApEn at the ankle. Specifically, the younger group had significantly higher values Post Occlusion as compared with the older and younger groups at baseline. Also, the older group Post Occlusion had significantly higher ApEn at the ankle compared with the younger group at baseline.

(continued)

box
9.1

Continued.

Our results demonstrate significant gait variability alterations for all lower extremity joints Post Occlusion based on the LyE and ApEn in both healthy younger and healthy older individuals. The direction of differences are similar to a previous study comparing gait variability of healthy matched controls and patients with PAD[2]. Specifically, the differences indicated an increase in noise and irregularity while walking after vascular occlusion and may reflect a diminished capacity of the neuromuscular system to achieve a stable gait. However, direct comparison of the magnitude of change in LyE values show that interruption of blood flow does not account for the total amount of changes in gait variability exhibited by patients with PAD. To compare values directly, the mean differences from the healthy baseline condition (younger and older combined means) were expressed as percentage change averaged across all joints for the Post Occlusion condition and for PAD patients as compared to the healthy baseline condition. The Post Occlusion condition had an average increase in LyE values of 11.5%, while the PAD patients had an average increase of 41.3%[2]. Thus, our findings support the idea that interruption of blood flow results in significant gait alterations in otherwise healthy individuals, but patients with PAD experience additional alterations in variability that are likely due to underlying cellular abnormalitites in the lower extremity muscles and nerves that have been demonstrated in these patients[6]. As a result of age, there was only one significant group effect of the six variables tested, while restricted blood flow caused significant differences in all variables (Table 1). This suggests that altered blood flow status, as seen in PAD, is a greater determinant of gait function than age.

SUMMARY

Collectively, our study shows that reduced blood flow, in the absence of pathology significantly alters gait variability patterns. However, the change in the gait variability patterns was not as severe as previously documented in symptomatic patients with PAD during pain free ambulation. These results support the hypothesis that additional neuromuscular problems in the lower extremities of patients with PAD contribute to gait alterations in

these patients. Nevertheless, blood flow is one mechanism contributing to altered gait variability patterns in patients with PAD and individuals with risk factors for PAD should be screened and treated immediately to prevent potential mobility problems (i.e. falls) and the development of more severe pathophysiological changes that have been observed in symptomatic PAD patients.

REFERENCES

1. American Heart Association, American Stroke Association. *Heart disease and stoke statistics*, 2007.
2. Myers S et al. *J Vasc Surg,* **49**, 924-31, 2009
3. McDermott M et al. *JAMA,* **286**,1599-606, 2001.
4. Sprott J, and Rowlands G. *Chaos data analyzer: The professional version*, American Institute of Physics, 1995.
5. Pincus S. *Chaos,* **5**, 110-7, 1995.
6. Pipinos I et al. *Vasc Endovascular Surg,* **42**, 101-12, 2008.

ACKNOWLEDGEMENTS

American Society of Biomechanics Graduate Student Grant-in-Aid, AAHPERD Graduate Student Grant-in-Aid, the Nebraska Research Initiative, and NIH (K25HD047194 and F31AG032788).

Table 1: Group means for the largest Lyapunov Exponent (LyE) and the approximate entropy (ApEn) for younger (Y) and older (O) groups during the Baseline (B) and Post Occlusion (PO) conditions. All values are reported mean ± standard deviation.

Condition	Ankle	Knee	Hip
LyE			
Y-B	.069 ± 0.02	.066 ± 0.02	.066 ± 0.02
Y-PO	.088 ± 0.02	.081 ± 0.02	.076 ± 0.02
O-B	.076 ± 0.02	.074 ± 0.02	.071 ± 0.02
O-PO	.080 ± 0.01	.084 ± 0.02	.080 ± 0.02
Significance	*	*	*
ApEn			
Y-B	.712 ± 0.13	.431 ± 0.08	.307 ± 0.06
Y-PO	.858 ± 0.17	.504 ± 0.08	.374 ± 0.08
O-B	.762 ± 0.14	.482 ± 0.08	.349 ± 0.08
O-PO	.822 ± 0.13	.527 ± 0.09	.406 ± 0.09
Significance	*, ‡, §, ‖,¶	*	*

* $p<0.05$, significant difference, B vs. PO
‡ $p<0.05$, significant difference, Y vs. O
§ $p<0.05$, significant interaction, Y-B vs. O-PO
‖ $p<0.05$, significant interaction, Y-B vs. Y-PO
¶ $p<0.05$, significant interaction, Y- PO vs. O-B

An abstract presented at the American Society of Biomechanics.

Huisinga, J. M., & Stergiou, N. (2011). Persons with multiple sclerosis show altered joint kinetics during walking after participating in elliptical exercise. *Journal of Applied Biomechanics.* Epub Oct. 3.

INTRODUCTION

Multiple Sclerosis is a progressive neurological disease that is associated with a wide range of symptoms including motor weakness, increased falls, exaggerated fatigue, poor balance, spasticity, vision problems, heat sensitivity, decreased physical activity, cognitive deficits, and depression [1]. Exercise has been shown to improve overall quality of life and mobility in MS patients [2, 3]. However, the most effective exercise modality to improve mobility in MS patients is unknown. In order to determine whether gait-simulating exercise training is a viable treatment option for MS patients, biomechanical analysis of gait is necessary to quantitatively determine whether changes in gait mechanics occurs as a result of the training. Therefore, the purpose of this study was to determine the effect of a short-term aerobic, gait-simulating exercise intervention on the functional movement status of MS patients. It was hypothesized that the training would result in joint torques and powers that were closer to those of healthy controls.

METHODS AND PROCEDURES

Eighteen MS patients (46.1 ± 10.1 yrs; EDSS 2.4 ± 0.7) and 18 healthy matched controls (40.7 ± 11.3 yrs) walked through a 10 meter walkway at their self-selected walking pace, while kinetics and kinematics were collected for 10 trials with a Kistler force plate (600Hz) and an 8-camera Motion Analysis system (60 Hz). Data collection was performed on the MS patients before and after individuals participated in a total of 15 exercise session over a period of six weeks. The exercise modality used by all patients was an elliptical exercise machine which allowed weight-bearing, sagittal plane motion with joint kinematics similar to walking [4]. Each training session consisted of 30 minutes of cumulative exercise. Healthy controls underwent only one gait analysis. Joint torques and powers were calculated from the ground reaction forces and the kinematics for each participant. Maximum flexor and extensor torques and maximum power absorption and generation were identified for the hip, knee, and ankle joints. Paired t-tests were used to compare within MS patients pre- and post-training while a linear mixed model was used to compare outcome measures between MS patients pre- and post-training to healthy controls with velocity as a covariate.

RESULTS

MS patients before training compared to healthy controls exhibited significantly decreased walking velocity, decreased ankle dorsiflexor torque (ADT), decreased ankle plantarflexor torque (APT), decreased knee extensor torque (KET), and decreased hip flexor torque (HFT). In addition MS patients had significantly decreased ankle dorsiflexor power absorption during early stance (A1), decreased ankle plantarflexor power generation during late stance (A2), decreased power absorption at the knee during early stance (K1), decreased hip extensor power generation during early stance (H1), and decreased power absorption of the hip flexors during late stance (H2) (Table 1). Velocity did not have a significant effect on any of these outcome variables. As a result of training, within the MS patients significant increases occurred in APT, HET, A1, A2, and

(continued)

box

9.2

Continued.

K1 such that after training, significant differences were not present for these variables between MS patients and controls.

DISCUSSION

Baseline differences between healthy controls and MS patients in joint torques and powers were present prior to the training which indicated that MS patients had significantly decreased flexor and extensor torques and decreased power generation and absorption at all three joints. Following the elliptical exercise training program, significant increases were found for both joint torques and powers such that the MS patients gait parameters moved closer to those of the healthy controls and were no longer significantly different. These results agree with our hypothesis and provide exhilarating support for the use of elliptical exercise training as a rehabilitation tool for MS patients. The significant improvements are occurring during early and late stance specifically. During early stance both ankle (A1) and knee (K1) power absorption are increased which indicates improved weight acceptance during the transition from double to single support. During late stance, there is increased plantarflexor torque (APT) as well

as increased power generation at the ankle (A2). During late stance/pre-swing, muscle activity at the ankle enables the leg to enter the swing phase with sufficient propulsion to move the body mass forward. Clinicians refer to gait powered by ankle push-off as using an "ankle strategy", which is thought to be the preferred walking strategy for healthy young adults [5]. Thus, as a result of short term (6 weeks/15 sessions) elliptical training, MS patients seem to have adopted a gait strategy that is similar to the preferred strategy of healthy adults. These findings provide support for the use of an elliptical exercise machine, which is a gait-simulating exercise, as a tool to improve gait mechanics in MS patients in a relatively short amount of time.

REFERENCES

1. Noseworthy et al. (2000) *N Engl J Med* 343(13):938-52.
2. Snook & Motl (2009) *Neurorehabil Neural Repair* 23(2):108-116.
3. Motl & Gosney (2008) *Mult Scler* 14(1):129-35.
4. Burnfield et al (2010) *Phys Therapy* 90(2):289-305.
5. Kerrigan et al. (1998) *Arch Phys Med Rehabil* 79(3):317-22.

ACKNOWLEDGEMENTS

ASB Grant-In-Aid, the MARS Foundation and the Nebraska Research Initiative.

		Pre-training mean (S.D)	Post-training mean (S.D.)	Control mean (S.D.)	*p-value* pre-con; pre-post; post-con
	Velocity (m/s)	1.11 (0.22)	1.12 (0.24)	1.24 (0.26)	0.023*; 0.212; 0.023*
Joint Torques (N*m/kg)	ADT	-0.277 (0.076)	-0.2844 (0.082)	-0.412 (0.197)	0.013*; 0.571 0.018*
	APT	1.189 (0.140)	1.266 (0.127)	1.341 (0.264)	0.016*; 0.004*; 0.166
	KET	0.542 (0.176)	0.549 (0.188)	0.705 (0.273)	0.020*; 0.333; 0.050*
	KFT	-0.269 (0.145)	-0.274 (0.168)	-0.292 (0.232)	0.833; 0.837; 0.835
	HET	0.611 (0.201)	0.688 (0.158)	0.802 (0.273)	0.123; 0.006*; 0.333
	HFT	-0.781 (0.188)	-0.763 (0.028)	-1.048 (0.306)	0.007*; 0.568; 0.003*
Joint Powers (Watts/kg)	A1	-0.394 (0.035)	-0.477 (0.042)	-0.661 (0.243)	0.002*; 0.003*; 0.060
	A2	2.499 (0.118)	2.81 (0.134)	3.193 (0.869)	0.017*; 0.003*; 0.177
	K1	-0.711 (0.056)	-0.807 (0.072)	-1.068 (0.432)	0.013*; 0.040*; 0.146
	K2	0.457 (0.048)	0.458 (0.051)	0.561 (0.323)	0.430; 0.959; 0.502
	K3	-0.497 (0.038)	-0.480 (0.042)	-1.057 (0.646)	0.153; 0.572; 0.093
	H1	0.410 (0.038)	0.438 (0.032)	0.660 (0.325)	0.036*; 0.396 0.036*
	H2	-0.687 (0.037)	-0.652 (0.039)	-0.990 (0.429)	0.025*; 0.345; 0.008*
	H3	0.490 (0.025)	0.464 (0.025)	0.784 (0.340)	0.108; 0.229; 0.131

Table 1: Joint torque and joint power variables; *Sig ($p < 0.05$).

more relevant for students and provide valuable insights into biomechanics research results.

In the research domain, human movement will be studied to a greater extent using virtual reality. The use of virtual reality takes biomechanical research beyond the laboratory settings to simulating actual environments from which natural human movement responses can be detected. Examples are the VENLab at Brown University, the Medical Virtual Reality Center format at the University of Pittsburgh, and the Nebraska Biomechanics Core Facility at the University of Nebraska at Omaha (Exhibit 9.13).

As new research technologies continue to emerge, wireless transmission will have a major impact on biomechanics. Using wireless systems, research activities normally conducted in laboratories can be expanded outside the laboratory to a larger monitored range of human activity. For example, a wireless biomedical gait device, Gait-O-Gram®, was developed at the Nebraska Biomechanics Core Facility to study human gait variability (Exhibit 9.14).

In sports and exercise research, an increasing emphasis is being placed on obtaining accurate measures to determine the outcomes of various training protocols. Computer modeling, simulation, and virtual reality can be used to evaluate a training protocol that is designed to enhance athletic performance. For example, an athlete can practice specific movements in virtual reality to get a cognitive edge. Such advanced biomechanical methodologies can optimize performance and further improve the design of training programs. In the future, successful training in sports and exercise will rely on both computer technology and various biomechanical measurements of movement.

WWW

Virtual Reality Sites

*www.cog.brown.edu/Research/
ven_lab/*

www.mvrc.pitt.edu/index.html

http://biomech.unomaha.edu

The virtual reality system at the Nebraska Biomechanics Core Facility at the University of Nebraska at Omaha.

exhibit   9.13

The wireless Gait-O-Gram® device was developed in the Nebraska Biomechanics Core Facility to study human gait variability.

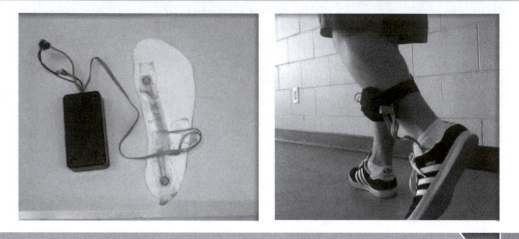

In clinical settings, biomechanical approaches and methods will commonly be used by physicians, physical therapists, and other specialists. The goals will be to examine pathological human movement and develop more effective treatments for patients to regain their quality of life by using motion analysis and gait evaluations that can be conducted away from the laboratory with inexpensive wireless technology. This technology will also be incorporated into standard clinical examinations in hospitals to increase the precision of the clinical diagnoses.

In occupational science, biomechanically designed environments will be the norm. Currently, the focus is on the engineering of the workplace; however, it is slowly being realized that the interface between the human and the machine is equally important. Thus, biomechanists are needed to work with engineers to design more biologically sound workplace layouts that are safe and will improve productivity.

As the scientific and clinical professions using biomechanical analysis of human movement expand further, the development of new training protocols for athletes and an exploration of new treatments and rehabilitation procedures for patients will follow. The advanced biomechanical technology will become essential to human movement studies in the future.

SUMMARY

Biomechanics is a discipline that uses a wide variety of instruments, techniques, and technologies to study movement. Biomechanists work in a number of areas including developmental biomechanics, biomechanics of exercise and sport, rehabilitative biomechanics, occupational biomechanics, and forensic biomechanics. Because of this diversity, a broad range of knowledge is required. Therefore, many students of biomechanics pursue advanced expertise in master's and doctoral programs. As a result of the variety of applications related to biomechanics, employment opportunities are extremely varied. These opportunities include positions in academia as well as industry and government.

study / QUESTIONS

1. Explain the focus of developmental biomechanics.
2. The safety and mechanical efficiency of tools would most likely be evaluated by which type of biomechanist?
3. List and describe some optical recording devices.
4. Define biomechanics.
5. Is biomechanics a discipline? Explain.
6. Why do we need to study movement using an interdisciplinary approach?
7. What is the difference between biomechanics and kinesiology?
8. Define kinetics, kinematics, dynamics, and statics.
9. Identify the major areas of research in biomechanics.
10. Give five examples of biomechanical applications.
11. What is a force platform?
12. Name five journals where biomechanists publish their research.

Visit the IES website to study, take notes, and try out the lab for this chapter.

learning \ ACTIVITIES

1. Go to either the International Society of Biomechanics in Sport website (www.isbs.org) or the Canadian Society of Biomechanics website (www.csb-scb.com). Write a brief description of the website's contents.
2. Find two different professional journals that publish articles related to biomechanics. Retrieve one article from each. In your own words, write an abstract for each article.
3. Explore (using the Internet and/or written sources) the job market for biomechanics, and write a brief report on one potential career opportunity.

suggested / READINGS

Adrian, M. J., & Cooper, J. M. (1995). *Biomechanics of human movement* (2nd ed.). New York: McGraw-Hill.

Alexander, R. M. (1992). *The human machine*. New York: Columbia University Press.

Chaffin, D. B., Andersson, G. B. J., & Martin, B. J. (1999). *Occupational biomechanics* (3rd ed.). New York: John Wiley & Sons.

Hall, S. J. (2006). *Basic biomechanics* (4th ed.). New York: WCB/McGraw-Hill.

Hamill, J., & Knutzen, K. M. (2006). *Biomechanical basis of human movement* (2nd ed.). Media, PA: Williams & Wilkins.

McGinnis, P. M. (2004). *Biomechanics of sport and exercise* (2nd ed.). Champaign, IL: Human Kinetics.

Nordin, M., & Frankel, V. H. (2012). *Basic biomechanics of the musculoskeletal system* (4th ed.). Philadelphia: Lippincott Williams & Wilkins.

Stergiou, N. (2004). *Innovative analyses of human movement*. Champaign, IL: Human Kinetics.

references

Alt, F. (1967). *Advances in bioengineering and instrumentation.* New York: Plenum Press.

Atwater, A. E. (1980). Kinesiology/biomechanics: Perspectives and trends. *Research Quarterly in Exercise and Sport, 51,* 193–218.

Bates, B. T. (1974). The fourth international seminar on biomechanics. *Journal of Health, Physical Education, and Recreation, 45,* 69–70.

Bates, B. T. (1991). The need for an interdisciplinary curriculum. In *Third National Symposium on Teaching Kinesiology and Biomechanics in Sports Proceedings,* pp. 163–166. Ames, IA.

Bernstein, N. (1967). *The coordination and regulation of movement.* New York: Pergamon Press.

Bogert, T. V., & Gielo-Perczak, K. (1992). Letter to the Editor: BIOMCH-L: An electronic mail discussion forum for biomechanics and movement science. *Journal of Biomechanics, 25,* 1367.

Charles, J. M. (1994). *Contemporary kinesiology: An introduction to the study of human movement in higher education.* Englewood, CO: Morton.

Chen, S. J., Pipinos, I., Johanning, J., Huisinga, J. M., & Myers, S. A. (2006). The effect of claudication on joint movements during walking. *Proceedings of the 30th Annual Meeting of the American Society of Biomechanics.* Blacksburg, VA.

Cooper, J. M. (1971). *Selected topics on biomechanics.* Chicago: Athletic Institute.

Dillman, C. J., & Sears, R. G. (1978). *Proceedings of the National Conference on Teaching Kinesiology.* Urbana-Champaign: University of Illinois.

Fenn, W. O. (1929). Mechanical energy expenditure in sprint running as measured in moving pictures. *American Journal of Physiology, 90,* 343–344.

Fenn, W. O. (1931). A cinematographical study of sprinters. *Science Monthly, 32,* 346–354.

Hamill, J. (2007). Biomechanics curriculum: Its content and relevance to movement sciences. *Quest, 59,* 25–33.

Hay, J. G. (1973). *Biomechanics of sports techniques.* Englewood Cliffs, NJ: Prentice Hall.

Higgins, J. R. (1977). *Human movement: An integrated approach.* St. Louis, MO: Mosby.

Higgins, S. (1985). Movement as an emergent form: Its structural limits. *Human Movement Science, 4,* 119–148.

Huisinga, J. M., Pipinos, I.I., Stergiou, N., & Johanning, J. M. (2010). Treatment with pharmacological agents in peripheral arterial disease patients does not result in biomechanical gait changes. *Journal of Applied Biomechanics, 26,* 341–348.

Huisinga, J. M., & Stergiou, N. (2010, August). Elliptical exercise improves walking mechanics in multiple sclerosis patients. *Proceedings of the 34th Annual Meeting of the American Society of Biomechanics.* Providence, Rhode Island.

Judkins, T. N., Oleynikov, D., & Stergiou, N. (2009). Electromyographic response is altered during robotic surgical training with augmented feedback. *Journal of Biomechanics 42*(1), 71–76.

Kurz, M. J., & Stergiou, N. (2005). An artificial neural network that utilizes hip joint actuations to control bifurcations and chaos in a passive dynamic bipedal walking model. *Biological Cybernetics, 93*(3), 213–221.

Kurz, M. J., & Stergiou, N. (2007). Hip actuations can be used to control bifurcations and chaos in a passive dynamic walking model. *Journal of Biomechanical Engineering, 129*(2), 216–222.

Myers, S. A., Johanning, J. M., Pipinos, I. I., & Stergiou, N. (2010, August). Vascular occlusion affects gait variability patterns of healthy younger and older individuals. *Proceedings of the 34th Annual Meeting of the American Society of Biomechanics.* Providence, Rhode Island.

Myers, S. A., Pipinos, I. I., Johanning, J. M., & Stergiou, N. (2011). Gait variability of patients with intermittent claudication is similar before and after the onset of claudication pain. *Clinical Biomechanics, 26,* 729–734.

Narazaki, K., Oleynikov, D., & Stergiou, N. (2006). Robotic surgery training and performance: Identifying objective variables for quantifying the extent of proficiency. *Surgical Endoscopy, 20*(1), 96–103.

Nelson, R. C. (1980). Biomechanics: Past and present. In J. M. Cooper & B. Haven (Eds.), *Proceedings of the biomechanical symposium,* pp. 4–13. Bloomington, IN: The Indiana State Board of Health.

Nigg, B. M., & Herzog, W. (1994). *Biomechanics of the musculoskeletal system.* New York: John Wiley & Sons.

Rodgers, M. M., & Cavanagh, P. R. (1984). Glossary of biomechanical terms, concepts, and units. *Physical Therapy, 64,* 1886–1902.

Suh, I. H., Mukherjee, M., Schrack, R., Park, S. H., Chien J. H., Oleynikov, D., & Siu, K. C. (2011). Electromyographic correlates of learning during robotic surgical training in virtual reality. *Studies in Health Technology and Informatics, 163,* 630–634.

Terauds, J. (1982). *Biomechanics in sports: Proceedings of the international symposium of biomechanics in sports.* Del Mar, CA: Academic Press.

Wilkerson, J. D. (1997). Biomechanics. In J. D. Massengale & R. A. Swanson (Eds.), *The history of exercise and sport science,* pp. 321–365. Champaign, IL: Human Kinetics.

Wurdeman, S. R., Huisinga, J. M., Filipi, M., & Stergiou, N. (2010). Multiple sclerosis affects the frequency content in the vertical ground reaction forces during walking. *Clinical Biomechanics.* Epub ahead of print. doi: 10.1016/j.clinbiomech.2010.09.021.

Motor Control and Motor Learning

DAVID E. SHERWOOD

DEFINITIONS IN MOTOR LEARNING AND MOTOR CONTROL

motor learning ■

Have you ever watched an elite snowboarder such as Shaun White and been impressed with the precision, style, and power of his performance? How did he get to the point where his performance seems so effortless and smooth, when we know that in actuality his heart must be racing? How do we design practice schedules to develop these skills in elite athletes? What kind of feedback do we give novices or elite performers to maximize their performance? These questions are central to the study of the acquisition of motor skills or **motor learning**.

At the same time, have you ever wondered how the human nervous system can control the elegant and complex movements of an ice skater? Or how you find yourself dropping a hot frying pan before even knowing that it was too hot to handle? How does the nervous system know what muscles to activate, in what time sequence, while minimizing activity in muscles that would interfere with the chosen activity? What specific structures in the nervous system are responsible for controlling movement? What happens when these structures are damaged by injury or disease? All these questions are asked by investigators

motor control ■

in **motor control,** the study of how the nervous system controls movement.

Even though the terms *motor learning* and *motor control* were introduced in separate paragraphs, they are very closely linked. When we talk about motor learning, we are really talking about how one learns to control the proper muscles and coordinate the limbs to produce the chosen action. So to understand how one learns motor skills one also needs to have an understanding of how actions are produced by the nervous system.

MOTOR LEARNING AND MOTOR CONTROL ACTIVITIES

As with the other areas of exercise science described in this book, the areas of motor learning and motor control are complex and can be studied from a number of different perspectives. At the most global level, specialists in these areas can study motor learning and control at the behavioral level by observing the change in the actual performance as the level of skill increases. Investigations at this level might focus on how the movements of the joints and limbs (i.e., biomechanics) change with practice. Or questions about learning and control at a level "closer" to the nervous system itself by studying the electrical signal associated with muscle contraction (electromyography, EMG) may also be addressed. One might assess changes in the timing or amplitude of the EMG signal from various muscles over practice trials. Finally, specialists might investigate control and learning issues by recording from structures within the nervous system itself (typically done with animal subjects) or by using positron emission tomography (PET) scans (see Chapter 4) to assess the areas of the brain that are most active during movement.

Another way to outline the characteristics of this field of study is shown in Box 10.1. Here the learning process is divided into three phases: before practice, during practice, and after practice. Within each of these phases, the issues that would be faced by the instructor are outlined. Each issue in each phase is a research area in motor learning and motor control.

Issues in motor learning and motor control across the learning process.

BEFORE PRACTICE

1. How do I want to present the skill to be learned (live demonstration, video, verbal explanation)?

2. How do I motivate learners so that they will want to practice?

3. What kind of knowledge do I want learners to have before they practice (rules, strategies, physical principles, biomechanics)?

4. How do I want to organize the practice session? Do I use blocked, random, or variable practice? Massed or distributed practice? How much practice time should be devoted to each task?

5. Do I break down the skill and teach it in parts or as a whole unit?

6. What kind of individual differences should I expect?

DURING PRACTICE

1. How do I give feedback during practice? What should I give feedback about, how often, and how precise should the information be?

2. How do I keep motivation up during practice? How much rest should I give between trials?

3. What should the learners be paying attention to as they practice?

4. Should I have them evaluate their own errors?

AFTER PRACTICE

1. What kind of postperformance feedback should I give, video feedback or verbal feedback?

2. How do I help them remember what they learned today?

3. How much retention should I expect?

HISTORY OF MOTOR CONTROL AND MOTOR LEARNING

The goal in this section is not to present an exhaustive history of motor control and motor learning but to highlight the people and historical events that shaped our modern-day thoughts about how movements are controlled and learned. The focus is on the following issues. First, how did we come to understand how the nervous system causes muscle contraction? It was a question that was pondered for over 1,500 years until it was resolved in the mid-1800s. Second, how did we come to know about **cerebral localization,** or the idea that specific mental, motor, and sensory processes are correlated with discrete regions of the brain? Finally, why did it take so long for a theory of motor learning to emerge?

■ *cerebral localization*

Animal Spirits or Bioelectricity?

The most basic issue in motor control is to discover how the nervous system can control the contraction of the muscles. The view advanced by the Roman physician Claudius Galen (129–199 CE) was that the nervous system controlled muscular contraction with a hydraulic system whereby the passage of fluids (he called them "animal spirits") down the nerves caused the muscles to inflate. When the fluid was evacuated, the muscle relaxed (Jeannerod, 1985). This hydraulic model was clearly in evidence as late as the mid-1600s, when the French philosopher René Descartes (1596–1650) proposed his model of muscle activation (Wozniak, 1996). Exhibit 10.1 shows his model. According to Descartes, movement was stimulated by a sensory signal that caused the influx of animal sprits, which were present in the heart and arteries, selectively into the muscles required

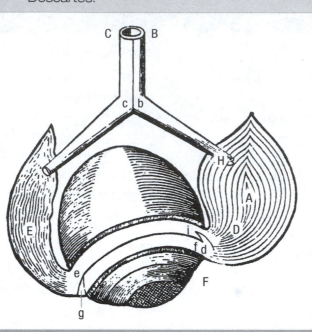

Animal spirits by nervous tubes *B* and *C*. In the case presented here, animal spirits inflate muscle *A*, while muscle *E* relaxes. A movement (here, of the ocular globe) is produced toward muscle *A*. To explain this reciprocal innervation mechanism by the hydraulic model, Descartes had to postulate the existence of a complicated system of valves that allowed for the evacuation or retention of animal spirits. In the case presented here, valve *H* closes, which allows muscle *A* to be filled, while muscle *E* can freely empty by evacuation canal *e*.

From *The Brain Machine,* by Marc Jeannerod (tr. David Urion). Cambridge, MA: Harvard University Press, 1985.

for the movement. Even though scientists of the time demonstrated evidence against the hydraulic model by showing that nerves were not tubes, liquid did not run out when a nerve was severed, and muscle volume was constant before and after a contraction (Jeannerod, 1985), the hydraulic model persisted until the late 1700s, when it was replaced by the notion of bioelectricity.

The shift toward a bioelectric explanation for the control of muscle was instigated by scientists who noticed that some animals, like eels, were capable of giving shocks when touched. This observation "sparked" the notion that animals could generate electricity in their bodies. Around 1780, Luigi Galvani noted that an electric current applied to the muscle or nerve would cause a contraction of the muscle of a frog. He also noted that muscular contractions occurred when the frog preparation was connected to lightning rods during thunderstorms as well as when a circuit was completed using other means in the absence of thunderstorms. Galvani concluded that certain tissues were capable of generating animal electricity that caused muscle contraction. Later, working with his cousin Giovanni Aldini (1762–1834), Galvani demonstrated a muscle contraction in one frog by touching it with a nerve from a different frog, establishing the existence of bioelectricity (Sabbatini, 1998). The paradigm shift was now complete. Nerves were not water pipes or channels, as Descartes had thought; rather, they were electrical conductors. Information within the nervous system was carried by electricity generated directly by the organic tissue (Sabbatini, 1998).

One of the first to study animal electricity was the Italian physician Luigi Galvani (1737–1798) from Bologna.

Cerebral Localization

Even though the general idea of cerebral localization had been present for many years, it was not until the 1800s that the attempt to show empirical support for localization was made. The first empirical efforts came from Franz Josef Gall (1728–1828), a German neuroanatomist and physiologist, who noted apparent relationships between unusual talents and striking differences in facial and/or cranial appearance. Based on the assumptions that the size and shape of the cranium reflected the size and shape of the underlying regions of the brain and that the level of development of a given ability was a reflection of the size of the cerebrum, Gall argued that a correlation between a well-developed ability and a particularly well-developed part of the cranium was evidence of localization of that ability in that portion of the cerebrum (Wozniak, 1996).

The correlational methods of Gall were replaced by the neurosurgical techniques utilized by the child-prodigy Marie-Jean-Pierre Flourens (1794–1867), who earned a medical degree before he turned 20. Flourens completely uncovered the brain and then removed a specific portion of the brain (called ablation) and noted the effect on the behavior of the animal (a pigeon, in this case). He was able to localize a motor center in the medulla oblongata and stability and motor coordination in the cerebellum (Wozniak, 1996). However, when he ablated the cerebrum, many of the higher cognitive functions were damaged, leading Flourens to conclude that the functions of intelligence, perception, and drive were distributed throughout the cerebrum.

David Ferrier (1843–1928) mapped areas of the sensory cortex and motor cortex in many species, confirming the concept of cerebral localization for sensory and motor processes.

The next breakthrough was made possible by a technological development pioneered by Gustav Fritsch (1838–1927) and Eduard Hitzig (1838–1907) in the area of electrical stimulation. They developed a method whereby one could electrically stimulate one area of the cerebral cortex and note the effect on the behavior of the animal. They demonstrated that stimulation of certain areas of the cortex resulted in movements of the contralateral (opposite side) limbs and that ablation of these areas led to weakness of these limbs.

Theoretical Developments in Motor Learning

Motor learning and control are thought to be younger areas of exercise science because theoretical developments in these subdisciplines were delayed relative to other areas. How did this come about?

One problem with the early work in motor learning and control was that researchers focused on understanding the performance of the skill, rather than on the factors that influenced the long-term retention or learning of the skill. For example, in the late 1800s and early 1900s researchers investigated issues such as the contribution of visual information to accuracy of hand movements (Bowditch & Southard, 1882) and speed–accuracy trade-offs in rapid movements (Hollingworth, 1909). Although motor skills were the focus of these studies, they shed little light on the processes underlying the learning of skills. The other major roadblock to the development of a motor learning theory was the research emphasis on specific skills and the solving of practical problems. For example, research in telegraphy, typing, and other vocational skills dominated this time period.

During the 1920s and 1930s, some researchers, mostly from psychology departments, began to focus on more basic research issues, rather than on the acquisition of specific skills. Studies on how to organize practice schedules appeared (Hunter, 1929) as well as studies on the transfer of training from one skill to another (McGeoch, 1931), the retention of skills (Book, 1925), and individual differences in motor skills (Kincaid, 1925). One of the most debated topics of the time was on the existence of *plateaus* in the learning curve, where gains in performance stalled for some time before gains were again noted. Although some evidence was shown for plateaus (Bryan & Harter, 1897), many studies failed to replicate the earlier studies (Kincaid, 1925). Also, the well-known psychologist E. L. Thorndike (1874–1949) published his *law of effect,* which would guide researchers' work in knowledge of results for years to come (Thorndike, 1927). The law states that responses that are rewarded will be repeated but that those actions followed by punishment will be extinguished. It would be many years until this law was replaced in the minds of many people as to how skills were learned. Even though the beginnings of theory were noted during this time, much of the research focused on industrial applications, as in earlier years. Studies of time–motion and efficiency in shoveling coal or mixing mortar were common (Schmidt, 1982).

FOCUS POINT

The first scientific journal dedicated to research in motor control and learning (*Journal of Motor Behavior*) was founded by Richard A. Schmidt in 1969 and has become one of the most well-respected journals in the field.

The major impact on research in motor skills during the 1940s and 1950s came from World War II. The military spent significant amounts of money on research related to pilot and military training. For example, the Air Force began a psychomotor testing program to help to identify potential pilots by correlating motor, perceptual, and intellectual abilities with flying ability. After the war, military spending in motor skill research continued, but with a broader focus that included the teaching, transfer, and retention of motor skills (Adams, 1987). The second factor that had a major impact on motor learning research was the emergence of general learning theories from psychologists such as C. L. Hull. Hull believed that his theory covered all kinds of behavior, both verbal and motor, so many of the experiments used to test the theory used motor skills as the learning task (Hull, 1943). Even though Hull's theory was later shown to be incorrect, it did stimulate research and thinking about motor skills.

The 1960s were an exciting time in motor learning because the discipline finally began to come into focus. Individuals like Franklin Henry, Alfred Hubbard, Arthur Slater-Hammel, and Jack Adams developed highly active university research laboratories dedicated to the study of motor skills. They trained graduate students like Richard A. Schmidt, George Stelmach, Ronald Marteniuk, and Walter Kroll, who had major impacts on the field themselves.

During the 1970s, interest in motor skills reached a peak when Jack Adams published his paper "Closed-Loop Theory of Motor Learning" in 1971, outlining the first true theory specific to motor learning (Adams, 1971). Throughout the rest of the 1970s, a number of papers were published testing the predictions of Adams's theory, which in general held up reasonably well to scientific scrutiny. In 1975, Richard A. Schmidt published the second theory of motor learning in his paper "A Schema Theory of Discrete Motor Skill Learning," which challenged Adams's theory on several points (Schmidt, 1975). For the next 10 years or so, the battle between the two theories was fought on the pages of the *Journal of Motor Behavior* and *Research Quarterly for Exercise and Sport*. It was an intellectually challenging and thrilling time to be a graduate student in the field (more about these theories later).

Another major paradigm shift was also under way, away from the more traditional stimulus–response (SR) approach championed by Thorndike toward the information-processing approach sparked by the work of people like U.

Neisser (Neisser, 1967). In the newer approach, the human was modeled as an active processor of information who needed to code sensory information, store it, and plan actions based on environmental information. Researchers focused on the stages of information processing (stimulus identification, response selection, and response programming) and short- and long-term memory stores. The information-processing approach continues to be a focus for many motor skill researchers today.

THEORETICAL APPROACHES

Now that you are familiar with how the field of motor control and learning developed, we can return to the issues presented at the beginning of the chapter. That is, how are movements controlled and learned? What are the current ideas about how the nervous system controls movement? How do we plan teaching strategies to maximize learning? As this information is presented, you will understand the various theoretical approaches that are used to help guide our investigations in the area.

Theories of Motor Control

Several theories have been developed to explain how the nervous system controls movement, including multilevel movement control, open-loop and closed-loop control theories, and dynamic pattern theory.

Understanding the theories requires a basic understanding of the nervous system and its two parts: the central nervous system (CNS) and the peripheral nervous system (PNS). The central nervous system, which includes the brain and spinal cord, coordinates the activities between the various parts of the body. The peripheral nervous system consists primarily of nerves extending from the brain and spinal cord, linking the body and the CNS. The PNS can be divided into a sensory or afferent division, which detects changes in the environment and conducts nerve impulses from the various sensory receptors toward the CNS, and a motor or efferent division, which transmits impulses away from the CNS to the effectors (muscles and glands). The combination of the nervous system and the muscles that work together to permit movement is referred to as the *neuromuscular system*.

Multilevel movement control

One approach that has been taken to help us understand the motor control process has been to conceptualize the neuromuscular system as having a number of levels. Each level of the system involves unique physiological structures that contribute to the control of movement. The upper level is composed of the brain structures that are responsible for the planning and initiation of movement. For example, the **supplementary motor cortex** has been shown to be involved in the movement planning process, whereas movement initiation is controlled by both the **basal ganglia** and the **motor cortex**. Specifically, the basal ganglia initiate action and also control movement amplitude or distance (Jeannerod, 1985). The motor cortex is involved in determining which muscles are involved in the action and the particular level of force required for the action. Also, the motor cortex is organized *somatotopically,* which means that each region in the motor cortex is dedicated to the control of a certain part of the body. Parts of the body that require very fine muscular control (e.g., the

■ *supplementary motor cortex*
■ *basal ganglia*
■ *motor cortex*

fingers and lips) are represented by more nerve cells (neurons) than muscles that are involved in gross movement (e.g., trunk muscles). The somatosensory cortex, which lies just posterior to the motor cortex, is involved in processing the sensory feedback from sensory receptors for touch, vision, hearing, and proprioception. The somatosensory cortex is also somatotopically organized. The **cerebellum**, located at the base of the brain (Exhibit 10.2), helps to regulate coordination and the control of fine movements, like touching your finger to your nose with your eyes closed.

cerebellum ■

Damage to the cerebellum can result in a loss of muscular strength and coordination.

How do these structures work together to plan and initiate an action? Suppose that you want to throw a dart to a bull's-eye. The movement plan is sent from the supplementary motor cortex to the motor cortex, where the relevant muscles are chosen for the task. The basal ganglia provide the activation for the movement and arm amplitude information. The movement commands from the motor cortex are also sent to the cerebellum, allowing for adjustments in the movement program. The pathway from the motor cortex to the cerebellum and back again is called the cerebro-cerebellar loop, and it provides for very rapid adjustments (10 milliseconds) in the original movement commands. The motor commands that move the arm are sent down to the next lowest level, the spinal level, through efferent pathways.

Two major efferent pathways connect the upper level of the nervous system to the spinal level, the *pyramidal tract* and the *extrapyramidal tract*. The upper motor neurons (or first-order neurons) of the pyramidal tract descend without synapse from the motor cortex to the spinal cord (Exhibit 10.3). Some nerve fibers cross over the midline of the body in the medulla, forming the lateral corticospinal tract, while some fibers remain on the same side of the body, forming the ventral corticospinal tract. The upper motor neurons synapse with the lower motor neurons (second-order neurons or alpha motor neurons) that

exhibit / 10.2   Motor areas of the cortex.

Note that the area labeled "motor areas involved with the control of voluntary muscles" is the motor cortex. The supplementary motor cortex (not labeled) is just anterior of the motor cortex toward the frontal lobe. The basal ganglia (also not labeled) are deep within the cerebral cortex. The area labeled "sensory areas involved with cutaneous and other senses" refers to the somatosensory cortex.

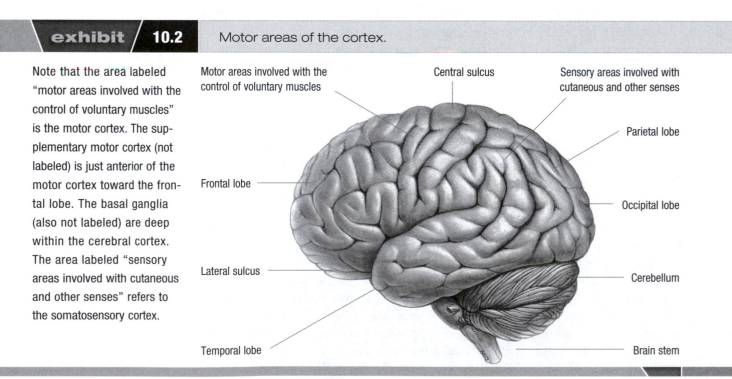

The pyramidal motor pathways.

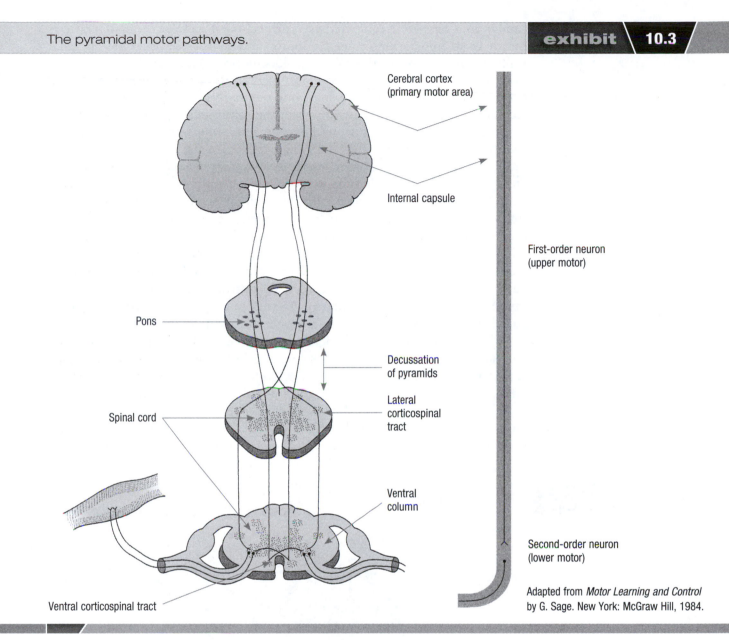

Cerebral cortex
(primary motor area)

Internal capsule

First-order neuron
(upper motor)

Pons

Decussation
of pyramids

Lateral
corticospinal
tract

Spinal cord

Ventral
column

Second-order neuron
(lower motor)

Ventral corticospinal tract

Adapted from *Motor Learning and Control*
by G. Sage. New York: McGraw Hill, 1984.

travel from the spinal cord to the muscle. Damage to the pyramidal tract causes paralysis in the muscles. The extrapyramidal tract is a very complicated tract that involves many of the structures already discussed in the upper level. The first-order neurons originate in many areas of the cerebral cortex, including the motor cortex, and synapse on several cortical and subcortical areas, including the basal ganglia, cerebellum, thalamus, and brain stem. Second-order neurons descend to the spinal level from some of these structures. It is thought that the extrapyramidal system helps to refine movements initiated by the pyramidal tract and acts to control posture and balance.

The middle level in the model is the spinal level, which is where the upper motor neurons synapse with the lower motor neurons in the spinal cord. Also, sensory receptors in the muscle send nerve fibers back into the spinal cord, where they synapse with lower motor neurons. Early ideas about the spinal cord held that it was merely a relay station between the brain and the muscles similar to a telephone cable. However, the current view of the spinal cord is that it is an integration center for motor and sensory information and that it plays a major role in the control of locomotion. Much of the evidence for the current view of the spinal cord as a locomotor control center comes from experimental work on animals involving the midbrain preparation. With this technique, the spinal cord is severed in the midbrain, separating the middle level of the nervous system from the upper level where voluntary movements are controlled. In this state the animal is unable to sense any stimulation from the body and is also unable to perform voluntary movements of the limbs. However, if the animal is supported on a treadmill and is stimulated by an electrical current to the spinal cord, the animal begins stepping movements similar to normal gait patterns. Interestingly, the animal continues stepping even when the electrical stimulus is turned off. In addition, stepping can be initiated by turning on the treadmill, and stepping speed can be increased by increasing treadmill speed. This work has given rise to the concept of a central pattern generator in the spinal cord that controls gait patterns without the involvement of the higher centers of the nervous system. Clearly, the spinal cord is much more complex than a simple relay station, as once believed.

The lowest level of the model includes the muscles, tendons, ligaments, and sensory receptors in the muscles involved in movement control. One way that the spinal level and the lower level interact is through the control of reflexes. For example, we have all had our reflexes tested by tapping the knee with a small mallet, which should result in a small kick of the foot. Muscle receptors called **muscle spindles** (Exhibit 10.4) that lie parallel with the main skeletal muscle fibers, called *extrafusal muscle fibers,* mediate this *monosyn-*

muscle spindle ■

---

exhibit / 10.4   Muscle spindle.

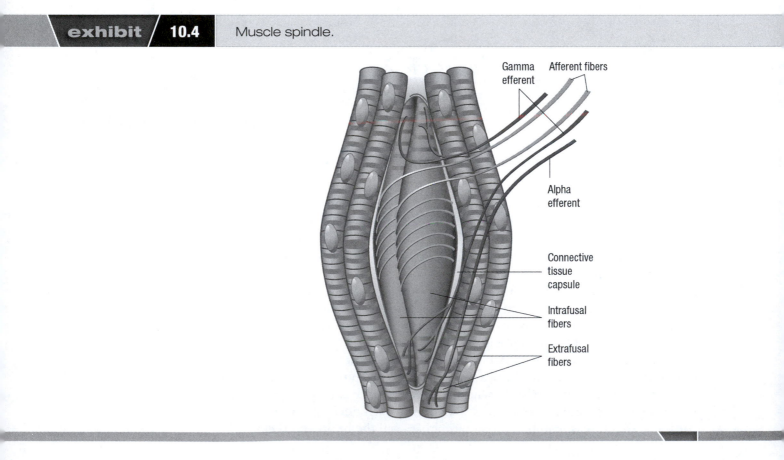

Gamma efferent

Afferent fibers

Alpha efferent

Connective tissue capsule

Intrafusal fibers

Extrafusal fibers

exhibit 10.5

Diagram of a two-neuron reflex, from a spindle in a muscle, back to the muscle fibers of the same muscle.

exhibit \ **10.5**

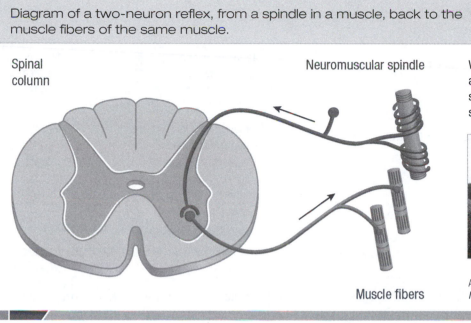

Spinal column

Neuromuscular spindle

Muscle fibers

When the patellar tendon is tapped with a rubber mallet, muscle spindles are stretched, resulting in the myotatic (or stretch) reflex and the knee-jerk response.

Adapted from E. Gardner, *Fundamentals of Neurology*, 2nd ed. © 1958.

aptic stretch reflex (Exhibit 10.5). The polar ends of the muscle spindle are composed of contractile tissue called *intrafusal muscle fibers*. From the nuclear bag and nuclear chain fibers in the central part of the muscle spindle emerges the *Ia afferent fiber,* which carries sensory information about the amount of stretch on the spindle to the spinal cord. When the patellar tendon is tapped, the quadriceps muscle is stretched, stretching both the extrafusal muscle fibers and the muscle spindles within the muscle. Because the muscle spindle is sensitive to muscle stretch, the Ia afferent fiber increases its firing rate in this situation. The signal is passed along the Ia afferent fiber to the spinal cord, where it synapses with the alpha motor neurons for the quadriceps, resulting in a small contraction and thus the kicking action. The muscle spindle is also sensitive to the velocity or speed of muscle stretch, which is signaled by the group II afferents.

As you can see, all levels of the nervous system are involved in the control of movement. Voluntary movements utilize all levels of the system, from the upper level where movements are planned and initiated, to the lower level where the alpha motor neurons for the appropriate muscles are activated. For reflexive movements, in which a stimulus leads to an involuntary response, only the spinal and lower levels may be involved.

Open-loop and closed-loop control theories

Another way to conceptualize how the nervous system organizes movement is to consider whether movements are controlled with an open- or closed-loop system (Exhibit 10.6). In an **open-loop control** system the higher centers are responsible for the planning and initiating of the movement, the selection of the relevant muscles, and the output of the efferent signals to the spinal and the lower levels. Some of the best evidence for open-loop control comes from animal studies showing that monkeys could climb and move about in their cages even after **deafferentation** (cutting only the sensory nerves entering the spinal cord) (Taub, 1976). Because feedback from the limbs was not available due to

■ *open-loop control*

■ *deafferentation*

exhibit / 10.6   Open- and closed-loop control.

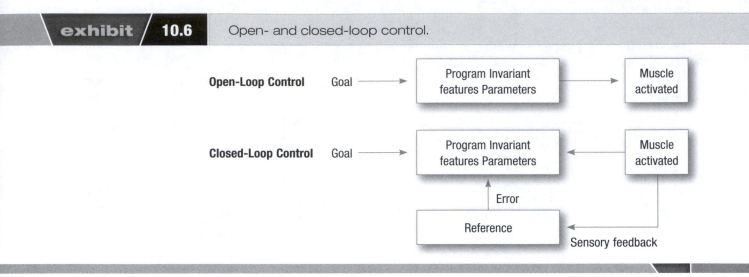

deafferentation, control must have been achieved by the higher centers using efferent commands exclusively. Another example of open-loop control comes from *motor program theory,* championed by Schmidt (1982). According to Schmidt, practicing motor skills results in the learning of stored motor programs that control the action without the influence of peripheral feedback. The motor program selects the muscles involved and controls the timing and the sequence of movements in the action, all without the need for sensory feedback. Schmidt has also suggested that the motor program is **generalized** to control a class of actions such as throwing or kicking. In this way, a separate program does not have to be stored for every possible movement that we can make, thus avoiding a storage problem for the brain. According to this idea, all movements within the general class of movements share the same invariant characteristics, those features that do not change from movement to movement. The program can be flexible by using different parameters (e.g., force, time, and amplitude) to meet the goals of the task, even though the invariant features (the overall movement pattern) remain the same.

generalized motor program ■

closed-loop control ■

    Closed-loop control, in contrast, uses both efferent and afferent information to control the action. As with open-loop control, the higher centers plan and initiate the action, but, in addition, closed-loop control utilizes sensory feedback from the relevant muscles to make corrections in the original movement plan. For example, the spinal feedback loop involving the muscle spindles requires 30 to 60 milliseconds and provides rapid, small-amplitude corrections to the movement. Feedback loops involving higher centers require 60 to 120 milliseconds, depending on the type of correction involved. The other major difference between the open- and closed-loop systems is the need for a reference mechanism in the closed-loop system. The reference mechanism is a perceptual–motor template of the desired action that is stored in the higher centers. For the motor system to detect errors, feedback from the limbs must be compared with the reference. If there is a mismatch between the incoming feedback and the reference, an error is detected, and the higher centers can correct the error with additional efferent signals.

    One model that utilizes closed-loop control is the equilibrium point model (EP) (Feldman, 1986). Unlike the motor programming theory in which the level of force is part of the program commands, the EP model claims that the relative tension between the agonist and antagonist muscles is what is controlled by the higher centers. Suppose that you want to move a limb from a stationary position to another position. According to the EP model, a limb is stationary because the tensions created by the agonist and antagonist muscles are equal. To move to another position, the relative tensions between the agonists and the antagonists must be changed. For example, the force in the biceps could be increased relative to that in the triceps, resulting in forearm flexion. To stabilize the limb at a new position, the triceps force would have to increase so that the forces could be brought into equilibrium. Sensory feedback from the muscles and joints is used to help keep the limb at the equilibrium point, so the EP model can be classified as a closed-loop model. Box 10.2 is an abstract of a research study in motor control.

Dynamic pattern theory

A relatively recent theory of motor control is the dynamic pattern theory introduced by Kelso and others (1981). This theory focuses on the coordination between components within the nervous system, using the principles of nonlinear dynamics and chaos theory (Wallace, 1996). Even though the details of nonlinear dynamics are far beyond the scope of this chapter, some examples of how these ideas have been applied to motor control are presented. The chapter by Wallace (1996) is an excellent introduction into this area.

One major focus of dynamic pattern theory is how patterns of coordination change as a function of some outside variable called a control parameter. Suppose that you are walking on a treadmill and the treadmill speed is gradu-

---

box 10.2

Abstract of a research study in motor control.

Lin, C.H., Winstein, C. J., Fisher, B. E., & Wu, A. D. (2010). Neural correlates of the contextual interference effect in motor learning: A transcranial magnetic stimulation investigation. *Journal of Motor Behavior, 42*(4), 223–232.

The authors applied transcranial magnetic stimulation (TMS) to investigate the causal role of the primary motor cortex (M1) for the contextual-interference effect in motor learning. Previous work using a nonfocal TMS coil suggested a causal role for M1 during high-interference practice conditions, but this hypothesis has not yet been proven. In the first experiment, participants practiced three rapid elbow flexion-extension tasks in either a blocked or random order, with learning assessed by a delayed retention test. TMS was delivered immediately after feedback during practice using a circular coil, centered over the contralateral M1. Each participant practiced with one of three TMS conditions: no TMS, real TMS, or sham TMS. Although no significant differences were observed between groups during acquisition, retention of the random group was better than the blocked group. The learning benefits of random practice were attenuated in the real-TMS condition, but not in the sham-TMS or no-TMS conditions. In the second experiment, the authors studied the effects of suprathreshold TMS and subthreshold TMS over M1, lateral premotor cortex, and peripheral arm stimulation using a focal figure-8 coil on motor learning under random practice conditions. The authors found that only suprathreshold TMS on M1 produced significant disruption of retention compared to the other stimulation conditions. Results suggest that a high-threshold neuronal population within M1 is causally important for enhanced retention following random, but not blocked practice. Results also support the early inter-trial interval as a critical period of M1 activity during practice. Overall, these results suggest neural circuits within M1 contribute to motor learning processing that depends on learners' training experience. Results contribute to knowledge of the critical and specific role that M1 plays in generating a learning advantage following high-interference practice conditions.

ally increased (the control parameter). At some critical speed, you will change from a walking pattern to a running pattern. The change in patterns seems to happen automatically, without thinking about it. One idea is that as the treadmill speed is increased, the walking pattern becomes unstable or more variable, and the switch is made to the more stable, less variable running pattern. In dynamic pattern theory, the motor output is not simply a function of what was programmed by higher centers, as in the motor programming theory. The control of the movement and the shift from one pattern to another are complicated functions of afferent input, efferent commands, and many other factors (anatomical, psychological, biomechanical, and biochemical).

Theories of Motor Learning

Turning now to the issue of how we learn motor skills, the next section briefly discusses two theories of motor learning, Adams's closed-loop theory (1971) and Schmidt's schema theory (1975).

Closed-loop theory

Adams's closed-loop theory arrived in 1971 and sparked a renewed interest in research in motor learning. Adams's theory assumes a closed-loop approach to motor control and focuses on how we acquire slow positioning movements (see Exhibit 10.7). Adams states that we form a reference of the correct movement, called a perceptual trace, over repeated practice trials. Early in practice the perceptual trace is weak because the learner has not achieved many correct responses. But as the learner receives verbal feedback from the instructor termed **knowledge of results (KR),** the learner is able to correct his or her movement errors. KR provides error information about the result of the event like "Your serve was 2 feet long" or "Your golf ball sliced 35 yards." Once the learner corrects major errors and begins to repeat the correct response on a regular basis, the perceptual trace gains strength. After a great deal of practice, the perceptual trace is strong and can be used as a reference mechanism in a closed-loop control system. For example, during an action like a tennis serve, the sensory feedback from the moving limbs (called intrinsic feedback) is compared with the perceptual trace. If there is a mismatch, then an error is registered, and the higher centers can issue a correction. Once the perceptual

knowledge of results ■

---

exhibit / 10.7   A closed-loop approach to motor control.

Feedback/Knowledge of results (KR)

INPUT → **Processing and Execution**

Perception → Decision-making → Motor program initiation

→ OUTPUT

trace is strong, Adams claims that the learner can continue to improve without KR, since learners can detect and correct their own movement errors with the perceptual trace. Adams also proposes a mechanism called the memory trace that is responsible for movement initiation. According to Adams's theory, the best way to strengthen the perceptual trace and the memory trace is to use constant practice, that is, to attempt to repeat the correct movement time and time again, with KR on every practice trial. Box 10.3 is an abstract of a research study in motor learning that involves practice with different KR delays.

Schema theory

The next theory of motor learning appeared in 1975 when Schmidt published his paper on schema theory. Schmidt's main dissatisfaction with Adams's theory was that it implied that a distinct perceptual trace and memory trace need to be learned for every action that one can perform. If you want to learn to shoot a basketball, for example, you would have to practice shooting from each and every point on the court to be prepared for a game situation. This did not make sense to Schmidt and others in the field. Instead, Schmidt proposed that learners acquire rules (i.e., schemas) for producing movement and for evaluating performance that can be used in situations where novel movements are required. The *recall schema* is the rule used for producing movement, and the *recognition schema* is used to evaluate one's performance. The recall schema is developed by learning the relationship between the parameter (e.g., force or amplitude) used with the generalized motor program and the outcome of the action provided by KR. The recognition schema is developed by acquiring the relationship between the sensory feedback from the movement and the outcome of the action.

How might the recall schema, for example, develop with practice? Let's say that you want to teach basketball shooting to a novice. On each practice trial, the learner chooses the force parameter that he or she thinks will be required to get the ball to go the appropriate distance. If the ball is short or long, the performer adjusts the force parameter appropriately to correct the error on the previous trial. When moving to different positions on the court, different force parameters are required for the different distances involved.

Abstract of a research study in motor learning.

box 10.3

Badets, A., & Blandin, Y. (2010). Feedback schedules for motor-skill learning: The similarities and differences between physical and observational practice. *Journal of Motor Behavior, 42*(4), 257–268.

In two experiments, the authors assessed different knowledge of results (KR) schedules for observational and physical practice. In Experiment 1, participants had to learn a sequence-timing task under either a bandwidth (KR being delivered when participants' performance was outside a predefined bandwidth or range) or yoked (same number of KRs provided as the bandwidth group) KR procedure. The results show that for both practice conditions the bandwidth KR schedule was more effective in promoting learning than the yoked schedule. During Experiment 2, a KR frequency was controlled (100% or 33% KR) and the data indicate that a reduced KR frequency only enhanced the learning of observers. Because a low KR frequency improves the sensory process controlling motor learning, the authors propose that action observation may be perceptual in nature.

variable practice ■ This is called **variable practice,** and Schmidt believes that it is the best way to strengthen the recall and recognition schemas relative to constant practice. With variable practice, a wide range of force parameters is used, so the relationship between the parameter and the outcome is strong and can be used to estimate the parameter needed for a novel distance. Constant practice does not allow for a strong rule to be formed, because only one parameter is used. In fact, the major prediction of schema theory is that novel variations of the movement can be produced more effectively following variable, as opposed to constant, practice. The Future Directions section at the end of the chapter discusses whether these theories are still viable today.

TECHNOLOGY AND MOTOR CONTROL

Technology has had a tremendous effect on the study of motor control, particularly in providing information about the areas of the brain that are responsible for the control and coordination of movement. In addition, recent surgical techniques have been used to alleviate symptoms of serious conditions such as Parkinson's disease. This section gives a brief review of the latest technological advances in the study of motor control.

EEG (electroencephalography) is used to identify electrical activity of brain neurons by placing electrodes on the surface of the scalp. Brain activity is typically classified by the frequency of neuronal firing. For example, beta waves fire at the fastest rate and indicate an activated cortex, while delta waves fire quite slowly and indicate deep sleep. Researchers in motor control have used EEG to study brain activation patterns in skilled athletes in a variety of sports, including pistol shooting, dart throwing, and golf. The magnetic fields created by neuronal activity are detected with magnetoencephalography (MEG). Up to 150 sensors are placed close to the scalp to record the minute magnetic signals generated by brain neurons. MEG is better than EEG in localizing the sources of brain function and is used in the identification of cognitive functions and some language disorders.

Two brain-scanning techniques that have been used to investigate motor control issues are the earlier-mentioned positron emission tomography (PET) and functional magnetic resonance imaging (fMRI). In the PET procedure, patients ingest a radioactive solution with positively charged electrons that interact with electrons in the blood, producing electromagnetic radiation. Scanners sensitive to this level of radiation identify more active brain areas. The fMRI scanner is sensitive to increases in brain blood flow, with the more active parts of the brain showing greater blood flow than less active areas. One recently developed technique that is designed to disrupt normal neuronal activity is transcranial magnetic stimulation (TMS). TMS involves a short burst of magnetic waves that are directed to a particular part of the brain. If the pulse of activity causes a disruption to motor control, one can infer that a particular part of the brain is crucially involved in the control of movement. To see information on the various brain-scanning techniques go to http://www/pbs.org/ and search for "brain scanning."

Technology has also been used to treat symptoms of neurological diseases. For example, deep brain stimulation (DBS) has been used to treat symptoms of Parkinson's disease such as gait disruptions and muscular tremor and rigidity. DBS involves inserting into the brain a thin wire electrode that is controlled by a surgically implanted battery pack. The signals from the battery pack activate the electrode, blocking the electrical signals that cause the symptoms of the disease. We are just beginning to use technology to unlock the fascinating mysteries of how the brain controls movement, and it is exciting to imagine what the future holds in this endeavor.

EDUCATIONAL PREPARATION

Motor control and motor learning are subjects students may be interested in exploring further at a graduate level. Most doctoral students take classes in motor learning, motor control, neurophysiology, cognitive psychology, and exercise and sport psychology, but their research emphasis is usually in either motor learning or motor control. Programs are usually housed in kinesiology or exercise science departments, except for those teaching or focusing on neurophysiological techniques, for which the program is in a biology or physiology department or a medical facility.

Many exercise science students pursue a master's degree in kinesiology or exercise science with an emphasis on motor learning and motor control and then continue with training in other related areas such as human factors or physical therapy. In addition, many teachers in this field and coaches take graduate classes in motor learning and motor control to advance their own careers and to keep current on the rapidly expanding knowledge base.

EMPLOYMENT OPPORTUNITIES

Students interested in expanding their knowledge base in the academic subdiscipline in motor learning and motor control should pursue a doctoral degree and aim for employment at the college or university level. Another vocational avenue for students with an interest in motor learning and motor control is to use their knowledge in some applied field. As suggested earlier, some students might be interested in applying their knowledge about human learning in an industrial setting by continuing their work in human factors. Individuals involved in human factors help to design workplace environments to increase productivity and minimize the possibility of injury. Physical therapy is another area in which the background knowledge in motor learning and motor control is invaluable for rehabilitating injuries and reteaching motor skills. Motor control and motor learning are effective areas for persons in teaching and coaching careers as well.

PROFESSIONAL ASSOCIATIONS

American Alliance for Health, Physical Education, Recreation and Dance (AAHPERD) www.aahperd.org

Canadian Society for Psychomotor Learning and Sport Psychology (CSPLSP) www.scapps.org

North American Society for the Psychology of Sport and Physical Activity (NASPSPA) www.naspspa.org

International Society of Motor Control (ISMC) www.i-s-m-c.org

Psychonomic Society www.psychonomic.org

Society for Neuroscience www.sfn.org

PROMINENT JOURNALS

Brain Research

Experimental Brain Research

Human Movement Science

Human Performance

Journal of Experimental Psychology (Human Learning and Memory)

Journal of Experimental Psychology (Human Perception and Performance)

Journal of Human Movement Studies

Journal of Motor Behavior

Motor Control

Neuroscience

Perceptual and Motor Skills

Quarterly Journal of Experimental Psychology

Research Quarterly for Exercise and Sport

FUTURE DIRECTIONS

In motor control research, Rosenbaum (1991) identified four main questions that still provide much of the research direction for current and future researchers. The first deals with the degrees-of-freedom problem. Movements are very complex and involve many muscles and joints. How does the nervous system coordinate and control all of the components? Is the control achieved by a motor program or by some other controlling structure? Or do dynamic principles play a large role, with little involvement of the higher centers? This continues to be an important topic of research. A second main question deals with the serial-order problem; that is, how are long sequences of our actions controlled? The motor program theory states that movements of 500 to 800 milliseconds might be controlled by a single program, but how about longer sequences of actions? Dynamic systems theory can explain shifts in coordination patterns, but little is said about how the actions are actually controlled. A third issue deals with the perceptual–motor integration problem. Here the issue is how information from the environment is used to plan and adjust our movements. How does sensory information influence an ongoing motor program or the stability of a coordination pattern? Finally, how does a coordination pattern change with learning? What are the changes in the nervous system that underlie the change in the coordination pattern? These questions clearly indicate the strong link between motor control and motor learning and the difficulty in trying to study one subarea without considering the other.

In motor learning, two major findings in recent decades shook the once solid beliefs of many researchers in the area and provided a huge stimulus to reexamine some older issues. The first finding, in 1990, was that by reducing the amount of KR given during practice one could actually improve the long-term retention of a task relative to a 100 percent KR schedule (Winstein & Schmidt, 1990). This finding flew in the face of Adams's closed-loop theory and Schmidt's schema theory, which both held that KR should be provided on every trial to strengthen the perceptual trace, memory trace, recall schema, and recognition schema. Since 1990, a number of researchers have investigated the generality

box 10.4

Abstract of a research study in motor learning.

Van Tilborg, I. A. D. A., & Hulstijn, W. (2010). Implicit motor learning in patients with Parkinson's and Alzheimer's disease: Differences in learning abilities? *Motor Control, 14,* 344–361.

Experimental studies show intact implicit motor learning in patients with Alzheimer's disease (AD) but the results for patients with Parkinson's disease (PD) are inconclusive. This study tests implicit sequence learning in AD and PD patients, and healthy controls, using the classical Serial Reaction Time Task (SRTT), and a somewhat similar Pattern Learning Task (PLT), which involves stylus movements in different directions, and which allows detailed movement analysis. As expected, the time measures showed less implicit motor learning in the PD patients relative to the other groups in both tasks, but their error percentages increased when the sequence changed from a fixed to a random order, which *is* indicative of implicit learning. The AD patients showed a reversed pattern of results. Arguably, errors and time measures may reflect the involvement of separate processes, e.g., spatial and motor components, which could be differently affected in AD and PD.

of the original finding and explored the optimal KR frequency schedule for a number of tasks. The issue is still debated, but it is clear that KR must not be given so often that learners become dependent on it for error detection, rather than focusing on their own intrinsically based error-detection mechanism.

The second main issue deals with how to organize a practice session when multiple motor programs must be acquired (e.g., forehand, backhand, and volley in tennis). For many years, drills were designed that used **blocked practice,** where one skill was repeated over and over again until it was stamped in, before moving on to the next skill. However, research since 1979 indicates that **random practice,** in which a different program is required on each trial, is more effective for learning than blocked practice (Shea & Morgan, 1979). Current research deals with whether this finding generalizes to all tasks and learners of different levels (Magill & Hall, 1990). Box 10.4 is an abstract of a research study in motor learning that investigates implicit motor learning in Parkinson's and Alzheimer's patients.

■ *blocked practice*

■ *random practice*

The area of observational learning has also become an important issue in motor learning research. Long ignored by the theories of motor learning, the processes by which we learn by watching someone else perform motor skills has finally been recognized as an important part of the motor learning process. Based on Bandura's social learning theory (Bandura, 1977), research has shown that we can learn motor skills even when KR or KP (**knowledge of performance** [KP]) is not given (McCullagh & Caird, 1990). This finding also shook the confidence in closed-loop theory and schema theory, both of which hold that KR is required during practice for learning to take place.

■ *knowledge of performance*

SUMMARY

Motor control and motor learning are different, yet very closely related. Motor learning deals primarily with how one learns to control the proper muscles and coordinate the limbs to execute a movement. Motor control, however, involves understanding how actions are produced by the nervous system.

It is important for exercise science students to study motor control and motor learning, because they are related to physical activity in both healthy individuals such as athletes and injured or ill patients such as those in rehabilitative settings. For example, a strength and conditioning coach can use the principles of motor control and motor learning to teach the proper techniques for olympic lifting. A physical therapist, however, may use related principles to help a stroke patient regain mobility. Motor control and motor learning have applications in many areas of exercise science.

study / QUESTIONS

Visit the IES website to study, take notes, and try out the lab for this chapter.

1. What are the differences between motor learning and motor control?
2. What is the law of effect?
3. How are the following structures involved in movement control: motor cortex, cerebellum, basal ganglia, spinal cord, muscle spindle?
4. What is the difference between open-loop and closed-loop control?
5. What are the two main vocational avenues for people in motor learning and motor control?

learning \ ACTIVITIES

1. Go to the International Society of Motor Control (ISMC) website (www.i-s-m-c.org). Describe the benefits of membership and what the cost is. Identify when and where the annual convention will be held.

2. Go to the *Motor Control* (the official journal of ISMC) website (www. humankinetics.com/MC/journalAbout.cfm). Search for articles (from *Motor Control* only) containing information concerning the various practice methods mentioned in the chapter. Write a brief description of what you found.

3. Search online to discover the spectrum of research being conducted by professionals in motor control and motor learning. Find an article published in the past year and write a brief synopsis.

4. Research (using online and/or printed sources) possible career options related to motor learning and motor development for students in exercise science.

suggested / READINGS

Christina, R. W. (1989). Whatever happened to applied research in motor learning? In J. S. Skinner, C. B. Corbin, D. M. Landers, P. E. Martin, & C. L. Wells (Eds.), *Future directions in exercise and sport science research* (pp. 411–422). Champaign, IL: Human Kinetics.

Christina, R. W. (1997). Concerns and issues in studying and assessing motor learning. *Measurement in Physical Education and Exercise Science, 1,* 19–38.

Haywood, K. M., & Getchell, N. (2009). *Life span motor development* (5th ed.). Champaign, IL: Human Kinetics.

Kelso, J. A. S. (1991). *Dynamic patterns.* Cambridge, MA: MIT Press.

Schmidt, R. A., & Lee, T. D. (2011). *Motor control and learning: A Behavioral emphasis* (5th ed.). Champaign, IL: Human Kinetics.

references

Adams, J. A. (1971). A closed-loop theory of motor learning. *Journal of Motor Behavior, 3,* 111–149.

Adams, J. A. (1987). Historical review and appraisal of research on the learning, retention, and transfer of human motor skills. *Psychological Bulletin, 101,* 41–74.

Bandura, A. (1977). *Social learning theory.* Englewood Cliffs, NJ: Prentice Hall.

Book, W. F. (1925). *The psychology of skill.* New York: Gregg Publishing.

Bowditch, H. P., & Southard, W. F. (1882). A comparison of sight and touch. *Journal of Physiology, 3,* 232–254.

Bryan, W. L., & Harter, N. (1897). Studies in the physiology and psychology of the telegraphic language. *Psychological Review, 4,* 27–53.

Feldman, A. G. (1986). Once more on the equilibrium-point hypothesis (lambda model) for motor control. *Journal of Motor Behavior, 18,* 17–54.

Hollingworth, H. L. (1909). The inaccuracy of movement. *Archiv für Psychologie, 13*(whole No. 13), 1–87.

Hull, C. L. (1943). *The principles of behavior.* New York: Appleton-Century.

Hunter, W. S. (1929). Learning: II. Experimental studies of learning. In C. Murchison (Ed.), *The foundations of experimental psychology* (pp. 564–627). Worcester, MA: Clark University Press.

Jeannerod, M. (1985). *The brain machine.* Cambridge, MA: Harvard University Press.

Kelso, J. A. S., Holt, K. G., Rubin, P., & Kugler, P. N. (1981). Patterns of human interlimb coordination emerge from the properties of nonlinear, limit-cycle oscillatory processes: Theory and data. *Journal of Motor Behavior, 13,* 226–261.

Kincaid, M. (1925). A study of individual differences in learning. *Psychological Review, 32,* 34–53.

Magill, R. A., & Hall, K. G. (1990). A review of the contextual interference effect in motor skill acquisition. *Human Movement Science, 9,* 241–289.

McCullagh, P., & Caird, J. K. (1990). Correct and learning models and the use of model knowledge of results in the acquisition and retention of a motor skill. *Journal of Human Movement Studies, 18,* 107–116.

McGeoch, J. A. (1931). The acquisition of skill. *Psychological Bulletin, 28,* 413–466.

Neisser, U. (1967). *Cognitive psychology.* New York: Appleton-Century-Crofts.

Rosenbaum, D. A. (1991). *Human motor control.* New York: Academic Press.

Sabbatini, R. M. E. (1998). The discovery of bioelectricity. *Brain and Mind, 2,* 1–4.

Schmidt, R. A. (1975). A schema theory of discrete motor skill learning. *Psychological Review, 82,* 225–260.

Schmidt, R. A. (1982). *Motor control and learning.* Champaign, IL: Human Kinetics.

Shea, J. B., & Morgan, R. L. (1979). Contextual interference effects on the acquisition, retention, and transfer of a motor skill. *Journal of Experimental Psychology: Human Learning and Memory, 5,* 179–187.

Taub, E. (1976). Movement in nonhuman primates deprived of somatosensory feedback. In J. Keogh & R. S. Hutton (Eds.), *Exercise and sport sciences reviews* (pp. 335–374). Santa Barbara, CA: Journal Publishing Affiliates.

Thorndike, E. L. (1927). The law of effect. *American Journal of Psychology, 39,* 212–222.

Wallace, S. A. (1996). The dynamic pattern perspective of rhythmic movement: A tutorial. In H. N. Zelaznik (Ed.), *Advances in motor learning and control.* Champaign, IL: Human Kinetics.

Winstein, C. J., & Schmidt, R. A. (1990). Reduced frequency of knowledge of results enhances motor skill learning. *Journal of Experimental Psychology: Learning, Memory, Cognition, 16,* 677–691.

Wozniak, R. H. (1996). Mind, brain, and adaptation: The localization of cerebral function. In *René Descartes and the legacy of mind/body dualism.* Available at http://serendip.brynmawr.edu/Mind/Descartes.html.

Exercise and Sport Psychology

RICHARD J. SCHMIDT

DEFINITIONS IN EXERCISE AND SPORT PSYCHOLOGY

Exercise and sport psychology involves the study of human behavior in exercise- and sport-related environments, in both individual and group contexts. Fundamentally, exercise and sport psychology addresses two primary questions: (1) how do exercise and sport affect one's psychological makeup and (2) how can the principles of psychology be used to improve sport performance and exercise, adoption, and adherence (Abernethy et al., 1997)?

Exercise psychology is defined by Rejeski and Thompson (1993) as the

> application of psychology to the promoting, explaining, maintaining, and enhancing of the parameters of physical fitness. . . . It is concerned with cognitions, emotions, and behaviors that are related to the perception of and/or objective changes in muscular strength and endurance, range of motion, cardiopulmonary endurance, and body composition.

Sport psychology, in contrast, is concerned with the application of psychological principles to the various areas of sport.

The study of exercise and sport psychology focuses not only on apparently healthy, asymptomatic children and adults who exercise and/or are involved in sports, athletics, or other active endeavors, but also on those individuals who are in special populations such as those with cardiovascular, pulmonary, orthopedic, endocrinologic, metabolic, oncologic, immunologic, psychologic, or neuromuscular disorders.

Basic research in exercise and sport psychology involves studying the fundamental relationships among human behavior, exercise, and sport. Applied research in exercise and sport psychology addresses practical problems or questions in exercise and sport, such as the following: How does precompetition anxiety affect a national-class volleyball team's performance on the day of the national championship? Does either short-term or long-term aerobic exercise have a significant effect on reducing anxiety or depression? What are the effects of anaerobic sprint training or, perhaps, weight training on the same variables? Does participation in K–12 physical education increase students' self-esteem? Do athletes in different sports possess differing personality or mood state profiles that influence their success? What factors need to be considered in developing effective cohesion within a sports team? How can exercise adherence be improved for individuals who are obese or are cardiac rehabilitation patients? What are the most effective ways to reduce unwanted aggression in sports? What are the psychobiological indicators of overtraining and staleness? Can these indicators be used to improve exercise and sport performance as well as to facilitate recovery during rehabilitation? What are the best strategies to help athletes overcome substance abuse in sports? Information obtained from such studies is used to understand how psychological factors affect exercise and sport performance and how participation in exercise and sport affects one's psychological development, health, and well-being.

PROFESSIONAL DUTIES OF EXERCISE AND SPORT PSYCHOLOGISTS

Exercise and sport psychologists work with the academic, applied, or clinical aspects of exercise and sport.

Academic exercise and sport psychologists strive to expand and disseminate the knowledge base through teaching and critical research. Their research may address issues such as how mental imagery affects performance, the role of exercise in anxiety reduction and depression in cardiac rehabilitation patients, the factors that influence exercise adherence, or the relationship between exercise and/or sport programs in the development of children's self-concept and self-esteem. Much of the research conducted in higher education is shared with other professionals through publication of their findings in scientific research journals or at their presentation of research findings at professional meetings.

- *academic exercise and sport psychologist*

Applied exercise and sport psychologists apply the knowledge base in real-world situations. They provide information about the role of psychological factors in sport, exercise, and physical activity to individuals, groups, and organizations. They may, for example, assist with exercise adherence, wellness communication, or exercise program development and evaluation. In addition, they teach participants specific mental, behavioral, psychosocial, and emotional control skills applicable in sport and physical activity contexts. They may, for example, focus on relaxation, concentration, or the use of imagery.

- *applied exercise and sport psychologist*

Clinical exercise and sport psychologists specialize in helping athletes solve issues related to mental health, anxiety, and drug dependence.

- *clinical exercise and sport psychologist*

HISTORY OF EXERCISE AND SPORT PSYCHOLOGY

A commonly quoted phrase is found in most introductory texts in the profession of physical education: *mens sana in corpore sano,* or "a sound mind in a sound body." Despite this early acknowledgment of the inseparability of the mind–body dyad, exercise and sport psychology is a relatively new area of academic study and research in exercise science. In the United States, exercise and sport psychology had its beginnings in the late 19th and early 20th centuries.

In 1884, Conrad Rieger published what is considered by some to be the first article related to psychology and exercise after he investigated the effects of hypnotic catalepsy on muscular endurance (Morgan, 1972). Shortly thereafter, in 1897, Norman Triplett published the first true experimental study in exercise psychology (Triplett, 1898). While a professor of psychology at Indiana University, Triplett was intrigued by the observation that the performance of some competitive cyclists appeared to be enhanced by the "wheel-to-wheel rival" competition of other

The ancient Greeks, well noted for the primacy that they placed on love of wisdom and athletics, were among the first to recognize and write about the inseparable dichotomy of the mind and body (Ziegler, 1964).

cyclists, while the performance of others seemed to be impaired. Based on these observations, Triplett (1898) designed a study that compared the performance scores between two competitive groups. Employing a self-designed hand-cranked cycle ergometer, the subjects of one group cycled alone, while the others worked in competition with one another. As a result of this study, Triplett concluded that "we infer that the bodily presence of another individual contestant participating simultaneously in the race serves to liberate latent energy not ordinarily available" (p. 523). Rejeski and Thompson (1993) indicated that Triplett's study was also the first to observe the adverse effects of anxiety on competition. This study is also noted as being the first experiment in social psychology (West & Wicklund, 1980).

Other scholars in the late 1800s and early 1900s, such as George W. Fitz (1895), William G. Anderson (1899), E. W. Scripture (1899), G. T. W. Patrick (1903), and Robert A. Cummins (1914), investigated topics such as reaction time, the effects of physical training, cross education, the psychology of football, and the effects of basketball practice on motor reaction attention and suggestibility, respectively, as they pertained to sport. It is noteworthy that in 1908 the American Psychological Association president, G. Stanley Hall, issued a report highlighting the psychological benefits resulting from participation in physical education.

Except for Triplett's research, the majority of the exercise studies conducted up until the early 1920s focused on the relationship between psychology and motor learning.

The first investigator to conduct systematic sport psychology research was Coleman R. Griffith, who began to study the psychological factors in basketball and football in 1918 as a doctoral student at the University of Illinois. Through his work and with the assistance of the athletic director of the University of Illinois at that time, Griffith was appointed as the director of the newly developed Athletic Research Laboratory in 1925. In his new position, Griffith established himself as the pioneer researcher in the United States in the field of exercise and sport psychology. His research interests were in the areas of learning, psychomotor development, and personality research. He taught sport psychology classes, published numerous research articles, and wrote two classic texts: *Psychology of Coaching* (1926) and *Psychology and Athletics* (1928). During his years at Illinois, Griffith was able to do collaborative research on such notables as Red Grange, Knute Rockne, and Dizzy Dean in investigating topics related to motor learning, athletic motivation, and personality. Unfortunately, financial issues caused the Athletic Research Laboratory to close in 1932. Griffith, however, continued at the University of Illinois as a professor in the Department of Educational Psychology. He also maintained his close ties with sport psychology when he was hired by Philip Wrigley in 1938 as a team sport psychologist for the Chicago Cubs. As a result of the influence and impact of Coleman Griffith's work, he is often recognized as the Father of American Sport Psychology (Kroll & Lewis, 1970).

In 1938, Franklin Henry assumed a faculty position in the Department of Physical Education at the University of California–Berkeley and established the psychology of physical activity graduate program. His primary areas of research and teaching were motor learning and sport psychology. He is noted for being the leading proponent in the scientific development of the field of exercise and sport psychology (Weinberg & Gould, 2011).

Celeste Ulrich was one of the pioneer women in exercise and sport psychology. During a long and prolific career in physical education, much of her research investigated the influence of stress on athletic performance. Dr. Ulrich was president of the American Alliance for Health, Physical Education, Recreation and Dance from 1976 to 1977.

The 1960s and 1970s saw the maturation of exercise and sport psychology as a true discipline. This is evidenced by the establishment of the majority of professional exercise and sport psychology organizations in the United States and other countries and the development and publication of numerous texts and scholarly journals devoted to sport psychology (Wiggins, 1984; Williams & Straub, 1986). Research studies during this time period focused on aggression, causal attributions, personality, arousal and anxiety, team cohesion, imagery, and achievement motivation (Callois, 1961; Cox, Qui, & Liu, 1993;

Roberts, 1959). Arthur T. Slater-Hammel of the University of Indiana and John Lawther of Penn State University began to offer course work in sport psychology at their respective universities. Also during this time, Bruce Ogilvie and Thomas Tutko wrote their historic book entitled *Problem Athletes and How to Handle Them* (1966). As a result of his work, Bruce Ogilvie has often been referred to as the Father of North American Applied Sport Psychology (Williams & Straub, 1986). It was Henry's, Lawther's, and Slater-Hammel's programs that produced graduates who were to become some of the most prolific researchers and teachers in exercise and sport psychology.

The 1980s saw the development and expansion of critical research in exercise and sport psychology. Major emphases in research were the psychological aspects of exercise (Browne & Mahoney, 1984; Rejeski & Thompson, 1993) and the maximization of athletic performance through psychological intervention (Browne & Mahoney, 1984). Rejeski and Thompson (1993) noted that studies in this area are historically categorized into one of the following 10 areas: (1) fitness and mental health, (2) body image and esteem, (3) stress reactivity, (4) fatigue and exertion, (5) motivation, (6) exercise performance and metabolic responses, (7) sleep, (8) cognition, (9) the corporate–industrial environment, or (10) exercise addiction (Rejeski & Thompson, 1993; Seraganian, 1993).

In 1983, the U.S. Olympic Committee established an official sport psychology committee and a registry with three categories of clinical, educational, and research sport psychology. Eleven prominent sport psychologists were assigned to U.S. Olympic teams as part of the Elite Athlete Project. The sport psychologists along with their assigned teams were John Adderson (boxing), Herbert Fensterheim (fencing), Andrew Jacobs (cycling), Dan Landers (archery and shooting), Michael Mahoney (weight lifting), Rainer Martens (Nordic skiing), Jerry May (alpine skiing), Robert Nideffer (men's track and field), Bruce Ogilvie (volleyball), Richard Suinn (women's track and field), and Betty Wenz (synchronized swimming) (Silva & Weinberg, 1984).

In 1987, exercise and sport psychology was first recognized by mainstream psychology with the formation of Division 47 (Exercise and Sport Psychology) of the American Psychological Association (Williams & Straub, 1986).

The 1990s saw the continued growth and development of research and practice in exercise and sport psychology. In exercise psychology, researchers are continuing to investigate such topics as exercise adoption and cognition, adherence, motivation, mental health, body image, eating disorders, stress, and fatigue as they relate to exercise and sport. In sport psychology, investigators are continuing their efforts to better understand the relationships between psychology and athletic performance, skill development and acquisition, motivation, goal setting, sport socialization, group dynamics, and psychometrics. The future promises additional emphasis on the applied aspects of exercise and sport psychology. Although applied sport and exercise psychology must be driven by basic research, it appears that most employment opportunities will be working as professionals in school and university settings, sport and health clubs, sports medicine clinics, and counseling centers, and as independent consultants.

It has been estimated that there are over 2,700 individuals working in the field today in over 61 countries (Salmela, 1992). Most exercise and sport psychologists live in Europe and North America, but major increases in activity have occurred in Latin America, Asia, Africa, and the Middle East in the last decade.

PARENT DISCIPLINES OF EXERCISE AND SPORT PSYCHOLOGY

psychology ■

E xercise and sport psychology has two primary parent disciplines: psychology and physical education. Academic training in exercise and sport psychology crosses the boundaries of both disciplines. **Psychology** involves the study of human behavior and includes developmental, abnormal, counseling, clinical, experimental, personality, and physiological psychology, as well as learning and motivation.

The second parent discipline is physical education. Undergraduate training in physical education normally includes courses such as anatomy, biomechanics, exercise physiology, exercise testing and prescription, and motor learning. For physical educators, the knowledge gained from the study of psychology can be used to improve health and enhance human performance during physical activity, exercise, and athletic participation.

AREAS OF STUDY

F ollowing are examples of several current areas of study, research, and practice in exercise and sport psychology. These overviews will serve to give you a general orientation to each topic, importance to the field, current status, examples, current research findings, and implications for practice. It is important to remember that although exercise psychology and sport psychology are often viewed as two separately distinct domains in terms of teaching, research, and actual practice, they do share some commonality between and within specific areas (motivation, emotion, goal setting, anxiety, overtraining, and others).

Exercise Psychology

According to Lox, Martin, and Petruzzello (2010), exercise psychology "represents the convergence of exercise science and psychology" and "is concerned with (1) the application of psychological principles to the promotion and maintenance of leisure physical activity (exercise) and (2) the psychological and emotional consequences of leisure physical activity" (p. 4). Studying the psychological principles for promoting and maintaining exercise behavior is important given the role physical activity plays in mental and physical health. Studying the psychological and emotional consequences is important in order to design exercise activity interventions that decrease negative and increase positive psychological/emotional states.

Exercise psychology addresses a number of areas, such as psychological effects of exercise, exercise adoption, exercise adherence, exercise and motivation, and theoretical models of exercise behaviors. A brief overview of three of these areas, exercise and mood state, exercise adherence, and exercise dependence syndrome are presented next.

Exercise and mood state

One of the most researched areas in exercise psychology is the effect of acute and chronic exercise on mood states. Although almost everyone who exercises on a regular basis reports feelings of well-being, or positive affect, either as a result of an acute bout of exercise or through participation in a regular program of physical activity, researchers are as yet unclear as to the mechanism(s) underlying these perceptions. Several mechanisms have been hypothesized to account for the increases in positive affect following an acute bout of exercise (Brown, 1991; deVries et al., 1968; Ransford, 1982; Steinberg & Sykes, 1985): an increase in circulating endorphins resulting in feelings of euphoria; the monoamine hypothesis, which holds that increased levels of central monoamine neurotransmitters give rise to feelings of positive affect; the thermogenic hypothesis, which holds that elevation in body temperature accompanying exercise contributes to the perception of positive affect; the distraction hypothesis, which holds that it is not the exercise itself, but rather the psychological distraction or break that an exercise bout gives from the trials and tribulations of daily life that is responsible for bringing about changes in affect; and the mastery hypothesis, which holds that exercise may increase one's sense of self-mastery or accomplishment, thereby leading to improved affect.

One of the most popular instruments used by researchers to assess changes in mood states following exercise is the Profiles of Mood States (POMS) questionnaire developed by McNair, Lorr, and Droppelman (1971/1981). The POMS measures the mood states of tension/anxiety, depression/dejection, anger/hostility, vigor/activity, fatigue/inertia, and confusion/bewilderment. In using this instrument, researchers have generally found that exercisers and athletes tend to have a more favorable mental health mood state profile than nonexercisers and nonathletes. A more favorable mental health profile is represented by low scores on tension, depression, anger, fatigue, and confusion and a high score on vigor.

In the area of athletics, Morgan et al. (1987) have used the POMS to develop a mental health model useful in predicting athletic success. The model suggests that positive mental health is directly related to athletic success and high levels of performance. Elite athletes in a variety of sports (swimmers, wrestlers, oarsmen, runners) are characterized by what Morgan calls the **iceberg profile.** The iceberg profile of a successful elite athlete is formed by scoring high on the variable of vigor and low on the variables of tension, depression, anger, fatigue, and confusion (compared to the population 50th percentile; see Exhibit 11.1). Less successful athletes have a flatter profile, scoring at or below the 50th percentile on all six psychological factors.

■ *iceberg profile*

The iceberg profile (Morgan et al., 1987).

exhibit \ **11.1**

Exercise adherence

exercise adherence ■

An area of great concern for exercise professionals is the high rate of attrition commonly seen in exercise programs. Specifically, **exercise adherence** refers to the degree to which an individual follows the recommended frequency, intensity, and duration. More generally, adherence to exercise has most often been defined for research purposes as a percentage of attendance. Lack of exercise adherence affects asymptomatic children and adults as well as individuals in cardiac, pulmonary, and other chronic disease rehabilitation programs. Research has shown that approximately 50 percent of those who begin exercise programs drop out within the first 6 months (Wankel, 1987). The dropout rate is similar for cardiac patients (Erling & Olderidge, 1985). Exercise psychologists are concerned with why there is a discrepancy between wanting to exercise and the ability to adhere to an exercise program.

Research has shown that a multitude of psychological, physiological, cultural, socioeconomic, and program factors affect exercise adherence. Some of these factors are prior exercise history, recent exercise behaviors, active versus inactive leisure time, current level of fitness, and smoking versus nonsmoking. Physiological factors include body weight, body fat, angina pectoris, and left ventricular ejection fraction (Markland & Ingledew, 2007; Olderidge et al., 1983). Psychological factors include aspects of personality such as self-motivation, attitudes toward exercise, and health knowledge and beliefs (Willis & Campbell, 1992). Social factors include marital status, spousal and family social support, peer social support, and work demands (Willis & Campbell, 1992). Program factors include enjoyment, convenience, quality of the exercise facility and equipment, program social support, group versus individual programs, program leadership, and program intensity (Edmunds, Ntoumanis, & Duda, 2008; Willis & Campbell, 1992).

Exercise dependence syndrome

exercise dependence ■
syndrome

Another phenomenon of concern to exercise professionals is **exercise dependence syndrome.** This syndrome is "a craving for leisure-time physical activity, resulting in uncontrollable excessive exercise behavior, that manifests in physiological (e.g., tolerance/withdrawal) and/or psychological (e.g., anxiety, depression) symptoms" (Hausenblas & Symons Downs, 2002, p. 90). It is possible to distinguish between primary and secondary exercise dependence, with the main distinction derived from the individual's objective for exercising (Pierce, 1994).

primary exercise ■
dependence

In **primary exercise dependence,** the exercise is an end in itself. Other features associated with primary exercise dependence include exercise tolerance, manifested as a progressively increasing intensity, duration, or frequency of exercise; or lying to a spouse about how much or when one exercises. In **secondary exercise dependence,** exercise is used exclusively to control body composition, as is seen often in individuals with eating disorders (e.g., anorexia nervosa).

secondary exercise ■
dependence

Several psychobiological mechanisms have been proposed as explanations for exercise dependence (Hamer & Karageorghis, 2007; Thompson & Blanton, 1987; Yates, Leehey, & Shisslak, 1983): the affect regulation hypothesis, which holds that exercise acts to enhance positive affect and reduce negative affect and that the habitual exerciser experiences mood disturbances upon withdrawal from exercise; the anorexia analogue hypothesis, which posits that compulsive exercise serves as a male counterpart to the eating disorder anorexia nervosa (which is a predominantly female disorder); the endorphin hypothesis, which posits that the individual exercises to excess because of an actual physical dependence on the chemicals released during exercise; the psychophysiological hypothesis (also referred to as the energy conservation–sympathetic arousal hypothesis), which holds that because the effect of training is a decrease in sympathetic nervous system output, an increase in fitness can potentially result in a state of lethargy and fatigue, motivating the individual to increase the training.

Sport Psychology

Sport psychology addresses a number of areas, such as psychological characteristics and high-level performance; skill acquisition; group dynamics; motivation; overtraining, staleness, and burnout; and psychological techniques for individual performance. A brief overview of two of these areas, personality and sport and overtraining, staleness, and burnout, are provided next.

Personality and sport

Coaches and sport psychologists have long been interested in the relationship between **personality** (the collective pattern of one's psychological traits and states) and sports performance. Early research posited a relationship between certain aspects of one's personality and level of athletic success (Fisher, 1984). Several theories have emerged in an attempt to explain this relationship.

   Weinberg and Gould (2011) described three theories in this regard: (1) trait theory, (2) the situational approach, and (3) the interactional approach. Basically, **trait theory** contends that one's personality consists of identifiable and measurable stable psychological characteristics and that the assessment of these traits will allow investigators to predict athletic performance in a variety of settings. The **situational approach**, which is based on social learning theory (Bandura, 1977), suggests that an athlete's behavior in a given setting is shaped or molded by the specific situation or environment. The **interactional approach** states that an athlete's behavior is a function of the interaction between the environmental situation and his or her psychological traits.

■ *personality*

■ *trait theory*

■ *situational approach*

■ *interactional approach*

Overtraining, staleness, and burnout

All forms of stimuli act as a stressor on the body. Whether it be exercise, injury, or a very emotionally charged reaction, the body responds to all these forms of stimuli in a general way. Selye (1976) first defined this response to such stressors as the **general adaptation syndrome.** He characterized the body as responding in three general stages depending on the duration that the stressor was applied. These three stages are the **alarm stage** (the body mobilizes its mechanisms to meet the demands of the stress), the **resistance stage** (stress syndrome disappears with the body being more resistant to the stressor), and the **exhaustion stage** (stress syndrome reappears and the body enters a state of decline). These three stages are characterized by a syndrome consisting of (1) adrenal enlargement, (2) thymus and lymphatic shrinkage, and (3) bleeding ulcers in the digestive tract.

■ *general adaptation syndrome*

■ *alarm stage*

■ *resistance stage*

■ *exhaustion stage*

   Athletes and exercisers of all ages and at all levels of involvement have the potential to incur staleness and/or burnout should a chronic imbalance (inordinate amount of stress) develop in their training or conditioning program. We know that principles of conditioning specify that one's systems must be overloaded on a systematic and progressive basis to make improvements in physiological adaptations and therefore performance. Scientific application of the variables of frequency, intensity, duration, mode, and progression must be followed to bring about desired outcomes in training and/or performance. At the same time, a fine balance must be struck among these variables and adequate rest and nutrition.

overtraining ■   **Overtraining** has been defined as "a stimulus consisting of a systematic schedule of progressively intense physical training of a high absolute and relative intensity" (Singer, Murphey, & Tenant, 1993, p. 842). Overtraining, in effect, describes the application of an incorrect dose of frequency, intensity, duration, and mode in a training and conditioning program. When a chronic imbalance exists in these variables, inappropriate responses such as staleness or, in more severe cases, burnout may become manifest (Thomson et al., 1998).

staleness ■   **Staleness,** characterized by increased negative mental health and decreased performance, is an undesirable outcome of overtraining. Although individuals experiencing staleness may still be highly motivated in training, they tend to suffer decrements in physiological adaptations with resultant decreases in performance. Although an athlete or exerciser experiencing staleness generally exhibits a variety of behavioral disturbances, the primary disturbance is

burnout ■   depression (Morgan et al., 1987). **Burnout,** while sharing some of the same symptoms as staleness, "possesses the central features of loss of interest and motivation" (Singer et al., 1993, p. 842).

Although staleness and burnout are caused by a complex interaction of physiological and psychological factors, Raglin and Morgan (1989) ranked the following causes as being primarily responsible for the development of these syndromes: (1) too much stress and pressure, (2) too much practice and physical training, (3) physical exhaustion and all-over soreness, (4) boredom because of too much repetition, and (5) poor rest or lack of proper sleep.

Mild staleness may be treated by reducing training intensity and/or volume, but more severe cases of staleness and burnout usually require qualified medical and psychological intervention (Barron et al., 1989).

THEORETICAL APPROACHES

The study of exercise and sport psychology employs specific theoretical orientations and research methodologies. The specific theoretical orientations are generally classified as behavioral, psychophysiological, and cognitive–behavioral (Weinberg & Gould, 2011).

Behavioral

The behavioral orientation views the primary determinants of an athlete's or exerciser's behavior as coming from the environment. In this approach, participants are viewed as being primarily motivated by factors external to themselves (Weinberg & Gould, 2011).

Psychophysiological

The psychophysiological orientation suggests that the best way to study exercise and sport is to examine the physiological processes of the brain and their influences on the physical activity (Weinberg & Gould, 2011). This approach largely involves measuring physiological variables such as heart rate, electromyography, electroencephalography, blood lactate levels, galvanic skin response, and eye movement response patterns and then correlating these measures with exercise and sport behavior.

Cognitive–behavioral

The cognitive–behavioral orientation assumes that the behavior of individuals is determined by their cognitive mental (or "thinking") processes (Weinberg & Gould, 2011). Specific cognitive variables, such as self-confidence, self-efficacy, self-esteem, anxiety, fear, motivation, need for success, and fear of failure, are thought to be the determinants of the behavior that an exerciser or athlete may exhibit in any given situation.

RESEARCH METHODOLOGIES

Research methodologies for exercise and sport psychology include both qualitative and quantitative approaches. *Qualitative research* involves using any one of the five main traditions; that is, the biographical, phenomenological, grounded theory, ethnographic, or case study approach (Creswell, 1998; Johnson, 1988). *Quantitative research* involves employing strict experimental control procedures to study the effect of the manipulation of an independent variable (e.g., various intensities of exercise training) on a dependent variable (e.g., changes in cardiorespiratory fitness; Hyllgard, Mood, & Morrow, 1997).

A variety of quantitative research methodologies are used to study exercise and sport psychology. To begin with, one may employ any of the several theories or theoretical constructs available within the disciplines of psychology, sociology, anthropology, physical education, sport, or exercise science. With appropriate training and qualifications, one may use psychological tests or questionnaires on either an individual or group basis in quasi-experimental or experimental research design settings. The use of the introspective or phenomenological approach may be of value when other approaches seem inadequate or contraindicated. Box 11.1 is an abstract of a research study that employed the use of quantitative methodologies to study exercise and sport psychology. Box 11.2 is an abstract of a research study that used qualitative methodologies to study exercise and sport psychology.

Abstract of a research study that used quantitative methodologies.

box 11.1

Markowitz, S. M., & Arent, S. M. (2010). The exercise and affect relationship: Evidence for the dual-mode model and a modified opponent process theory. *Journal of Sport and Exercise Psychology, 32*(5), 711–730.

This study examined the relationship between exertion level and affect using the framework of opponent-process theory and the dual-mode model, with the Activation-Deactivation Adjective Checklist and the State Anxiety Inventory among 14 active and 14 sedentary participants doing 20 min of treadmill exercise at speeds of 5% below, 5% above, and at lactate threshold (LT). We found a significant effect of time, condition, Time × Condition, and Time × Group, but no group, Group × Condition, or Time × Group × Condition effects, such that the 5% above LT condition produced a worsening of affect in-task compared with all other conditions whereas, across conditions, participants experienced in-task increases in energy and tension, and in-task decreases in tiredness and calmness relative to baseline. Posttask, participants experienced mood improvement (decreased tension, anxiety, and increased calmness) across conditions, with a 30-min delay in the above LT condition. These results partially support the dual-mode model and a modified opponent-process theory.

Abstract of a research study that used qualitative methodologies.

box
11.2

Mosewich, A. D., Kowalski, K. C., Sabiston, C. M., Sedgwick, W. A., & Tracy, J. L. (2011). Self-compassion: A potential resource for young women athletes. *Journal of Sport and Exercise Psychology, 33*(1), 103–123.

Self-compassion has demonstrated many psychological benefits (Neff, 2009). In an effort to explore self-compassion as a potential resource for young women athletes, we explored relations among self-compassion, proneness to self-conscious emotions (i.e., shame, guilt-free shame, guilt, shame-free guilt, authentic pride, and hubristic pride), and potentially unhealthy self-evaluative thoughts and behaviors (i.e., social physique anxiety, obligatory exercise, objectified body consciousness, fear of failure, and fear of negative evaluation). Young women athletes (N = 151; Mage = 15.1 years) participated in this study. Self-compassion was negatively related to shame proneness, guilt-free shame proneness, social physique anxiety, objectified body consciousness, fear of failure, and fear of negative evaluation. In support of theoretical propositions, self-compassion explained variance beyond self-esteem on shame proneness, guilt-free shame proneness, shame-free guilt proneness, objectified body consciousness, fear of failure, and fear of negative evaluation. Results suggest that, in addition to self-esteem promotion, self-compassion development may be beneficial in cultivating positive sport experiences for young women.

TECHNOLOGY AND RESEARCH TOOLS

Because exercise and sport psychologists are interested in measuring exercise intensity, electronic devices that provide objective data are used in the quantitative and qualitative research. Software programs help the researchers analyze their data.

Electronic Devices

Many electronic devices provide direct measures of exercise intensity and duration (e.g., exercise heart rate, distance covered) and indirect estimates of the energy expended (e.g., calories burned, metabolic units). Because these devices provide objective data that are not subject to the falsified feedback or memory-fade problems that arise when using self-report tools, they are more expensive to purchase and maintain and can be somewhat complex to use.

Heart rate monitors. Using a transmitter that emits a signal displayed on a special wristwatch, a heart rate monitor attached to a chest band placed over the heart provides constant pulse readings. More advanced models provide a recording of the heart rate at regular intervals and allow the user to program a desired intensity range with accompanying auditory feedback.

Pedometers. Typically attached to either the waistband or shoe, this small device works like a car's odometer, providing such data as the number of steps and the distance covered over a period of time. Some advanced models can approximate the number of calories burned when body weight is entered, but because of differences in body physiology and fitness levels, the estimate's accuracy is poor. Also, stride length increases as a person moves faster, so the distance reported may be underestimated. Conversely, distance may be overestimated if a person is walking at a slower than average pace.

Accelerometers. This small device detects the acceleration of a leg or an arm and provides data related to the amount of activity performed over time. Accelerometers vary in price as well as their sensitivity to movement. Similar to pedometers, accelerometers may overpredict energy expenditure during walking and underpredict energy expenditure in more intense activities and arm ergometry.

Global positioning systems. GPS technology is commonplace; it is used in cars, cell phones, and increasingly to monitor outdoor activities, including those involving running, biking, and walking. Similar to the GPS in cars, those used to monitor physical activity transmit continuous microwave signals via satellites to a GPS receiver that computes estimated energy expenditure by tracking speed, slope, and duration of physical activity. The units can also be bundled with additional sensors for monitoring heart rate or pedal revolutions in cycling, for example.

Software

Software such as SPSS, Statistical Package for the Social Sciences, for quantitative research (descriptive and inferential statistics) has been available for some time. Other software offers computerized assistance to analyze data obtained in qualitative research studies. One such program is QSR NUD*IST, which is an acronym for nonnumerical unstructured data indexing, searching, and theorizing (Qualitative Solutions and Research, 1996). This software helps researchers manage nonnumerical and unstructured data in qualitative analysis by supporting indexing, searching, and theorizing functions.

EDUCATIONAL PREPARATION

Students interested in academic study in exercise and sport psychology usually begin their preparation at the graduate level. The American Psychological Association's (APA) Division 47 (Exercise and Sport), the Association for the Advancement of Applied and Sport Psychology, and the North American Society for the Psychology of Sport and Physical Activity (NASPSPA) have information available for prospective students, which they disseminate in a pamphlet entitled "Graduate Training and Career Possibilities in Exercise and Sport Psychology" (American Psychological Association, 1994). Graduate programs of study are normally housed in physical education or exercise science departments, where students usually major in a specialty area of human performance and take related course work offered by departments of psychology.

Currently, there are over 100 master's and doctoral degree programs related to study and research in sport psychology in the United States, Great Britain, Canada, Australia, and South Africa (Sachs, Burke, & Loughren, 2007). Doctoral students complete course work in such areas as clinical psychology, personality theory, clinical assessment, psychometric theory, group processes, psychotherapy, motivation and emotion, learning processes, education, and human development. Master's students take most of their course work in physical education, sport, or exercise science and elective course work in psychology and/or sociology. Typical courses in a master's program address such areas as the psychological bases of human movement, exercise adherence, or, perhaps, psychological kinesiology.

WWW

**Exercise and Sport Psychology
American Psychological
Association**
*www.apa.org/about/division/
div47.aspx*

Typically, four academic tracks are available in exercise and sport psychology at the doctoral level. Track I is targeted toward those who want to teach and conduct research into the use of cognitive strategies for improving the performance of athletes. A doctoral degree (Ph.D.) in sport sciences with a specialization in sport psychology and a significant proportion of course work in psychology or counseling is required. Professionals may find employment in academic positions at colleges or universities, as researchers in sport research institutes or medical research laboratories, or as coaching educators within college or university physical education departments or sport organizations. Work in this track may include employment as a scientist, scholar–educator, or performance-enhancement specialist working in the areas of youth sport (motivational factors, ideal experiences, or optimal learning periods), learning and expertise (learning processes, expert systems, and the like), or performance enhancement (mental preparation strategies, motivation, intervention techniques) (APA, 1994; Singer, 1996).

Track II focuses on teaching and research in psychology, as well as working with athletes. A doctoral degree in psychology with a significant proportion of course work in exercise and sport sciences is required for this track. Individuals may find employment in academic positions within colleges or universities or as researchers in sport research institutes or medical research laboratories. Opportunities in Tracks I and II may include part-time consulting with amateur and professional athletes and teams and, on rare occasions, full-time consulting. As in Track I, work in Track II may also include employment as a scientist, scholar–educator, or performance-enhancement specialist working in the areas of psychometrics (sport-specific psychological test construction, diagnosis, and prediction of success) and performance enhancement (APA, 1994; Singer, 1996).

Track III focuses on those who have an interest and aptitude in providing clinical or counseling services to various populations, including athletes. A doctoral degree from an APA-accredited clinical or counseling psychology program with a significant proportion of course work in sports psychology and related sport sciences is required to work in this track. Primary employment may be found in private psychology practice, clinical or counseling psychology programs in a university counseling/health center, sports medicine clinics as a psychological consultant, or as a university-based substance-abuse specialist. Individuals in this track may opt to do part-time consulting for either amateur or professional sports teams (APA, 1994; Singer, 1996). Please note, however, that few positions occur for working with elite athletes.

Track IV focuses on health promotion and working with athletes but not necessarily in sport psychology. A master's degree in clinical/counseling psychology with a significant proportion of course work in exercise and sport science or a master's degree in sport or exercise science with a significant proportion of course work in psychology is required to work in this track. Some employers may require a doctoral degree. Primary employment may be found in college/university athletics; in health promotion, wellness, and rehabilitation programs; or in coaching. For those interested in exercise psychology, this track will provide opportunities for promoting physical activity among a variety of individuals in health care, wellness, and rehabilitation settings.

If you are interested in obtaining more specific information concerning academic programs and/or employment possibilities in exercise and sport

www

Graduate Training and Career Possibilities in Exercise and Sport Psychology
www.appliedsportpsych.org/students/graduate/training

psychology, you may wish to obtain *Directory of Graduate Programs in Applied Sport Psychology* (Sachs, Burke, & Loughren, 2007), or consult the AAASP website.

CERTIFICATIONS

In 1991, the Association for the Advancement of Applied Sport Psychology (AAASP) began a Certified Consultant AAASP program that requires advanced training in both psychology and the sport sciences to ensure that individuals have the necessary sport science and psychological training to consult in exercise and sport psychology in the United States. A doctoral degree with appropriate course work in psychology, health, exercise physiology, performance, health, psychopathology, ethics, statistics, research design, cognitive behavior, and the biological bases of behavior is required. Additional skills in counseling and a supervised practicum are also required (McCullagh & Noble, 1993).

The U.S. Olympic Committee (USOC) maintains its own sport psychology registry. Registered professionals are qualified to work with Olympic athletes as well as national teams. To be on the registry, one must be a member of the APA and a Certified Consultant (CC) of the AAASP. Other countries, such as Australia, Britain, and Canada, have established certification criteria for those who provide services in sport psychology within their respective countries.

WWW

AAASP Certified Consultants
www.appliedsportpsych.org/consultants/become-certified

EMPLOYMENT OPPORTUNITIES

Employment opportunities in exercise and sport psychology are quite variable at the present time. Most positions available are in applied exercise and sport psychology at the university level, where one works as an **educational sport psychologist.** The next most popular employment areas are consultant positions with individual athletes, sports teams, and sport–health clubs or positions as qualified clinical sport psychologists. Job announcements may be found at the major annual conventions sponsored by the APA, the AAASP, the American College of Sports Medicine, and the North American Society for the Psychology of Sport and Physical Activity. In addition, many of the association websites post jobs in the field. See the Professional Associations section later in the chapter for web addresses.

■ *educational sport psychologist*

Higher education

This is the primary occupation for individuals trained in the field of exercise and sport psychology. At the university level, job responsibilities generally consist of teaching academic courses and conducting research related to the field.

Primary/secondary education

Elementary through high school physical education instructors and coaches use principles of behavioral modification and group dynamics for teams and physical education classes. In addition, knowledge of exercise psychology principles might enable an instructor to increase the self-esteem of a student or provide support for someone experiencing body image concerns (Lox et al., 2010).

Fitness and wellness

The fitness and wellness field includes personal trainers as well as directors of corporate fitness and wellness programs. In these positions, the ability to apply motivational techniques and adherence strategies would be particularly valuable (Lox et al., 2010).

Rehabilitation

Rehabilitation personnel include athletic trainers, physical therapists, and cardiac rehabilitation staff. The ability to increase confidence and reduce stress in an individual participating in rehabilitation would be extremely useful in this setting (Lox et al., 2010).

Consulting

A consultant in exercise and sport psychology generally works with athletes for the purpose of improving athletic performance. This type of consulting may involve developing cognitive behavioral strategies or imagery training schema to enhance performance. It may also involve working with sports medicine groups to develop strategies to control pain in injured athletes or to reduce the severity and incidence of athletic injuries. Consultation may take the form of working with athletes who have eating disorders such as anorexia nervosa, bulimia nervosa, or anorexia athletica. In addition to working with athletic programs, consultants in exercise and sport psychology work with K–12 physical education programs to design them in such a way as to instill in students lifelong habits toward regular physical activity and proper nutrition.

PROFESSIONAL ASSOCIATIONS

 number of organizations currently serve exercise and sport psychology researchers and professionals. The following are the most prominent organizations related to the field.

American Psychological Association Division 47 (Exercise and Sport Psychology). This division of the APA focuses on furthering the scientific, educational, and clinical foundations of exercise and sport psychology.

Association for the Advancement of Applied Sport Psychology. Founded in 1986, the AAASP promotes the development of psychological theory, research, and intervention strategies in the sport, exercise, and health psychology fields. The organization's focus is on three areas of interest: intervention/performance enhancement, health and exercise psychology, and social psychology.

AAASP
www.appliedsportpsych.org

The Canadian Society for Psychomotor Learning and Sport Psychology (SCAPPS). In Canada, SCAPPS promotes the study of motor control, motor learning, motor development, and sport/exercise psychology by encouraging the exchange of

SCAPPS
www.scapps.org

views and scientific information in fields related to psychomotor learning and sport/exercise psychology.

European Federation of Sport Psychology (FEPSAC). This organization comprises national European societies that deal with sport and exercise psychology, including the German Association of Sport Psychology (ASP) and the British Association of Sport and Exercise Sciences (BASES).

International Society of Sport Psychology (ISSP). The ISSP, the only worldwide organization of sport, exercise, and health psychology scholars, promotes the study of human behavior of individuals and groups associated with sport and physical activity.

North American Society for the Psychology of Sport and Physical Activity (NASPSPA). Focused on three interest areas—sport and exercise psychology, motor development, and motor learning/control—the NASPSPA seeks to advance the scientific study of human behavior in the sport and physical activity arenas.

Sport and Exercise Academy (Division of AAHPERD). This organization has as its mission to extend the knowledge of exercise and sport psychology in sport and physical education. The Academy publishes a newsletter and gives an annual award for the best sport and exercise psychology dissertation.

WWW
FEPSAC
www.fepsac.com

WWW
ISSP
www.issponline.org

WWW
NASPSPA
www.naspspa.org

WWW
Sport and Exercise Academy
www.aahperd.org/naspe/about/leaders/Sport-Exercise-and-Psychology-Academy.cfm

PROMINENT JOURNALS AND RELATED PUBLICATIONS

International Journal of Sport Psychology

Journal of Applied Sport Psychology

Journal of Sport and Exercise Psychology

Journal of Sport Behavior

Medicine and Science in Sports and Exercise

Pediatric Exercise Science

The Gerontologist

The Sport Psychologist

Women in Sport and Physical Activity

The following journals are published by the APA, Division 47 (Sport and Exercise Psychology) and Division 38 (Health Psychology).

Health Psychology

Journal of Applied Psychology

Journal of Counseling and Clinical Psychology

Journal of Counseling Psychology

Journal of Personality and Social Psychology

Perceptual and Motor Skills

Psychology and Aging

FUTURE DIRECTIONS

In exercise psychology, there will be a continued need for research in the area of exercise and mental health. Additional areas for further research include exercise adherence, the therapeutic effects of exercise, exercise addiction, and exercise and cognitive functioning (Katz et al., 1985; Sachs, 1981; White-Welkley et al., 1998).

In sport psychology, future research needs to be targeted toward research in the area of psychological skills training (PST) (Singer et al., 1993). Although current research has indicated the effectiveness of PST in improving sports performance, little is known about the mechanisms of this effect. Research into youth sport and cross-cultural sport will serve to address issues related to potential sport-related child abuse (Cox & Noble, 1989) and to answer questions regarding the relationship between sport and culture (Duda, 1980), respectively. Additional areas in which further research is needed include self-confidence, children and aggression in sport, the psychology of burnout, character development through sport, and gender issues in sport and exercise.

Of equal importance to these topical areas, gains must be made in constructing proper research designs to answer critical questions relevant to exercise and sport psychology. Constructs in exercise and sport psychology need to be accurately defined. Only in this way can researchers validly compare the results of one study with another investigating the same phenomenon under similar conditions. Research designs that have real-world application must be employed so that results will have applicability to real populations (Seraganian, 1993).

SUMMARY

Exercise and sport psychology involves the study of human behavior in exercise- and sport-related environments. Both exercise psychology and sport psychology use the principles of psychology to examine (1) how exercise or sport affects psychological makeup and (2) methods for improving exercise or sport performance. Exercise psychology applies psychology to the parameters of physical fitness, whereas sport psychology applies psychological principles to the various areas of sport. Because psychological factors affect exercise and sport performance and participation in exercise and sport affects psychological development and health, it is important for exercise science students to develop a clear understanding of this aspect of the discipline.

study / QUESTIONS

Visit the IES website to study, take notes, and try out the lab for this chapter.

1. What is sport psychology?
2. What is exercise psychology?
3. Describe three theoretical approaches used in exercise and sport psychology. What are some research methodologies used in exercise and sport psychology?
4. Identify two general objectives of exercise and sport psychology.
5. Describe three roles of exercise and sport psychology specialists.
6. What career opportunities are there in exercise and sport psychology?

7. What are current areas of research in exercise and sport psychology?

8. Define overtraining, staleness, and burnout in sport.

learning \ ACTIVITIES

1. Go to the Association for the Advancement of Applied Sport Psychology (AAASP) website (www.appliedsportpsych.org).

   a. What audiences has this site been designed to provide information for?

   b. What types of membership are available?

   c. What are the benefits of membership?

   d. What are the requirements for certification?

2. Go to the American Psychological Association Division 47 website (www.apa.org/about/division/div47.aspx).

   a. Why did this division form?

   b. What are the benefits of student membership?

3. Go to the North American Society for the Psychology of Sport and Physical Activity (NASPSPA) website (www.naspspa.org).

   a. What are the society's three functions?

   b. Where is the upcoming national convention? How much does it cost to attend as a student or as a professional? What does your registration cover (all benefits)?

4. Go to the International Society of Sport Psychology (ISSP) website (www.issponline.org).

   a. What is the ISSP mission?

   b. What benefits are gained by becoming a member?

   c. What types of membership are available?

suggested / READINGS

American Psychological Association. (1996). *Exploring sport and exercise psychology.* Washington, DC: Author.

Andersen, M. (2000). *Doing sport psychology.* Champaign, IL: Human Kinetics.

Biddle, S. J. H. (Ed.). (1995). *European perspectives on exercise and sport psychology.* Champaign, IL: Human Kinetics.

Gill, D. (2008). *Psychological dynamics of sport and exercise* (3rd ed.). Champaign, IL: Human Kinetics.

Hill, K. (2001). *Frameworks for sport psychologists: Enhancing sport performance.* Champaign, IL: Human Kinetics.

Lox, C. L., Martin, K. A., & Petruzzello, S. J. (2010). *The psychology of exercise: Integrating theory and practice* (3rd ed.). Scottsdale, AZ: Holcomb Hathaway.

Roberts, G. (2001). *Advances in motivation in sport and exercise.* Champaign, IL: Human Kinetics.

references

Abernethy, B., Kippers, V., Mackinnon, L. T., Neal, R. J., & Hanrahan, S. (1997). *The biophysical foundations of human movement.* Champaign, IL: Human Kinetics.

American Psychological Association. (1994). *Graduate training and career possibilities in exercise and sport psychology.* Washington, DC: Author.

Anderson, W. G. (1899). Studies in the effects of physical training. *American Physical Education Review, 4,* 265–278.

Bandura, A. (1977). Self-efficacy: Toward a unifying theory of behavioral change. *Psychology Review, 84,* 191–215.

Barron, J. L., Noakes, T. D., Levy, W., Smith, C., & Millar, R. P. (1989). Hypothalamic dysfunction in overtrained athletes. *Journal of Clinical Endocrinology and Metabolism, 60,* 803–806.

Browne, M. A., & Mahoney, M. J. (1984). Sport psychology. *Annual Review of Psychology, 35,* 605–625.

Brown, J. D. (1991). Staying fit and staying well: Physical fitness as a moderator of life stress. *Journal of Personality and Social Psychology, 60,* 555–561.

Callois, R. (1961). *Man, play, and games.* New York: Free Press.

Cox, P. H., Qiu, Y., & Liu, Z. (1993). Overview of sport psychology. In R. N. Singer, M. Murphey, & L. K. Tenant (Eds.), *Handbook of research in sport psychology,* pp. 3–31. New York: Macmillan.

Cox, R. H., & Noble, L. (1989). Preparation and attitudes of Kansas high school head coaches. *Journal of Teaching Physical Education, 8,* 329–241.

Creswell, J. W. (1998). *Qualitative inquiry and research design: Choosing among the five traditions,* pp. 7–8. Thousand Oaks, CA: Sage Publications.

Cummins, R. A. (1914). A study of the effect of basketball practice on motor reaction attention and suggestibility. *Psychology Review, 21,* 356–369.

deVries, H. A., Beckman, P., Huber, H., & Dieckmeir, L. (1968). Electromyographic evaluation of the effects of sauna on the neuromuscular system. *Journal of Sports Medicine, 8,* 61–69.

Duda, J. (1980). Achievement motivation among Navajo students: A conceptual analysis with preliminary data. *Ethos, 8,* 131–155.

Edmunds, J., Ntoumanis, N., & Duda, J. L. (2008). Testing a self-determination theory-based teaching style intervention in the exercise domain. *European Journal of Social Psychology, 38,* 375–388.

Erling, J., & Oldridge, N. B. (1985). Effect of a spousal support program on compliance with cardiac rehabilitation. *Medicine and Science in Sports and Exercise, 17,* 284.

Fisher, A. C. (1984). New directions in sport personality research. In J. M. Silva & R. S. Weinberg (Eds.), *Psychological foundations of sport,* pp. 70–80. Champaign, IL: Human Kinetics.

Fitz, G. W. (1895). A local reaction. *Psychological Review, 2,* 37–42.

Griffith, C. R. (1926). *Psychology of coaching.* New York: Scribners.

Griffith, C. R. (1928). *Psychology of athletics.* New York: Scribners.

Hamer, M., & Karageorghis, C. I. (2007). Psychobiological mechanisms of exercise dependence. *Sports Medicine, 37,* 477–484.

Hausenblas, H. A., & Symons Downs, D. (2002). Exercise dependence: A systematic review. *Psychology of Sport and Exercise, 3,* 89–123.

Hyllgard, R., Mood, D. P., & Morrow, Jr., J. R. (1997). *Interpreting research in sport and exercise science.* St. Louis: Mosby.

Johnson, M. L. (1988). Qualitative effects of youth sport camp experience (Abstract). *Journal of Sport and Exercise Psychology, 20,* S21.

Katz, J. F., Adler, J. C., Mazzarella, N. J., & Ince, L. P. (1985). Psychological consequences of an exercise training program for a paraplegic man: A case study. *Rehabilitation Psychology, 30,* 53–58.

Kroll, W., & Lewis, G. (1970). America's first sport psychologist. *Quest, 13,* 1–4.

Lox, C. L., Martin, K. A., & Petruzzello, S. J. (2010). *The psychology of exercise: Integrating theory and practice* (3rd ed.). Scottsdale, AZ: Holcomb Hathaway.

Markland, D., & Ingledew, D. K. (2007). The relationship between body mass and body image and relative autonomy for exercise among adolescent males and females. *Psychology of Sport and Exercise, 8,* 836–853.

McCullagh, P., & Noble, J. M. (1993). Education and training in sport and exercise psychology. In P. Seraganian (Ed.), *Exercise psychology: The influence of physical exercise on psychological processes,* pp. 377–394. New York: John Wiley & Sons.

McNair, D. M., Lorr, M., & Droppelman, L. F. (1971/1981). *Manual for the profile of mood states.* San Diego, CA: Educational and Industrial Testing Service.

Morgan, W. P. (1972). Hypnosis and muscular performance. In W. P. Morgan (Ed.), *Ergogenic aids and muscular performance,* pp. 193–231. New York: Academic Press.

Morgan, W. P., Brown, D. R., Raglin, J. S., O'Connor, P. J., & Ellickson, K. A. (1987). Psychological monitoring of overtraining and staleness. *British Journal of Sports Medicine, 21,* 107–114.

Ogilvie, B. C., & Tutko, T. A. (1966). *Problem athletes and how to handle them.* London: Pelham Books.

Olderidge, N. G., Donner, A., Buck, C. W., Jones, N. L., Anderson, G. A., Parker, J. O., Cunningham, D. A., Kavanaugh, T., Rechnitzer, P. A., & Sutton, J. R. (1983). Predictive indices for dropout: The Ontario exercise heart collaborative study experience. *American Journal of Cardiology, 51,* 70–74.

Patrick, G. T. W. (1903). The psychology of football. *American Journal of Psychology, 14,* 104–117.

Pierce, E. F. (1994). Exercise dependence syndrome in runners. *Sports Medicine, 18,* 149–155.

Qualitative Solutions and Research. (1996). *QSR NUD*IST user guide.* Thousand Oaks, CA: Sage Publications.

Raglin, J. S., & Morgan, W. P. (1989). Development of a scale to measure training induced distress. *Medicine and Science in Sports and Exercise, 21*(Suppl.), 60.

Ransford, C. P. (1982). A role for amines in the antidepressant effect of exercise: A review. *Medicine and Science in Sports and Exercise, 14,* 1–10.

Rejeski, W. J., & Thompson, A. (1993). Historical and conceptual roots of exercise psychology. In P. Seraganian (Ed.), *Exercise psychology: The influence of physical exercise on psychological processes,* pp. 3–35. New York: John Wiley & Sons.

Roberts, J. M. (1959). Games in culture. *American Anthropologist, 61,* 597–605.

Sachs, M. L. (1981). Running addiction. In M. H. Sachs & M. L. Sachs (Eds.), *Psychology of running,* pp. 116–121. Champaign, IL: Human Kinetics.

Sachs, M. L., Burke, K. L., & Loughren, E. A. (2007). *Directory of graduate programs in applied sport psychology* (8th ed.). Morgantown, WV: FIT.

Salmela, J. H. (1992). *The world sport psychology sourcebook.* Champaign, IL: Human Kinetics.

Scripture, E. W. (1899). Cross-education. *Popular Science Monthly, 56,* 589–596.

Selye, H. (1976). *Stress in health and disease.* Boston: Butterworth.

Seraganian, P. (1993). Current status and future directions in the field of exercise psychology. In P. Seraganian (Ed.), *Exercise psychology: The influence of physical exercise on psychological processes,* pp. 383–390. New York: John Wiley & Sons.

Silva, J. M., & Weinberg, R. S. (1984). Psychological foundations of sport. Champaign, IL: Human Kinetics.

Singer, R. N. (1996). Future of sport and exercise psychology. In J. L. Van Raalte & B. W. Brewer (Eds.), *Exploring sport and exercise psychology.* Washington, DC: American Psychological Association.

Singer, R. N., Murphey, M., & Tenant, L. K. (Eds.). (1993). *Handbook of research in sport psychology.* New York: Macmillan.

Steinberg, H., & Sykes, E. A. (1985). Introduction to symposium on endorphins and behavioral processes: Review of literature on endorphins and exercise. *Pharmacology, Biochemistry Behavior, 23,* 857–862.

Thompson, J. K., & Blanton, P. (1987). Energy conservation and exercise dependence: A sympathetic arousal hypothesis. *Medicine and Science in Sports and Exercise, 19,* 91–99.

Thomson, W. C., Wade, V. K., Jones, J., & Flor, K. (1998). Avoiding burnout: Hardiness as a stress buffer in college athletes. *Research Quarterly for Exercise and Sport, 69*(Suppl.), S116.

Triplett, N. (1898). The dynamogenic effects of pacemaking and competition. *American Journal of Psychology, 9,* 507–533.

Wankel, L. M. (1987). Enhancing motivation for involvement in voluntary exercise programs. In M. L. Maehr & D. A. Kleiber (Eds.), *Recent advances in motivation and achievement, Vol. 5. Enhancing motivation.* Greenwich, CT: JAI Press.

Weinberg, R. S., & Gould, D. (2011). *Foundations of sport and exercise psychology* (5th ed.). Champaign, IL: Human Kinetics.

West, S. G., & Wicklund, R. A. (1980). *A primer of social psychology theories.* Monterey, CA: Brooks/Cole.

White-Welkley, J. E., Dunn, E. C., Nowicki, S., Duke, M., & Price, L. (1998). Excessive exercise, psychopathologic symptoms and eating attitudes among female non-athletic adults. *Journal of Sport and Exercise Psychology, 20*(Suppl.), S97.

Wiggins, D. K. (1984). The history of sport psychology in North America. In J. M. Silva & R. S. Weinberg (Eds.), *Psychological foundations of sport,* pp. 9–22. Champaign, IL: Human Kinetics.

Williams, J. M., & Straub, W. F. (1986). Sport psychology: Past, present, and future. In J. M. Williams (Ed.), *Applied sport psychology,* pp. 1–13. Palo Alto, CA: Mayfield.

Willis, J. D., & Campbell, L. F. (1992). *Exercise psychology.* Champaign, IL: Human Kinetics.

Yates, A., Leehey, K., & Shisslak, C. M. (1983). Running—an analogue of anorexia? *New England Journal of Medicine, 308*(5), 251–255.

Ziegler, E. F. (1964). *Philosophical foundation for physical, health and recreation education.* Englewood Cliffs, NJ: Prentice Hall.

Glossary

AAHPERD American Alliance for Health, Physical Education, Recreation and Dance.

Abstract A brief summary of the main elements of a scientific article. Abstracts usually also include a purpose statement, description of the methods, results, and conclusions.

Academic exercise and sport psychologist Professional who works to expand and disseminate the exercise science knowledge base through teaching and critical research.

Academy of Nutrition and Dietetics (the Academy) Formerly known as the American Dietetic Association; the world's largest organization of food and nutrition professionals and an excellent resource for individuals interested in becoming an RD or a DTR.

Accelerometer A transducer that measures acceleration. It usually consists of an inertia mass that exerts a force against an element, whose resulting strain is then measured.

ACE American Council on Exercise.

ACSM American College of Sports Medicine.

Adaptation Long-term change in the body due to exercise training.

Adenosine triphosphate (ATP) A molecule in which energy (e.g., for muscle contraction) is stored in high-energy phosphate bonds.

Aerobic exercise Exercise that primarily depends on ATP production involving the use of oxygen.

Affective (or psychological) domain Area concerned with objectives of interests, attitudes, values, and the development of appreciations.

Alarm stage The first of the three stages of the **general adaptation syndrome;** occurs at the onset of stress and is typified by increased physiological arousal.

Allied health A field of study and practice that includes hospital and other clinical settings that promote a positive state of well-being. These settings provide a number of employment opportunities for the exercise scientist.

AMA American Medical Association.

Anabolic steroids A class of drugs that are derived from testosterone; used as an ergogenic aid in strength/power sports.

Anatomy The study of the parts of an organism and their relationship to each other.

Antioxidant Naturally occurring or synthetic substance that helps protect cells from the damaging effects of oxygen free radicals, highly reactive compounds created during normal cell metabolism.

Applied exercise and sport psychologist Professional who applies sport-specific and general psychological theories to sport settings in an attempt to increase the psychological well-being, health, and performance of athletes.

Arteriosclerosis Hardening of the arteries; degenerative condition of the arteries resulting in a loss of their elasticity and the development of thicker walls.

ATEP Athletic training education programs.

Atherosclerosis A disease in which fatty deposits in artery walls lead to a reduction in blood flow through the artery; can lead to heart attack and stroke.

Athletic trainer Medical professionals who are experts in injury prevention, assessment, treatment, and rehabilitation, particularly in orthopedic and musculoskeletal disciplines.

Autonomic nervous system The branch of the nervous system that controls the involuntary functions of the body.

Basal ganglia A collection of subcortical nuclei that are responsible for movement initiation.

Basal metabolic rate (BMR) The minimal amount of energy required for maintenance of life. The BMR is typically measured under strict laboratory conditions: 12 hr after eating, after a restful sleep, no exercise or activity preceding the test, elimination of emotional excitement, and in a comfortable temperature.

Basic Standards for the Professional Preparation in Exercise Science A document developed by the Applied Exercise Science Council of NASPE. It was designed to provide guidance for curricular development for college and university programs that prepare undergraduate students for careers in exercise science.

Biomechanics The study of the human body in motion.

Blocked practice The type of practice in which the learner repeats practice trials using one motor program before the acquisition of a different program.

Blood doping Techniques used to increase red blood cell content to enhance endurance performance.

BOC Board of Certification.

Bomb calorimeter Instrument used to determine the energy value of foods and nutrients.

Burnout A condition characterized by increased negative mental health, decreased performance, and loss of interest and motivation.

CAAHEP Committee on Accreditation of Allied Health Education Programs.

CAATE Commission on Accreditation of Athletic Training Education.

Calorimetry The determination of heat loss or gain; a calorimeter is used to measure the amount of heat exchanged in a chemical reaction or by the body under certain conditions.

Cancer A family of diseases, all of which result from uncontrolled growth and spread of abnormal cells.

Carbohydrate loading A dietary method used by endurance athletes to increase the carbohydrate (glycogen) stores in the muscles and liver.

Cardiovascular disease Any disease that affects the cardiovascular system; for example, coronary heart disease and peripheral artery disease.

Case-control study A study in which the subjects are selected based on the presence of a disease of interest and matched with controls without the disease.

CAT scan Computerized axial tomography, a body-imaging technique utilizing X-rays and computers to provide cross-sectional images of the body.

Cerebellum A structure located at the base of the brain that is involved in the regulation of coordination and the control of fine movements.

Cerebral localization The mapping of the cerebral cortex into areas and the correlation of the various areas with cerebral function.

Cerebrovascular disease Any disease that results in obstruction or narrowing of the arteries that supply blood to the brain.

CEU Continuing education unit.

Cholesterol A steroid molecule found in the blood that can contribute to lipid deposition and atherosclerosis of artery walls.

Cinematography A technique that provides a sequence of images that can be displayed as a motion picture or viewed one by one.

Clinical education Athletic training students are required to participate in a minimum of two years of academic clinical education to provide meaningful hands-on experiences associated with a variety of different patient populations in a variety of settings. Clinical experiences provide practice under the direct supervision of qualified clinical instructors or other credentialed health care professionals.

Clinical exercise and sport psychologist Professional who is specifically trained to address emotional problems and personality disorders experienced by athletes.

Clinical instruction Hands-on instruction in athletic training clinical settings such as high schools, colleges, clinics, and hospital-based facilities.

Clinical rehabilitation A career opportunity that involves an exercise scientist working in a hospital or other clinical setting and using exercise as the primary mode for rehabilitating patients following disease, injury, or surgery.

Closed-loop control A type of motor control through which sensory feedback from the limbs is used to correct errors in the initial movement plan or program.

Cognitive domain Area concerned with objectives that deal with the recall or recognition of knowledge and the development of intellectual skills and abilities.

Comparative anatomy Type of anatomy that compares structural similarities and differences in animals, including humans.

Computerized dynamic posturography A process used to measure the control of posture and balance in upright stance.

Concentric contractions Muscle action that involves the production of force while the muscle is shortening, such as when curling a barbell to the chest.

Conclusions Relationships among the original purposes of a study that were specified in the introduction to the analysis and discussion of the findings.

Construct validity The degree to which a test measures an intangible quality or attribute (e.g., sportsmanship or creativity).

Content validity The extent to which the items on a test adequately sample the subject matter and abilities that the test was designed to measure.

Coronary heart disease Narrowing of the coronary arteries, usually caused by atherosclerosis (the build-up of fatty plaques on the artery walls), that prevents adequate blood and oxygen supply to the heart.

Corporate (or agency) fitness An exercise science career opportunity that involves developing and/or supervising fitness programs in various workplaces and community centers.

Creatine supplementation Creatine is often ingested by athletes as a supplement to increase muscle mass. The rationale for creatine supplementation is to boost either total creatine stores or creatine phosphate or phosphocreatine stores within muscle. Supplementation increases the rate of resynthesis of creatine phosphate following exercise. Forms and methods of ingestion vary.

Criterion validity The extent to which a test correlates with another valid measure of the same concept.

Cross-sectional survey A survey that measures both risk factors and the presence or absence of the disease at the same time. They are often called prevalence studies.

Deafferentation A surgical technique whereby the afferent nerves are severed to prevent sensory information from reaching the central nervous system. Usually only performed on animals.

Densitometry The determination of the density (mass/volume) of the body. Body mass may be measured using an accurate physician's scale, while body volume is commonly measured using the hydrostatic (underwater) weighing technique.

Developmental anatomy The study of the anatomical changes that occur from birth to the end of life.

Diabetes A disease of the insulin system in which insufficient insulin is produced (type 1 diabetes) or the body is insensitive to insulin (type 2 diabetes).

Dietetics The science of applying food and nutrition to health and disease.

Discussion The use of inductive reasoning to interpret the findings of a study as well as a comparison of these findings with those of previous studies for the purpose of integration into a larger theoretical model.

Dual energy X-ray absorptiometry (DXA) An X-ray using more than one wavelength and a special filter that varies the energy peaks. Useful for estimating amounts of fat, muscle, and bone.

Dynamics A branch of mechanics that investigates bodies, masses, and forces in motion.

Dynamography A technique that provides kinetic data. A dynamograph is a device used for measuring forces produced during an activity.

Eccentric contraction A muscle contraction in which the muscle actively lengthens under tension.

Educational sport psychologist Professional who communicates the principles of sport psychology to athletes and coaches.

Electromyography A technique that provides data on muscle activity by recording the electrical changes that occur in a muscle during or immediately before contraction.

Electrotherapeutic devices Machines that use electrical energy in the treatment of disease or injury. Those commonly used by the athletic trainer include transcutaneous electrical nerve stimulation (TENS), ultrasound, galvanic stimulators, neuromuscular electrical stimulation (NMES), shortwave and microwave diathermy, and interferential electrical muscle stimulation.

Embryology The study of anatomical changes in tissues from conception to birth.

Endocrine gland A ductless gland that secretes hormones into the blood.

Epidemiology The study of the occurrence and prevalence of disease among the population.

Ergogenic aid A substance, device, or treatment that is believed to enhance athletic performance.

Ergolytic A substance, device, or treatment that can impair performance.

Evaluation A judgment of merit based on a comparison of various measurements, impressions, and other evidence of some standard.

Exercise adherence Ability to comply with the prescribed frequency, intensity, duration, mode, and progression of a physical activity until a stated outcome goal is achieved.

Exercise dependence syndrome   According to Lox (2010, p. 90) "a craving for leisure-time physical activity, resulting in uncontrollable excessive exercise behavior, that manifests in physiological (e.g., tolerance/withdrawal) and/or psychological (e.g., anxiety, depression) symptoms."

Exercise epidemiology   The study of factors associated with participation in physical activity and of how physical activity affects the probability of disease or injury.

Exercise physiology   The study of how the body, from a functional standpoint, responds, adjusts, and adapts to exercise.

Exercise science   The study of how and why the body responds to physical activity.

Exhaustion stage   The final of three stages of the general adaptation syndrome; if the stressor continues, the individual eventually enters the last stage, characterized by low levels of arousal. As the ability to cope with the stress deteriorates, the individual may become fatigued or ill.

External reviewers   Individuals who have academic background and training similar to the authors, and who rate and scrutinize a manuscript and recommend acceptance, rejection, or improvement for publication in a journal.

Fast-twitch glycolytic (FG) fibers   Fatigable muscle fibers that favor glycolytic (anaerobic) methods of energy production; also known as type IIb fibers.

Fast-twitch oxidative glycolytic (FOG) fibers   Intermediately fatigue-resistant muscle fibers that utilize both oxidative (aerobic) and glycolytic (anaerobic) methods of energy production; also known as type IIa fibers.

Fatigue   A state of exhaustion or a loss of strength or endurance, as may follow strenuous physical activity.

Food science   Science that applies principles of the biological and physical sciences to study the nature of foods, the causes of food deterioration, and the principles underlying the processing and preparation of food.

Force platform   An electromechanical device that provides electrical signals proportional to the components of force acting on it.

General adaptation syndrome   Hans Selye's theory concerning the typical reaction to stress that remains constant with various stressors. GAS consists of three stages: alarm, resistance, and exhaustion. (1) Alarm stage: Occurs at the onset of stress and is typified by increased physiological arousal. (2) Resistance stage: As the stressor continues, the individual tries to cope. Arousal is initially high but declines until it reaches lower than normal levels. (3) Exhaustion stage: If the stressor continues, the individual will eventually enter the last stage, characterized by low levels of arousal. As the ability to cope with the stress deteriorates, the individual may become fatigued or ill.

Generalized motor program   A stored set of movement commands that activate the proper muscles in the correct sequence with the correct timing without the influence of sensory feedback. Variables such as overall duration and force can be varied from trial to trial with a parameter modification.

Glycogen   The storage form of carbohydrate found in the liver and in the muscles.

Goniometer   A device that provides kinematic data on joint positioning; is used to measure static positions of limb segments with respect to a joint axis.

Gross anatomy   The study of those body structures that can be seen without the aid of a microscope.

Hemiparesis   A loss of motor control (including strength) and sensation on one side of the body.

Hemoglobin   A blood protein involved in the transport of oxygen and carbon dioxide.

Higher education   An exercise science career opportunity that usually involves teaching and/or research at the college or university level.

Histology   The microscopic study of the anatomy of tissues and their cellular basis.

Hormone   A chemical released from an endocrine gland into the blood that exerts its biological effect elsewhere in the body.

Hyperlipidemia   An elevated level of lipids (fats) in the blood.

Hypertension   Persistently high arterial blood pressure that may have no known cause, or it may be associated with another primary disease. It is a risk factor for the development of heart disease, peripheral vascular disease, stroke, and kidney disease.

Hypothesis   A tentative proposal made to explain certain observations or facts that require further investigation to be verified.

Iceberg profile   Using the Profile of Mood States (POMS), it was determined that high-level competitive athletes normally displayed mood states above the mean in the Vigor-Activity category, and below the mean in the Tension-Anxiety, Depression-Dejection, Anger-Hostility, Fatigue-Inertia, and Confusion-Bewilderment categories. The graphic representation of these data produces a characteristic shape that resembles an iceberg.

Incidence rate   The frequency, or number of cases that occur over a defined time period, divided by the average size of the population at risk. They are often used in exercise epidemiology to provide a measure of the rate at which a population develops a disease.

Indirect calorimetry   The measurement of energy expenditure via determination of oxygen consumption and carbon dioxide production.

Instrumented staircase   Assessment equipment typically equipped with multiple force platforms; designed to accurately measure the amount of force applied on each step during stair ascent and descent and can detect the usage of handrails during stair negotiation.

Instrumented treadmill   A treadmill with force platforms embedded below the belt to allow biomechanists to measure the amount of force applied while walking or running on the treadmill. Its split-belt design can provide a different speed for each belt or even two different directions, creating a more challenging environment for studying human locomotion.

Insulin   A hormone released from the pancreas that functions to facilitate glucose transport from the blood into cells.

Interactional approach   When studying stress and coping, this research model considers the interaction between an athlete's personality and the situation in which the athlete is involved. The impact of the environment on the athlete is potentially far more powerful than a particular personality disposition.

Interval measurement   A level of measurement resulting in values that permit the making of statements of equality of intervals in addition to statements of sameness or difference (nominal) or greater than or less than (ordinal).

Introduction   Section of an article or manuscript that specifically identifies the problem and often states the research hypotheses.

Ischemic heart disease   A pathologic condition of the myocardium caused by a lack of oxygen in the tissue cells.

ISSN   International Society of Sports Nutrition.

JRC–AT   Joint Review Committee–Athletic Training.

Keywords   Words from a manuscript or an article that identify the key concepts in a particular research question.

Kilocalorie   The amount of heat necessary to raise the temperature of 1 liter of water 1° Celsius.

Kinematics   A branch of mechanics that investigates motion without reference to masses or forces.

Kinesiology   The parent discipline of biomechanics; a science that investigates movement.

Kinetics   A branch of mechanics that investigates the actions of forces in producing or changing the motion of masses.

Knowledge of performance   A source of feedback that indicates errors in the learner's movement pattern, not the outcome.

Knowledge of results   A source of feedback that indicates whether the outcome of the practice trial was successful in reaching or achieving the goal.

Magnetic resonance imaging   A noninvasive medical diagnostic technique that uses a magnetic field to produce anatomical pictures of the living body.

Measurement   The process of assigning numerical or symbolic values to members of a group for the purpose of distinguishing among the members on the basis of the degree to which they possess the characteristic being assessed.

Meta-analysis   A technique of literature review that contains a definitive methodology and quantifies the results of various studies to a standard metric that allows the use of statistical techniques as a means of analysis.

Metabolic syndrome X   A condition characterized by diabetes, hypertension, and hyperlipidemia. It is a major risk factor for coronary heart disease.

Metabolism   The sum total of all physical and chemical changes that occur in the body. Metabolism involves two processes: anabolism (the building-up or synthesizing processes) and catabolism (the tearing-down or degrading processes).

Methods   This section describes the data-gathering steps of the scientific method in such detail that the study can be replicated.

Modeling   A technique used to provide a prediction of kinematic and kinetic data.

Motion recording device   Captures body motion using optical lenses to provide permanent recorded images of movement.

Motor control An area of study that deals with how the nervous system controls movement.

Motor cortex A cortical brain region responsible for movement initiation and where most of the upper motor neurons originate.

Motor learning An area of study that deals with how we acquire and retain motor skills.

Muscle spindle A sensory receptor located in parallel with the main (extrafusal) muscle fibers that is sensitive to the amount of muscle stretch.

Narrative review A subjective summary and interpretation of research results from most, if not all, of the studies in a particular area.

NASPE National Association for Sport and Physical Education. This is an association of the American Alliance for Health, Physical Education, Recreation and Dance.

NATA National Athletic Trainers' Association.

NATABOC National Athletic Trainers' Association Board of Certification.

Nominal measurement A level of measurement that permits only the making of statements of sameness or difference.

Nonscientific literature Anything published in a book, magazine, newspaper, or online that is not peer-reviewed for scientific content.

NSCA National Strength and Conditioning Association.

Nutraceuticals Nutrients that exhibit druglike properties when taken in appropriate dosages.

Nutrigenomics The study of the interaction of nutrients with the human genome; also called nutrition genomics.

Nutrition The science of food that is generally described as the sum total of the processes involved in the intake and utilization of food substances by living organisms, including ingestion, digestion, absorption, and metabolism of food.

Objectivity The aspect of test reliability that is concerned with the variability in scores resulting from different individuals administering and scoring a test.

Open-loop control A type of control whereby the entire movement is controlled by the higher centers without the influence of sensory feedback from the lower centers.

Ordinal measurement A level of measurement that permits the ordering of the individuals measured in addition to statements of sameness or difference (nominal).

Osteoporosis A disease characterized by very low bone mass and deterioration of bone tissue that results in brittle bones and an increased risk for fractures.

Overtraining Exceeding a physical and psychological optimal volume and intensity over time that results in disturbed mood and staleness. Usually associated with highly competitive and highly trained endurance athletes.

Parasympathetic nervous system The branch of the autonomic nervous system that is most active at rest and is involved in restorative functions.

Pathological anatomy The study of anatomical changes that occur in tissues as a result of disease.

Peer-review process Subjecting an author's scholarly work or ideas to the scrutiny of others who are experts in the field.

Personal training Using an individualized approach to assess, motivate, educate, and train clients regarding their health and fitness needs.

Personality The collective pattern of one's psychological traits and states.

PET scan Positron emission tomography; a body-scanning procedure that uses injected radioactive substances to measure the metabolic activity of a tissue or an organ.

Physician extender Allied health care professional trained to perform many of the duties previously done by a physician.

Physiology The study of the processes and functions of the human body.

Phytochemical Chemical substances found in plants that possess medicinal properties that help prevent chronic disease.

Pressure insole A device that consists of a matrix of small force transducers. It provides detailed information concerning load distribution.

Primary exercise dependence Occurs when the exercise is an end in itself; associated features include exercise tolerance, manifested as a progressively increasing intensity, duration, or frequency of exercise, or lying to a spouse about how much or when one exercises, for example.

Primary reference Original data and/or ideas that are generally the first published record of an investigation. Examples include research articles, research monographs, preprints, patents, dissertations, and conference proceedings.

Private consulting A career opportunity that involves sharing one's expertise in exercise science with others (law firms, hospitals, fitness centers, private individuals) so that they can benefit from the information.

Prospective cohort study   A study where subjects are selected at random from a defined population. Baseline information on potential risk factors is then collected, and the subjects are followed over time to track the incidence of disease.

Psychology   The science of mental processes and behavior.

Psychomotor domain   Area concerned with objectives that deal with movement and factors that influence movement.

Random practice   A type of practice schedule in which the learner performs a different motor program on each trial (e.g., tennis forehand, tennis backhand, and tennis volley).

Randomized controlled trial   A study where the subjects are randomly assigned to one of two groups: an experimental treatment group or a control group. Measurements are made before and after the intervention in both groups to assess differences between the groups in the outcomes of interest. It is considered the gold standard of research designs.

Ratio measurement   A level of measurement that permits the making of statements of equality or ratios, such as one value is twice another, in addition to statements of sameness or difference (nominal), greater or lesser (ordinal), and equality of intervals (interval).

Recommended dietary allowance (RDA)   Established by the Food and Nutrition Board; represent the levels of intake of essential nutrients considered to be adequate to avoid deficiencies and meet the known nutritional needs of practically all healthy people of similar age and gender.

References   Sources used to support various statements in a manuscript or an article.

Regional anatomy   A system of study in which everything about a specific region of the body is studied together; e.g., all the bones, muscles, nerves, and vessels of the upper limbs are learned before moving on to another body area.

Reliability   The extent to which a test consistently yields the same results when repeated under the same conditions.

Resistance stage   The second of three stages of the general adaptation syndrome; as the stressor continues, the individual tries to cope. Arousal is initially high but declines until it reaches lower than normal levels.

Response   An acute or short-term change in the body that is associated with exercise.

Results   The findings of a research study from the data analysis.

Science   A systematic attempt to establish theories to explain observed phenomena and the knowledge obtained through these efforts.

Scientific literature   Reports of original empirical and theoretical work (or summaries thereof) in the natural and social sciences.

Secondary exercise dependence   Occurs when exercise is used exclusively to control body composition, as is seen often in individuals with eating disorders (e.g., anorexia nervosa).

Secondary reference   Information about primary sources, usually a compilation or synthesis of various ideas and data. Secondary sources may rearrange, modify, or summarize data, which include book chapters, narrative reviews, and meta-analyses.

Simulation   A technique used to provide a prediction of kinematic and kinetic data.

Situational approach   When studying stress and coping, this hypothesis assumes that individuals have different situation-specific anxiety levels and a repertoire of coping options available to them from which they can choose, depending on the characteristics of the situation.

Slow-twitch oxidative (SO) fibers   Fatigue-resistant muscle fibers that favor oxidative (aerobic) methods of energy production; also known as type I fibers.

Social cohesion   Degree of interpersonal attraction among team members.

Sonography (ultrasound)   Use of sound waves to assess body tissues.

Spasticity   A condition of excessive muscle tone and resistance to stretch.

Staleness   A condition characterized by increased negative mental health and decreased performance.

Statics   A branch of mechanics that investigates bodies, masses, and forces at rest or in equilibrium.

Stroke   Loss or impairment of body function due to injury or death of brain cells from insufficient blood supply.

Supplementary motor cortex   A brain area anterior of the motor cortex responsible for the planning of movement.

Surveillance system   A system used to track behavior trends in a population over time. They are often used in exercise epidemiology to track physical activity over time.

Sympathetic nervous system   The branch of the autonomic nervous system that is most active during periods of stress and activity.

Systemic anatomy   A method of study in which each of the systems of the body is studied independently before moving on to the next system; e.g., the skeletal system is studied first, then the muscular system, nervous system, and so on until the 11 body systems are covered.

Teacher/athletic trainer   An individual who has completed the requirements for both a teaching credential and entry-level athletic training.

Temporal analysis   A technique that uses time as the basis for examining motion.

Theory   A comprehensive explanation of a given set of data that has been repeatedly confirmed by observation and experimentation and has gained general acceptance within the scientific community but has not yet been decisively proven.

Trait approach/trait theory   Most personality research with athletes is grounded in this theory, which states that more or less enduring traits comprise the basic personality structure. Trait theory is based in large part on the work of Raymond B. Cattell, who saw traits as a hypothetical construct inferred from the objective observation of behavior. These traits produce the basic elements of behavior, of which understanding is vital to any prediction about people. Cattell described 16 basic traits and developed a standardized test to quantify them: the 16 Personality Factor Questionnaire (16PF). Cattell's instrument, which assigns a value of 1 to 10 to each of these factors, has been useful in sport-specific personality research. Three assumptions shared by traditional trait psychologists are: (1) people are cross-situationally consistent; (2) our behavior displays a temporal stability; and (3) there is a co-occurrence of behavioral manifestations referring to the same underlying trait.

Type 1 diabetes   A form of diabetes in which the body's immune system destroys the pancreatic cells that produce insulin. As a result, type 1 diabetics cannot produce adequate amounts of insulin.

Type 2 diabetes   A form of diabetes in which the cells of the body do not use insulin properly. As the need for insulin increases over time, the pancreas loses its ability to produce adequate amounts of insulin.

Ultrasound sonography   A noninvasive technique that uses sound waves to assess body tissues.

Validity   The degree to which a test measures what it is intended to measure.

Variable practice   Practice involving the use of different program parameters (e.g., force, overall duration), instead of only one (constant practice).

Videography   A technique that provides a sequence of images that can be displayed as a motion picture or viewed individually. The images are recorded on videotape and are most commonly taken at a rate of 30 frames per second. High-speed video can be taken at 60 or more frames per second.

$\dot{V}O_2$ max   The maximal rate at which an individual can take in and utilize oxygen.

Index